READING THE EPISTLE TO THE HEBREWS

Society of Biblical Literature

Resources for Biblical Study

Tom Thatcher
New Testament Editor

Number 66

READING THE EPISTLE TO THE HEBREWS
A Resource for Students

READING THE EPISTLE TO THE HEBREWS

A Resource for Students

Edited by

Eric F. Mason

and

Kevin B. McCruden

Society of Biblical Literature
Atlanta

READING THE EPISTLE TO THE HEBREWS
A Resource for Students

Library of Congress Cataloging-in-Publication Data

Reading the Epistle to the Hebrews : a resource for students / edited by Eric F. Mason
and Kevin B. McCruden.
     p. cm. — (Society of Biblical Literature resources for biblical study ; no. 66)
   Includes bibliographical references and indexes.
   ISBN 978-1-58983-608-2 (paper binding : alk. paper) — ISBN 978-1-58983-609-9
   (electronic format)
   1. Bible. N.T. Hebrews—Textbooks. I. Mason, Eric Farrel. II. McCruden, Kevin B.
   BS2775.55.R43 2011
   227'.8706   2011033812

Printed on acid-free, recycled paper conforming to
ANSI/NISO Z39.48-1992 (R1997) and ISO 9706:1994
standards for paper permanence.

CONTENTS

Acknowledgments

The editors of this project are indebted to numerous people who have made this book possible. We are delighted that this volume is part of the Resources for Biblical Study series, published by the Society of Biblical Literature and Brill, and we gratefully acknowledge the guidance and encouragement of the RBS New Testament editor Tom Thatcher. We first contacted Tom with the idea for a rather different kind of student-friendly introduction to the study of Hebrews, but he asked us to consider reenvisioning the project loosely along the lines of an existing RBS volume edited by David L. Barr, *Reading the Book of Revelation: A Resource for Students* (2003). The timing of the conversation was fortuitous, as Tom had recently begun formulating plans to extend the series by commissioning volumes like Barr's on other New Testament books. We easily were convinced of the merits of his suggestion, and we happily reconfigured our project in a way consistent with the spirit of the Barr volume yet also sensitive to the distinctive challenges of studying Hebrews. While certainly any deficiencies of the volume remain our own, we have benefitted much from Tom's advice as well as from comments offered by the anonymous readers of the book proposal. Likewise, we have received excellent guidance at each step from the SBL publication staff, especially Leigh Andersen, Bob Buller, and Kathie Klein.

Naturally, the success of a project such as this hinges largely on the cooperation of those who write the various chapters. We are extremely grateful to our contributors, an invigorating mix of junior and senior scholars, and we are humbled by their willingness to participate in this endeavor. All of them took very seriously our joint task of explaining this complex biblical text in ways accessible to students and other nonspecialist readers. Likewise, all were very conscientious of the timeline of the project and graciously took care to adhere to this in the midst of the many other demands on their individual schedules. We realize as editors that we were very fortunate to work with such outstanding scholars and persons.

We are indebted to the editors of two journals for their kind permission to include revised versions of previously published materials. Chapter 4 in this volume is adapted from Eric F. Mason, "Hebrews and the Dead Sea Scrolls: Some Points of Comparison," *Perspectives in Religious Studies* 37 (2010): 457–79; and chapter 6 is revised and updated from Craig R. Koester, "Hebrews, Rhetoric, and the Future of Humanity," *Catholic Biblical Quarterly* 64 (2002): 103–23. Likewise, we are grateful to Edmondo Lupieri, the John Cardinal Cody Chair of Theology at Loyola University Chicago, for hosting a seminar in honor of this volume on 10 February 2011. This was an enjoyable and invigorating opportunity for discussion of three of the chapters in this collection, those by the editors and Mark A. Torgerson, and we appreciate very much the responses to our papers by Loyola graduate students Amanda Kunder, Jeremy Miselbrook, and Amy Pezderic.

Finally, we would be remiss if we failed to express appreciation to those persons who have most supported us in this project, our wives Jacqueline Mason and Kerry McCruden, and our children Anastasia Mason and Liam and Samuel McCruden. Without their faithful encouragement and love, we could not have persevered.

Eric F. Mason
Kevin B. McCruden

Abbreviations

Greek and Latin Sources

Aelius Theon
    Progym.   *Progymnasmata*
Albinus
    Epit.   *Handbook of Platonism*
Apollonius of Tyana
    Ep.   *Letters*
Aristotle
    Eth. nic.   *Nichomachean Ethics*
    Rhet.   *Rhetoric*
Athanasius
    C. Ar.   *Orations against the Arians*
Augustine
    Conf.   *Confessions*
Barn.   *Barnabas*
Cicero
    De or.   *De oratore*
    Div.   *De divinatione*
    Flac.   *Pro Flacco*
    Inv.   *De inventione rhetorica*
    Nat. d.   *De natura deorum*
    Off.   *De officiis*
    Part. or.   *Partitiones oratoriae*
    Quint. Fratr.   *Epistulae ad Quintum fratrem*
Clement of Alexandria
    Ecl.   *Extracts from the Prophets*
    Quis div.   *Salvation of the Rich*
    Strom.   *Miscellanies*

Cyril of Alexandria
    Adv. Nest.   *Against Nestorius*
Demosthenes
    1–2 Aristog.   *1–2 Against Aristogeiton*
    1–3 [4] Philip.   *1–4 Philippic*
    Cor.   *On the Crown*
    Exord.   *Exordia*
Dio Chrysostom
    Or.   *Discourses*
Dionysius of Halicarnassus
    1–2 Amm.   *Epistula ad Ammaeum i–ii*
Epictetus
    Diatr.   *Diatribai (Dissertationes)*
Euripides
    Herc. fur.   *Madness of Hercules*
Eusebius
    Praep. ev.   *Preparation for the Gospel*
Herodotus
    Hist.   *Histories*
Hesiod
    Theog.   *Theogony*
Irenaeus
    Haer.   *Against Heresies*
Isocrates
    Hel. enc.   *Helenae encomium (Or. 10)*
John Chrysostom
    Hom. Heb. *Homiliae in epistulam ad Hebraeos*
Josephus
    Ag. Ap.   *Against Apion*
    Ant.   *Antiquities*
    J.W.   *Jewish War*
Justin
    Dial.   *Dialogue with Trypho*
Lucian
    Merc. cond. *Salaried Posts in Great Houses*
    Philops.   *The Lover of Lies*
    Sacr.   *Sacrifices*
Marcus Aurelius *Meditations*

Maximus of Tyre
    Diss.   *Dissertationis*
Origen
    Cels.   *Against Celsus*
    Hom. Exod.   *Homiliae in Exodum*
Philo
    Abr.   *On the Life of Abraham*
    Aet.   *On the Eternity of the World*
    Cher.   *On the Cherubim*
    Conf.   *On the Confusion of Tongues*
    Congr.   *On the Preliminary Studies*
    Contempl.   *On the Contemplative Life*
    Decal.   *On the Decalogue*
    Deus   *That God is Unchangeable*
    Ebr.   *On Drunkenness*
    Gig.   *On Giants*
    Her.   *Who Is the Heir?*
    Hypoth.   *Hypothetica*
    Ios.   *On the Life of Joseph*
    Leg.   *Allegorical Interpretation*
    Legat.   *On the Embassy to Gaius*
    Migr.   *On the Migration of Abraham*
    Mos.   *The Life of Moses*
    Opif.   *On the Creation of the World*
    Plant.   *On Planting*
    Post.   *On the Posterity of Cain*
    Praem.   *On Rewards and Punishments*
    Prob.   *That Every Good Person is Free*
    Prov.   *On Providence*
    QE   *Questions and Answers on Exodus*
    QG   *Questions and Answers on Genesis*
    Sacr.   *On the Sacrifices of Cain and Abel*
    Somn.   *On Dreams*
    Spec.   *On the Special Laws*
Philostratos
    Ep.   *Epistulae*
    Gymn.   *De gymnastica*
    Vit. Apoll.   *Vita Apollonii*

Pindar
    Nem.   *Nemean Odes*
Plato
    Leg.   *Laws*
    Phaed.   *Phaedo*
    Phaedr.   *Phaedrus*
    Resp.   *Republic*
    Tim.   *Timaeus*
Pliny the Younger
    Ep.   *Epistulae*
Plutarch [and Pseudo-Plutarch]
    Cat. Maj.   *Cato the Elder*
    Def. orac.   *De defectu oraculorum*
    E Delph.   *De E apud Delphos*
    Exil.   *De exilio*
    Frat. amor. *De fraterno amore*
    Garr.   *De garrulitate*
    Is. Os.   *De Iside et Osiride*
    [Lib. ed.]   *De liberis educandis*
    Mor.   *Moralia*
    Quaest. conv. *Quaestionum convivialum libri IX*
    Sept. sap. conv. *Septem sapientium convivium*
    Sol.   *Solon*
    Superst.   *De superstitione*
Quintilian
    Inst.   *Institutio oratoria*
Rhetorica ad Herennium
    Rhet. Her. *Rhetorica ad Herennium*
Seneca
    Ben.   *De beneficiis*
    Ira   *De Ira*
    Prov.   *De providentia*
Strabo
    Geogr.   *Geography*
Suetonius
    Claud.   *Divus Claudius*
    Nero   *Nero*
Tacitus
    Ann.   *Annales*

Hist.	*Historiae*
Tertullian	
Marc.	*Against Marcion*
Theodore of Mopsuestia	
Cat. hom.	*Catachetical Homily*
Theophrastrus	
Char.	*Characteres*
Xenophon	
Cyr.	*Cyropaedia*
Mem.	*Memorabilia*

Dead Sea Scrolls

DJD(J)	Discoveries in the Judaean Desert (of Jordan)
ar	Aramaic
CD	Damascus Document (versions A and B from the Cairo Genizah)
1QapGen	Genesis Apocryphon
1QpHab	Pesher Habakkuk
1QM	War Scroll
1QS	Rule of the Community
1QSa	Rule of the Congregation
1QSb	Rule of the Blessings
1QpPs	Pesher Psalms
4Q174	Florilegium
4Q175	Testimonia
4Q177	Catena manuscript a
4Q255–264	Rule of the Community
4Q266–273	Damascus Document
4Q285	War Rule
4QMMT (394–399)	MMT ("Some of the Works of the Law")
4Q400–407	Songs of the Sabbath Sacrifice
4Q491–496	War Scroll
4Q543–549	Visions of Amram
5Q11	Rule of the Community
5Q12	Damascus Document
6Q15	Damascus Document
11Q13	Melchizedek
11Q14	War Rule

11Q17	Songs of the Sabbath Sacrifice
11Q29	Rule of the Community?
Mas1k	Songs of the Sabbath Sacrifice (found at Masada)

Pseudepigrapha

| 1 En. | 1 Enoch |
| Jub. | Jubilees |

Rabbinic Literature

b.	Babylonian Talmud
B. Qam.	Bava Qamma
Ber.	Berakot
Gen. Rab.	Genesis Rabbah
m.	Mishnah
Meg.	Megillah
Pesiq. Rab.	Pesiqta Rabbati
Roš. Haš.	Roš Haššanah
Šabb.	Šabbat
Sanh.	Sanhedrin
Sukkah	Sukkah
t.	Tosefta
Ta'an.	Ta'anit
y.	Jerusalem Talmud

Other

ANF	*Ante-Nicene Fathers*. Edited by Alexander Roberts and James Donaldson. 10 vols. Repr., Peabody, Mass.: Hendrickson, 1994. [orig. 1885–1887]
BDAG	Bauer, W., F. W. Danker, W. F. Arndt, and F. W. Gingrich. *Greek-English Lexicon of the New Testament and Other Early Christian Literature*. 3rd ed. Chicago: University of Chicago Press, 1999.
BiPa	Biblia Patristica. Index des citations et allusions bibliques dans la littérature. Paris, 1975–
ca.	circa

KJV	King James Version
LCL	Loeb Classical Library
LXX	Septuagint
LW	*Luther's Works*. American Edition. Edited by Jaroslav Pelikan and Helmut T. Lehman. 55 vols. Philadelphia: Muehlenberg and Fortress; St. Louis: Concordia, 1955–1986.
MT	Masoretic Text
NAB	New American Bible
NASB	New American Standard Bible
NLT	New Living Translation
NPNF 1	*The Nicene and Post-Nicene Fathers*, series 1. Edited by Philip Schaff. 14 vols. Repr., Peabody, Mass.: Hendrickson, 1994. [orig. 1886–1889]
NPNF 2	*The Nicene and Post-Nicene Fathers*, series 2. Edited by Philip Schaff and Henry Wace. 14 vols. Repr., Peabody, Mass.: Hendrickson, 1994. [orig. 1890]
NRSV	New Revised Standard Version
OG	Old Greek
RSV	Revised Standard Version
SIG	*Sylloge inscriptionum graecarum*. Edited by W. Dittenberger. 4 vols. 3rd ed. Leipzig, 1915–1924.
s.v.	*sub verbo* ("under the word")
TDNT	*Theological Dictionary of the New Testament*. Edited by G. Kittel and G. Friedrich. Translated by G. W. Bromiley. 10 vols. Grand Rapids: Eerdmans, 1964–1976.
WUNT	Wissenschaftliche Untersuchungen zum Neuen Testament

INTRODUCTION

Eric F. Mason

The title of this book is *Reading the Epistle to the Hebrews: A Resource for Students*, and the phrases on both sides of the colon are vital to convey the intent for this volume. This is a book about the Epistle to the Hebrews, which has been called "the Cinderella" of New Testament studies (Guthrie 2004, 414; following McCullough 1994, 66). This designation accurately reflects the explosion of interest in the book in recent decades—since the publication in 1989 of Harold W. Attridge's landmark commentary in the Hermeneia series—after years of relative neglect. For centuries, most interpreters assumed Paul was the author; once scholarship rejected that traditional identification, the anonymous author of Hebrews was essentially sidelined as eccentric and rarely included in discussions of profound early Christian voices. Rudolf Bultmann virtually ignored the book, for example, in his classic *Theology of the New Testament* in the mid-twentieth century (1951–1955). In recent years, however, Hebrews has reemerged as a text of significant interest, so much so that now many would affirm Frank J. Matera's assessment that the author is "one of the great theologians of the New Testament … equal in theological stature" with those of the Pauline and Johannine traditions (Matera 2007, 333).

Most of the contributors to the present volume are recognized specialists on the study of Hebrews, as a perusal of the volume's bibliography will demonstrate. Others have not normally published on Hebrews but bring particular expertise from another field or discipline to the study of this text, thereby enriching this collection with contents ranging beyond the topics normally addressed in academic biblical studies. Together these essays examine numerous important issues for reading Hebrews, such as the author's conceptual influences and engagement with Scripture and other traditions, the book's structure, its major theological themes, emerging interpretative methods for engaging the text, and the use of

Hebrews (both positively and negatively) by subsequent generations of readers.

Our assumption is that most readers of this book will study it alongside a standard commentary. As such, rather than seeking to duplicate what those volumes do best (treatment of standard issues such as authorship, date, and so forth, plus detailed exegesis of the biblical text), our focus has been to provide extended discussions of important issues that go beyond what is feasible in a typical commentary. Our hope is that readers will find the chapters in this book both illuminating and provocative as they ponder Hebrews in the company of our contributors.

This leads naturally to consideration of the second half of this book's title: "a resource for students." Our contributors have been charged not just to write chapters that engage the best of contemporary scholarship on Hebrews but to do so with the needs and concerns of student readers at the forefront. We have sought to write with an advanced undergraduate readership in mind, but also in ways that will be beneficial for more advanced students in seminary or graduate school and indeed for any educated reader studying Hebrews for the first time. This means we have been intentional about defining specialized terminology, providing relevant historical and cultural background information, and explaining tenets of the methodologies we utilize. While Hebrews is the subject of several very readable introductory commentaries and handbooks written by esteemed scholars (including some excellent volumes by contributors to this book), we are aware of no other student-oriented book on Hebrews that addresses the breadth of issues with the range of perspectives that the present volume offers. We trust that students and other readers of Hebrews will find the essays here to be understandable, instructive, and enlightening.

* * *

Hebrews is a difficult, mysterious, and sometimes even cryptic book, elements that have contributed both to its neglect and appeal. We cannot know the identity of its author, though (despite early reservations in the West) from the fourth through sixteenth centuries interpreters overwhelmingly assumed it was Paul until Erasmus and Martin Luther reopened the question (for an excellent survey of the history of interpretation of Hebrews, see Koester 2001, 19–63). Other suggestions by ancient and modern readers have included Barnabas, Apollos, and even Priscilla;

extensive arguments for Luke (Allen 2010) and a Pauline pseudepigrapher (Rothschild 2009) have recently appeared. Most contemporary scholars, however, concede that we cannot know the author's personal identity but that we can discern several things about him from the text. His heartfelt, pastoral "word of exhortation" (13:22) was preserved as a letter (albeit one lacking a typical epistolary beginning) but exhibits fine homiletic qualities. He wrote eloquent Greek, normally described as the most refined in the New Testament (see Trotter 1997, 163–84, for a very accessible survey of the author's literary sophistication and style), and he was equally comfortable with the canons of Greek rhetoric and the *middot* of Second Temple period Jewish exegetical traditions. This resulted in sometimes complex, often creative, and always profound interpretations of the Septuagint as he urged his audience to remain faithful to its Christian commitment in the midst of adversity in the latter part of the first century C.E.

We do not know exactly what sort of issues the audience faced, and even among the contributors to this volume explanations will differ. Formerly most interpreters assumed that the recipients were Jewish Christians who struggled over the relationship between their heritage and their faith in Jesus, thus they were either hesitant to break away from the synagogue or else inclined to return. Such interpretations have deep roots in tradition, in part due to the heavy use of sacrificial and priestly imagery in the book, and this contributed both to the title later added to the book ("To the Hebrews") and the assumption among many early readers that it was intended for the Jerusalem church. Increasingly, however, modern interpreters argue that nothing in Hebrews demands a reading so dependent on Jewish ethnicity; instead, the problem is discouragement and apathy in the midst of withering social opposition and (sometimes) persecution. Still, however, scholarly reconstructions of the precise setting continue to vary. Regardless, almost all interpreters now agree that the text was sent to friends still in Rome ("those from Italy send you greetings," 13:24).

Detailed consideration of these matters need not detain us here because such things are covered in significant detail in most critical commentaries. Instead, as noted above, the purpose of this volume is to examine major issues for interpretation of Hebrews that go beyond the scope of the typical commentary yet are vital for beginning readers of the text. Our subjects may be grouped in five categories: issues of conceptual and historical background, structure of the text, emerging methodological approaches, major theological issues, and reception history.

Conceptual and Historical Background

The question of the conceptual background that most influenced the author of Hebrews is one with a long history of discussion, and virtually any commentary includes some discussion of three major proposals: Middle Platonic thought (especially as represented by Philo of Alexandria), Palestinian Judaism, or Gnosticism. While the latter of these has largely been abandoned in recent decades, especially in English-language scholarship, one still finds ardent defenses for the other two suggestions, unfortunately often couched in either-or terms. Both remaining options, however, largely still concern the Jewish context of the author, whether more akin to the Platonizing Judaism of Philo of Alexandria or more Palestinian strains as represented by the Qumran sectarians and other apocalyptic groups. More recently, a number of interpreters have begun to consider how interpretation of Hebrews is impacted when read explicitly as a text addressed to a Roman audience.

Four essays in this volume address issues related to the conceptual and historical backgrounds of Hebrews. While each contributor considers these questions from a different perspective, all four agree that the author of Hebrews draws on a rich and varied font of traditions.

In "Hebrews among Greeks and Romans," Patrick Gray addresses the fundamental question of "why it is necessary to know anything about Greece or Rome in a letter to 'Hebrews.'" Gray explains that, regardless of the ethnicity of the recipients of the book, they lived in the Greco-Roman world, and "several aspects of the argument of Hebrews stand out more vividly when viewed against the background of Greek and Roman culture." Gray provides a lucid consideration of numerous issues, including language and rhetoric, philosophy, causes of and responses to persecution, understandings of brotherly love, imagery from athletics, political discourse, and conceptions of sacrifice. Throughout he demonstrates how an understanding of the Greco-Roman world illuminates interpretation of Hebrews—and thus also how both the author and his audience were immersed in the broader culture of their era.

The next chapter, by James W. Thompson, is titled "What Has Middle Platonism to Do with Hebrews?" and addresses more specifically the influence of philosophical thought on the book's author. Thompson observes that in the early centuries of the church both critics and proponents of Christianity noted numerous "irreconcilable differences" between Platonism and Christianity, including the eschatological expectations of the latter, yet Christian thinkers frequently "employed Platonic language and categories in varying degrees to explain Christian beliefs." The question of whether the author of Hebrews also drew upon Middle Platonic philosophical thought remains debated, but Thompson provides a careful, articulate defense of that position. He first offers a very helpful survey of Middle Platonic thought, especially as expressed by its Jewish proponent Philo. Thompson then considers key passages in Hebrews and explains how the author utilized philosophical thought and language in his argumentation. He concludes that, while the author of Hebrews was not a thoroughgoing Platonist, nevertheless, "like the Christian theologians who came after him, he employed Platonic assumptions for his own pastoral purposes."

Eric F. Mason addresses another major suggestion for the conceptual background of Hebrews in "Cosmology, Messianism, and Melchizedek: Apocalyptic Jewish Traditions and Hebrews." Like Thompson, Mason argues that the author of Hebrews utilized ideas from a number of traditions, both philosophical and eschatological. But just as some interpreters deny the presence of Middle Platonism in Hebrews, others reject the idea that the book has parallels with ideas expressed in apocalyptic Jewish traditions like those reflected in the Dead Sea Scrolls. Mason surveys the complicated history of attempts to relate the Scrolls to Hebrews, then cautiously considers similarities in three areas: cosmology, particularly conceptions of the heavenly sanctuary and divine throne; messianism, especially ideas about a messianic priest; and Melchizedek, specifically interpretations that portray him as a heavenly, angelic figure. In each case, Mason notes both similarities and differences in Hebrews and the Qumran texts, but he concludes that "these points of contact establish the importance of understanding the broader Second Temple Jewish context for reading this epistle."

David M. Moffitt considers the author's Jewish context in a different way in "The Interpretation of Scripture in the Epistle to the Hebrews." Moffitt sets two major goals for his investigation: to survey issues important for understanding how the author interprets Scripture, and to analyze selected examples of his exegesis that indicate something of his conception of Scripture. Moffitt undertakes the first of these by explaining the nature of the biblical text (the Septuagint) utilized by the author of Hebrews—in the process providing a very helpful primer on textual criticism—then discussing several important Jewish interpretative techniques known from the Dead Sea Scrolls and rabbinic literature. Next, he makes his way through key passages in Hebrews, explaining how the author deals with biblical citations and how such compares with techniques current in contemporary Judaism. Throughout his discussion Moffitt reflects recent scholarship on Hebrews' methods of biblical interpretation (especially that of Susan Docherty 2009). He concludes that the author of Hebrews considers Scripture "a repository of divine speech," words "living and active" that speak "about Jesus, the Son, and the community that confesses Jesus' name." Drawing on contemporary exegetical methods, he can recast "scriptural words in new ways," yet "the words themselves also place constraints on him" that demand careful attention.

Structure of the Text

Interpreters of Hebrews have long struggled to explain how the book is structured. Still there is no consensus, though the five-part outline proposed by Albert Vanhoye (1976 [first ed. 1963]), arranged concentrically around a central emphasis on sacrifice in 5:11–10:39, has been especially influential. Normally interpreters have sought to organize the book in a linear fashion based on verbal or thematic cues in the text, but others have utilized insights from disciplines such as discourse analysis with varying results (Guthrie 1994; Westfall 2005). The book's sermonic qualities have prompted still other scholars to analyze the book in light of rhetorical or homiletical models, and two chapters here explore such possibilities from very different perspectives.

Craig R. Koester, in "Hebrews, Rhetoric, and the Future of Humanity," notes that consideration of the structure of Hebrews is vital because "the way that interpreters perceive the book's structure reflects the way they understand its message." He argues that the book is best understood when considered through the lens of Greco-Roman rhetoric. Koester provides an introduction to the canons of classical rhetoric while presenting Hebrews as a text with an exordium (1:1–2:4), a proposition (2:5–9), three series of arguments (2:10–12:27), a peroration (12:28–13:21), and an epistolary postscript (13:22–25). Throughout he illustrates his approach with copious examples from classical literature and explains how each section of the text would function to appeal to the audience. Also, he interacts with other scholars' suggestions about the book's structure and features. He concludes that the author, addressing "a Christian community in decline … focused his speech on the way that the hope of inheriting glory in God's kingdom seemed to be contradicted by the inglorious experience of Christian life in the world." The author assures his audience that God is faithful and that the ministry of Jesus ensures the fulfillment of their promised inheritance.

In the next chapter, "Hebrews, Homiletics, and Liturgical Scripture Interpretation," Gabriella Gelardini offers an alternative approach. She observes that the author of Hebrews makes extensive use of biblical quotations but varies the methodology and concentration of citations from section to section in the book, a technique most closely paralleled in synagogue homilies. Gelardini provides a very helpful introduction to ancient synagogue practices, architecture, and liturgy before turning to describe the nature of and expectations for synagogue homilies. In her reading, the key biblical passages undergirding the homily we now call Hebrews were Exod 31:18–32:35 (the Torah text, or *sidrah*, with the theme of covenant breaking) and Jer 31:31–34 (the related reading from the Prophets, the *haptarah*, on covenant renewal). The overall structure is that of a three-part *petichta* homily with elaborate expectations for the use of scriptural citations in each section. Gelardini asserts that the key texts from Exodus and Jeremiah were paired in the reconstructed ancient Jewish "trienniel reading cycle between the two fast days from Tammuz 17 and Av 9," the former commemorating the destruction of the law tablets by Moses in response to the golden calf incident and the latter the rebellion at Kadesh-barnea. Both also were associated with the destruction of the First Temple by the Babylonians, with Tisha be-Av also related to the fall of the Second Temple and the failure of the Bar Kokhba revolt. As the lowest points on the Jewish calendar, they are "shadow images" of its highest point, Yom Kippur, and this explains the importance of the Day of Atonement rite for the author of Hebrews.

EMERGING METHODOLOGICAL APPROACHES

Recent decades in biblical scholarship have been marked by the emergence of new methodologies beyond the traditional historical-critical modes that have long characterized academic biblical studies. Hebrews has not normally been a prominent text under consideration by practitioners of new approaches, especially compared to the attention received by other New Testament texts such as the Gospels and Pauline Epistles, but that does not mean it is not fertile ground for such investigations.

One might argue that social-scientific interpretation of the New Testament no longer is an "emerging" field, but analyses of Hebrews remain few, and there is much internal debate among practitioners about the proper appropriation of such techniques for biblical interpretation. (For Hebrews, see especially deSilva 2008 [orig. 1995] and 2000, both examples of sociorhetorical interpretation, and the rather different approach of Whitlark 2008.) Jerome H. Neyrey, a veteran social-scientific interpreter who earlier examined Jesus' role in the Gospel of John using the model of a "broker" (Neyrey 2007), analyzes Hebrews' portrait of Jesus as priest in "Jesus the Broker in Hebrews: Insights from the Social Sciences." Neyrey explains the importance of patron-client relationships in the ancient Mediterranean world and the vital role played by brokers, go-betweens who "bring the client's needs to the attention of the patron, as well as the benefactions of the patron to the clients." Next he considers the presentation of Jesus as priest/broker in Hebrews through the lens of five questions: How does one become a broker? What makes one successful? What does one broker? Why a broker, and why this one? What tariff does a broker receive? In the course of his discussion, Neyrey also considers how Hebrews presents Jesus as priest in ways akin to the ancient rhetorical categories students learned in *progymnasmata* exercises.

Kenneth Schenck considers a different emerging methodology in "Hebrews as the Re-presentation of a Story: A Narrative Approach to Hebrews." Others have applied this approach to study of New Testament letters—most notably Richard Hays (2002 [orig. 1983]) on Galatians—with the assumption that Paul "was arguing with his opponents *over a story*"; such a foundational narrative understanding of the gospel and its implications included various elements both shared and disputed by the apostle and his detractors. Schenck surveys the application of literary criticism to the New Testament in recent decades and considers critiques of the approaches used by Hays and others, then asserts that the author of Hebrews also has in mind a story that undergirds his message in the epistle. Schenck rejects the idea that Hebrews was written to Jewish Christians "tempted to return to mainstream Judaism and its Levitical means of atonement" in the years before the destruction of the temple. Instead, he argues that the author of Hebrews offers consolation after the destruction of the temple in 70 C.E. to Christian believers of any ethnicity who might question their faith in the aftermath of that event. In order to do this, the author draws upon a shared body of assumptions from the biblical "story" he shares with the recipients and re-presents them in "a radical reinterpretation of key events in the common Christian-Jewish story." This motive explains the author's significant interest in things and ideas such as sanctuaries, atonement, exaltation, and priesthood. As such, "the author builds on the audience's current understanding and common Christian traditions and re-presents them in striking terms."

Major Theological Issues

Hebrews is a profoundly theological book, and as noted earlier the significance of this has been increasingly recognized in recent decades. Frank J. Matera offers an overview of the theology of the book in "The Theology of the Epistle to the Hebrews." Matera notes that "the task of New Testament theology is to provide a thick and rich description of the theology in the New Testamant so that what was written in the past will have meaning and relevance for the future," yet this task is difficult because the New Testament texts were not intended as theological treatises. Nevertheless, they are steeped in religious thought, and one may consider their contents using classic theological categories, provided that one remains cognizant of the original nature of the texts under discussion. Matera finds in Hebrews "the most systematic presentation of the person and work of Jesus in the New Testament" but also challenges, including its distinctive presentation of Jesus as priest, its emphasis on Jesus' death but relative silence on the resurrection and parousia, and its self-description as a "word of exhortation." Matera explicates the theology of the book in three parts: consideration of its doctrinal exposition (chiefly on the person and work of Christ) and its moral exhortation (especially concerning what one may know of the audience and their hope for the future), then reflections on the significance of Hebrews' theology for contemporary Christian faith and thought.

Next, Kevin B. McCruden explores more specifically a particular theological issue in Hebrews in "The Concept of Perfection in the Epistle to the Hebrews." Perfection terminology occurs eighteen times in Hebrews, yet McCruden notes that it is difficult to ascertain exactly how the author understands this idea. He undertakes his investigation with "the methodological assumption that a larger narrative world or theological story informs this ancient sermon," one very comprehensible to an ancient audience but likely "profoundly alien" to modern readers. He proceeds to explain this story, particularly with respect to the role that perfection plays in the "human career" of Jesus, and finds many parallels between Hebrews and the *kenōsis* hymn in Phil 2:6–11. Also, McCruden draws links between the perfection of Jesus and the perfection of his faithful people. He concludes, "while the event of Jesus' exaltation comprises one aspect of what Jesus' perfection means for the author of Hebrews, the personal faithfulness of Jesus also plays a significant role in the perfecting of the Son as eternal high priest." Likewise, "the faithful ultimately experience perfection in the age to come," yet "even now … perfection understood as communion with God is an experiential reality that has been made possible through the personal sacrifice of Jesus that cleanses the believer from within."

Reception History

Traditionally Hebrews has been overshadowed by other New Testament books in the history of Christian thought, especially the Gospels and Pauline Epistles (even though it was long considered among the latter). Nevertheless, Hebrews has had considerable influence in certain ways. Sometimes this has been positive, as in the development of key christological doctrines, and at other times it has been negative, as when read as a text espousing Christian supersessionism. Also, Hebrews has been used in varying ways in the history of Christian worship. Three chapters in this last major section of the book explore these varied topics.

Rowan A. Greer, author of a classic volume on patristic interpretation of Hebrews (Greer 1973), examines the use of Hebrews in christological controversies in "The Jesus of Hebrews and the Christ of Chalcedon." After considering broadly the use of Scripture by early Christian interpreters, he turns to consider two difficulties for understanding the identity of Christ posed by Hebrews: "If Christ is 'the exact imprint of God's very being,' does this mean that he is divine in such a way as not to compromise monotheism? Further, if Christ is divine, why would he need to 'learn obedience by what he suffered'? Indeed, how could a divine being possibly suffer at all?" Greer finds these two issues respectively at the heart of two crucial debates in early Christianity, the Arian controversy and the resulting Nicene Creed (381 c.e.), with Athanasius of Alexandria and Theodore of Mopsuestia offering opposing arguments, and the fifth-century Nestorian controversy, prompted by the Trinitarian affirmations in the creed and now engaged by Cyril of Alexandria and Nestorius. Greer carefully considers the issues in both debates and the use of Scripture by each of the four proponents. Greer concludes, "Describing some of the interpretations of Hebrews put forth during the period of the first four general councils underlines the importance of the theological frameworks that shape them. Nevertheless, all the interpreters claim that their presupposed frameworks spring from Scripture. If we take these claims seriously, there is a circularity or reciprocity binding exegesis and theology together." With this he offers a challenge to the assumptions of modern biblical interpreters as well.

Alan C. Mitchell then considers a very different history of interpreting Hebrews in "'A Sacrifice of Praise': Does Hebrews Promote Supersessionism?" Mitchell notes that, "from the second century C.E., Christians have used [Hebrews] to promote the view that Christianity, according to God's plan, had replaced Judaism," and he concedes that much in Hebrews can be read in that light. He cautions against such interpretations that may promote anti-Semitism, however, especially in light of the Holocaust. Mitchell argues that "Hebrews itself is not inherently supersessionist," despite the long history of interpretation otherwise. He offers a definition of supersessionism and surveys its various expressions, examines three key passages in Hebrews (7:1–12; 8:8–13; 10:1–10) often read to support that view, and offers a different approach to the book that avoids such conclusions. The context of the book of Hebrews itself is a major factor for Mitchell's argument: the New Testament books were written "before Christianity had split definitely from Judaism. When one understands the rich variegation of Judaism in the first century C.E. and the processes of self-definition each of the various Jewish sects undertook, then texts that appear as polemical need not be seen as anti-Semitic or supersessionist." Instead, they are documents of intra-Jewish debate, even if addressed to Gentiles who have attached themselves to this Jewish messianic movement.

Finally, Mark A. Torgerson approaches the traditional interpretation of Hebrews from yet a third perspective, that of a liturgist examining the history of Christian worship. In "Hebrews in the Worship Life of the Church: A Historical Survey," Torgerson considers how Hebrews has been utilized in multiple aspects of ecclesial life, including preaching, baptism, Eucharist, ordered ministry, lectionaries, hymnody, service books, and visual art. He includes copious examples documenting the role of Hebrews in each of these areas, drawing from a diverse range of Christian traditions both ancient and modern. Torgerson notes that Hebrews "has occupied a unique niche" in Christian worship life: "Though the Epistle to the Hebrews has not had a large role to play in the development and practice of Christian worship, it has remained an enduring source of inspiration and theological interpretation." Perhaps more surprising, Torgerson illustrates that the influence of Hebrews in Christian worship has risen in recent years in many circles, especially when gauged by its increased presence in lectionary cycles.

Given his instrumental role in the present wave of interest in Hebrews, it is only appropriate that the volume's epilogue is penned by Harold W. Attridge. Attridge offers trenchant comments on each essay, reflecting both on their individual contributions and the questions they raise for future study. He especially notes the "intertexts" considered by each contributor, evaluating how they approach Hebrews in relation to other ancient literature and ideas. He writes, "Their use of these various lenses through which to read Hebrews is a marvelous illustration of the challenges inherent in making sense of this biblical book." Elsewhere he states that this volume's essays "should certainly serve to engage a new generation of students" of Hebrews. If so, the goals inherent in both phrases of the book's title will be fulfilled.

HEBREWS AMONG GREEKS AND ROMANS

Patrick Gray

The author of the Letter to the Hebrews shares with the apostle Paul a conviction that the death of Jesus marks a decisive intervention into human history by the God of Israel. "Christ crucified," however, is "a stumbling block to Jews and foolishness to Gentiles" (1 Cor 1:23). That Christianity spread as quickly as it did is surprising, given that its central message struck a jarring note with every conceivable demographic—the categories "Jew" and "Gentile," after all, cover all of humanity. The story of Christianity begins with the execution of a Jewish teacher, but it is also important to remember that he was killed by Roman authorities and that the earliest descriptions of the fledgling sect were written in Greek. From the outset, then, the Christian movement cut across ordinary ethnic, cultural, social, and linguistic boundaries.

Sometimes the encounter between the Jews who were Jesus' first followers and the Greco-Roman world is quite explicit, as when the Gospel of John (19:20) notes that the sign over the cross declaring Jesus "King of the Jews" was written in Greek, Hebrew, and Latin or when the Gospel of Luke (3:1) mentions the names of specific Roman officeholders at the time of John the Baptist. In the Letter to the Hebrews, the influence of Greek and Roman culture is less conspicuous but no less profound. In their attempts to articulate their newfound faith, the author and audience of Hebrews were engaged with other Christians in the crucial process of creating a distinctively Christian identity. But it was not creation *ex nihilo*. Although novel claims about Jesus were the proverbial leaven in the lump, Christian identity was formed from preexisting elements in the cultural contexts of those who converted. This essay will survey a selection of concepts, images, and motifs from the Greco-Roman milieu in which Christianity emerged and will illustrate their significance for understanding Hebrews.

One may wonder why it is necessary to know anything about Greece or Rome in a letter to "Hebrews." This question has two answers.

(1) While the prevailing view among scholars is that Hebrews is addressed to a Jewish-Christian or perhaps a mixed audience, a number of commentators believe that a non-Jewish audience is more likely (e.g., Moffatt 1924, ix; Weiss 1991, 70–72; Ehrman 2000, 378–79). Theories of a Jewish-Christian readership, they argue, rely too heavily on the superscript (or title) *pros Ebraious*, which was not a part of the original text. This superscript first appears in a papyrus copy of the letter (P^{46}) dating to the late second or early third century. It may reflect no more than an educated guess about the intended audience by early copyists based on the letter's contents.

Certain clues about the readers and their relationship with God suggest that the author may have a non-Jewish audience in mind. The term "Hebrew" never occurs in the text, and there is never any specific warning against reverting to Judaism, only of forsaking Christ (2:1–2; 6:6; 10:29). The pressing Jew-Gentile tension that runs through Acts and Paul's letters is entirely absent; thus Hebrews may belong to a stage in history when the Christian movement is predominantly Gentile (Scott 1923, 18–19). Further proof that the author is not describing the readers' former life in Judaism but in paganism is sometimes seen in the fact that the alternative to progress in faith is described as "falling away from the living God" and a return to the performance of "dead works" (3:12; 6:1; 9:14), a way of speaking that is more difficult to reconcile with a Jewish background (Weiss 1991, 71–72). In support of this interpretation, a number of scholars have pointed to the similarities between Heb 6:1–2 and the missionary preaching aimed at pagans in Acts and 1 Thessalonians. Parallels between the elements mentioned by the author as foundational and the basic instruction for Gentile proselytes to Judaism in the Second Temple period also support this view (Braun 1984, 157–60). The thoroughly scriptural character of Hebrews' argument is not seen as a problem by proponents of a non-Jewish audience, since the Gentile church adopted the Septuagint (the Hebrew Bible translated into Greek) as its own Scripture at an early stage. One need only look to Paul's letters to the Galatians and Corinthians for examples of a very similar use of Jewish Scripture in addressing a Gentile audience. As a result of this reliance on biblical writings, the author's discussion of Judaism has a bookish feel about it (Eisenbaum 2005b, 213–37);

rather than discussing contemporary Judaism and railing against the still-standing Jerusalem temple, as one sees in the Dead Sea Scrolls, Hebrews is concerned with the tabernacle in use more than a millennium earlier and the priestly ordinances as set out in the Pentateuch.

(2) A Jewish audience for the letter nevertheless remains a strong possibility. But even if Hebrews was sent to a group of Jews, some familiarity with the Greco-Roman environment in which it was written remains necessary for understanding the author's assumptions and manner of thinking. In this respect, they would be no different from the majority of Jews living in the first century. After the destruction of the temple in 586 B.C.E., most Jews went into exile, and their descendants never returned to the land. Jews in the Diaspora still outnumbered those in Palestine when Hebrews was written.

Engagement with Hellenistic culture was unavoidable beginning in the fourth century B.C.E., when Alexander the Great established Greek military control over much of the region and Greek became the common language of the Mediterranean basin. Jerusalem was not exempt from Hellenistic influences, nor were those who actively sought to escape it. The case of the Maccabean revolt against the Seleucid king Antiochus IV provides a poignant illustration. Although the Maccabees succeeded in driving the pagans from Jerusalem after the desecration of the temple, they won the battle, so to speak, only to lose the war: the story of their struggle to resist the encroachment of Hellenistic culture has survived not in Hebrew but only in manuscripts translated into Greek. The Christian faith one encounters in Hebrews is born out of a Judaism that has been immersed in Greek and Roman culture for centuries.

HEBREWS AND GRECO-ROMAN CULTURE

Several aspects of the argument of Hebrews stand out more vividly when viewed against the background of Greek and Roman culture.

LANGUAGE AND RHETORIC

The letter begins with the declaration that "God speaks." It should come as no surprise that someone with a special interest in divine speech is himself an especially eloquent writer. Of all the New Testament authors, the author of Hebrews is perhaps the most polished Greek prose stylist. His vocabulary is wide-ranging and not limited to the language of the Septuagint, the

Greek translation of the Old Testament to which the author refers when he quotes the Bible. Approximately 150 words are found in Hebrews and nowhere else in the New Testament.[1] Literary devices used by Hellenistic writers abound in Hebrews: etymological wordplay (2:10; 7:9; 9:6–17; 12:2); alliteration (1:1; 4:16; 12:21); anaphora (the repetition of "by faith" throughout ch. 11); antithesis (7:18–20; 10:11–12); assonance (1:1–3; 12:9); and litotes (4:15; 6:10; 7:20), among others (Attridge 1989, 20–21). Hebrews is not at all a typical "letter," and its syntax has all the structural and rhythmic qualities one would expect in a composition intended for oral delivery.

The author describes his work as a "word of exhortation" (13:22), a term also used in Acts 13:15 in reference to a synagogue homily. Surviving synagogue homilies do not constitute a very strictly defined literary genre, but their general structure shares certain formal properties with the speeches of Greek and Roman orators. Ancient rhetorical handbooks such as those of Aristotle, Demetrius, and Quintilian classify speeches as forensic, deliberative, or epideictic. Forensic rhetoric aims at persuading an audience to make a judgment about past events. Deliberative rhetoric seeks to persuade an audience to choose a particular course of action in the future. Epideictic rhetoric typically focuses on the present and seeks to convince an audience that a person, group, or idea is worthy of praise or blame.

Hebrews is not an example of forensic rhetoric, since it does not ask its readers to determine the guilt or innocence of the figures it mentions. The author's glorification of Jesus in comparison with the angels, Moses, and the Levitical priests resembles epideictic rhetoric, as does the lengthy roll call of the heroes and heroines of faith in Heb 11. By exhorting his readers to follow the example of Jesus in persevering through hard times (12:1–3), to press on toward perfection (6:1–2; 10:38–39), and to avoid the fate of those who fall away (2:1–3; 3:7–4:11; 6:4–6; 10:19–31), elements of deliberative rhetoric are also present. It may be that the deliberative and the epideictic are aimed at different groups within an audience that includes members who are firm in the faith and members whose commitment is waning. While it may not be possible to fit Hebrews neatly

---

1. E.g., *metriopatheō*, "to moderate one's emotions" (5:2); *eulabeia*, "reverence" (5:7; 12:28); *apatōr*, "without father" (7:3); *tympanizō*, "to torture" (11:35); *euperistatos*, "easily ensnaring" (12:1).

into one category, it is clear that the author is acquainted with the basic topics and techniques found in ancient rhetoric.[2]

GREEK AND ROMAN PHILOSOPHY

Wherever the author received his education, it is clear that he was particularly gifted in rhetoric. There are indications that philosophy is also among the subjects with which he is familiar. When he chides the readers for their sluggishness in 5:11–14, for example, he uses terminology shared with Greek philosophers concerned with the pursuit of virtue. They still need milk, he says, not solid food. Only the mature (*teleioi*) can handle solid food because they have attained a state (*hexis*) wherein they can distinguish good from evil. This evaluation of their progress corresponds with the description of the moral life found in Aristotle (*Eth. nic.* 2.1.1–8; 2.5.6), who sees all human activity as aiming toward a *telos* ("end" or "purpose") and who uses *hexis* to denote the cultivated character traits or settled disposition that results from habitual practice (Lee 1997, 158–59).

But the most pervasive philosophical influence may be in the area of metaphysics rather than ethics. Many scholars see in Hebrews the earliest instance of Platonic influence on Christian thought, perhaps through the conduit of a Hellenistic Jewish writer such as Philo of Alexandria, who calls Plato "the sweetest of all writers" (*Prob.* 13) and quotes frequently from his dialogues (Thompson 1982; Sterling 2001). Plato's worldview is strongly dualistic. He sees reality as divided between two distinct "worlds": the material world, perceived through the senses and characterized by corruption and change; and the world of ideas or "Forms," perceived by the mind and characterized by permanence and incorruptibility (*Phaed.* 78c–79d; 80b). Only knowledge of the latter is true knowledge, as its object is changeless and eternal, whereas the physical world is fleeting and less "real." Visible objects are "real" only to the degree that they imitate the Forms, which serve as a sort of blueprint for objects encountered in the realm of space, time, and matter (*Tim.* 28a). Plato's "Allegory of the Cave" in the seventh book of *The Republic* (514a–520a) provides the most famous explanation of the relationship between the two worlds. Objects encountered in the physical world, as well as particular examples of quali-

---

2. Detailed discussion of the rhetorical features of the letter may be found in Craig R. Koester's essay in this volume. For an approach to Hebrews as a synagogue homily, see Gabriella Gelardini's essay.

ties such as justice and courage, are described as shadows or dim reflections of the Forms.

A number of passages in Hebrews recall key aspects of Plato's theory of Forms. The author consistently contrasts the heavenly realm that will abide forever and the earthly realm that is passing away (1:10–12; 10:34; 12:27–28). In Heb 8:5, for example, Jewish priests serve in a tabernacle described as "a copy and a shadow of the heavenly sanctuary" that has been made according to a "pattern" showed to Moses by God. The tabernacle in which Jesus serves as high priest is one "not made with hands" (9:11). Ancient Israelite rituals take place in a "sanctuary made with hands … a copy of the true," and employ "copies of the heavenly things" (9:23–24). The law, too, contains a "shadow" but "not the very image" of "good things to come" (10:1). According to the well-known definition in Heb 11:1, faith is likewise a function of the relationship between the visible world and the invisible.

One critical difference between Hebrews and this Platonic outlook has to do with history. Events in history, that is, in the human world of time and space, are of little ultimate significance. Hebrews, by contrast, sees history reaching back into the Israelite past as well as headed toward a climax with the return of Christ, the establishment of God's kingdom, participation in a Sabbath rest, and the fulfillment of God's promises (4:1–10; 9:15, 27–28; 10:35–39; 11:16, 39–40; 12:28; 13:14). This future depends for its realization upon certain pivotal events having taken place in the physical world, namely, the death and resurrection of Jesus, whose bodily suffering is essential to the exercise of his priestly office (2:14–18; 5:7–10; 10:10). It is through the "veil" of his flesh that believers enter the heavenly sanctuary (10:20). In this way, Hebrews turns Platonism "on its side," so that the contrast between type and antitype is framed in terms of the past, on the one hand, and the present and future, on the other (Johnson 2006, 20). The spatial antithesis (this world/the heavenly world) corresponds to a temporal antithesis (in which the past is prologue to or foreshadowing of a glorious future).[3]

---

3. On the distinction between the Middle Platonism one finds in the first century and in Plato's own writings, see James W. Thompson's essay in this volume.

Social Setting: Persecution

Although very little about the audience is known with certainty, one aspect of the social-cultural context for the letter is clear: the perceived existential crisis the author is addressing is related to some experience of persecution (10:32–34). They have "endured a hard struggle with sufferings, sometimes being publicly exposed to abuse and persecution, and sometimes being partners with those so treated." Their possessions have been plundered. Some have been imprisoned. The author's description of their plight strongly implies that their profession of Christian faith has provoked this ill treatment, though he nowhere identifies the perpetrators.

What motivated religious persecution in the first century? The earliest surviving references to Christianity made by Roman writers provide a clue. A common thread appears in the brief comments found in Suetonius, Tacitus, and Pliny, Roman historians writing early in the second century. Tacitus, in describing the fire at Rome during Nero's reign, speaks of Christianity as a "pernicious superstition" breaking out after being temporarily checked by the death of Jesus (*Ann.* 15.44). Recounting Nero's punishment of the Christians, whom the emperor blamed for the fire, Suetonius calls them "a class of men given over to a new and mischievous superstition" (*Nero* 16.2). Pliny the Younger, in a letter to Trajan, similarly describes the Christians of Bithynia as adherents of "a degenerate superstition carried to extravagant lengths" (*Ep.* 10.96). "Superstition" (Greek: *deisidaimonia*; Latin: *superstitio*) is the standard category in the first-century Mediterranean for denigrating "debased" religiosity. As it does in English, superstition in antiquity includes a wide range of irrational beliefs and customs and old wives' tales (Theophrastus, *Char.* 16; Strabo, *Geogr.* 7.3.4). Especially in Roman sources, superstition is connected to foreign cults and, as a result, is often considered politically subversive (Cicero, *Div.* 2.72.148; Livy 10.39.2; Suetonius, *Claud.* 25.5). For this reason as well as for their practice—puzzling to non-Jews—of abstaining from pork, many writers apply this label to the Jews (Cicero, *Flac.* 67; Tacitus, *Hist.* 5.13).

The emotion of fear in religion receives special emphasis in Greco-Roman definitions of superstition (Polybius 6.56.6; Lucian, *Philops.* 37). Believing the gods to be wrathful rather than beneficent, the superstitious are gripped by a paralyzing fear (Plutarch, *Superst.* 165d, 167c–f). The strategy of invoking God's fearfulness is on frequent display in Hebrews. God is "a consuming fire" who must be approached "with reverence and godly fear" (12:28–29). Judgment is a source of hope for the faithful but a "fearful prospect" for those who fall away; thus "it is a fearful thing to fall into the hands of the living God" (10:27, 31). No one can hide from God; everything is "open and laid bare to the eyes of the one with whom we have to do" (4:13). Jesus' own prayers, according to Heb 5:7, are answered only on account of his "godly fear."

On the other hand, Jesus' death in Heb 2:14–16 is said to effect liberation from life-long fear of death inspired by the devil. The result for the readers is compared favorably with that of Moses, who is terrified by what he sees at Sinai and says, "I tremble with fear" (12:18–24). In recounting the circumstances surrounding Moses' birth and subsequent flight from Egypt (11:23–28), the author mentions his parents' and his own fear-lessness. The intended result of the moral instruction listed in 13:1–5 is that the audience may say, "The Lord is my helper; I will not be afraid" (13:6), and maintain the "confidence" that enables them to "draw near to the throne of grace" (4:16; cf. 3:6; 10:19, 35). It may be that prior to their conversion the author and audience held fairly typical views of "aberrant" religion—as silly, irrational, obsessive in matters of ritual or behavior, and above all conducive to fear and anxiety—but now they feel a need to articulate their newfound faith in terms that address the perception that they are superstitious, whether by denial or by challenging the conventional wisdom (Gray 2003, 215–27).

RESPONDING TO SUFFERING

The precise reasons for their persecution remain obscure because the author has no need to rehearse details that are surely known to his readers (10:32–33). He focuses instead upon their response to this experience of suffering. They may look at their suffering as ultimately meaningless, or, still worse, they may look on it as a punitive sign of God's displeasure. The author of Hebrews urges his readers in 12:5–11 to regard their hardships as a necessary part of their education as God's children:

> And you have completely forgotten the exhortation that reasons with you as sons: "My son, do not disregard the *discipline* of the Lord, nor be discouraged when rebuked by him. For the one he loves the Lord *disciplines*, and he chastens every son whom he accepts." Endure for the sake of *discipline*. God is dealing with you as sons, for what son is there that a father does not *discipline*? But if you are without *discipline*, in which all have a share, then you are illegitimate and not legitimate sons. More-

over, we have had our natural fathers as *disciplinarians*, and we respected
them. Should we not all the more be subject to the father of spirits and
live? For they applied *discipline* for a short while as they thought best, but
he does so for our benefit so that we might share in his holiness. Though
for the moment all *discipline* appears to be not joy but grief, later it yields
a peaceful fruit of righteousness in those who have been trained by it.
(my translation)

Some form of the Greek word *paideia* appears in this passage eight times
(see the italicized words in the translation above). It can denote the physical discipline of an errant child or, more generally, the process of education
in Greek culture. Hebrews employs it to explain why bad things happen to
good people, a perennial question pondered by thinkers of all times and in
all places, including Stoic philosophers writing in the first century such as
Seneca and Epictetus.

Little in this passage, apart from the quotation from Prov 3:11–12,
would strike a Greek or Roman reader as out of the ordinary. The depiction of certain family dynamics would seem especially familiar. Illegitimate
children were often the offspring of a slave and were thus automatically at
a legal disadvantage in comparison with their legitimate half-siblings. The
silver lining in the dark cloud of illegitimacy had to do with the exemption of bastard children from the power of the *paterfamilias* (Braun 1984,
413–14). The institution of *patria potestas* invested the oldest male in
Roman families with almost absolute power over all of his descendants
(Crook 1967, 113–22; Eyben 1991, 114–43). All legitimate children were
under this jurisdiction, and reaching the age of majority did not abro-
gate the obligations it imposed. Only death, formal *emancipatio*, adoption
into another family, or the father's insanity suspended *patria potestas*. A
paterfamilias possessed power of life and death (*ius vitae necisque*) over
his children, who could not technically own their own property or make
legally valid wills. A father could deny marriage, compel divorce, and even
sell his children.

Although the image of the Roman family as little more than a paternal
despotism may be an exaggeration, the caricature appears often in ancient
sources and would have conditioned how this language in Hebrews was
heard, all the more so since the *paterfamilias* was responsible for the rear-
ing and education of children. Hebrews presupposes on the part of the
audience an experience of parental discipline that corresponds to what one
finds reflected in contemporaneous Greek and Roman moralists. Seneca

(*Ira* 2.21.1–6) believes that fathers should not be too strict with their children, but, for the children's sake, neither should they be too lenient. He contends that a father's love and his severity with his children are in direct proportion to one another (*Prov.* 1.5). Maximus of Tyre (*Diss.* 4.7) likewise argues that the desire to give pleasure is an unreliable indicator of true parental affection.

Discipline was occasionally delegated to slaves. According to Plutarch, however, Cato the Elder himself undertook his son's education because he thought it unseemly for his son to be disciplined by a slave (*Cat. Maj.* 20.4–7). Hebrews has in mind just such a scrupulous parent. The author reminds the audience that they had fathers—not slaves—as disciplinarians. Many failed to find the right balance between severity and affection. Too many fathers

> in their eagerness that their children may the sooner rank first in everything, ... lay upon them unreasonable tasks, which the children find themselves unable to perform, and so come to grief; besides being depressed by their unfortunate experience, they do not respond to the instruction they receive. (Ps.-Plutarch, *Lib. ed.* 9b)

Good fathers nevertheless have the best interests of their children at heart. The analogy between the human and the divine found in Heb 12:5–11 is matched closely by Seneca's description of God as a loving father who says of humanity, "Let them be harassed by toil, by suffering, by losses, in order that they may gather true strength" (*Prov.* 2.6), a sentiment echoed in Heb 10:32–39 as well (see Croy 1998, 147–50).

Though spared many of the unpleasant aspects of *patria potestas*, bastards occupied a precarious position in Roman society because they were usually left out of a father's will and had few rights should the father die intestate (Dixon 1992, 62). Unless explicitly and intentionally left out of a will, by contrast, all legitimate children had a share in the father's estate. The privileges of legitimate sonship hinted at in the rhetorical question in Heb 12:8 serve as a reminder of their heavenly inheritance as God's children, thus supplying the motivation to endure the hardships they face. "The peaceful fruit of righteousness" and the prospect of "sharing in his holiness" (12:10–11) should enable the audience to face their present persecution with the confidence that they will receive "the promise" (10:35–36). As Aristotle remarks, the roots of *paideia* are bitter, but the fruit is sweet (Diogenes Laertius 5.18).

In its conception of what constitutes true *paideia* and a worthy inheritance, Hebrews is obviously far from typical in the Greco-Roman world. But Hebrews also diverges from Jewish thinking in two ways: (1) "inheritance" does not refer to "the promised land," as it usually does in the Old Testament; and (2) it comes through Jesus, who is "the mediator of a new covenant, so that those who are called may receive the promised eternal inheritance" (9:15). The readers' willingness to be dispossessed is an indication that they perceive their sufferings as firm but loving discipline administered by God the father.

BROTHERLY LOVE

If God is the father of the faithful in Hebrews (12:7, 9) and Jesus is God's son (1:2; 5:8; 6:6), then the audience and Jesus are related as siblings. Jesus, because he is the "firstborn" (1:6), is their older brother. This relationship between Jesus and the readers is most explicit in Heb 2:10–18. Jesus is "not ashamed to call them brothers." Fraternal empathy is said to be a prerequisite for the office of high priest (2:17): "He therefore had to become like his brothers in every respect so that he might be a merciful and faithful high priest in God's service." Hebrews probes the image of Christ as brother more deeply than any other New Testament writer. A closer look at the expectations associated with brotherhood in Greco-Roman literature throws into relief the nature of Jesus' priesthood in Hebrews. The most systematic discussion is found in Plutarch's essay "On Brotherly Love" (*De fraterno amore*).

Brothers look out for and protect one another. As Cyrus tells his son, there is no need for a man with a great and powerful brother to fear any harm (Xenophon, *Cyr.* 8.7.15). Unfortunately, examples of enmity between brothers are as easy to find as examples of solidarity. Familiarity can breed contempt, which too often takes the form of slander (Plutarch, *Frat. amor.* 479b).[4] Unlike the brother who nurses a grudge, Jesus, who has put up with all manner of abuse (Heb 12:3), ensures that his brothers' sins will

---

4. Plutarch repeatedly uses the same word for "slander" (*diabolos*: cf. *Frat. amor.* 481b, 490c–f) as is used in Heb 2:14, where it refers to the devil. In the biblical tradition, the devil is often called the "accuser" or "slanderer" (Job 1–2; Zech 3). To be sure, Plutarch does not use the term with the same "diabolical" connotations, but it is nonetheless striking that in both texts *diabolos* poses a threat that a model brother is able to neutralize.

be remembered no more by the father (8:12; 10:17). He accomplishes this by sacrificing himself. This is especially fitting since the anxiety caused by fraternal strife is most acute at family gatherings where sacrifices are made, when "that voice which has been beloved and familiar from boyhood [becomes] most dreadful to hear" (*Frat. amor.* 481d).

Brothers are not always equal in terms of age, status, or talent. Some sink into disgrace through resentment or envy of a brother's accomplishments (*Frat. amor.* 485e–486f). How may this problem be overcome? The superior brother "conform[s] his character" to that of the inferior and makes him a partner in his undertakings whenever it is possible (484d). True to form, Jesus humbles himself and becomes like his brothers in all respects (Heb 2:9, 14, 17) except for sin (4:15) and is thereby able to "deal gently" with them (5:2). He also resembles the mythical Pollux, who refuses to become a god and instead becomes a demigod so that he can participate in his brother's mortality and share with Castor a portion of his own immortality.[5] Yet younger brothers are still advised to emulate, reverence, and even obey the older. Obedience is the most highly esteemed of the signs of respect a younger brother shows to an elder (Xenophon, *Cyr.* 8.7.16; Cicero, *Quint. fratr.* 1.3.3). The audience of Hebrews is likewise urged to obey and imitate Jesus; indeed, their salvation depends on it (5:9; 13:13).

Judged by Hellenistic standards, Jesus is the consummate older brother. Flawed brothers are much easier to find. Fraternal reprimands, however, should come only after defending the wayward brother before the father and, if necessary, bearing the father's wrath in his place (Plutarch, *Frat. amor.* 482e–483c). This duty recalls the description of the atonement in Hebrews, which the author sees as a vicarious act (see 2:9; 9:24–26). As mediator (7:25; 9:15; 12:24), Jesus diverts God's furious judgment of sin (10:27) from his brothers to himself.

Even in harmonious relationships, the problem of inheritance looms as a potential source of friction (Bannon 1997, 12–61). Plutarch describes the man who ingratiates himself with the parents and in so doing cheats his brother of "the greatest and fairest of inheritances," the parents' goodwill (*Frat. amor.* 482e). The most valuable portion of the inheritance, he adds, is the brother's friendship and trust (483e; cf. Xenophon, *Mem.* 2.3.1–4).

---

5. Castor and Pollux are also renowned for their willingness to help the pious (Cicero, *Nat. d.* 2.2.6; Pindar, *Nem.* 10.54) and are often referred to as "saviors" (Plutarch, *Superst.* 169b; see Burkert 1985, 212–13).

One finds no trace of rivalry in Jesus' relationship with his brothers. In stark contrast to the negative examples of brotherhood in Hebrews—Cain (11:4; 12:24) and Esau (12:16–17)—he has made them his "partners" (3:1, 14). Jesus is "the heir of all things" (1:2) and "has inherited a name" more excellent than that of the angels (1:4). He sits at the right hand of the one who sends angels "for the sake of those who are to inherit salvation" (1:14). Apart from the mediation of their devoted sibling, Hebrews contemplates no other way by which the readers will receive the promises. Here and throughout the letter, then, the admonition in Heb 13:1 to "let brotherly love continue" is no mere afterthought but goes to the heart of the author's message.

ATHLETICS

Athletics is another of the author's sources for metaphors and analogies. Philosophers found in the sporting life a wide range of material fit for illustrating important truths about the life of virtue. Demosthenes (*1 Aristog.* 25.97), Aristotle (*Eth. nic.* 1.8.9; 3.9.3–4), Epictetus (*Diatr.* 3.15.1–7; 3.22.51, 58), and Marcus Aurelius (3.4.3; 4.18) are representative in their use of the *agōn*, or "contest," as a metaphor for moral and spiritual pursuits.

While Hebrews has already referred to the readers' plight as a "great contest" (*pollēn athlēsin*) in 10:32, athletic imagery is most relevant to the author's point in Heb 12:1–13. The author exhorts the audience to "run the race with perseverance" in the presence of a "cloud of witnesses." This description clearly evokes the setting of a track meet taking place in a large stadium full of spectators. Succeeding in this race will require them to put off any extraneous weight (12:1) in addition to maintaining a rigorous training regimen that will test their resolve (12:11). Near the end of the race they must take care not to let their hands "droop" or their knees go weak (12:12), or else they will lose the prize. By offering his encouragement, the author is like Eryxias, the coach of the famed wrestler Arrichion (Philostratos, *Gymn.* 21). When Arrichion begins to fade, Eryxias goads him on to victory by shouting out that he will have a glorious epitaph at his grave that reads, "He did not give up at Olympia!" Jesus is their role model (12:2) who, like Arrichion, emerges victorious even as he dies.

To what further use does the author put this imagery? The heroes of faith from Heb 11 constitute the "cloud of witnesses" in 12:1 said to be watching the audience as they endure present difficulties. They have already run their race and now can only look on as the readers run theirs. But they are not disinterested spectators, since so much depends upon the outcome. These faithful saw "from afar" the promises they died without receiving (11:13). That these promises remain unfulfilled is again mentioned in 11:39, with the cryptic comment in 11:40 that "apart from us they should not be made perfect." This cloud of witnesses, who appear one by one in the preceding chapter, reemerges in 12:1 as a crowd cheering the readers on as they "run the race." Their perfection, the fulfillment of "what was promised," is now beyond their control and is in the hands of the audience. The author ties the fate of the patriarchs and matriarchs to that of his audience. If the audience does not get to the finish line, according to the logic of 11:40, then no one gets there. The consequences of the readers' actions in 12:1–13 thus extend far beyond themselves to all those mentioned in chapter 11. With this remarkable move the author raises the stakes considerably and seeks to impress upon his audience the gravity of the situation—this is no mere track meet, he implies—and the crucial role they play in salvation history.

POLITICAL DISCOURSE

Paul (Rom 13:1–7) and 1 Peter (2:13–17) explicitly address Christian attitudes toward the state. Largely absent from the argument of Hebrews is anything resembling political commentary. Wherever and whenever it was written, it is nonetheless certain that Hebrews was produced in the context of the Roman Empire, and some scholars believe that, by reading between the lines, it is possible to detect hints of this overarching political reality.

For example, the opening paean to Christ as Son of God who reflects divine glory (1:2–3) and the invitation to seek aid by approaching the throne of grace through the Son (4:16) offers an alternative to the vision promoted in much imperial propaganda that assigns these roles to the emperor (Koester 2001, 78–79). Critique of the Roman imperial cult is usually associated with the book of Revelation, but it has been suggested that Hebrews' emphasis on the superiority of Christ's priesthood over the Levitical system serves a comparable function, namely, to offer tacit resistance to the emperor's claim as Pontifex Maximus to be the preeminent mediator between his subjects and the gods (Muir 2008, 170–86). In the same vein, some see a subtle response to ideology and iconography affiliated with the Roman conquest of Judea that resulted in the temple's destruction in 70 C.E. (Aitken 2005, 136–46). Among the accolades bestowed upon Vespasian and his son Titus—a victorious general who also became emperor—were parades, the building of the Temple of Peace in Rome, and the erection of the Arch of Titus at the highest point on the Via Sacra. The real triumph belongs to Jesus in this reading, and the true temple is the one in heaven, where he now serves as priest.

SACRIFICE

Performance of various sacrifices was a central component of Greek and Roman religion. Hebrews refrains from making sacrifice as popularly conceived a Christian duty. The only concrete instruction on sacrifice comes at Heb 13:15–16: "Through him then let us continually offer up a sacrifice of praise to God, that is, the fruit of lips that acknowledge his name. Do not neglect to do good and to share what you have, for such sacrifices are pleasing to God" (RSV). Praise and benevolence as modes of sacrifice are not ideas peculiar to Hebrews, nor is the author alone in his endorsement of "spiritual" sacrifice (Ferguson 1980, 1151–89). This notion often appears as a positive alternative in critiques of the sacrificial mindset. In the Old Testament, prophetic critiques emphasize the inadequacy of animal sacrifices unaccompanied by obedience to Mosaic law (1 Sam 15:22; Jer 7:21–23; Amos 5:21–24; Sir 34:18–35:11).

Greek and Roman writers direct similar attacks against their own cults. Lucian of Samosata puts it bluntly in the opening paragraph of his essay *On Sacrifices*:

> In view of what the dolts do at their sacrifices and their feasts and processions in honour of the gods, what they pray for and vow, and what opinions they hold about the gods, I doubt if anyone is so gloomy and woe-begone that he will not laugh to see the idiocy of their actions. Indeed, long before he laughs, I think, he will ask himself whether he should call them devout or, on the contrary, irreligious and pestilent, inasmuch as they have taken it for granted that the gods are so low and mean as to stand in need of men and to enjoy being flattered and to get angry when they are slighted.

Popular sacrificial practices reflect unworthy notions of the gods as dependent upon the offerings of mortals for sustenance and responsive to bribes rather than sincere piety (Apollonius of Tyana, *Ep.* 26; Euripides, *Herc. fur.* 1345; Plato, *Phaedr.* 279b–c; Maximus of Tyre, *Diss.* 11). Especially noxious is the horrific practice of human sacrifice (Plutarch, *Superst.* 171b–e).[6] If the gods are free from emotion or otherwise immutable, as the Stoics and Platonists claim, respectively (Plutarch, *E Delph.* 393c; *Def. orac.* 420e), it is pointless to expect them to change their minds on account of an especially fine offering; further, if inexorable fate rules the universe, then the gods cannot—even if they were so inclined—alter the preordained course of events so as to benefit the worshiper. Moreover, such ministrations are undignified and, because they are material, are ineffective for acquiring moral purity, which alone is pleasing to the gods (Lucian, *Sacr.* 15; Diogenes Laertius 6.42).

Much in Hebrews' discussion of the ancient Israelite worship conforms to this line of thought on matters of purity and sacrifice. Above all, the author's preference for the new covenant can be seen in his insistence that the normal sacrifices required as a part of the old covenant could not sufficiently repair the damage done by the sin on account of which they were instituted. Under the provisions of the old covenant, "gifts and sacrifices are offered that cannot perfect the conscience of the worshiper" (9:9, 13–14). Its sacrifices cannot perfect those who would draw near to God nor do away with the consciousness of sin that places a barrier between the individual and God (10:22).

This emphasis on the interior state of the individual fits with the philosophical preference for "rational" worship. It is important to keep in mind, however, that Hebrews stops short of condemning outright the sacrificial system of the old covenant. After all, God had instituted it, so nonperformance was not really an option. The author seeks instead to show that the purity requirements of the Israelite cult have now been fulfilled by Jesus in such impeccable fashion that any further blood offerings are superfluous. Levitical ritual had its proper time and place (see 7:12, 18; 8:6–7), but after the resurrection and exaltation of Christ the situation has changed dramatically. Hebrews' analysis of the old covenant and its way of dealing with moral pollution thus hinges on a highly distinctive understanding of history—they have entered "the last days" (1:2); the first covenant "is becoming obsolete, growing old, and is ready to vanish" (8:13; see also

---

6. Many scholars believe that reports of human sacrifice in ancient Greece are almost always mythical or imaginative exaggerations, though archaeological evidence suggests that, on occasion, life perhaps imitated myth (Hughes 1991, 185–93; see also 13–24, 60–65).

10:9); Jesus' self-sacrifice comes "at the end of the age" (9:26)—alien to most Greeks and Romans.

CONCLUSION

This essay has surveyed a sampling of the main motifs, concepts, and images from the Greco-Roman world that help the reader make sense of the sometimes complicated argument of Hebrews. Many more could be included. It has been argued, for example, that Jesus in Hebrews resembles the Greek hero Heracles, who descended into Hades, overcame the the power of death, and became a deity who offers aid to those who request it (Aune 1990, 3–19). Confusion about Sarah's role in the conception of Isaac in Heb 11:11 has led some to study ancient theories about embryology (van der Horst 1990, 287–302). Hellenistic assumptions about what constitutes a true god have been invoked to make sense of the comparison of Jesus and Melchizedek in Heb 7:3 (Neyrey 1991, 439–55). The call to extend hospitality to strangers, "for thereby some have entertained angels unawares" (13:2), recalls for many readers the story of Baucis and Philemon related by the Roman poet Ovid.

Not all such theories are equally conclusive or of equal importance for reading the epistle. But the more one knows about the context in which it was written, the easier it will be to notice points of continuity and discontinuity with that context. Jesus may well be "the same yesterday and today and forever" (Heb 13:8), but the author explains Jesus' significance in the terms of a very specific historical-cultural setting. Like most thinkers in Greco-Roman antiquity, Hebrews finds the old and the customary to be trustworthy and is cautious about anything new and unfamiliar. For all the similarities he shares with the broader culture, the author cannot deny that something novel and different has taken place with Jesus and the "new covenant" he has inaugurated. He strives mightily to show that Jesus, while representing God's new way of dealing with humanity, nonetheless fits perfectly with the divine plan disclosed under the old covenant. It is the peculiar pattern according to which the strange—socially, culturally, philosophically, theologically—mingles with the familiar that gives Hebrews its distinctive character.

What Has Middle Platonism to Do with Hebrews?

James W. Thompson

Celsus, a Middle Platonist known to us only through Origen's *Contra Celsum*, launched a major attack on Christian belief in the second century. Well acquainted with various Christian groups, he saw irreconcilable differences between Platonism and Christianity. He had harsh words against the doctrines of creation and resurrection (*Cels.* 8.49) and ridiculed the Christian insistence on faith rather than knowledge (1.9). He gave an extended critique of the doctrine of the incarnation, insisting that such a change would be contrary to the nature of the immutable God (4.2, 14). Christian writers recognized some of the same conflicts between Christianity and Platonism, maintaining that the doctrines of creation, incarnation, and eschatological triumph were incompatible with the Platonic views of God and the world. Nevertheless, while Christians recognized the conflict between their credo and Platonism, they also employed Platonic language and categories in varying degrees to explain Christian beliefs (Meijering 1974, 17; de Vogel 1985, 27–28). The apostolic fathers (Wyller 1996, 26:697), the apologists (Andresen 1954, 159–95; Edwards 1991, 17–34), and the later Christian tradition all employed Platonic categories to articulate their convictions while holding to beliefs that were in conflict with the Platonic tradition (Thompson 1998, 317). Platonic categories were the common property not only of the elite but of all educated people (Backhaus 1996, 262).

The refined language of the Epistle to the Hebrews leaves no doubt that the author belonged to the educated circles among whom the tenets of Platonism were commonplace. Moreover, scholars have recognized the similarities between the Platonic language of Philo of Alexandria and Hebrews, especially in the description of the heavenly tabernacle in Heb 8:1–10:18. The author cites the instructions to Moses, "See that you make everything according to the archetype [*typos*] shown you on the mountain"

(Heb 8:5, citing Exod 25:40). The heavenly archetype is the "true tent" in heaven (8:2), while the one on earth is a "copy [*hypodeigma*] and shadow [*skia*]" (8:5). The language evokes Plato's theory of ideas (*Resp.* 514–517; *Leg.* 1.643c), according to which earthly matters are shadows of heavenly archetypes (*typoi*). Philo gave a Platonic interpretation to Exod 25:40 (*QE* 2.52; *Leg.* 3.100–102; *Plant.* 26–27; *Mos.* 2.71–75), and the later church fathers would also read the passage with Platonic lenses (Origen, *Hom. Exod.* 9.2; Eusebius, *Praep. ev.* 12.19.1–9).

To what extent was the author of Hebrews a Platonist? His interaction with Platonism has been one of the most disputed issues in the scholarship on the homily in the last century. Some scholars insist that Heb 8:1–10:18 does not reflect a Platonic ontology (see Gäbel 2006, 121–27) but is derived from apocalyptic depictions of a heavenly sanctuary. Other scholars have observed that the author's affirmation of the Christian credo was incompatible with Platonism and deny any significant connection between the author and Philo (Mackie 2007, 83–104; Hurst 1990, 38–42). The belief in the divine work in creation (1:2; 2:10; 11:3) and the explicit references to the preexistent Son, who was "a little while lower than the angels" (2:9) and lived in the flesh (5:7–8) before his exaltation (see 1:3, 13), are contrary to Platonic teachings about the deity. The traditional Jewish belief in the two ages, which is also incompatible with Platonism, is a consistent feature of the homily. God has spoken "in these last days" (1:2), and believers have "tasted the powers of the coming age" (6:5; see also 9:9–10). They anticipate the final apocalyptic shaking of the heavens and the earth (12:26–28).

The eschatological features of Hebrews do not preclude the presence of Platonic thought, however, for patristic writers offer abundant evidence that Jewish eschatological expectations and Platonic metaphysics, despite their apparent incompatibility, commonly existed alongside each other. Justin and Clement of Alexandria, for example, affirmed a Christian eschatology while expressing themselves in the language of Platonism (Thompson 2007, 580; Daly 2003, 20–22, 44–47). Justin speaks frequently of the second advent (*Dial.* 31.1–3; 110.2–4; 111.1; 118.1; 121.3) and insists that the "great and terrible day" (49.2) is coming soon (32.4). Christ will "appear in Jerusalem" (85.7) and destroy all his enemies (121.3), including the "man of sin" (32.4). Although Clement of Alexandria tried to harmonize apocalyptic thought with Greek cosmology, he maintained a hope for the end, speaking of "the resurrection for which we hope; when, at the end of the world, the angels … receive into the celestial abodes those who repent" (*Quis div.* 42; *ANF* 2:604). After the second coming of Christ, all of the righteous will be taken up into heaven (*Ecl.* 56–67). One may ask, therefore, to what extent the author of Hebrews anticipated the patristic employment of concepts from Middle Platonism alongside eschatological perspectives. If the author employed ideas from Middle Platonism, a related question emerges: Which of the two perspectives is predominant? This essay will explore these questions.

PHILO AND MIDDLE PLATONISM

Since Hugo Grotius first identified parallels between Hebrews and the works of Philo in the seventeenth century (*In Hebr.* 4.10; cited in Spicq 1952, 1:39; see also Sterling 2001, 191), numerous works have examined the relationships between them, noting their common use of Platonic language. Philo was, however, a major representative of a larger movement, Middle Platonism, which emerged in the first century B.C.E. after the Platonic tradition turned from the skepticism of the Academy to a renewed interest in metaphysics (Klauck 1994, 59). While several names of Middle Platonists are known to us, few works have remained. Philo (ca. 20 B.C.E.–ca. 50 C.E.) and Plutarch of Chaeroneia (ca. 45–124 C.E.), both of whom have left a substantial body of literature, are the major sources of our knowledge of this school of thought. Philo applied the Middle Platonic framework to the allegorical interpretation of Scripture, while Plutarch applied it to Greek myths. Thus our understanding of the intellectual climate of Hebrews requires that we compare this homily not only with Philo but also with those who shared Philo's approach to religious traditions.

While Middle Platonists shared common ground with other philosophical schools, the distinguishing features and dominant concerns of Middle Platonists were the transcendence of God, the existence of the ideas, and the immortality of the soul (Klauck 1994, 59; see also Dillon 1996, 48–49). Philo describes God as the One (*Opif.* 171), the Monad (*Leg.* 2.3; *Her.* 183; *Cher.* 87) and the truly existent (*ho ōn ontōs, Opif.* 172; *Decal.* 8; *Spec.* 1.28). The corollary to the transcendence of God is the chasm separating God and the incorporeal world of ideas from the material world and human weakness. Middle Platonists described this duality as the distinction between Being and becoming. True Being in the intelligible world exists in timeless eternity (*aiōn*), while the perceptible world is subject to constant becoming (*genesis*). The latter is subject to change and never remains in the same state (Philo, *Opif.* 12). Philo indicates that everything in creation must change, while immutability is the property of God alone

(*Leg.* 2.33). The supreme God is "motherless," "unbegotten," and "abiding" (*Opif.* 100; see also *Mos.* 2.12). Plutarch asks, "What is real Being? It is the eternal and unbegotten and imperishable, without beginning and without end, to which [a length of] time, not even one, brings change" (*E Delph.* 392e). In *The E at Delphi*, he comments on the E at the entrance of the temple of Apollo, suggesting that E signifies the Greek "You are" (*ei*), which is the appropriate address to God, who is unchanging and uncontaminated by matter (*E Delph.* 392f), while humankind inhabits the world of becoming and is subject to change, decay, and mortality. "Everything of a mortal nature is at some stage between coming into existence and passing away" (*E Delph.* 392b). Thus Plutarch says that the antithesis to "you are" (*ei*) is "know thyself" (*gnōthi sauton*). He explains that the address "you are" is an utterance addressed in awe to the god who exists through all eternity, while "know thyself" is a reminder to mortals of their own weaknesses (*E Delph.* 394c).

Consistent with their distinction between the two realms of reality, Middle Platonists distinguish between the One, which transcends the universe, and the Indefinite Dyad, the principle of duality, which is infinitely divisible. The One belongs to the intelligible world, while the latter can be seen throughout nature (Dillon 1996, 46). Middle Platonists identify the transcendent God with the One, who stands above the principle of multiplicity that is associated with the realm of becoming. Whereas God is one and unmixed (see Philo, *Abr.* 122), humans belong to the world of becoming that is characterized by multiplicity. Indeed, Philo frequently employs words for multiplicity to describe the inferiority of things that belong to the material world (*Plant.* 44; *Somn.* 2.14). Plutarch's distinction between being and becoming/eternity and time corresponds to his distinction between the one and the many. God is stable and unitary, and the human, subject to becoming, is in a state of constant change and therefore lacks unity (Whittaker 1981, 56). God is One, and humankind is many and always in the state of birth and decay (*E Delph.* 392).

The major challenge for Middle Platonists was to overcome the radical separation between the transcendent deity and the material world (Backhaus 1996, 263). In order to preserve the transcendence of the divine Being, they claimed an intermediate principle that mediated between the first principle and the material world (Cox 2007, 43). Philo claims that God created the world through the *logos* (*Sacr.* 8), who serves the deity by providing links between God and everything else (*Deus* 57). He uses the same language to describe wisdom (*sophia, Conf.* 146–147). Similarly,

Plutarch identifies such a figure with Isis, who mediates between the transcendent and material realms (Dillon 1996, 46). Beneath this intermediate being the Platonic cosmos was filled with subordinate intermediate beings. Philo describes the angels who exist below the transcendent God, while Plutarch speaks of a cosmos populated by daemons (see below).

The bridging of the chasm between the two realms became the challenge of Middle Platonism in another respect. The possibility of knowledge of God became the starting point of Middle Platonic philosophy (Andresen 1978, 3:55). Human knowledge of God comes by perception. God is immutable, and humans are inherently unstable. The task is for humans to overcome the instability of their existence and to know God.

This philosophical framework was welcome in Alexandrian Judaism and in its heir, Alexandrian Christianity. The emphasis on transcendence was the central feature that made Middle Platonism popular to Jews of the Diaspora, providing the means for combining this principle with their traditional belief in the sovereignty of God (Cox 2007, 30). Just as Middle Platonism preserved the transcendence of God by positing an intermediary principle, Alexandrian Judaism incorporated intermediaries into their cosmology. Philo spoke of both wisdom (*sophia*) and word (*logos* also means reason).

Hebrews and Middle Platonism

Like Philo and Plutarch, the author of Hebrews is the interpreter of religious traditions. He addresses second-generation believers who are discouraged because they have not seen the eschatological triumph of God and are weary from a long journey that has not reached its goal because the promises remain unfulfilled. The recipients of Hebrews have experienced the dissonance between the Christian claim and the reality they experience, for they do not see the world in subjection to the Christ (Thompson 2008, 10). The author acknowledges this crisis. After celebrating the exalted place of Christ above the cosmos (1:5–13) and declaring of the Son, "He has put all things under his feet" (2:8), he acknowledges, "We do not yet see all things in subjection to him" (2:8b), expressing the frustration of readers whose experience conflicts with their confession. The passage of time and the experience of marginalization (see 10:32–35) have led the readers to ask if the commitment is worth the price that they continue to pay. Indeed, the unstable situation of the readers is evident in the concern over whether they will "drift away" (2:1), "fall away" (3:12; see also 6:4–6), or be "carried away" (13:9). Even in their own communities, they are as insecure as "refugees" (6:18).

The author's challenge is to rebuild their symbolic world and provide stability for people who waver from their original confession. His frequent exhortation to "hold firmly" (*katechein*, 3:6, 14; 10:23; *kratein*, 4:14; 6:18) appears in the context of assurances that the community has a stable possession that it may grasp. Indeed, as the central section of the homily indicates, they may hold firmly because of the entry of Christ into the heavenly world (4:14–16; 6:18–19; 10:19–23). Thus the refugee community can now grasp the anchor of the soul that is stable (*asphalē*), certain (*bebaia*), and entering beyond the curtain that separates heaven and earth (6:18–19). The frequent use of forms of *bebai-* ("certain," "unwavering," "firm," BDAG, 172–73) reflects the critical need to find stability for the wavering readers. This "word of encouragement" is essentially a reassurance that the community has a stable possession to which it can hold.

The author provides certainty with a series of comparisons that are interspersed with exhortations. He employs "better" (*kreittōn*) thirteen times in the homily, in addition to other comparisons. Indeed, Hebrews is a series of comparisons between the Christ-event and the people and institutions of the Old Testament. These comparisons do not reflect a polemic against the Old Testament or Judaism but are rhetorical devices that demonstrate the greatness of the work of Christ. Comparison (Greek *synkrisis*) is a common rhetorical device among ancient orators, as Aristotle indicates in describing the importance of *synkrisis* in speeches in praise of a distinguished person:

> And you must compare him with illustrious personages, for it affords ground for amplification and is noble, if he can be proved better than men of worth. Amplification is with good reason ranked as one of the forms of praise, since it consists in superiority, and superiority is one of the things that are noble. (*Rhet.* 1.9.38–39)

In contrast to the ancient orator's use of *synkrisis*, the distinguishing feature of this rhetorical device in Hebrews is its use in the comparison of beings and realities that belong to two levels of reality. That is, transcendent beings and realities are better than earthly counterparts. Christ is "better" than the angels (1:4) as a result of his exaltation, and the order of Melchizedek to which he was appointed at the exaltation (see 5:6, 10; 6:20) is greater than the Aaronic priesthood (7:7). Because Christ offers better sacrifices (9:23) in a greater tabernacle (9:11–14), believers have a greater covenant (7:22; 8:6), a greater hope (7:19; see also 10:34), and greater promises (8:6; 11:40) than their earthly counterparts. Believers have not come to Mount Sinai, which "may be touched" (12:18), but to the heavenly Mount Zion (12:22). Believers, therefore, belong to a reality that is not perceptible to the senses, for it is both invisible (11:1, 27) and untouchable (12:18). The author describes the transcendent world by a variety of terms. It is the promised rest (4:3, 9), the heavenly sanctuary (8:1–5; 9:1–14, 23), the heavenly city (11:10, 16; 12:22; 13:14), the homeland (11:14), and the unshakable kingdom (12:28), all of which have earthly counterparts.

Similar comparisons appear in the works of Philo and Plutarch. Plutarch says that "that which really is and is perceptible and good is superior [*kreittōn*] to destruction and change" (*Is. Os.* 373a). Similarly, Philo commonly compares the heavenly with the earthly, insisting that the heavenly reality is better (see *Opif.* 140; *Her.* 89; *Ios.* 147). Philo describes God as "greater than the good, more venerable than the Monad, purer than the unit" (*Praem.* 40; see also *Contempl.* 2). The mind of the universe is "supremely pure and undefiled, superior to excellence and superior to knowledge, and even superior to the good itself and the fair itself" (*Opif.* 8).

The Prologue: Hebrews 1:1–4

The opening words of Hebrews establish the major themes of the homily, as the author summarizes in poetic form the path of the preexistent Son from his primordial state to his earthly existence ("when he made purification for sins") and subsequent exaltation to "the right hand of the majesty on high" (1:3). The claim that God has spoken "in these last days" expresses the eschatological perspective that will be a recurring theme of the homily (see 6:4–6; 9:27; 12:27–28). The contrast between the "many and various ways" that God has spoken in the past with God's speaking in a Son "in these last days" suggests a qualitative distinction between the provisional and the final, anticipating the argument of 7:1–10:18. The author also introduces the ontological status of the Son with the description of him as the instrument of God's work in creation, the reflection (*apaugasma*) of God's glory, exact representation (*charaktēr*) of God's being, and the one who "bears all things by his powerful word" (1:2–3). All of these attributes are associated with the mediator in the literature of Middle Platonism (Cox 2007, 56–140). The preexistent Son both shared the divine nature and interacted with the creation. The affirmation that he "made purification for sins" anticipates the later reference to his solidarity with humankind (2:14–17; 4:15; 5:7–10) and the extended section on his sacrificial death (8:1–10:18). This event "during the days of his flesh" (5:7) was a stage in his journey from descent to earth to the exaltation, when he sat down at the right hand of God on high (1:3; cf. Ps 110:1), returning to his primordial status in the transcendent realm.

The reference to the exaltation and allusion to Ps 110 introduce the dominant thread of the homily. While the author acknowledges the solidarity of the Son with humankind, it is only a stage in the path toward his exaltation. The words of Ps 110 provide a unifying thread (see 1:3, 13; 6:20; 7:3, 23–24; 8:1; 10:12) for declaring the transcendence of the Christ, who sat down at the right hand of God. The author later elaborates, indicating that he "passed through the heavens" (4:14) and entered behind the curtain separating heaven and earth (6:19; 10:19) into the heavenly sanctuary (9:11–14, 23). Having entered the transcendent reality, he opens the way for believers to follow (see 2:10; 4:14–16; 6:20; 10:19–23).

The claim that the exalted Son is "greater than angels" (1:4) anticipates the author's regular use of *synkrisis* and the argument based on the two levels of reality. In this initial allusion to Ps 110:1, he introduces the transcendence of the Son, anticipating the later description of the transcendent high priest (see 4:14–16; 6:20; 8:1–10:18). This *synkrisis* suggests, contrary to much of the Jewish tradition, that angels do not share in the exaltation. "Better" (*kreittōn*) is used here, as elsewhere, to suggest the spatial contrast between the heavenly and the earthly, inferior reality (see 9:11–14, 23; 10:34). The suggestion that angels do not share in the Son's exalted status is the first in a series of *synkrises* between the transcendent one and the objects of comparison.

THE SON, ANGELS, AND CREATION: HEBREWS 1:5–13

The author demonstrates the superiority of the Son to the angels in the catena of citations in 1:5–13, carefully arranging the passages to support his claim and recapitulating the themes of creation (1:10), incarnation (1:9), and exaltation (10:8–13) first introduced in the prologue. The citation of Ps 110:1 in 1:3, 13 forms an *inclusio* (rhetorical "bookends") indicating that the exaltation provides the framework for reading the citations. Drawing on Old Testament imagery, the author cites two well-known messianic texts (Ps 2:7; 2 Sam 7:14) to affirm that the exaltation is also the coronation of Jesus as Son (1:5; see also 5:5–6, 10) when all of the angels worship him (1:6). This claim is of special importance to the author, for whom it is axiomatic that the inferior pays homage to the superior (7:4–8; Thompson 1982, 132).

Having cited three passages to demonstrate that the Son is better than the angels (1:5–6), the author now provides the basis for the argument (1:7–12). The sequence of the citations indicates how the exaltation makes the Son better than the angels. The contrasting statements to the angels (1:7) and to the Son (1:8–13) suggest their fundamental difference. Whereas God "makes the angels into winds" (cf. Ps 104:4), he says to the Son, "Your throne, O God, is forever and ever" (cf. Ps 44:7 LXX). Unlike the rabbis who cited Ps 104:4 to demonstrate the transcendence of God or the might of the angels, the author contrasts the eternity of the Son (1:8) with the mutability of angels. Because they do not share the exaltation, they are inferior to the Son.

The place of angels within creation is analogous to the role of intermediate beings in the thought of Middle Platonists, for whom the radical separation of the deity from the material worlds necessitated the existence of the daemons to mediate (Dillon 1996, 216; Busch 2000, 26) with the realm of the senses. Plutarch speaks of those beings who live on the boundary between gods and humans who are subject to human emotions and involuntary changes (*Def. orac.* 416). They are a "ministering class, midway between gods and men" (*Is. Os.* 361c; *Def. orac.* 417a; cf. "ministering spirits" in Heb 1:14). The angels in Philo have a similar role (see *Gig.* 16). They are the proper inhabitants of the air (16) and are subject to change (17). In his interpretation of the story of Jacob's ladder, he indicates that angels "ascend and descend" (*Somn.* 1.333) throughout the universe.

Because the exalted Son shares the ontological status with God, the author does not hesitate to cite passages originally addressed to God as words spoken to the Son. The extended citation suggests that in 1:8–9 (cf. Ps 44:7 LXX) the author understands the exaltation as God's anointing to a new status after the incarnation. Indeed, the Son is God (1:8), and he is now "forever" (*eis ton aiōna tou aiōnos*). This designation introduces a major theme of the homily (5:6; 7:23–24, 28; see also 7:3; 10:12).

The author reinforces the distinction between the eternal Son and the changeable angels in the extended citation in 1:10–12 (cf. Ps 102:26–28), a statement that originally described God's sovereignty over creation. Once more a passage originally addressed to God becomes God's address to the Son. The words "You are from the beginning, you established the earth, the works of your hands are the heavens" recall the description of the role of the preexistent Son at the creation in 1:2–3. The chiastic structure of the psalm in 1:11–12 introduces the sharp contrast between the Son and the created order. In contrast to the creation, which is subject to destruction, aging, and change (1:11a, c–12ab), the Son abides (*diameinei*, 11:b) and is the same (*ho autos*, 1:12c). The fact that both angels and the creation are subject to change suggests that angels belong to the creation. The Son, however, is exalted above the creation; thus he is not subject to destruction or aging. He abides and is the same.

By using Ps 102:26–28 as an exaltation text, the author has introduced the two levels of reality into the argument. This distinction is reminiscent of the Platonic view according to which "becoming" (*genesis*) is the characteristic of this creation, while eternal being is characteristic of the intelligible world and the deity. One may compare Philo's argument that this world is subject to destruction (*Leg.* 3.101) in contrast to those things above the creation, which are abiding (*monimoi*) and sure *(bebaioi)* and eternal (*aidioi*).

The affirmation "but you abide" (*su de diameneis*) contrasts the eternity of the exalted Son with the transitory nature of the creation. Indeed, the author apparently alters the future "he will remain" in the Septuagint to the present tense in order to emphasize the eternity of the Son. That Christ "remains" is of central importance to Hebrews (Thompson 1982, 138; see also 7:3, 24; 13:8). The author also speaks of a transcendent possession that "abides" (*menei*, 10:34; 12:27; 13:14) The frequent use of *menein* in theologically significant passages indicates that the author has chosen Ps 102 because it coheres with the theme of the eternity of the exalted one and the transitory nature of the material world.

The claim that only the exalted Christ abides (*diamenei*) corresponds to the Platonic view of the intelligible world and the deity. For Plato the ideal world abides (*Tim.* 37d). According to Philo, God stands the same, remaining (*menōn*) immutable (*Somn.* 2.221), and individuals find their stability only in him. Philo quotes approvingly the words of Philolaus: "There is, he says, a supreme ruler of all things, God, ever One, abiding, without motion, like unto himself, different from all others" (*Opif.* 100). Similarly, Plutarch maintains that the deity is commonly called the Monad because God abides (*menei*, *Garr.* 507a). For both writers the verb connotes the immutability of God.

The divine voice also says to the exalted Christ, "You are the same [*ho autos*], and your years will never end" (1:12c). Here also the author attributes to Christ the quality that Philo and Plutarch ascribe to the deity. Philo also says that God remains the same (*ho autos*), while the heavenly bodies are in constant motion (*Post.* 19–20). Similarly, Plutarch, argues that the appropriate way to address God is with the word "you are" (*ei*) because only true Being remains the same (*ho autos*, *E Delph.* 392e), while the rest of the creation is subject to change. Thus while the author of Hebrews employs the psalm to declare that the exalted Christ is *ho autos*, Middle Platonists employed this designation alongside other terms for the immutability of the deity.

The author anticipated the church fathers in reading Ps 102:26–28 with the lenses of Middle Platonism. In commenting on this psalm, Eusebius (*Praep. ev.* 11.10.15) argues that Plutarch's claim that "you are" is the appropriate way to address God is actually a commentary on the words of Exod 3:14 ("I am the one who is") and Ps 102:28 ("you are the same").

The contrast between the eternity of the exalted Son and the creation's subjection to dissolution anticipates the culminating *synkrisis* of the homily (12:18–29), which contrasts the transitory creation with the unshakable kingdom that abides (see below). Thus near the beginning and end of the homily the author assumes a metaphysical dualism that was the distinguishing feature of Middle Platonism. His challenge is to reassure wavering readers of the transcendent reality that they do not see (2:8b). Anticipating the later argument, he identifies this reality as God's transcendent rest (3:7–4:11) that is available for believers.

CHRIST AND THE PRIESTHOOD OF AARON: HEBREWS 4:14–10:31

The exaltation also provides the framework for the central section of Hebrews (4:14–10:31), which begins with the affirmation that the exalted Son is also the "high priest who passed through the heavens" (4:14) and concludes with the claim that he entered behind the curtain into the heavenly sanctuary (10:19–23). While the author proceeds from his portrayal of Jesus as Son to his work as high priest, he maintains the focus on Christ as the exalted one. In 4:14–5:10, the author reiterates the claim of the descent and ascent of the Son, first announced in 1:1–4. Jesus first sympathized with human weakness (4:15) and suffering (5:7–8) before he was appointed high priest according to the order of Melchizedek at the exaltation. Jesus' sufferings during the time that he was below the angels recalls once more (see 1:2–3) the role of the Platonic daemons, who also suffer and sympathize (Plutarch, *Is. Os.* 360e; *Def. orac.* 416d) with humankind (Busch 2000, 28).

After a paraenetic interlude (5:11–6:12), the author reaffirms that the exaltation was also the appointment to the priesthood of Melchizedek (6:19–20). As the reference to the exaltation indicates, this priesthood is transcendent. The exalted high priest serves in a heavenly tabernacle where he offered the ultimate sacrifice. The distinction between the two spheres of reality is evident in the author's *synkrisis* in describing the sanctuary.

made by the Lord (8:2)	not made by man (8:2)
archetype (8:5)	copy and shadow (8:5)
worldly (*kosmikos*, 9:1)	greater and more perfect tent (9:11)
	not made by hands (9:11, 24)

Similarly, the author distinguishes between the animal sacrifices offered on earth and the sacrifice of Christ, who offered himself in heaven (9:1–14). The former cleanse only the flesh, but the latter cleanses the conscience (9:9–10). The entire presentation is built on the *synkrisis*, declaring the superiority of the heavenly over the earthly. The author does not merely contrast the old with the new but demonstrates the superiority of the transcendent reality to the earthly system. Thus the author's argument in 7:1–10:18 rests on the ontological dualism by which he contrasts the work of the high priest in the heavenly sanctuary with the high priests of the earthly sanctuary (Thompson 2007, 569).

As the author indicates in 6:19–20, the heavenly high priesthood of Melchizedek (Heb 7) is the anchor for the wavering readers. Citing Gen 14:18–20 and Ps 110:4, the two Old Testament passages that mention this mysterious figure, the author elaborates on the nature of this priesthood to demonstrate that he is "like the Son of God" (7:3). After the brief description of the etymology of Melchizedek's name and the brief summary of the encounter between Abraham and Melchizedek (7:1–2), the author describes the major attributes of Melchizedek in four parallel lines (7:3). When the author describes Melchizedek as "without father [*apatōr*], without mother [*amētōr*], without genealogy [*agenealogētos*]" and "without beginning of days or end of life" in the first two lines, he is not merely employing the common rabbinic argument from the silence of Scripture but developing an important theme, as the fourth line indicates (7:3d). Here the author cites Ps 110:4, which declares that this priesthood is "forever" (*eis ton aiōna*). The previous use of this phrase (see 1:8; 6:20) indicates its significance for the author, who adds to it "he abides [*menei*]." The three lines that precede 7:3d may be understood as an interpretation of the claim that "he abides forever."

Ancient readers would have recognized that one who is "without father" and "without mother" is a divine being. Philo refers to the "motherless and virgin Nike" (*Opif.* 100). He maintains that the number seven is the image of the supreme God and is "motherless," "unbegotten," and "abiding." In *The Life of Moses*, Philo describes the creation of the Sabbath, claiming it was

> in the first place motherless, exempt from female parentage, begotten by the Father alone, without beginning, brought to the birth, yet not carried in the womb. Secondly, he saw not only these, that she was all lovely and motherless, but that she was also ever virgin, neither born of a mother nor a mother herself, neither bred from corruption nor doomed to suffer corruption. (*Mos.* 2.10)

The reference to Melchizedek as "without father, without mother, without genealogy" also employs the negative theology (later known as *via negativa*) of Middle Platonists, who maintained that one can most appropriately describe God using negation (Dillon 1996, 284; Neyrey 1991, 441), denying of God a series of qualities that belong to other beings in order to demonstrate the deity's superiority to the latter (Dillon 1993, 107). Plutarch speaks of deities who are unbegotten (*agennētos*, *Is. Os.* 359cd; *Quaest. conv.* 718; *Sept. sap. conv.* 153), uncreated (*agenētos*, *E Delph.* 392e), and incorruptible (*aphthartos*, *Is. Os.* 359c, 373d). Negative theology became especially important to patristic writers (Neyrey 1991, 441).

The statement that Melchizedek is "without beginning of days or end of life" also echoes the philosophical description of the deity, indicating that the divine (*apatōr, amētōr*) is eternal. The phrase has its clearest analogies in philosophical descriptions of the deity. Plutarch says of true Being that it "has no beginning nor is it destined to come to an end" (*E Delph.* 393a; see also 392e; *Is. Os.* 359c). The author elaborates on the phrase with the citation of Ps 110:4, "He abides a priest forever." As in 1:5–13, he understands the exaltation to mean that Christ, in the heavenly world, abides (cf. *diamenei*, 1:11). *Menei*, used in 7:3 for the order of Melchizedek, is used regularly in Hebrews for heavenly realities (see 10:34; 12:27; 13:14). This description is analogous to Philo's depiction of God as the one who abides (*Somn.* 2.221). Thus, just as *menein* is used in Platonism for the immutability of the deity, it is used in Hebrews for the immutability of Christ (Thompson 1982, 121).

The eternity of the high priest becomes the dominant theme in Heb 7, which is an elaboration on the abiding priesthood (7:3) in the form of a *synkrisis*. In 7:4–10 the author indicates the superiority of the priesthood of Melchizedek to the Levitical order, contrasting "the one who lives" with "dying men" (7:8). The author develops this contrast further, focusing on the psalm's use of the term "order" (*taxis*) and comparing the "order of Aaron" (7:11) with the "order of Melchizedek" (7:11). Not only does the announcement of the latter indicate a change from one to the other, but the latter is ontologically superior. This comparison of two orders of priesthood reiterates the earlier comparison between the exalted Son and the angels (1:4–13), indicating in both instances that the transcendent one abides ([*dia*]*menei*), while angels and earthly priests belong to the realm that is subject to change, destruction, and death. The former is "fleshly" (*sarkinē*), while the latter possesses an "indestructible life" (7:16) because of the exaltation. The treatment of Melchizedek reaches the culmination in the comparison between those priests who were not able to abide (*paramenein*) in contrast to the one who abides forever (*menei eis ton aiōna*, 7:23–24).

The comparison between the eternal order (*taxis*) of the priesthood of Melchizedek with the impermanent order of Aaron is reminiscent of the distinction between the celestial and the earthly orders (*taxeis*) in Philo and among Middle Platonist writers. Philo speaks of the "category [*taxis*] of the incorporeal and intelligible" (*Opif.* 34) and of the transcendent order (*Praem.* 42). The priesthood according to the order of Melchizedek is not only superior because it is later in time; it is qualitatively and metaphysically superior. The Levitical priesthood belongs to the sphere of the flesh and of death (see 7:8), while the priesthood of Melchizedek belongs to the heavenly and unchangeable sphere. Just as the exalted Son is greater than the angels and creation (1:6–12) because he alone is immutable and abiding, the exalted high priest is greater than mortal high priests.

This *synkrisis* corresponds to a fundamental principle of Middle Platonism: the distinction between the eternity of the transcendent realm and the change and impermanent character of the creation (see *Is. Os.* 369d). The comparison between the high priest who is "without father, without mother, without genealogy" and "without beginning of days or end of life" corresponds to Plutarch's distinction between the eternal deity and the material world, which is subject to birth and decay (see above)

A significant feature of the dualistic framework of Hebrews is the distinction between the finality of the work of Christ in the heavenly sanctuary and the incompleteness of the sacrificial ministry on the earth. Consistent with the contrast between the "many and various ways" in which God spoke to the fathers and the ultimate revelation in the Son (1:1–2), a primary focus of 7:1–10:18 is the repeated use of *hapax* (or *ephapax*) for the work of Christ. The term, which can have the simple meaning "once," is used in Hebrews for a single event that is "once for all" in contrast to multiple occurrences (BDAG, 97). The importance of this focus on the "once for all" quality of the Christ-event is evident in the fact that the term is used more in Hebrews than in all other New Testament books combined. This distinction is implicit in the use of the descendants of Levi and the one man in 7:5 and 7:20–21. It becomes explicit in the use of the "many" and the one high priest in 7:23–24. Here the many belong to the sphere of death (see 7:8, 23), signifying the imperfection of the Levitical order (Weiss 1991, 415; Grässer 1993, 2:258). In contrast to the many high priests of the earthly sphere who are prevented by death from remaining, the work of the exalted high priest is *ephapax*. The author's distinction is rooted in the metaphysical distinction between two levels of reality (Thompson 2007, 579). The distinction between the one and the many is the context for the claim that the sacrifice of Christ was *ephapax* (7:27) in contrast to sacrifices offered "each day." The author elaborates on the significance of *ephapax* in the parallel statement in 7:27, summarizing the argument of chapter 7 with the contrast between "those who are subject to weakness" and the one who was "made perfect forever" (*eis ton aiōna teteleiōmenon*). With the singular event of the exaltation, the priest according to the order of Melchizedek entered into eternity and abides forever.

This contrast between the one and the many extends into the description of the cultus in 9:1–10:18 as the author continues to contrast the two levels of reality. In the earthly sanctuary (9:1) that is "made with hands" (9:11, 24), priests offer sacrifices continually (*dia pantos*, 9:6) in the outer court (9:7). Christ entered into the sanctuary "not made with hands" (9:12) to offer a sacrifice that was *ephapax* (9:12). The author clarifies his point in 9:25, indicating that an earthly sacrifice must be offered again and again (*pollakis*), whereas the sacrifice of Christ is *hapax* (9:26). With the repetition of "each year" (10:1, 3) and "each day" (10:11) to describe sacrifices offered many times (*pollakis*, 10:11), he concludes the central section of the homily with the contrast to the one who offered a single sacrifice "for all time" (*eis to diēnekes*; cf. 7:3). Alluding to Ps 110:1, he claims the finality of the work of Christ by contrasting those who stood offering sacrifices with the one who sat down at the right hand of God (10:12). This contrast is the basis for the conclusion of this central section and the claim that "by a single sacrifice he has perfected for all time [*mia gar prosphora teteleiōen eis to diēnekes*] those who are sanctified" (10:14). At the conclusion, therefore, the author explicitly contrasts the one and the many. Only the priestly activity that belongs to the heavenly world is forever.

The author's vertical dualism invites a comparison with his Platonic contemporaries, for whom the distinction between the one and the many was fundamental. Philo, for example, insists that God created the world in six days (*Opif.* 13). However, "God once for all [*hapax*] made a final use of six days for the completion of the world and had no further need of time-periods" (*Decal.* 99). Thus Philo's distinction between the "once" and the successive time periods is consistent with the delineation between time and eternity. The high priest, who enters the sanctuary once each year, symbolizes the entry into the unseen. No one may enter but one who is

> free from all defects, not wasting himself with any passion great or small but endowed with a nature sound and complete and perfect in every respect. To him it is permitted to enter once a year and behold the sights which are forbidden to others, because in him alone of all resides the winged and heavenly yearning for those forms of good which are incorporeal and imperishable. (*Ebr.* 136)

Similarly, in Philo's *De gigantibus*, the high priest Reason (*ho archiereus logos*) is permitted to resort to the sacred doctrines only "once a year" (*Gig.* 52), signifying the stability that accompanies the contemplation of the "Indivisible Unity." On the other hand, the many never find stability because only those people who have disrobed themselves of all created things may come near to God. Thus Philo interprets the cultic activity of the high priest within a cosmological dualism that distinguishes between the two levels of reality.

Plutarch also distinguishes the one and the many, associating the former with the intelligible world and the latter with the material world. This distinction is evident in his treatment of Isis and Osiris. The heavenly Osiris represents the one, while Isis represents the many, as symbolized in their robes, for the robes of Isis are variegated in color, while the robes of Osiris have only one color (*Is. Os.* 382c). The variety in the colors of Isis's robe indicates her association with matter and the many, while the singular color in the robe of Osiris represents the purity of the one. Therefore, when they have once (*hapax*) taken off the robe of Osiris, they guard it and ensure that it remains untouched, while they use the robe of Isis many times over. Plutarch explains in *Is. Os.* 382d:

> for in use those things that are perceptible and ready at hand afford many disclosures of themselves and opportunities to view them as they are changed about in various ways. But the appreciation of the conceptual, the pure, and the simple, shining through the soul like a flash of lightning, affords an opportunity to touch and see but once [*hapax*].

Plutarch's distinction between the one and the many reflects his dualism between Being and becoming. He expresses Osiris's association with the intelligible world of timelessness with the contrast between the event that is *hapax* and those that are repeated numerous times. The former points to the intelligible world, while the latter describes events in the material world. One may compare Plutarch's claim, noted above, according to which "He, being One, has with only one 'now' completely filled 'for ever'" (*E Delph.* 393a–b). Plutarch's use of *hapax* indicates a moment when linear time becomes concentrated in one unsurpassed moment when the cycle of events is transcended by timelessness (Eiserle 2003, 420).

The distinction between the one and the many in the works of Philo and Plutarch provide the background for the comparison in Hebrews between the many priests and sacrifices and the ultimate sacrifice of the exalted Christ. While the references to a historical event distinguish Hebrews from the Middle Platonists, the author of Hebrews nevertheless works within the two levels of reality to affirm that the work of Christ is *ephapax* and beyond multiplicity in a way that is analogous to the ontology of the Middle Platonists. The assurance of the transcendence and eternity of the Christian possession serves the author's paraenetic purpose of providing stability for insecure believers.

SEEING THE INVISIBLE ONE: HEBREWS 11

The appropriate response to the work of Christ in the transcendent sanctuary is "the full assurance of faith" (*plērophoria pisteōs*, 10:22) rather than the lack of faith (*apistia*) exhibited by Israel (3:12, 19; 4:2). Both the description of ancient Israel's lack of faith and the extended section in 10:32–12:11 indicates that faith is inseparable from endurance in Hebrews. The author says to the readers, "You endured sufferings" (10:32, *hypemein-ate pathēmatōn*) in the early days, and "you need endurance" (*hypomonē*) before giving the positive examples of faith in chapter 11. All of the exemplars of faith endured deprivations similar to those of the readers. Thus faith, like the Hebrew equivalent *'mn*, involves standing firm under all circumstances.

Endurance is only one dimension of faith, however, as the working definition indicates in 11:1. In contrast to Paul, the author does not speak of faith in Christ, for Jesus is himself the pioneer of faith (*tēs pisteōs archēgos*, 12:2). The parallel phrases "assurance [*hypostasis*] of things hoped for" and "conviction [*elenchos*] of things not seen" point to the second dimension of faith. *Hypostasis*, literally "to stand under" (Grässer 1965, 48), is used metaphorically in philosophical literature and in Hebrews (see 1:3; 3:14) for reality, equating reality with a firm place to stand. Thus faith involves taking one's stand, not on the visible realities, but "on things hoped for." Similarly, *elenchos* means "proof" or "conviction" and in Heb 11:1 means "a proving (or conviction about) unseen things" (BDAG, 315). "Things hoped for" and "things not seen" are the author's equivalent of the earlier "not made by hands, not of this creation" (9:11) and the subsequent "what can(not) be touched" (12:18) and "what cannot be shaken" (12:27–28). Faith, therefore, is finding a place to stand in the invisible, transcendent reality. The author encourages readers, who do not see the world in subjection to the Son (2:8b), to recognize that reality is not to be found in the visible world.

The author offers numerous equivalents for "things unseen" in his portrayal of the heroes of faith. The heroes sought an inheritance (11:8), a "city having foundations whose maker and builder is God" (11:10, 16), a homeland (11:14), a promise (11:9, 13), and a reward (11:26), but, like the readers, never saw the transcendent reality. However, they had special powers of perception to recognize the reality of the unseen world, as the references to knowing and seeing indicate. In the first place, they know of the reality of the unseen: "We know that the worlds were created by the word of God, so that what is seen was made from things that are not visible" (11:3). The readers themselves were able to endure the confiscation of their property because they knew that they had an abiding possession (10:34). In the second place, the heroes had the capacity to see the unseen. They saw the heavenly homeland from a distance (11:13). Moses "looked to the reward" (11:26) and left Egypt, not fearing the edict of the king, for "he endured as seeing the invisible one" (11:27).

The images of knowing and seeing invisible realities are commonplace in the literature of Middle Platonism. In describing God's role in creating the intelligible world as a pattern for the world of the senses, Philo describes the former as "a world discernible only by the mind" and the latter as "the world which our senses can perceive" (*Opif.* 19). Although the heavenly city is invisible for Philo, it is perceptible to the one who has the special capacity to see the invisible (*Post.* 15; *Deus* 3; *Plant.* 17; *Praem.* 27). He speaks of the apprehensions of reality gained by the "soul's eye" (*Migr.* 39; see also *Her.* 89). Similarly, Alcinous (= Albinus) describes the deity as ineffable and graspable only by the intellect (*Epit.* 10.4).

According to Heb 11, the knowledge that reality is not in the phenomenal world makes one a stranger to this world (Käsemann 1984, 17–20). The author transforms the story of Abraham as a literal "stranger and alien" (Gen 23:4), declaring that the patriarch and his family were "strangers and aliens on the earth" (11:13). The author emphasizes Abraham's alien existence, indicating that he "went out," not knowing where he was going (11:8), sojourned as an alien (*allotrios*), and lived in tents (11:9). Similarly, Moses, in looking beyond temporary pleasure and the treasures of Egypt to the invisible one (11:25–27), chose to suffer with his people. At the conclusion of the list of heroes, the author describes faithful people who "wandered in deserts and mountains, in caves and holes in the ground," declaring that the world was not "worthy" of them (11:38). Their actual home, as the author insists, is not on earth, but a "city that has foundations, whose maker and builder is God" (11:10; see also 11:16), and a heavenly homeland (11:14, 16). Thus they were strangers in an ontological, not a sociological, sense (Backhaus 2001, 175). Having an invisible homeland in heaven made them strangers on earth. This portrayal of faith is consistent with the author's earlier view that believers are on a journey toward the heavenly rest (3:7–4:11) and that the exalted Christ has opened the way (2:20; 6:20; 10:19–23).

A familiar theme in Middle Platonism is the alien existence of those whose homeland is in the invisible world. According to Philo, the wise are appropriately called sojourners (*paroikountes*). The heavenly region, the place of their citizenship, is their native land; the earthly region is a foreign country in which they live as sojourners (*Conf.* 75–78; see also *QG* 4.74; *Somn.* 1.181). Those who migrate from their homes place their faith in God (*Her.* 99). According to *De congressu* 84–87, our task is to recognize our duty to hate the habits and customs of the lands in which we live, which are symbolized as Egypt and Canaan (Thompson 1982, 60). Jacob's temporary residence with Laban is symbolic of the soul's expectations of a city (*Somn.* 1.46).

The idea that one is a stranger on earth has deep roots in the philosophic tradition (Feldmeier 1992, 27–38). Plutarch's essay *De exilo* describes the situation of literal exiles before concluding with reflections about exile as a metaphor for human existence. He cites the ancient words of Empedocles, "All of us ... are sojourners here and strangers and exiles" (*Exil.* 607d). Because the soul has come from elsewhere, one may say that "the soul is an exile and a wanderer" (607e).

The portrayal of the object of faith as "seeing the invisible one" (11:27; see also 11:1) is an appropriate pastoral response to readers who "do not see everything in subjection to the Son" (2:8b). In the list of heroes, the author reminds the readers of others who did not see God's handiwork on earth but endured marginalization because of their capacity to see the transcendent homeland. Although the author does not incorporate a complete Platonic ontology, he employs those aspects of Middle Platonism that advance his purpose, maintaining that the reality on which believers should rely is the unseen world.

Eschatology and Ontology: Hebrews 12:14–29

This reality is not only unseen, as the recapitulation of the homily in 12:14–19 indicates. The author presents Esau as the negative alternative to the heroes in chapter 11 (12:16–17). Unlike Moses, who chose the unseen reality over the temporary pleasures of sin (11:26), Esau chose the temporary—a single meal—over the eternal. The author encourages the readers not to be like Esau, adapting the familiar contrast between Mount Sinai and Mount Zion from Jewish literature. The parallel "you have not come to what may be touched ... you have come to Mount Zion, the city of the living God, the heavenly Jerusalem" (12:18, 22) once more contrasts material and transcendent realities. The description of Mount Sinai as "what may be touched" may reflect the use of Exod 19:12–13, which promises death to anyone who touches the mountain. The author of Hebrews, however, characterizes the entire Sinai theophany as tangible, suggesting that believers have approached the untouchable transcendent realm, the city that the ancient faithful people saw only in the distance. This comparison corresponds to the Platonic distinction between the sense-perceptible and intelligible realities. For Plato that which is touchable belongs to the sphere of sense perception (*Phaed.* 99e; *Tim.* 28b, 31b). Indeed, God is described in other Hellenistic literature as "untouchable" (*apsēlaphētos*; for texts, see Thompson 1982, 45). The author of Hebrews writes that Christians, however, have approached the transcendent city.

This dualistic distinction between two realms leads the author to contrast the word (12:19) on earth (12:25) that the Israelites heard from Sinai with the voice that believers now hear from heaven (12:24–25). Citing Hag 2:6, the author recalls the promise of an eschatological earthquake, a familiar theme in apocalyptic literature, in which God will "shake not only the earth but also the heaven" (12:26). In the interpretation in 12:27, the author departs from the usual apocalyptic expectation, contrasting the heavens and the earth that will be shaken with those things that cannot be shaken and indicating that the latter will abide. He further characterizes those things that will be shaken as "made." Thus he distinguishes between two levels of reality. The "heavens and the earth" that will be shaken belong to the material world. One may compare Philo's use of the term *saleuein*, used primarily for things in the earthly sphere (*Post.* 22–23; *Somn.* 2.221, 37). For the author, that which is shakable belongs to the world of sense perception: "He knows two worlds already possessing full reality, one of which is material, and therefore shakable; the other is not material, and is unshakable. When the material world appears, only the world that is presently unseen (11:1) and untouchable (12:18) remains" (Thompson 1982, 50). The author has thus maintained an apocalyptic tradition but has interpreted it in Platonic terms, focusing on the stability of the heavenly world. Anticipating the Christian Middle Platonists who followed him, he brought together apocalyptic thought and Platonic ontology.

CONCLUSION

What does Middle Platonism have to do with Hebrews? Just as we now recognize that Judaism and Hellenism did not exist in separate worlds, we have abundant evidence that Jewish eschatology and Platonic ontology could exist alongside one another and intersect in a variety of ways. The author of Hebrews demonstrates neither a profound knowledge of Platonism nor a belief in all of the major tenets of its point of view (Sterling 2001, 210). However, like the Christian theologians who came after him, he employed Platonic assumptions for his own pastoral purposes. Responding to the readers' loss of confidence in the eschatological hope, the author provides stability for their existence by reassuring them of the eternal and transcendent Christ (1:10–12; 7:3, 23–24), who alone is the anchor for their insecure existence (6:19–20). With his focus on what is eternal rather than transitory, he appeals to the major theme of Middle Platonism. While he maintains the traditional Jewish eschatological hope, he shifts the emphasis to the stable, invisible, and untouchable reality that provides certainty for wavering people (Eisele 2003, 142). With Philo, he maintains that wavering humans can find security in proximity to one who is immutable.

Cosmology, Messianism, and Melchizedek: Apocalyptic Jewish Traditions and Hebrews

Eric F. Mason

As James Thompson has noted in the previous chapter, the author of Hebrews draws upon Middle Platonic philosophical traditions at several points in his argumentation. Alongside that, however, the author also demonstrates much familiarity with apocalyptic Jewish traditions. One's first reaction to this statement may be that Hebrews is not an apocalypse, like the New Testament book of Revelation or parts of Daniel in the Hebrew Bible in which human figures are shown heavenly scenes and secrets. That certainly is true, but a text need not be of the apocalypse genre to share the apocalyptic mindset. John J. Collins notes, for example, that relatively few texts of the apocalypse genre are found among the Dead Sea Scrolls, yet one might rightfully call the Qumran sect an "apocalyptic community" because of its tenets such as determinism of human behavior and dualism (good versus evil), its eschatology (the expectation of a final, climactic war between spiritual forces, often with participation by one or more messianic figures and the hope for eternal life), and its significant interest in angels (Collins 1997, 10–11).

As such, the Dead Sea Scrolls provide a helpful framework in which to consider the relationship between Hebrews and apocalyptic Jewish traditions. Scholars have long sought to relate the Dead Sea Scrolls to interpretation of the New Testament, and often Hebrews has taken center stage. Already several decades before the discovery of the first scrolls in the Qumran area in 1947, Solomon Schechter proposed a relationship between Hebrews and discussion of the "new covenant" in two medieval manuscripts of the Zadokite Work (later called the Damascus Document) that were discovered in the genizah (or storage area for worn manuscripts) of a Cairo synagogue (Schechter 1910; Brooke 1999, 62–63).[1] By the time the Qumran Scrolls were found, Hebrews had long since been separated from the Pauline collection in the evaluation of critical scholarship; its peculiarities thus stood in sharper relief, and the perplexing question of its conceptual background was a burning topic. Although Ernst Käsemann's suggestion in 1937 that the author of Hebrews had adapted gnostic mythology to explain Jesus as a cosmic redeemer found some traction (particularly in German scholarship; Käsemann 1984), the stronger reply came from those who proposed that the book reflected Middle Platonic thought, classically expressed by Ceslas Spicq (1952–1953).

Ironically, Spicq's magisterial commentary appeared just as a period of what George J. Brooke has called the "rapid expansion of activity" in Scrolls scholarship commenced (Brooke 1999, 64). Only a handful of Scrolls had been published by 1957, but already the Jewish scholar Yigael Yadin eagerly proclaimed that the Qumran sect provided "the missing link" for understanding Hebrews (1958, 38).[2] Yadin found numerous points of contact on subjects such as angels, the priestly messiah, Moses, and the eschatological prophet. He similarly observed that both Hebrews and the Scrolls displayed heavy dependence on the Pentateuch and proposed that the recipients of Hebrews were former members of the Qumran community. Assuming they retained some sectarian tenets even after their conversion to Christianity, he concluded: "There could be no stronger appeal to the hearts and minds of people descending from the DSS sect than in those metaphors which are abundant and characteristic in the Epistle to the Hebrew [sic]" (Yadin 1958, 55). Others expressed similar enthusiasm (Spicq 1958–1959, 389–90; Kosmala 1959, x).

Such proposals faced withering criticism in the early to mid-1960s. About this same time, however, A. S. van der Woude published the fragmentary text 11QMelchizedek; his 1965 edition in German (with only passing comments about its potential relevance for Hebrews and New Testament study) was quickly followed by an English study co-authored with Marinus de Jonge in which they claimed the scroll was crucial for interpretation of both Hebrews and the Gospel of John (van der Woude 1965; de Jonge and van der Woude 1965–1966). For the former, they

---

1. Today it generally is recognized that the Damascus Document and Hebrews use "new covenant" language in very different ways, with the Qumran usage more appropriately understood to mean "renewed covenant" (Talmon 1994; Lehne 1990).

2. This survey follows Mason 2008, 64–68; and Hurst 1990, 43–44.

noted especially how 11QMelchizedek was relevant for understanding the language about Melchizedek in Heb 7. They proposed that Melchizedek is an angelic warrior figure in the scroll, and though that text's "angelic warrior-soteriology" differed from Hebrews' emphasis on Jesus' suffering and priestly role, it did correspond with the description of Melchizedek as a heavenly, eternal figure in Heb 7:3. Unlike Yadin and earlier enthusiasts for a Qumran-Hebrews connection, they denied that the recipients of the epistle were Essenes; also, they rejected ideas that Heb 1–2 was intended to suppress worship of angels (but noted that the author was indeed careful to exalt the Son over angels, lest there be any confusion; de Jonge and van der Woude 1965–1966, 315–21). Nevertheless, Yadin claimed that 11QMelchizedek supported his Essene thesis and answered the remaining question of why Melchizedek was so prominent in Hebrews (Yadin 1965, 152–54).

Early reception of de Jonge and van der Woude's proposals was divided, both concerning their interpretation of Melchizedek as an angelic figure in 11QMelchizedek and that text's relevance for Hebrews. But despite early challenges to the former—several of which have reappeared in revised forms in recent years—their understanding of Melchizedek in the scroll now is very widely accepted (Mason 2009a). On the other hand, their suggestion about the scroll's relevance for interpreting Hebrews found some early support but became particularly unfashionable after a rebuttal by Fred L. Horton (1976).

At present, scholarly opinion is rather mixed on the issue of the conceptual background that best explains Hebrews. On one level, this is to be applauded, because it means that the futile quest to identify *the* key to interpretation of Hebrews—as if the author lived in a monolithic thought world—has largely been abandoned. Instead, most interpreters recognize that the author was very sophisticated and drew from a number of intellectual streams when crafting his text, including Middle Platonism.

Some scholars, however, remain wary of the idea that the author was influenced by apocalyptic Jewish traditions such as those present in many Dead Sea Scrolls texts. In part this is understandable, given the excessive claims of an earlier generation of scholars eager to identify the audience of the book with members of the Qumran sect. This recent skittishness frequently is manifested in discussions of three major issues: cosmology (for which understanding the ancient Jewish conception of a heavenly sanctuary served by an angelic priesthood is vital), messianism (particularly the royal and priestly roles at Qumran as they relate to the Christology of Hebrews), and Melchizedek traditions (especially the compatibility of portraits of the figure in the two literatures). Consideration of these three topics also allows for reflections on Day of Atonement imagery and a distinctive method of reapplying biblical citations in both the Scrolls and Hebrews. The procedure below will be to describe each of these traditions at Qumran, then to consider how certain key elements of Hebrews may be understood in light of this background (for a broader approach, see Attridge 2004 and 2006).

I write with the assumption that most readers will be more familiar with Hebrews than the various Dead Sea texts. Many questions are now raging about the nature of the Qumran site, the relationship between the site and the scrolls themselves, and the identity of the Qumran sect (assuming such is relevant). This is not the proper venue in which to consider those issues, but it is appropriate for me briefly to state my presuppositions about these things at the outset. I assume that the Qumran site was settled by a sectarian group identified with the Essenes and that the scrolls found in the caves were from the community's library, with some of them composed or copied by members of the sect while others were brought into the community from elsewhere. (See VanderKam 2010 for a current discussion of these issues.)

COSMOLOGY

For readers unfamiliar with the apocalyptic texts of Second Temple period Jewish literature, one of the most striking things about the Dead Sea Scrolls is the cosmology envisioned in many of these writings. Much more so than in most books of the Hebrew Bible, this is a world filled with angels and evil spirits, one in which earthly liturgies and sanctuaries have heavenly parallels. Jubilees and various parts of what later became the book 1 Enoch circulated elsewhere, but copies are found among the Qumran Scrolls; the importance in these texts of things such as Watchers traditions, visionary experiences, and the immediacy of contact between humans and angelic beings provides a backdrop for understanding the worldview of the Qumran sectarians. While that group had many ideas in common with the Jews responsible for those kinds of apocalyptically tinged texts, other motifs and expressions could be expressed by the sectarians in a distinctive way. Various texts found at Qumran describe the division of humanity into "lots" aligned with spiritual beings, both good and evil. Eschatological expectations include a war between the "sons of light" and the "sons of darkness," with angelic aid of various sorts expected by the Qumran community in those climactic days. While admittedly much could be said about the eschatological conflict anticipated in these texts, discussion here will focus instead on understandings of the heavenly sanctuary and angels with liturgical functions.

One of the richest texts in which to explore these issues is Songs of the Sabbath Sacrifice, preserved in fragments from Caves 4 (4Q400–407) and 11 (11Q17) and also found at Masada (Mas1k). The earliest Qumran copies date from about 100 B.C.E., but the Songs do not bear the marks of a Qumran sectarian text and may have been composed earlier (Newsom 1990). As such, it likely is a text predating the establishment of the Qumran community but which (like Jubilees and several Enochic booklets) never- theless was very influential on the community's thought (Newsom 2000, 2:887).

The text addresses liturgical concerns for Sabbath worship over a period of thirteen weeks, with the first five songs emphasizing the estab- lishment and duties of the heavenly priesthood (along with reflections on the relationship between human and angelic priestly worship), the next three describing praises and blessings in various groupings of seven, and the remaining five describing the heavenly temple and God's chariot throne (Newsom 2000, 2:887–88). Overall, the Songs are striking for their vivid (though regrettably very fragmentary) descriptions of the angelic priest- hood, praise, and liturgy in the heavenly sanctuary around the throne of God. The imagery owes much to Isa 6 and Ezek 1; God sits on a chariot throne and is surrounded by cherubim and other heavenly beings (as in the eleventh and twelfth songs in 4Q405 20–22 2:1–14). If certain widely accepted textual reconstructions may be assumed, Melchizedek is explic- itly named as one of these angelic priests and may serve as leader of the angelic priesthood (see further discussion of Melchizedek below; for a very different approach to this text, one that understands the priests not as angels but rather as humans transformed into heavenly, angelic beings, see Fletcher-Louis 2002). The texts speak frequently of angelic liturgical service in the heavenly sanctuary or inner sanctum in ways reminiscent of biblical descriptions of Levitical priestly functions, and some passages (e.g., 4Q405 23 2:7–11) describe the appearance of the angelic priestly robes. Other pas- sages (including 4Q403 1 2:11 and 4Q405 7 a–e 7) seem to imply the exis- tence of seven heavenly sanctuaries, but again the context is fragmentary.

Presumably the text was used liturgically in the Qumran commu- nity, in the words of Carol Newsom, "as the means for a communion with

angels in the act of praise, in short, as a form of communal mysticism"
(2000, 2:888). Similarly, Maxwell J. Davidson relates the community's use
of the Songs with their avoidance of the sacrificial rites at the Jerusalem
temple, which they considered to be compromised. Several scrolls discuss
vividly the conflict between the Jerusalem priesthood and the Qumran
community. For example, one reads about particular disputes concerning calendar and purity issues in 4QMMT, presumably a letter written
by the Teacher of Righteousness to the Jerusalem high priest of the time.
Also, the Pesher on Habakkuk seems to describe a hostile excursion of
the high priest to the Qumran community, something criticized both for
the priest's intent to harm the community's Teacher and its occurrence on
the Day of Atonement according to the community's liturgical calendar
(which differed from the calendar used in Jerusalem; see 1QpHab 11:4–8
and further discussion below). Given this sort of tension with the Jerusalem religious establishment, Davidson notes that the Songs allowed the
community

> to experience the validation of [the community's] claim to be a holy
> temple with a legitimate priesthood, whose service was parallel to that
> of the heavenly angels with whom they were closely associated.... Thus,
> as the Qumran worshippers praised God together with the angels, they
> would have been reassured in their belief that they were the legitimate
> and holy priesthood ... despite the contradictory evidence of their exclu-
> sion from the Jerusalem temple. (Davidson 1992, 237)

The Songs are rich for a number of reasons, but the most important
things to highlight for the present investigation are the conceptions of a
heavenly sanctuary intimately related to God's throne and the assumption
of heavenly liturgical service. Similar ideas are evident in 1 En. 14:15–23
and Jub. 31:13–15 (cf. 30:18), both of which are texts known at Qumran,
and the later Testament of Levi 3:4–6; 5:1 (cf. 2:10–12).[3]
    Like those texts, Hebrews describes a heavenly sanctuary and a heav-
enly sacrifice, but with some interesting differences. The author clearly
understands a heavenly setting in which God is enthroned and surrounded by angels, as is evident especially when he contrasts the Son and

---

3. Perhaps the fragmentary Qumran text Aramaic Levi, whose precise relationship to Testament of Levi is much debated, also described a similar heavenly setting in
a vision experienced by Levi.

angels with a series of biblical prooftexts in Heb 1:5–14. There he concludes the comparisons by noting that angels are "ministering spirits," but
with a different twist than one might expect in light of the discussion of
the Qumran texts above: angels are said to minister to humans, described
as those inheriting salvation, rather than as priests in a heavenly liturgical
setting.[4] Indeed, while Hebrews gives considerable attention to a heavenly
sacrifice and says much about Melchizedek (see below), it presents Jesus as
the incomparable heavenly high priest, contrasted not with angelic priests
but with earthly Levitical priests (especially in Heb 7–10; cf. the more positive discussion in 4:14–5:10). This is an important distinctive of Hebrews
and illustrates well that, while the author shares concepts with contemporary Jewish thought, he appropriately adapts such ideas to express his
theological message.

Such adaptations also occur when the author describes the heavenly
sanctuary. He makes much of its correlation with the earthly tabernacle of
the exodus period, drawing on Exod 25:40 to explain that God instructed
Moses to build it according to the heavenly model (Heb 8:5). Elsewhere in
Heb 8–10 he offers additional comparisons of the two sanctuaries and their
respective priestly service, and in the course of this discussion he develops
an important schematization. The earthly sanctuary, connected with the
Mosaic law (i.e., the "first covenant") and staffed by Levitical priests, is
contrasted with the heavenly sanctuary, related to the "second" or "new
covenant" and the place where Jesus as high priest offers his self-sacrifice.
The Levitical priests are many, their sacrifices are continually repeated,
and they lack ultimate effectiveness because they cannot cleanse the conscience. In contrast, Jesus' sacrifice is singular and final, the offering of the
one ultimate priest who himself was sinless, and his sacrifice cleanses the
conscience in fulfillment of Jeremiah's new-covenant promise that God's
law would be put in believers' hearts.[5]

Commentators routinely note that the author of Hebrews makes
much use of Middle Platonic thought in this comparison of the two
priesthoods and sanctuaries. The correlation of things spiritual and

---

4. Unless otherwise noted, all biblical translations reflect the NRSV.

5. This is implied in 10:16 ("I will put my laws in their hearts") and 10:22 ("let us
approach with a true heart in full assurance of faith, with our hearts sprinkled clean
from an evil conscience and our bodies washed with pure water"). Earlier the author
noted that the Levitical sacrifices, unlike Jesus' new-covenant action (see 9:14), were
unable to "perfect the conscience of the worshiper" (9:9).

material is a philosophical motif, as is the strong preference for the one rather than the many. The author's discussion of the two sanctuaries in Heb 8–10 is marked by the frequent use of philosophical terminology reminiscent of Plato or the first-century c.e. Jewish philosopher/exegete Philo of Alexandria, though often these words are used by the author of Hebrews rather differently than by his philosophical forbearers (Koester 2001, 98–99).

This mixture of apocalyptic Jewish and Middle Platonic elements has prompted several suggestions for how one might understand the worldviews of the author and recipients of Hebrews, especially whether the author's approach differs from that of the recipients and/or the author feels compelled to stress eschatology in light of his presentation of Jesus' activity (see especially Barrett 1956; MacRae 1978; Sterling 2001). Something frequently overlooked, however, is the foundational nature of the author's indebtedness to an apocalyptic Jewish cosmology, as evidenced by the central importance of the heavenly throne in the author's conception of the heavenly sanctuary.[6] The author repeatedly connects throne and sanctuary, as descriptions of Jesus' heavenly sacrifice are followed by the assertion that he then takes his seat at the right hand of God's throne (1:3; 8:1; 10:12–13; see also 12:2). As noted already, the throne is an integral part of apocalyptic Jewish descriptions of the heavenly sanctuary, whereas such an image is foreign to Philo's Middle Platonic approach. This implies that Hebrews' first impulse is to conceive of the heavenly sanctuary in an apocalyptic Jewish sense, then to build on that foundation his theological argument about its significance and Jesus' unique ministry there by means of Middle Platonic motifs. The latter certainly is an important part of Hebrews' thought and should not be denied, but the comparable descriptions of the heavenly sanctuary in the Dead Sea Scrolls and elsewhere remind us of the fundamental importance of the apocalyptic Jewish conception for this sophisticated early Christian theologian.

MESSIANISM

Few topics have drawn as much attention in Scrolls scholarship as the sect's various messianic ideas. One of the very first scrolls discovered, the

---

6. Others who notice this connection include Hay 1973 and Mackie 2007. I examine the importance of this throne language more fully in Mason 2012.

best-preserved copy of the Rule of the Community (dubbed the "Manual of Discipline" in the early days of Qumran scholarship), includes a reference to a prophet and the "messiahs of Aaron and Israel" (1QS 9:11), so immediately this messianic dualism (often called "bifurcated messianism") was assumed to be characteristic of the sect. As Qumran scholarship has matured, it has become evident to most interpreters that the situation is far more complicated, and the question of the number of messiahs expected by the community is just one of several vexing issues, along with questions such as who may be considered a "messiah" and how changing political fortunes affected the evolution of messianic thought in the community. As such, one should be cautious about the facile, overly exuberant claims for links between the Scrolls and Hebrews that plagued the late 1950s and early 1960s. Still, it is important to consider discussions of a priestly messiah at Qumran, since Hebrews so forcefully argues that the Messiah Jesus also is a priest.

It is impossible here to present the nuanced discussion of these texts and their varying versions that would be ideal, but such treatments are available in numerous other studies (e.g., Collins 2010, 79–122; Mason 2008, 64–137). Nor is it possible here to discuss in detail the possible foundations from which the Qumran idea of a messianic priest developed; it must suffice here to say that Aramaic Levi and Jubilees, two texts found at Qumran, give evidence of a tradition in which Levi's violence against Shechem in Gen 32 is reinterpreted in light of other texts that describe zealous actions by his descendants (Levites after the golden calf incident, Exod 32:25–29; Phinehas, Num 25:6–15; and Moses' blessing on the Levites, Deut 33:8–11) toward the conclusion that Levi is granted a covenant with God (Mal 2:4–7) and ultimately, in Second Temple period Levi traditions, an eternal priesthood (Kugler 1996, 9–21). Given what one finds otherwise in the Qumran texts, one would expect something as important as the expectation of a messianic figure to be rooted deeply in exegesis of biblical texts, but one does not find that for Qumran's messianic priest unless this is seen as an extension of the developing Levi tradition.[7] The discussion that follows will consider in a broad manner what sorts of ideas appear in Qumran texts about a messianic priest.

---

7. As noted below, on occasion the identity of the messianic priest may be connected to Deut 33:8–11 or Num 24:17, but the latter verse is utilized elsewhere in the Qumran texts in rather different ways.

As already noted, one finds mention of "the prophet and the messiahs of Aaron and Israel" in 1QS 9:11. The first of these messiahs is presumed to be priestly (because Aaron is Israel's first high priest in the Hebrew Bible) and the latter royal, though nothing is said about what either will do. This copy of Rule of the Community dates to 100–75 B.C.E., and two other texts (discussed below) were appended by the scribe on the same scroll. Ten fragmentary manuscripts from Cave 4 (4Q255–264) and one from Cave 5 (5Q11) also preserve portions of Rule of the Community, and these range in date from the second half of the second century B.C.E. to the first half of the first century C.E. (Metso 2007, 2–6; she also considers whether 11Q29 preserves this text). This rule text was composed in Hebrew and was a composite text, including (in 1QS, easily the longest surviving copy, with eleven columns) sections on admission into the community, the community's dualistic beliefs, rules for community life, and a hymn of praise. In addition, the variations between the contents of the several copies from Caves 1, 4, and 5 indicate that the text had a complicated history of revision and development, not always including the messianic reference. As such, Sarianna Metso argues that 1QS represents a late version of the rule that incorporates elements from two different trajectories in the text's development (Metso 1997; for discussion of other approaches, see Knibb 2000, 2:793–94; Metso 2007, 15–20).

The other major rule text found among the Scrolls, the Damascus Document, likewise is found in multiple versions.[8] We have already noted that two incomplete medieval manuscripts of CD were discovered in the Cairo genizah several decades before the Judean desert finds. Their contents sometimes diverge significantly in the same section of the text; as such, they are called manuscripts A and B. Qumran Cave 4 yielded remains of eight copies (4Q266–273) dating between the first century B.C.E. and first century C.E., and other fragments were found elsewhere (5Q12; 6Q15; Baumgarten 2000, 1:166–70).

The phrase "the messiah of Aaron and Israel" (or something very similar) appears four times in CD (A 12:23–13:1; A 14:19; B 19:10–11; B 20:1), but admittedly only the second of these four is preserved in the Qumran fragments (Baumgarten 1996, 72, 134). The phrase differs from that found

---

8. Most scholars who understand the Scrolls as the library of Essene male celibates at Qumran assume that the Rule of the Community was specific to life there, with the earlier Damascus Document serving a similar purpose for Essenes of both genders living in normal family arrangements elsewhere.

in 1QS 9:11, however, because the word "messiah" each time is singular in CD. Some read this as only a quirk of expression and argue that two distinct figures must be intended (as in 1QS), otherwise the identification "of Aaron and Israel" is redundant (VanderKam 1994, 228–31). Others demand that only one figure is in view (Abegg 1995). If so, the figure would seem to be a priest because he is linked with Aaron.

One passage in CD A 7:9–8:1 (different from the content at this point in the text in CD B, but partially preserved in 4Q266 3 3:18–22 and 4Q269 5 1–4) provides some insight on messianic thought at a certain stage in CD's development. The passage is an elaborate midrash, and in the most relevant section Amos 5:26–27 is interpreted in light of Num 24:17 ("a star has left Jacob, a staff has risen from Israel"). Though not yet quoted in the discussion, the interpreter appeals to the word "star" in Amos 5:26 and, reading it alongside the phrase from Numbers, determines that he is "the interpreter of the law who comes to Damascus" (CD A 7:18–19). The "staff" is then identified as a future militaristic figure (i.e., a royal messiah) in the next two lines.[9] The grammar is ambiguous as to when the "star" appears, whether in the past or in the future, but the activity of teaching the law accords with a function of a future priest in other scrolls (Xeravits 2003, 45–46).

One other passage deserves scrutiny. In three of the four places in CD where one finds the phrase "messiah of Aaron and Israel," one reads nothing about the activities of the messiah(s), just that a new era dawns with the arrival of the figure(s), as also is the case in 1QS 9:11. But in CD A 14:19, one finds reference to an act of atonement, though again the grammar is ambiguous. The lack of written vowels allows the possibility that the Hebrew *ykpr* may be translated as "[he] will make atonement" (*piel*) or as "atonement will be made" (*pual*; Collins 2010, 87–92; VanderKam 1994, 229–30). Admittedly many questions remain, but offering sacrifices for atonement certainly is a priestly function.

As mentioned above, two short texts are appended to the same scroll as 1QS, and both often have been cited as relevant to understanding Qumran's messianic priest. The first of these, Rule of the Congregation, announces an assembly "in the end of days" and details a number of regulations for participation. Attention then turns for the remainder of this short text (of only two columns) to description of an eschatological ban-

---

9. The translation is that of Edward Cook in Tov 2006.

quet (1QSa 2:11–22). The "messiah of Israel," a royal figure, is present, as is the "chief priest of the congregation." The latter is never called a messiah, but he takes precedence over the other figure in two ways: he is first to take his seat at the banquet table (though others also go ahead of the messiah in this procession), and he is the first to take the bread of the meal after having blessed it. The priest and messiah then bless the members of the congregation. It is not clear that this priest is understood as messianic, but he does function in the eschaton and takes precedence in these two ways over the royal figure.

The other text on this scroll is Rule of the Blessings, and how to interpret its five poorly preserved columns is much debated. Interpreters agree that this text is strongly influenced by the language of the priestly blessing of Num 6:24–25, but because of the gaps in the text one cannot be certain who is being addressed in various places. Building on an earlier proposal by Jacob Licht, Martin Abegg argues that 1QSb 4:20–5:19 (not all of which is extant) describes blessings on the high priest at the eschaton, preceded by blessings on the faithful, two unidentified groups or individuals, and the other priests, and followed by blessings on the "Prince of the Congregation," the royal messiah (Abegg 2003, 10–12). In 4:24–25, one reads that the high priest is "like the angel of the presence in an abode of holiness," and in the previous line he is said to be placed "at the head of the Holy Ones" (4:23), that is, the angels, with whom he serves "in the temple of the kingdom" (4:25–26; Abegg 2003, 11). The cosmology assumed in this text evokes that of Songs of the Sabbath Sacrifices, and a pairing of a priestly and royal figure seems implied. That said, the priest is never called "messiah" in the text that survives, and too much has been lost to allow for definitive conclusions.

Yet another text that mentions a priest in an eschatological context is the War Scroll, preserved in 1QM (easily the most complete), 4Q491–496, and perhaps also 4Q285 and 11Q14. These manuscripts date to between the first century B.C.E. and the first century C.E. (Duhaime 1994, 80–83).[10] Of all the texts surveyed here, the War Scroll is most explicit about the functions of a priest in the eschaton, but admittedly again the priest is not called a messiah. The setting is the climactic war between the "sons of light," led by the royal "Prince of the Congregation," and the "sons of dark-

---

10. Others argue that 1QM and the other manuscripts preserve two different war traditions (Davies 2000, 2:965–68).

ness," led by Belial. The war lasts thirty-five years, interrupted every seven years for a sabbatical year of rest. In 1QM 2:5–6, the high priest and other priests offer sacrifices "to atone" for the congregation during the "year of remission," or the sabbatical year (see Deut 15:1).

Elsewhere the high priest participates in the eschatological war in other ways, frequently exhorting the warriors with promises that God is with them and offering prayers (1QM 10:2–5; 15:4–16:1; perhaps also 13:1–14:1, assuming mention of the high priest has been lost from the end of column 12; cf. Deut 20:2–5) or reminding them of God's miraculous provisions for battle and promising angelic support (16:13–17:9). In 1QM 18:5–19:8, the high priest, other priests, and Levites bless God and utter a prayer of thanksgiving as the conclusion of the battle—and thus the realization of "everlasting redemption"—draws near. One should note that Num 24:17–19, a text used in CD (see above) and 4Q175 (see below), in both cases likely with messianic import, is used in 1QM 11:6–7 to emphasize God's deliverance without elaboration on any agents so used (thus no obvious interest in the identity of the "scepter" or "star"). Overall, however, the priest does function alongside what appears to be a royal messianic "Prince of the Congregation," so it may not be a stretch to compare this priest with the figure called "messiah of Aaron" in 1QS 9:11.

Some have suggested the possibility that a few other texts mention a messianic priest, but this survey will conclude with comments on Florilegium (4Q174) and Testimonia (4Q175). Both are examples of the thematic pesher genre, but they take different forms.[11] In the extant portions of the poorly preserved Florilegium, the author utilizes quotations from Deut 33; 2 Sam 7; and Pss 1, 2, and 7 as he discusses God's future deliverance of his "anointed" (Ps 2:2), here the faithful community in the last days rather than a messianic figure. Use of these texts in combination is not surprising (especially 2 Sam 7 and Ps 2; compare the use of Ps 2:7 and 2 Sam

---

11. The Hebrew term "pesher" ("interpretation") appears frequently in these kinds of texts when the author turns from citation to explanation, and such usage has prompted use of the word to denote a literary genre with three subcategories. Jonathan G. Campbell defines "thematic pesher" as referring to texts "consist[ing] largely of *pesher* units in which a variety of scriptural sources are employed to support an overarching theme," in contrast to continuous pesher, in which attention repeatedly returns to a certain base text, and isolated pesher, referring to short passages of interpretative material that appear in texts otherwise of a different genre (Campbell 2004, 13). Campbell helpfully notes, however, that these subcategories should be understood as points on a continuum rather than as clear-cut distinctions (2004, 15).

7:14 in Heb 1:5), though the text's identification of the "anointed" may be (Mason 2009b). Most important for the present investigation is mention of "the interpreter of the law," who will arise with the "shoot of David" in the last days (4Q174 1–2 1:11).[12] Nothing else survives to explain further the functions of this interpreter, but presumably again a priest is in view because the citation of Deut 33:8–11 earlier in the text concerns Levi's role of teaching the law (VanderKam 1994, 227–28).

Testimonia is very different—it is complete and consists of four quotations with very minimal additional comments, and it may even be the autograph of this text (Strugnell 1969–1970, 225). Its meaning is much debated and admittedly can only be inferred because of the lack of explanatory materials. The most common approach is that it is a series of three eschatological prooftexts, with citation of Exod 20:21 from a textual tradition like the Samaritan Pentateuch (= MT Deut 5:28–29 plus 18:18–19) for an eschatological prophet, Num 24:15–17 for a coming king, and Deut 33:8–11 (the same text used in Florilegium) to describe a priest. Finally, Josh 6:26 (a curse on anyone who rebuilds Jericho) appears, with vague editorial comments appended to apply this to a new situation. Most interpreters understand the curse as directed against a Hasmonean ruler who has combined two or more of the offices mentioned in the first three quotations (for various options, see Campbell 2004, 96–97). If the intent is to posit an eschatological priest in the third quotation, again one finds little about his function.

In summary, we can observe that some Qumran texts speak explicitly—at least in certain stages of their editorial development—about a priest who may be called "messiah." Several other texts describe a very prominent role for a high priest in the eschaton without directly identifying this figure with messianic language. Descriptions of the high priest's activities tend to be vague, though duties of priests described in the Bible predominate: making atonement, interpreting the law, and offering prayers and encouragement. While one might expect that a community itself led by priests would envision a central role for an eschatological high priest, it also seems likely that developing traditions about Levi's divinely commissioned priesthood undergirded these expectations.

---

12. The same language about a priest appears in 4Q177 11 5. Annette Steudel (1992) argues that 4Q174 and 4Q177 are two copies of different parts of the same longer composition.

Hebrews is characterized by its central presentation of Jesus as the messianic high priest, but as with the discussion of cosmology above, one finds here both similarities and differences with the parallel conception in the Scrolls. There the priest normally is paired with a Davidic figure; in Hebrews, Jesus himself is both king and priest. Indeed, the identity of Jesus as the Davidic Messiah is integral to Hebrews' assertion that he also is priest. Jesus is the divine Son of Heb 1:1–4, who then is contrasted with the angels in Heb 1:5–14. The author has multiple purposes here (including exalting the Son and preparing for subsequent discussion of the Sinai law and perhaps also his description of Jesus' humanity and Moses in Heb 2–3), but one thing he subtly executes is the correlation of the Son with both God and the Davidic Messiah by use of the quotations. In their original contexts, the quotations speak of God or the Davidic king, but now they are recast and applied to the Son, identifying him both as divine and messianic. (See also the comment in Heb 7:13–14 that Jesus is from the tribe of Judah.) The author begins and ends this litany with Ps 2:7 ("You are my Son," Heb 1:5) and Ps 110 (LXX 109):1 ("Sit at my right hand," Heb 1:13), essentially identifying Jesus as divine Son with the Davidic figure addressed in both decrees, then later in Heb 5:5–6 the author builds on this to assert that the same figure also is declared priest. Here Ps 2:7 again is evoked, now paired not with Ps 110:1 but rather 110:4, "You are a priest forever, according to the order of Melchizedek." Thus Jesus' status as Son is necessary to assert his priesthood, and all this is built on his identification as the Davidic king of these royal psalms.

Later the author of Hebrews explains why it is important that Jesus is a priest like Melchizedek (see below), but otherwise he is more interested in explaining the nature and benefits of Jesus' priestly service. Some of this was discussed above in relation to cosmology, and it will suffice here to add only brief comments. First, Hebrews' presentation is unique with its emphasis on the importance of Jesus' incarnation for his priesthood: he was prepared, or made "perfect" for this role, by means of his suffering, which allowed him to understand fully the human plight and thus be completely sympathetic toward those he came to deliver from death and the devil (2:5–18; 4:14–5:10; compare Kevin B. McCruden's discussion of perfection in this volume). Nothing of this sort is said of the messianic priest in the Qumran texts. Second, Jesus is contrasted to the Levitical priesthood. This also differs from the understanding at Qumran, where the presumption is that the messianic priest will be Levitical (or, more specifically, Zadokite). While that community certainly felt enmity toward the

Jerusalem priesthood, it was not an anti-Levitical stance. Rather, the community itself was led by Zadokite priests and (as noted above) likely based its own understanding of a messianic priest on traditions that God granted an eternal priesthood to Levi. Indeed, Henryk Drawnel has suggested that the author of Hebrews intentionally identified Jesus as the heavenly high priest *because* of his awareness of this Levi tradition. In large part this hinges on Drawnel's proposal that Levi is granted both priestly and royal offices in Aramaic Levi, matching the presentation in Hebrews of Jesus as both royal Son and priest (Drawnel 2004, 14, 307–9). Drawnel's interpretation of the royal language in Aramaic Levi is not shared by all, however, and one should also note that Hebrews lacks the sort of polemical tone that one might expect if the author were intentionally opposing this sort of Levi tradition (Mason 2008, 198–99; 2010a).

Drawnel's suggestion does, however, point in another very important direction. If nothing else, the conception of Levi's divine appointment to an eternal priesthood and the community's expectation of a messianic priest do provide a context in which the author of Hebrews could develop his priestly Christology (as does the expectation of a heavenly temple cult in the apocalyptic cosmology discussed above). Certainly there are differences in the Qumran and Hebrews conceptions of the messianic priest. But just as the Jewish context of early Christianity provided the expectation of a Davidic royal messiah (and saw it developed in a very different way), so also the author of Hebrews seems indebted on some level to an earlier priestly tradition that, like Hebrews, included divine appointment to an eternal role and the offering of atonement in the eschaton.

MELCHIZEDEK

Finally, we turn to discussion of Melchizedek traditions in the Dead Sea Scrolls, though it is important to consider first the biblical texts about the figure and how those are used in other Second Temple period interpretations. Melchizedek is mentioned only twice in the Hebrew Bible, Gen 14:18–20 and Ps 110:4, and the relationship between those passages is unclear. He is introduced very abruptly in Gen 14, so much so that most critical scholars assume that Gen 14:18–20 is an insertion in a preexisting narrative about Abram's return from rescuing his nephew Lot from the invading king Chedorlaomer and his allies. The king of Sodom went to meet Abram in the Valley of Shaveh (Gen 14:17), and they converse about the distribution of the spoils of the campaign (14:21–24). This is interrupted, however, in 14:18–20, where suddenly Melchizedek, king of Salem rather than Sodom, instead first encounters Abram. Bearing bread and wine, this "priest of God Most High" blessed Abram, and the scene concludes with payment of a tithe.

The name "Melchizedek" (*mlky-tsdq*) literally means either "my king is righteous" or, more likely in a Canaanite context, "my king is Sedeq." Also, his "God Most High" (*'l 'lywn*; Gen 14:18, 20) likely is the Canaanite deity El 'Elyon, but the biblical author understands Melchizedek as a follower of Israel's God instead (thus Gen 14:22, "Yahweh God Most High"; Fitzmyer 2004, 246–48). Although the Hebrew is ambiguous, virtually all interpreters past and present have assumed that Abram is the one who pays the tithe; most understand Salem as the later Jerusalem (a few prefer Shechem; see Mason 2008, 140 n. 4). Minor variations appear in the Septuagint, but these are not important for the present discussion (Fitzmyer 2000, 67; Mason 2008, 139–40).

Psalm 110 is a royal psalm, normally read as a preexilic text addressed to the ruler of the Davidic dynasty. Less clear is how to understand the granting of a priesthood in "the order of Melchizedek" (110:4) to a Hebrew king, given the normal biblical separation of the royal and priestly functions.[13] The relationship with Gen 14 is complex; there Melchizedek holds both royal and priestly offices, but why does the psalmist link a Davidic king with Melchizedek? Is it because of that combination of offices or an appeal to ancient (Jeru)salem traditions for legitimation of the Davidic dynasty? Some have argued that the psalm was composed in the postexilic—perhaps Hasmonean—era, reflecting later realities when priests took on royal roles (opposite of the order in the psalm), but they have found few followers (Mason 2008, 145–46).

This discussion assumes a translation of Ps 110:4 similar to that of the NRSV: "The LORD has sworn and will not change his mind, 'You are a priest forever, according to the order of Melchizedek.'" This is consistent with the rendering in the LXX. Some, however, have proposed different translations of the divine decree as a statement addressed to Melchizedek himself ("You are a priest forever by my order [or 'on my account'], O Melchizedek"), while others have read *mlky-tsdq* not as the name Melchizedek but as a comment on the addressee's personal nature or ruling characteris-

---

13. For a recent survey of the many problems concerning the setting, dating, and interpretation of Ps 110, see Allen 2002, 108–20.

tic ("a rightful king" [NJPS], "may justice reign," or "reign in justice").[14] Regardless of whatever else they might say about this figure, the Septuagiunt, Second Temple period authors, and author of Hebrews find the personal name Melchizedek when explicitly citing this verse.

Several Second Temple period authors mention Melchizedek, including that of the Genesis Apocryphon (1QapGen ar XXII 12–17), Pseudo-Eupolemus (preserved in Eusebius, *Praep. ev.* 9.17.5–6), Philo of Alexandria (*Abr.* 235; *Congr.* 99; *Leg.* 3.79–82), and Josephus (*J.W.* 6.438; *Ant.* 1.179–181). Melchizedek's name has been lost in Jub. 13:25, but comments about the tithe and Abram remain. Each of these accounts diverges to some extent from the information about Melchizedek in Gen 14, whether by offering etymologies for his name or office (Philo, Josephus), addressing awkward details such as his abrupt encounter with Abram (Genesis Apocryphon, Philo, Josephus), explaining this tithe as the origin of the practice supporting Levitical priests (Jubilees, Philo), allegorizing eloquently about friendship or the Logos (Philo), or even crediting this Canaanite with building Israel's temple (Josephus). But the more striking thing is that all these interpretations deal only with the Gen 14 story without demonstrating any concern for Ps 110:4 (Mason 2008, 146–63).

Although Genesis Apocryphon and Jubilees were found among the Qumran texts, three others discovered there present a very different understanding of Melchizedek. Unfortunately, they are very fragmentary, and in two of the three his name is found only through textual reconstruction. One of these texts, Songs of the Sabbath Sacrifice, was introduced earlier when discussing cosmology, so we need only consider a few relevant passages here. Newsom reads "Melchi]zedek, priest in the assemb[ly of God," in 4Q401 11 3 (Newsom 1998, 205; also Davila 2000, 162; García Martínez, Tigchelaar, and van der Woude 1997, 270). Melchizedek, a priest in both Gen 14 and Ps 110, appears now as a heavenly, angelic priest. James Davila adds that this section of 4Q401 appears to be part of the fifth song, "which describes an eschatological 'war in heaven'" (Davila 2000, 162, cf. 223). Melchizedek may also be mentioned in song 8, partially preserved in 11Q17 3 2:7, in the phrase "the chiefs of the princes of the wonderful priesthoods of Melchizedek" (DJD).[15] The context discusses the praises of heav-

---

14. A third possibility is to understand Melchizedek as the speaker (Milik 1972b, 125). For direct address, see Flusser 1966, 26–27; Kugel 1998, 279.

15. Translations marked DJD here and for 11QMelchizedek are from García Martínez, Tigchelaar, and van der Woude 1997.

enly priests serving in the heavenly sanctuary, and Melchizedek is said to head the heavenly priesthood (reminiscent of "the order of Melchizedek" in Ps 110:4). Both the DJD editors and Davila admit that other readings are possible, and Newsom rejects mention of Melchizedek here (Davila 2000, 132–33; García Martínez, Tigchelaar, and van der Woude 1997, 266, 269–70; Newsom 1998, 205; Davila 2000, 162–63 finds another reference to Melchizedek in 4Q401 22 3).

Another text, Visions of Amram, also seems to portray Melchizedek as a heavenly figure. This second-century B.C.E. Aramaic text is preserved in fragments of six (perhaps seven) Cave 4 manuscripts, 4Q543–549 (Stone 2000, 1:23–24). For now, 4Q544 (copy b) is most relevant. The text is a testament recounting a vision of Amram, the grandson of Levi, who dreams that two "Watchers" (one evil, the other good) are fighting over him, and he inquires about their identities and powers (Kobelski 1981, 24–25).[16] No letters of Melchizedek's name are preserved, but Józef Milik proposed that he indeed was mentioned and reconstructed the following parallel identifications of the two "Watchers" (Milik 1972a, 85–86):

4Q544 2 3:13: [And these are his three names: Belial, Prince of Darkness], and Melchireša'
4Q544 3 4:2–3: [My] three names [are Michael, Prince of Light, and Melchizedek][17]

Both lists of names are heavily reconstructed in light of conceptual parallels with 1QM and 11QMelchizedek, but Milik's suggestion is widely accepted in Qumran scholarship. The one extant name is Melchireša' ("my king is wicked"), which means the opposite of the name Melchizedek ("my king is righteous"). Melchizedek is identified as (or with) the angel Michael and the "Prince of Light." Michael, who appears elsewhere in Qumran texts as the opponent of Belial, is the "Prince of Light" in 1QM 13:10–11 (Larson 2000, 1:546–48).

---

16. Though "Watchers" often are evil in Second Temple period usage, as in 1 Enoch and Jubilees, Kobelski notes that the term "applies equally well to fallen angels as to holy ones" (Kobelski 1981, 28).

17. The text and line numbers are those of the standard Discoveries in the Judaean Desert edition by Puech, 2001. Milik cited the texts as 4Q544 3 2 and 4Q544 2 3. The translation is from Kobelski 1981, 28.

Both of these Qumran texts portray Melchizedek as a heavenly, angelic figure, with one emphasizing his identity as a priest and the other as a warrior. These descriptions also are key in 11QMelchizedek, a first-century B.C.E. manuscript in which Melchizedek is an eschatological priest and warrior acting on behalf of God, making atonement for God's people and delivering them while bringing judgment on God's foes. Portions of three columns have survived, probably from the latter part of the manuscript, and the second of these columns easily is the best preserved.

It is not feasible to consider all of the contents of column 2 in this article, but a few key things especially relevant to Hebrews may be noted. First, the author of this text utilizes numerous Scripture quotations and allusions, and in a way similar to the reapplication of biblical quotations to speak of the Son in Heb 1:5–14 (as discussed above), some passages clearly about God in their biblical context are recast so that they apply the term *'lwhym* to Melchizedek.[18] In fact, overall the author demonstrates a strong tendency to identify Melchizedek as *'lwhym* and God as *'l* (Mason 2008, 176–83). One example will suffice. The author quotes Ps 82:1 in line 10: "*'lwhym* shall stand in the assembly of *'l*" (DJD, adapted). In its original context, the passage echoes Canaanite mythological language, where it would be natural to find Baal speaking in the court of El. In Ps 82:1, Israel's God (*'lwhym*) rises to address the court of *'l*, whether understood as still reflecting Canaanite influence or now assimilated so that the two divine names both point to Israel's God (thus God speaking in God's own court; on the Canaanite background, see Smith 2004, 106–10). In the scroll, however, now it is Melchizedek as *'lwhym* who speaks in the court of Israel's God *'l*, something clarified in the subsequent lines. (A similar thing occurs later in the column with interpretation of Isa 57:2.) In the broader context of lines 10–14, Ps 7:8–9 and 82:2 also are utilized, and Melchizedek administers justice on behalf of *'l* against Belial and those of his lot. This language naturally has led to much speculation on the author's understanding of the identity and nature of Melchizedek, but given the flexibility of the term *'lwhym* in the Hebrew Bible to mean "angels" or "heavenly beings," the original assertion of van der Woude and de Jonge that Melchizedek is presented as a heavenly, angelic *'lwhym* remains most convincing (for discussion of other interpretations, see Mason 2008, 185–90; 2009a, 51–61).

---

18. The author of 11QMelchizedek uses the fuller (plene) spelling for this term, *'lwhym*, compared to *'lhym* in the Hebrew Bible.

Second, while Melchizedek is presented as a warrior, he also has a priestly role of making atonement in the eschatological age. Much is said about deliverance in column 2, and the author divides time into ten Jubilee units concluding with an eschatological Day of Atonement (line 7). In lines 2–9, Melchizedek delivers the "captives" (line 4) or "the inheritance of Melchizedek" (line 5). Discussion of the Jubilee in Lev 25:13 and Deut 15:2, read through the lens of Isa 61:1, is interpreted to speak of the eschaton; Melchizedek executes God's pronouncement and announces liberty in the first week of the tenth Jubilee "from the debt of all their iniquities" (line 6, DJD; the phrase has strong cultic overtones). Perhaps liberation occurs here, but more likely it points to the eschatological Day of Atonement at the end of the tenth Jubilee, when "atonement shall be made for all the sons of light and for the men of the lot of Melchizedek" (line 8, DJD). This Day of Atonement appears to be the "year of grace of Melchizedek" (line 9), and presumably he is the high priest conducting the eschatological sacrifice. (Another reference to the Day of Atonement in the context of a Jubilee may be found in line 25, where a figure blows a horn; see Lev 25:9.) Line 9 also speaks "of the administration of justice," and the extant text of line 8 implies that the righteous benefit from this judgment ("according to all their doings," DJD).

Before turning to consider why Melchizedek may have been understood this way, it is appropriate to consider briefly how Day of Atonement traditions are used elsewhere in the Qumran literature. The Qumran sectarians did not participate in the Yom Kippur rites at the Jerusalem temple, and it is unlikely that animal sacrifices were conducted by the community, yet observance of the nonsacrificial aspects related to the rite are documented in various kinds of texts. One of the most intriguing is 1QpHab 11:4–8, in which Hab 2:15 is interpreted to speak of the "Wicked Priest" (normally understood as a cipher for a Hasmonean high priest) who came after the "Teacher of Righteousness," presumably at Qumran itself, threatening him and disrupting the community's observance of the ritual fast. Only a few years after the discovery of the first scrolls (of which this was one), Shemaryahu Talmon noticed that these comments indicated what would later be recognized as a major cause for the tension between the sect and the Jerusalem establishment: they were using different calendars, otherwise the high priest would still have had cultic duties in Jerusalem and could not have traveled to Qumran (Talmon 1951). Some have argued that the Qumran community incorporated other sorts of ascetic observances with their fast, based on their interpretation of Lev

16:29 ("you shall afflict yourselves," NRSV "you shall deny yourselves" or alternately "you shall fast"; cf. observance of the term "Day of Affliction" as essential for members of the "new covenant" in CD 6:18–19; Baumgarten 1999, 188–91). Beyond this literal observance, the community could use the language and imagery of Yom Kippur to describe the greater conflict between good and evil. Both God (or Melchizedek) and Belial had their "lots," and aspects of the scapegoat ritual influenced discussion of fallen angels in Watchers traditions in numerous texts. With evil spirits now interpreted via the lens of Yom Kippur, their struggles in the present era were identified with the fast, and atonement with God's provision of eschatological bliss (Stökl Ben Ezra 2003, 98–99).

Clearly these three Qumran texts portray Melchizedek in a very different way than the others discussed earlier that essentially interpret Gen 14. The question naturally arises as to why this has occurred. As noted above, most interpreters have read Ps 110:4 as addressed to someone receiving a eternal priesthood *like* that of Melchizedek, though Flusser argues that some ancients may have found it directed *to* Melchizedek (Flusser 1966, 26–27). If Ps 110:4 is understood to grant Melchizedek an eternal priesthood, then he must also be the one enthroned at God's right hand (Ps 110:1) with dominion over his enemies (110:1–2) and bringing judgment (110:5–6). The latter could prompt the author of 11QMelchizedek to read Ps 82 as also about Melchizedek (Flusser 1966, 27; VanderKam 2000, 174). As noted above, Melchizedek is *'lwhym* in Ps 82 as quoted in line 10, and the text relates this final judgment with periods of Jubilee, sabbatical legislation, and the Day of Atonement. This pastiche of themes is rooted in Scripture: according to Lev 25:8–10, Jubilees (with the accompanying restoration of land and liberty) began on the Day of Atonement, and in Gen 14 Abram in essence enacts a "Jubilee" by returning captured persons and property in the context of his encounter with Melchizedek. In the words of James VanderKam, "it seems that the writer of 11QMelch used a series of biblical passages and themes that allowed him to connect Melchizedek, the day of atonement, and sabbatical and jubilee periods" (VanderKam 2000, 175–76).

The author of Hebrews uses both Ps 110:4 and Gen 14:18–20 in his discussion of Melchizedek, but as in the three scrolls just surveyed, the psalm takes priority. Melchizedek first appears in the aforementioned quotation of Ps 110:4 in Heb 5:6, and the author cites the relevant portion of that version twice more (5:10; 6:20) before finally explaining the connection in Heb 7. There the author reads the psalm in light of Gen 14, reporting on Melchizedek's encounter with Abraham and the tithe (7:1–2a), offers etymologies of his name and office (king of Salem) familiar from other Second Temple period traditions (7:2b), and asserts his heavenly nature as one lacking parentage, genealogy, or mortality, but instead "resembling the Son of God" and remaining "a priest forever" (7:3).[19] Having established the exalted nature of Melchizedek, next the author again appeals to Gen 14 to argue for the superiority of Melchizedek's priesthood over the Levitical line. With a playful tone, he argues that when Abraham paid the tithe to Melchizedek, his descendant Levi (and hence subsequently the priestly Levitical line) was still in his loins, thus he, too, recognized Melchizedek's priestly priority (7:4–10). With this new priestly hierarchy thus established, Jesus, whose priesthood shares with Melchizedek a lack of Levitical descent, an eternal office, and installation by divine oath (7:15–22), can now be said to have a priesthood superior to that of the Levites, too. Having been utilized by the author to make this point, Melchizedek falls from view in the epistle.

As implied above, the discussion of Melchizedek in Hebrews serves the ultimate purpose of allowing the author to explain how Jesus can be a priest outside the Levitical line and to validate his superiority over that esteemed lineage. Also, while the author is not interested in Melchizedek per se, he does find traditions about the figure useful for emphasizing the heavenly, eternal nature of Jesus' priesthood. Hebrews shares certain elements with the broader Second Temple period interpretive tradition, such as etymologies of Melchizedek's name and royal office, but the language of Heb 7:3 demands that Melchizedek also be understood as a heavenly figure as in 11QMelchizedek, Songs of the Sabbath Sacrifice, and Visions of Amram.

As with discussion above of the relationship between Hebrews and Qumran priestly messiah traditions, one does not find full agreement between the presentations of Melchizedek in both places. But certain key elements are consistent: both present Melchizedek as a heavenly figure, and both describe him in the context of Day of Atonement sacrifices.

---

19. Admittedly, Heb 7:3 can be read very differently, with some finding here only the assertion that Melchizedek lacks a *Levitical* lineage or that the author mere exploits on a *literary* level the silence about Melchizedek's origins and fate in the Hebrew Scriptures. I defend this interpretation of Melchizedek as a heavenly, angelic figure in Mason 2005 and 2008, 25–35, 199–203. See also the essays in this volume by David M. Moffitt and (for a different approach) Kenneth Schenck.

In 11QMelchizedek he seems to offer the eschatological rite, whereas in Hebrews Jesus, the priest like Melchizedek, offers himself as the ultimate sacrifice, described chiefly through the lens of Yom Kippur imagery. Melchizedek in Hebrews is no rival to Jesus, given the affirmations earlier in the book that the Son is superior to angels, yet traditions of his heavenly status like those found in the Qumran texts are useful for the author. As noted earlier, this tradition appears nowhere else outside the Scrolls among texts clearly dated to the first century c.e. Another text, 2 Enoch, knows of a heavenly Melchizedek; some argue forcefully for a first-century date, with the descriptions of Melchizedek in Hebrews and 2 Enoch understood as parallel (or perhaps polemical) developments from earlier traditions (Orlov 2007). Still, however, the date of 2 Enoch and its relationship to early Christian traditions remain much disputed (Macaskill 2007, 2:265). Gnostic traditions about Melchizedek seem to draw on Hebrews or the tradition preserved in 11QMelchizedek (Pearson 1998, 192–200).

Conclusion

On at least three points—cosmology, messianism, and Melchizedek traditions—the Qumran texts are useful for understanding the Epistle to the Hebrews, and they provide helpful comparisons on several others (including angels, Day of Atonement traditions, and use of Scripture). While admittedly much more could be said, these points of contact establish the importance of understanding the broader Second Temple Jewish context for reading this epistle, and they demonstrate the relevance of such without being hindered by speculative arguments about Essene ties for the author or audience of Hebrews or overly zealous assertions about literary dependence on the Qumran texts. Rather, in a broader way the ideas circulating at Qumran and in apocalyptic Judaism provided a very important—but admittedly not the only—conceptual background for the author of the epistle.

THE INTERPRETATION OF SCRIPTURE
IN THE EPISTLE TO THE HEBREWS*

David M. Moffitt

The anonymous author of the Epistle to the Hebrews drew extensively on the Jewish Scriptures—the texts he believed communicated the words of God to the people of God. In fact, Hebrews contains the longest citation of a passage from the canonical Old Testament in the whole of the New Testament (see the citation of Jer 31:31–34 [LXX 38:31–34] in Heb 8:8–12). Biblical quotations, allusions, concepts, and language are more a part of the fabric of this epistle than they are of any other New Testament book. The particular ways in which the writer appeals to and interprets Scripture, however, often seem foreign and artificial to modern readers.

This essay has two goals: (1) to provide an overview of some of the issues important for a historically contextualized understanding of the assumptions, methods, and texts underlying the author's interpretations; and (2) to examine and analyze a few significant instances of biblical citations in Hebrews in order to provide concrete examples that indicate something about the author's conception of Scripture.

CONTEXTUAL ISSUES AND ASSUMPTIONS

Two important areas of historical background that we must address to accomplish the first goal of our study are the form of the author's biblical text (i.e., the actual wording of a given verse as the author knew it) and the methods and assumptions that likely informed his understanding of how one interprets and argues from Scripture. We begin, then, with a brief

* I am grateful to my friend Rodrigo J. Morales for commenting on an earlier draft of this chapter.

examination of the complicated issue of the state of the textual form of Jewish Scripture in the author's time. This will involve us in a discussion of the translation of Hebrew Scripture most likely known to the author: the so-called Septuagint.[1]

THE USE OF THE SEPTUAGINT IN HEBREWS

The author of Hebrews worked with and from biblical *texts*. We do not know if he drew primarily from his memory or if he had direct access to biblical manuscripts.[2] The question of the form of these texts is nevertheless significant for our purposes. While a great many issues concerning Hebrews continue to be debated by experts, the conclusion that the author knew Scripture in Greek translation and not in the original Hebrew language has found wide acceptance. When he cites the Bible, the wording he uses and even at points the interpretative moves he makes (see, e.g., the discussions of Pss 8 and 40 below) suggest his dependence upon the Septuagint.

Unfortunately, this conclusion does not settle the issue of the form of any given text cited by the author. This is because the use of the definite article before the word *Septuagint* can be misleading. To refer to *the* Septuagint (or *the* Hebrew Bible, for that matter) leaves the impression that a uniform translation of Hebrew Scriptures existed and was in circulation in the ancient world. Such an impression fails to account for two important factors: the complex realities of producing and distributing texts before the invention of the printing press, and the reality of multiple forms of Hebrew scriptural texts in circulation.

Before the printing press, the duplication of any written artifact was performed by hand copying. Usually trained scribes were employed to produce copies of texts. The process of copying a text by hand, however,

---

1. The term *Septuagint*, which is derived from the Latin word for seventy (*septuaginta*), is often designated simply by the Roman numerals LXX. In this essay I use the designation LXX and the term *Septuagint* to denote a collection of Greek texts containing ancient translation traditions of Hebrew works, along with texts not found in the Hebrew Bible (e.g., the books known as the Apocrypha or Deuterocanonicals). This Greek collection, though not monolithic, was used by Jewish communities throughout the Diaspora and later became the Bible used by Greek-speaking Christians.

2. A combination of the two cannot be ruled out; for some reflection on this point, see Karrer 2006, 342–43.

inevitably results in discrepancies between the new copy and the exemplar (i.e., the manuscript that is being copied). The copyist is bound to make unintentional mistakes, particularly when copying lengthy texts. Words and letters can be accidentally transposed. Whole lines can be omitted or repeated simply because the scribe's eye inadvertently skipped ahead or back in the text. Nor was the alteration of a text always a passive/accidental process. Sometimes a scribe might see (or assume he sees) a mistake by an earlier copyist. The text does not make sense to him as it is. Scribes would sometimes correct these "mistakes" or add marginal notes aimed at explaining or clarifying the text. Scribes would also at times add marginal or interlinear notes they saw in their exemplar into the new copy they were producing. They did this under the assumption, which was sometimes correct, that the note had been added in order to correct a mistake in the exemplar.

The new copy, with all of its changes, was then taken to a particular location where it served as the Bible for the community of worshipers who gathered to hear it read. This is not to suggest that there was never any cross-pollination among communities and their manuscripts. To the contrary, people could travel widely in those days. Their memories, and sometimes even their copies of texts, went with them. Thus differences between manuscripts could be compared and variants could be harmonized or altered in other ways. This additional layer of complexity, however, does not alter the fact that a local community would know the Bible in the form that was read to them from the particular manuscripts their congregation possessed.[3]

Quite apart from the variety of issues related to producing and disseminating manuscripts, one must also consider the question of the original-language text that the original translator used when he rendered a biblical book into Greek (scholars refer to this original-language text as

---

3. Even with the standardization of a text's form that has come with the printing press, analogies can still be found in the modern world. Different churches, for example, may all agree on the importance of the Bible (they may even agree on the particular texts taken to be canonical) but nevertheless favor different translations. As a result, members of these congregations are likely to reflect upon and cite any given biblical passage in that version. The preferences of their denomination or local assembly, that is, can determine the form of the Bible that they know. The high rates of illiteracy in the ancient world and the limitations on the distribution of written texts just discussed would only have magnified this phenomenon.

the *Vorlage*). If one compares, for example, the version of Jeremiah in a modern edition of the Septuagint such as Rahlfs with the Hebrew Masoretic Text (MT: this is the Hebrew text upon which our modern English translations are based), the differences are quickly apparent. Not only is the LXX version shorter than the MT version by some 2,700 words, but one whole section of Jeremiah (chs. 46–51 in the MT) is located in a different place in the LXX (these chapters follow 25:13; Peters 1992, 1101).[4] Some of the differences between the MT and the LXX can be explained by factors such as the theological convictions of the translator (any translation involves some level of interpretation), the translation technique of the translator (was he more wooden/literal, perhaps even to the point of trying to preserve Hebrew word order and syntax in the translation, or was he more given to a looser or freer translation that altered Hebrew syntax in order to produce more polished Greek?), or scribal errors like those noted above.[5] The differences between Septuagint Jeremiah and the book's form in the MT, however, are so large and systemic that they suggest the translator had a Hebrew *Vorlage* that differed significantly from the Hebrew text of Jeremiah we now have in the MT.

The discovery of the Dead Sea Scrolls has clearly demonstrated that forms of Hebrew biblical texts other than those of the MT were in circulation during the Second Temple period. To put the matter differently, we now know that the standardization of the Hebrew text into the MT form we read had not taken place prior to the destruction of the Second Temple in 70 C.E. Proto-MT readings are found in abundance in the Qumran scrolls, but Hebrew readings that were previously known to us only in the Old Greek translations have also been discovered. In an age of printed texts, it may be difficult for us to comprehend, but the textual form of Scripture

---

4. Peters 1992 provides an excellent and succinct introduction to the complex issues concerning the Septuagint.

5. Contemporary analogies abound for the differences in translation technique. One need only place a version such as the NASB next to one like the NLT to see comparable differences in translation technique in some modern English versions. The key difference in the case of the LXX is that, whereas modern English translations of the Bible are often produced by a committee of scholars who agreed on the translation technique, the Old Greek translations of Hebrew books (the term *Old Greek* usually refers to the *original* translation of any given book from Hebrew into Greek) vary on a book-by-book basis. The LXX, that is, partly consists of a collection of Greek texts translated from Hebrew originals at different times in different places by different people.

was somewhat fluid at the time that early followers of Jesus began writing the letters and narratives that were later collected and canonized in the New Testament.[6]

The factors just discussed are significant for any consideration of the interpretation of Scripture in Hebrews. While it is not uncommon for scholars to assume that the author of Hebrews is rather freewheeling when he cites and interprets Scripture, the complexities of textual transmission and of the pluriformity of Scripture at the time the author wrote provide grounds for questioning that assumption. A judgment regarding the faithfulness of the author to Scripture *as he knows it* will never be as simple a matter as that of comparing the citation in Hebrews with the MT or the LXX or, even less, one of comparing the wording in a translation of Hebrews with a translation of the cited passage in a modern-language Old Testament. Indeed, it seems that a better default assumption would be to take the author's citations as renderings of the words of Scripture in the form that he and his original audience knew. As we will see below, the author's careful attention to the words of Scripture coheres with this assumption.[7]

JEWISH INTERPRETIVE PRACTICES

The second issue we must consider concerns the ways the author of Hebrews handles the texts he cites. He did not interpret Scripture in a cultural vacuum. Just as we bring (often implicitly) assumptions, traditions, strategies, and methods necessary for the task of interpretation when we attempt to elucidate the communicative potential of a text (or any communicative act), so also this ancient author lived in a cultural context that supplied him with the practices and beliefs that helped him make sense of and pose arguments from Jewish Scriptures. In order to help understand

---

6. For an especially helpful discussion of the fluidity of the Hebrew text form see McLay 2003, 119–22. It is worth noting here that even in the past few hundred years the work of textual critics to reconstruct the original form of biblical texts has led to continual updating of the standardized Greek and Hebrew texts underlying our modern translations. In other words, even in the age of the printing press, the forms of biblical texts remain somewhat fluid. For some examples of this, compare the footnotes in many modern English translations for passages such as John 7:53–8:11, the end of Mark 16, or 1 John 5:7 with older editions of English versions such as the KJV.

7. Docherty 2009 presents a sustained and compelling case for the conclusion that the author aims to be faithful to the wording of Scripture when he cites and interprets a passage.

those practices and beliefs, we will discuss some of the ways other Jews of his day were interpreting Scripture.

The cache of scrolls discovered in the Judean desert during the last century have greatly increased our knowledge of how Jews of the Second Temple period could read and interpret their Scriptures. Of special note for our purposes is the belief found in some of the scrolls that *the last days* had arrived. Some Jews of that time believed that history could be divided into discrete ages or periods. The period known as *the last days* was understood to be the penultimate age, the age just before God would finally and fully redeem his people, renew creation, and thereby fulfill all of his promises to his people. This was the period just before all the social, political, spiritual, and economic hopes of the Jewish people would finally come to fruition.

This season before the final redemption was often thought to be a time in which God's faithful ones would experience heightened suffering, a kind of darkest hour just before the dawn. Those who remained faithful during this period could count on being welcomed into the eternal inheritance about to be given to them. The mark of these faithful ones would be their steadfast obedience to God no matter what trials came their way.

Significantly, when the language of *the last days* occurs in the Dead Sea Scrolls, it is almost always used in the context of biblical interpretation (see especially Stuedel 1993, 225-46). The Scrolls indicate that their authors believed the Bible should be read in particular ways during the last days. The following important hermeneutical assumptions seem to be in play: (1) there are mysteries hidden in Scripture that only become clear to the faithful in the penultimate age; (2) the promises of God found in Scripture would begin to be fulfilled during this age, though their ultimate fulfillment would be in the world/age to come; and (3) the words of Scripture could be seen to apply directly to those living in the last days. These assumptions are nicely displayed throughout texts such as 1QpHab (esp. 7:1–14) and 1QpPs^a, commentaries on Habakkuk and Psalms. Scripture could, therefore, be viewed and correspondingly interpreted as a collection of divine utterances whose meanings would not become fully apparent until the penultimate age. The faithful who found themselves living during that time would be able to interpret the Scriptures correctly.

This is not to say that rules or methods for biblical interpretation were not applied. We know from rabbinic literature, which was written several centuries later than the texts at Qumran, that Jewish rabbis applied certain principles to the interpretation of Scripture. The use of rabbinic literature to illuminate earlier texts is always open to the problem of anachronism. Nevertheless, many of the principles (or *middot*) that we know of from early rabbinic texts describe practices we can identify in Second Temple period literature. We will not detail all the principles or their permutations (see Strack and Stemberger 1996, 15-30, for a detailed introduction to the various lists of *middot*), but two are especially important for our purposes. These are the argument by *qal wahomer* (basically an a fortiori argument: if the minor point x, then *even more* the analogous but weightier point y) and the argument by *gezerah shawah* (an argument by analogy that is based on the presence of an identical term or phrase in two different scriptural texts such that the two texts can be read together).

A few other important practices should also be mentioned here. Susan Docherty (2009, 143–60) has recently taken the descriptive work of Alexander Samely (among others) on rabbinic biblical interpretation and applied it to Hebrews.[8] Following Samely, Docherty notes that the rabbis were attracted to first-person speech in the Bible. This may be because it was easier to lift such speech out of its original context and recontextualize it in the setting of the rabbinic argument or conversation (Docherty 2009, 147, 177–78). Also, it was not uncommon in rabbinic discourse for longer citations to be "segmented" (Docherty 2009, 109, 177). That is to say, parts of a longer sentence—words or phrases—were sometimes isolated and examined one by one. The wording of the text was rendered faithfully, but particular words or phrases could be selected for special emphasis. Such a practice could supply new content for the words of a passage without altering the actual form of the text.

Summary

These preliminary comments regarding textual pluriformity and Jewish interpretive practices are far from exhaustive. Our goal has simply been to introduce some of the important background issues that need to be considered in the course of analyzing the ways in which the author of Hebrews has interpreted Scripture. With this introduction to these complex questions in mind, we now turn to look specifically at how Scripture is handled in Hebrews.

---

8. See Docherty 2009, 102–20 for her discussion of the descriptive work of Arnold Goldberg, Alexander Samely, and Philip Alexander.

BIBLICAL INTERPRETATION IN HEBREWS

In Heb 1:2 we find a clear expression of the author's conviction that he and his audience are living in the "last days." The emphasis he places throughout the epistle on motifs such as enduring testing/suffering faithfully (e.g., 2:18; 4:15–16; cf. 10:32–36; 12:3–4), inheriting the world to come/receiving the ultimate expression of God's promises (e.g., 2:5; 11:10, 15–16; 12:22–24, 28), and the final judgment (e.g., 6:2, 8; 10:24–27, 30–31; 12:27–29) cohere well with this belief. Thus it is unsurprising that in 1:2 he explicitly links his comment about "these last days" with the idea of God's revelatory speech *now* coming directly to the community he is addressing (God is *now* speaking "to *us*"). The idea that in the past God spoke one way (through the prophets) but now speaks another way (through a Son) probably indicates his belief that history is unfolding according to set periods predetermined by God. Moreover, the author's heavy reliance on biblical citation throughout the letter suggests that the word God now speaks to the audience through the Son is found in the words of the Jewish Scriptures.

This last suspicion finds corroboration in the fact that the dominant language the author uses to introduce scriptural citation is that of speech. The author identifies God as the primary speaker of biblical words (see 1:1–2, 5–13; 3:12; 4:3, 4–5; 5:5–6 [cf. 7:11–13]; 7:21; 8:8–12; 10:30; 12:5–6, 26; 13:5). The Holy Spirit is also explicitly said to speak scriptural words (3:7–11; 10:16–17), but this figure is indistinguishable from God (see 4:3, where "God" is identified as the speaker of the Spirit's words in 3:11; and 8:10, 12, where "God" [8:8] is the speaker of the words attributed in 10:16–17 to the Holy Spirit).

Jesus (or Christ) speaks words from Scripture in 2:12–13 and 10:5–9.[9] As with the Holy Spirit, Jesus is identified by a scriptural citation as God (see 1:8; cf. 1:10, where the Son is addressed, again by way of a biblical text, as Lord; cf. 2:3). Yet, unlike the Spirit, a clear distinction between God as Father and Jesus as Son is maintained in Hebrews (e.g., 1:1–2, 5–6; 5:5–6 [cf. 5:10; 7:28]).

Other figures are also identified. David (4:7) is named as the original speaker of the words from Ps 95. In keeping with Heb 3:7 and 4:3, though,

---

9. The practice of putting words from the psalms in the mouth of Jesus is not unique to Hebrews. For an excellent discussion of this phenomenon in other New Testament texts, see Hays 2005.

God is the real speaker (God, viz. the Holy Spirit, speaks "through" David). Moses is identified as a speaker of biblical words (9:20; 12:21).[10] The attribution of the words of Ps 8:4–6 to "someone" (2:6) is unique in the epistle.

It is not likely to be an accident, then, that the author begins his letter with a statement about God *speaking* to the audience through a Son. The point seems to be that "in these last days" (1:2) the word of God, especially as it is found in Jewish Scripture, is directly addressing the faithful community through the Son whom they confess. The author's notion of living in the penultimate age therefore helps explain the ease with which he applies biblical words to the contemporary situation of his audience. For example, in Heb 3–4 he pointedly addresses the language of Ps 95 to his present-day audience. Thus in 3:12–13 and 4:1–11 he applies the exhortations to hear God's voice "today" and to respond with obedience directly to the situation of his readers. As long as the present age lasts ("as long as it is called 'today,'" 3:13; see also 4:1), his audience has the opportunity to respond to God's voice, which is speaking directly to them, and to enter the promised rest.

In all likelihood, too, the author's belief that he lives in the penultimate age further implies that God's words in Scripture can now be understood more fully. In particular, he reads his Bible as revealing things about Jesus—the one he confesses as the Son/Messiah. The author, that is, reads his Bible with the assumption that the Son's true nature and work are to be learned by studying Scripture. His extensive appeals to biblical texts in relation to his discussion of Jesus as the heavenly high priest who offers himself in order to effect atonement (4:14–10:18) are attempts to instruct the audience from their Scriptures concerning who Jesus is (their heavenly high priest) and what he has done for them (offered himself to God in order to purify them from their sins and enable them to obtain God's promises). Even in Heb 1, words from Scripture (Deut 32:43 LXX//Ps 96:7 LXX) provide the audience with a glimpse into heaven, where God commands the angels to worship his Son (1:6). For the writer, God's words can be rightly understood "in these last days" to reveal truths about the Son.

With this general eschatological framework in view, we now focus our study on a few choice examples from different portions of Hebrews. In particular, we will look briefly at the catena of texts in Heb 1, the interpre-

---

10. In general, Moses is presented as the one who spoke the words of the law (7:14; 10:28), although see 2:3, where angels are likely thought to have been the agents through whom the law was spoken (see also Acts 7:38, 53; Gal 3:19).

tation of Ps 8 in Heb 2, the author's explication of Ps 110:4 in Heb 7, and, finally, the citation of Ps 40 in Heb 10.

Hebrews 1 largely consists of a litany of biblical citations presented as God speaking to and about the Son (1:5, 8–13) and to and about the angels (1:6–7). The scriptural texts he cites are Ps 2:7 (1:5), 2 Sam 7:14//1 Chr 17:13 (1:5), Deut 32:43 LXX//Ps 96:7 LXX (1:6), Ps 104:4 (1:7); Ps 45:6–7 (1:8–9), Ps 102:25–27 (1:10–12), and Ps 110:1 (1:13).

With so many citations laced together in these first few verses, we find ourselves quickly entangled in the web of complicated questions introduced above. We will not attempt to address all those issues. Suffice it to say that the author appears to be faithfully citing texts from the Septuagint, though probably in a form that contained some verses (e.g., Deut 32:43; Ps 102:25–27) that were translated from a Hebrew *Vorlage* that differed from the MT (see especially the discussion in Docherty 2009, 132–37).

I do, however, want to reflect a bit on the author's possible rationale for selecting these texts. We noted above the principle of connecting passages based on the fact that they contain the same word or phrase (*gezerah shawah*). Something like this principle provides a good explanation for the linkage of Ps 2:7 and 2 Sam 7:14//1 Chr 17:13 in Heb 1:5, as well as for the combination of Pss 104:4 and 45:6–7 in Heb 1:8. Specifically, the links are forged by the presence of the word "son" in the former passages and the words "angel" and "throne" in the latter ones.

Noting these correspondences does not allow us to assume that the writer's selections are arbitrary (i.e., based solely on the fact that they share the same words). On the contrary, the organizing ideas for why these texts were selected have already been introduced by the author in Heb 1:1–4. He is interested in showing from Scripture that God's Son (who is later identified as Jesus, 2:9) has the right to a position in heaven beyond that even of the angels—the position of ruling from the divine throne. The language of "Son," in other words, connotes *royalty* in this context, more specifically, Davidic royalty. The writer does not, therefore, randomly select texts with the word "son" in them. Instead, he cites verses from contexts where the word "son" is being used to refer to the divinely appointed king of Israel.[11] Nathan's oracle (2 Sam 7:4–17//1 Chr 17:3–15) not only identifies David as God's "son" but also states that the "throne" would be estab-

---

11. When the writer refers to the Son as the "firstborn" in 1:6, it is unsurprising that this very term is used in Ps 89:27 (see esp. 89:19–37) to refer to God's appointment of David and his line to be Israel's kings. Interestingly, Ps 89:1–37 contains a

lished for David's progeny "forever." The importance of this royal sense of "Son" for the writer, as well as the key terms "throne" and "forever" in Nathan's oracle, help explain why the author quotes the portion of Ps 45 that speaks of God's "throne" (now identified in the context of Heb 1 as the Son's throne) remaining "forever," the Son's royal scepter, and the Son being anointed by God.

The rationale for the passages selected by the author that contain the word "angel" is harder to discern at this point in his argument. That he wants to contrast the Son and the angels, and in particular to demonstrate the Son's greater status, seems clear enough (Heb 1:4). Certainly a text that refers to angels worshiping the Son would support this point. Furthermore, the writer's statement concerning the Son's role as the agent through whom God "made" (*epoiēsen*) the worlds (Heb 1:2) resonates with the creation motif in the citation of Ps 102:25–27 (Heb 1:10–12) and with Ps 104:4's identification of God as "the one who made" (*poiōn*) the angels. That is to say, if the Son participated in making/creating the angels, then the Son would likely hold a position in heaven above them.

Only at the end of Heb 1, however, do we begin to see more clearly why the author has cited Ps 104:4. In Heb 1:14 he explains what Ps 104:4 teaches his audience about what kinds of beings angels are. Angels, he states, are "ministering spirits." Unfortunately, most English translations of Ps 104:4 in Heb 1:7 obscure the connection between Heb 1:7 and the author's statement that angels are ministering or serving spirits in 1:14. English translations tend to render Heb 1:7 along the following lines: "Of the angels he says, 'He makes his angels winds [*pneumata*], and his servants [*leitourgous*] flames of fire'" (NRSV). The translation is not inaccurate. The problem is that *in the context of Heb 1* the decisions to translate the Greek word *pneumata* as "winds" and to render the Greek word *leitourgous* as "servants" in Heb 1:7 make it difficult for the English reader to see that the contrast in Heb 1:13–14 between God's invitation to the Son to sit on the heavenly throne (Ps 110:1) and the status of the angels hinges upon the fact that God made the angels as *spirits*. In Heb 1:14, when the author calls the angels "ministering spirits" (*leitourgika pneumata*), he is drawing upon the statement he found in Ps 104:4 that God *made* his angels

---

remarkable number of terms and themes that resemble the concerns of Heb 1 and the portions of Pss 45 and 102 that author cites in Heb 1:8–12.

as spirits (*pneumata*). That is to say, God made his ministers (*leitourgous*) as flames of fire.[12]

Two important points are implicit in this logic. First, the argument inherent in the coordination of texts cited in Heb 1 appears to work by way of a *qal wahomer* kind of comparison. If the angels are exalted, heavenly beings, how much greater is the Son who has been invited to sit at God's right hand?[13] Second, latent in the argument is the idea that the Son, whoever and whatever he is, has been invited to sit upon the divine throne because he is not a fiery, ministering spirit (if he were, he would not have been invited to sit on the throne). That this implication is precisely what the author wants to develop becomes clear when he cites and interprets Ps 8:4–6 in Heb 2:5–10.

Psalm 8:4–6 contains the key words "Son" and "angels" that, as we have just seen, contribute to the selection and interpretation of biblical citations found in Heb 1. A third important term is introduced with this new psalm citation: "man/human being" (*anthrōpos*). In the context of Hebrews, the "someone" who speaks the words of Ps 8:4–6 says, "What is man [i.e., humanity] that you [i.e., God] remember him, or the Son of man that you care about him? You made him for a little while lower than the angels. You crowned him with glory and honor. You subjected all things under his feet."[14]

While the principle of *gezerah shawah* is likely in play again, the choice of this passage is no more arbitrary than were the texts selected in Heb 1. The author is continuing to unpack the idea that the Son has been elevated above the angels, even to the point of being invited to rule from the throne at God's right hand. This is clear from the way in which the Ps 8 citation is introduced. The writer brings Ps 8 into his discourse in order to show that God has not given to angels the right to rule the "world to come." In Ps 8 the writer finds a divine word that he takes as a promise that the privilege

---

12. The point would be better grasped in English if Heb 1:7 were translated as follows: "But about the angels he says, 'He makes his angels *spirits*, and his *ministers* flames of fire.'"

13. Cf. 2:1–4, where the word given by angels is consequential, but the word of the Lord has even greater consequence.

14. It is a remarkable fact that in rabbinic writings Ps 8:4 is sometimes put on the lips of the "ministering angels" in heaven (see, e.g., b. Šabb. 88b–89a; cf. b. Sanh. 38b; Gen. Rab. 8:5–6).

of ruling creation in the coming age (the period of fulfillment after the last days) is reserved for humanity (and, thus, *not* for angels).

With the curious exception of a missing clause ("You established him over the works of your hands"), the form of Ps 8:4–6 in Hebrews is septuagintal. This is significant since the author's reliance on a Greek translation probably aided him in developing his particular interpretation of the relationship between the first two clauses of Ps 8:4. Specifically, the author appears to read these clauses as if they refer to distinct or discrete things. "Humanity" (*anthrōpos*) in Ps 8:4a and "the Son of man" in Ps 8:4b seem to be taken by him as making reference to different entities—a general group in the former case (human beings, as opposed to angels), but a particular individual in the latter instance (the Son, soon to be identified as the particular human being, Jesus). This is almost certainly *not* the meaning of the original Hebrew. In Hebrew, the two terms are near synonyms and mean something like "humanity" and "mortals," respectively.[15] Moreover, the syntax in the Hebrew is most naturally read as setting up the two clauses as synonymous parallels.

In the Septuagint tradition the conjunction "or" (*ē*), used to translate the Hebrew *waw* and thus to coordinate the two clauses in the version used by our author, introduces the potential for a more disjunctive interpretation of the relationship between the two clauses. This is only heightened in Hebrews by the writer's interest in the figure of the Son. That is to say, the argument thus far in Hebrews pushes toward interpreting the phrase "Son of man" not as a synonym for humanity in Ps 8:4a but in terms of *the* Son of Heb 1—the individual who now rules on the divine throne and has a status above that of the angels. (This need not imply, however, that the author of Hebrews knows the use of the term "Son of man" for Jesus in the Synoptic Gospels.) In fact, this is precisely what the author does in Heb 2:8–9. He grants, that is, that humanity in general cannot now be said to have dominion over all things, but there is one human being to whom this promise does currently apply—Jesus, who is, of course, the Son about whom the entire first chapter has been speaking.

---

15. The gender-neutral translation of Heb 2:6–7 in the NRSV works well for the likely sense of the Hebrew form of Ps 8:4–6. Unfortunately, however, the use of this approach here in Hebrews eliminates the crucial word "Son" from the context and occludes the semantic potential of the Greek, which is necessary to grasp the author's argument.

Thus the author presents Ps 8:4–6 as the culmination of his argument for the contrast he set up in the initial verses of the epistle between the Son and the angels. The Son has been advanced to the divine throne and elevated to a status above that of the angels *because he is a human being.* Or, to put it in the author's own terms, the Son is not one of the "ministering *spirits.*" He is a blood and flesh (Heb 2:14) human being who, being like the rest of humanity in every way (2:17), understands human weaknesses and suffering. He is therefore not ashamed to confess his kinship with humanity (2:12–13; Jesus' words are drawn from Ps 22:22, Isa 8:17//12:2, and Isa 8:18, respectively).

To summarize thus far, in the first two chapters of this epistle we find the author citing Scriptures that help him illuminate one of the main themes he announces at the beginning of the work: the exaltation of the royal Son above the angels. The passages he cites and interprets are both read in light of and used to illuminate this larger argument. Particular words, which are central to his case (especially "Son" and "angels"), help him in selecting the passages he cites. By bringing the context of these citations into the text he is creating, the author is able to build a biblically rooted argument for the Son's elevation above the angels around four key points. First, the Son's association with God clearly sets him apart from the created angels. Second, angels are divinely constituted as ministering spirits. Third, God ultimately intends for humanity to rule creation. Fourth, the Son is the blood and flesh human being Jesus. Thus because of his humanity, the Son, Jesus, has been invited to sit where no angelic spirit has ever been invited—on the throne at God's right hand.[16]

Within the argument just discussed lie a few implicit premises that the author explicates later in the epistle: the Son's obedience to God's will and the quality of his life after death. In order to follow these threads, we

---

16. In all likelihood the author is thinking about the elevation of humanity, and of Jesus in particular, in terms of the restoration to human beings of the divine glory and status that Adam originally possessed. We know of a legend about Adam, likely in circulation during the Second Temple period, that speaks of God sending the angel Michael to bring Adam up into heaven and then commanding all the angels to worship him. The rationale for this command appears to be that, as a human being, Adam was a kind of being that the angelic spirits were not: the visible *image* of God. This notion of Adam as God's image does not exhaust the meaning of the language used in Heb 1:3 to describe the Son as "the reflection of God's glory and the exact imprint of God's very being" (NRSV), but it does cohere remarkably well with this depiction. For more on these traditions about Adam, see Marcus 2003; Anderson 2000.

will jump over the extended reflection on Ps 95:7–11, along with several shorter citations and allusions, in Heb 3–4 and turn our attention to Heb 5–7 and specifically the writer's interpretation of Ps 110:4.

In Heb 4:14 the writer takes up one of the major topics of the whole epistle: Jesus' high-priestly office. He has alluded to this element of his Christology in 1:3 and explicitly mentioned it in 2:17 and 3:1, but his full development of the topic occupies most of the material from 4:14 to 10:25. One of his initial moves in this larger discussion occurs in Heb 5:5–6, where he links the word from Ps 2:7, "You are my Son; today I have begotten you" (see Heb 1:5), with Ps 110:4, which reads, "You are a priest forever according to the order of Melchizedek."

The link between the Son and the high-priestly office is hinted at in the epistle's opening sentences, which speak of the royal Son accomplishing an act reserved in Torah for Israel's high priests: making purification for sins (Heb 1:3). Interestingly, this comment about purification is immediately followed by an allusion to Ps 110:1 ("he sat down at the right hand of the Majesty on high," NRSV), a verse the writer explicitly cites later in chapter 1 (Heb 1:13).

This allusion to and citation of Ps 110:1 in Heb 1 already locate the psalm within the context of a discussion of the royal Son (even though the word "son" does not occur in the psalm). This is an important interpretive move that is probably not original to the author and that may provide insight into the rationale for the connection between the Son in Ps 2:7 and the priest of Ps 110:4.[17] Because the author now knows (in these last days) who is the ultimate royal Son who sits at God's right hand, he can readily associate other texts assumed to be about the royal Son with Jesus. While this observation may help explain how Ps 110:4 was applied to Jesus, it does not explain how the writer interprets or applies the verse.

The author presents both Ps 2:7 and Ps 110:4 as instances of the same kind of divine illocution. Both verses, that is, are taken to depict God's act of appointing or calling Christ to the respective offices mentioned in the verses. This coheres with the larger context. The author has just explained (Heb 5:1–4) that every high priest must be appointed to the office by God.

---

17. The Hasmoneans had already combined the offices of king and high priest into one. David Hay points out that their use of the language of "priest of God Most High" likely stems from their appeal to Melchizedek and Ps 110 as the model for the uniting of priestly and kingly duties (Hay 1973, 24–25). It is also worth noting that, like Ps 2, Ps 110 addresses a royal figure who triumphs over the nations.

Even Aaron received this honor by way of God's call. The same principle holds true in the case of Jesus. Just as God said to him "You are my Son" (Ps 2:7), God also said to him in another place, "You are a priest forever according to the order of Melchizedek."

Such a recontextualization of Ps 110:4 has the effect of legitimating Jesus' status as high priest. If God called him to be a high priest, then his status as high priest is something he has been given by divine fiat (see Heb 7:20–21). But did the high-priestly status of Jesus need to be legitimated? That is to say, is the writer engaged in an argument here? There are good reasons to think he is.

From the beginning of the letter Jesus has been assumed to function as, and has even explicitly been called, a high priest (1:3; 2:17; 3:1; 4:14). Apparently the author and his audience already confess Jesus as their high priest (3:13; 4:14), yet the writer also exhorts his audience in 4:14 to hold firmly to their confession. The author's concern to encourage his audience not to doubt or give up on their confession of Jesus as their high priest suggests that he is worried this might happen (whether or not some in the original audience were contemplating this kind of move). Why, though, might someone think of abandoning this confession?

One reason that is not hard to imagine is that the Mosaic law, that is, Scripture, explicitly limits priestly service to members of the tribe of Levi. Jesus, as a matter of historical fact for the author, belongs to the royal line of David, the tribe of Judah (Heb 7:14). While this latter point might help legitimate Jesus' royal status, it appears to prevent him from serving as a high priest (a fact that was not lost on the author; see 7:13–14). The confession of Jesus as high priest therefore poses an exegetical problem for the author and perhaps for some in his audience: In light of the law, how can Jesus the royal Son also be the high priest he is confessed to be?

The author's solution to this interpretive problem lies in Ps 110:4 and its reference to Melchizedek. To be sure, presenting Ps 110:4 as God's call to Jesus already begins to address the issue, but it is significant that the author is not content simply to cite Ps 110:4 as a word of God that trumps the word in the law. He goes on to work systematically through the words and phrases of Ps 110:4 in Heb 7:1–25 in order to demonstrate that Jesus can legitimately be the high priest he is confessed to be in spite of his tribal lineage.

He begins his discussion in Heb 7:1 by isolating the last word of Ps 110:4—Melchizedek. This enigmatic figure is mentioned in Torah (Gen 14:17–20). Right away the author highlights some pertinent information from Gen 14:18: Scripture identifies Melchizedek as both the king of Salem *and* as a priest of God Most High (Heb 7:1). Additionally, he notes that Melchizedek's priestly status is not based on his tribal lineage, because *Melchizedek has no genealogy.* This fact holds great importance for the writer. Not only does he deduce the idea that Melchizedek was neither born, nor died, from the Bible's silence on Melchizedek's genealogy, but he also pointedly contrasts the Levitical priests (whom he describes in genealogical terms as "those descendants of Levi," 7:5 NRSV), with Melchizedek, someone "who does not belong to their ancestry" (7:6 NRSV).[18] Melchizedek, in other words, is a legitimate priest of God *even though he is not a Levite.*

This suggests that there is an order of priests other than that of Aaron and the sons of Levi. This is exactly the issue the author considers next. In Heb 7:11–17, after discussing Melchizedek (whose name is the last word in Ps 110:4), he backs up a step in the psalm to consider the phrase "according to the order of." In Ps 110:4, which speaks of a priest "according to the order of Melchizedek," the author identifies a divine promise: there will be another priest—not an additional priest "according to the order of Aaron," but a different (*heteros*) priest, one who belongs to a different order, that of Melchizedek (Heb 7:11). This priest, who is Jesus, has not become a member of this other order by virtue of his genealogy (that is, he is not a priest on account of the law's prescriptions concerning physical descent) but by coming into possession of the kind of enduring life that Melchizedek has (Heb 7:16). Membership in Melchizedek's priestly order is not a matter of one's genealogy; it is a matter of the quality of life one possesses

---

18. A better translation of the latter quoted text would be "the one who has no genealogy." I note, too, that the addition of the word "man" to this clause in all the major English translations (e.g., "a man who does not belong to their ancestry," NRSV) is unfortunate. The author almost certainly does not think of Melchizedek as a man/human being. In fact, in Heb 7:8 he plainly contrasts Melchizedek (who has no beginning of days or end of life, 7:3) with human beings (*anthrōpoi*) who die. In all likelihood, the writer understands Melchizedek to be an angelic being (as he is in some Qumran texts). This is probably why Melchizedek's immortal life follows so easily and self-evidently for the author from the fact that Melchizedek lacks a genealogy in Genesis. Moreover, it is important to note that in Hebrews the angels are described in priestly terms (they are "ministers" [*leitourgoi*]; see Heb 1:7, 14; 8:2, 6; 10:11). For an excellent defense of the view that Melchizedek is an angelic being in Hebrews, see Mason 2008 and his essay in this volume. For a different approach, see the essay in this volume by Kenneth Schenck.

(Heb 7:15–16).[19] Jesus is a priest in the order of Melchizedek because of his indestructible life.

This last move in the argument pushes yet another step back in the wording of Ps 110:4. Being a priest in the order of Melchizedek is to be a *priest forever*. The words "priest forever" are probably, therefore, to be understood as receiving special emphasis in Heb 7:17 when the author repeats the part of Ps 110:4 that he cited in 5:6. Indeed, while the writer finally completes his systematic analysis of Ps 110:4 by emphasizing the fact that the divine word comes as an oath (he then cites the words at the beginning of the verse: "The Lord has sworn and will not change his mind, 'You are a priest forever,'" Heb 7:21), he continues in 7:24–25 to put emphasis on the idea that Jesus is no longer subject to death. Jesus holds his priesthood permanently because, like Melchizedek, he "remains forever" (7:24; cf. 7:3) and "always lives" (7:25; cf. 7:8).

Here, then, is the author's answer to the legitimacy of the confession about Jesus. Jesus can be a high priest *in spite of* his genealogy because, while the law limits priestly service to the tribe of Levi, Scripture speaks about another priesthood, one that depends *not* on tribal lineage but on the quality of life one possesses. Jesus, because he arose with the power of an indestructible life, is qualified to serve as the priest in that other, biblically sanctioned order. To make this case, the author interprets the words and phrases of Ps 110:4 beginning with the word at the end of the divine oath ("Melchizedek") and working back to the words at its beginning ("The Lord has sworn"). This kind of approach to a verse may seem strange to us today, but it is very much in line with the kinds of practices pointed out above by Docherty (and Samely). Specifically, the author has isolated an instance of first-person speech, cited the wording faithfully, and then segmented it in order to emphasize and explain the significance of individual words and phrases.

For our last example we consider the importance of the Son's obedience. As with the Son's quality of life, this was an element implicit in the logic of Heb 1–2. The point is more fully developed in 10:5–10. Here the author stresses the fact that the Son has a *body* that he presented to God.

---

19. I have argued elsewhere that this logic depends upon the confession of Jesus' resurrection. Jesus' life is known by the author to be indestructible precisely because, after he was crucified, he arose in the likeness of Melchizedek—he arose to a kind of life that will never again be subject to death (Moffitt 2008 and 2011).

The author appeals to Ps 40:6–8 to help establish the fittingness of this offering.

The first half of Ps 40:6 as cited in Hebrews reads as follows: "Sacrifices and offerings you have not desired, but *a body you have prepared for me*" (NRSV, emphasis added). The word *body* and the idea that *God* prepared that body are important elements to the author.[20] In Heb 10:10 it is God's will that atonement for sins be made by way of the offering of Jesus' body. Curiously, though, the initial clauses of Ps 40:6 in modern English translations of the Hebrew MT read something like: "Sacrifice and offering you do not desire, but *you have given me an open ear*" (NRSV, emphasis added). Instead of God preparing a *body* for the speaker, the psalmist claims to have received an *open ear* from God. What is going on here?

A likely explanation for the discrepancy between the MT version of the psalm and the version in Hebrews is that the author of Hebrews knows a Greek translation of the psalm that either interpreted the Hebrew word for "ear" in terms of a body or is based on a Hebrew *Vorlage* that differed here from the MT. We have already seen the care with which the writer cited the words of Ps 110:4. Remarkably, he did not change the wording of that psalm to fit his argument for the confession of Jesus as high priest, even though that psalm does not actually use the crucial word *high* priest. The psalm may be helpful in establishing the legitimacy of Jesus as a priest, but it says nothing (nor does the author force it to say anything) to suggest that Jesus is a high priest. Furthermore, the effective force of the writer's argument in Heb 10 would be significantly diminished if he altered the psalm. That is to say, if he changed the psalm to say something about a *body* instead of an *ear* in order to help establish from Scripture the importance of the offering of Jesus' body, anyone in his audience who knew Scripture as well as the rest of the epistle seems to assume they did would recognize the sleight of hand immediately. Notably, too, the most important LXX manuscripts of the psalm agree with the reading in Hebrews on this point (see especially Karrer 2002–2008, 2:194–96; Koester 2001, 432–33).

Nevertheless, the author has done a curious thing when he cites this text. He does not alter the words of Ps 40:7–8a, but he does change the syntax significantly. He stops his citation from the psalm at a point that shifts the relationship between the complementary infinitival phrase "to do your will, O God" and the verb whose meaning the phrase completes

---

20. The *you* referred to in Ps 40:6 is God (see 40:5).

in the LXX version. In Hebrews the verse reads, "Behold, I have come (in the scroll of the book it is written concerning me) to do your will, O God." In the LXX, the sentence continues on after "to do your will, O God." That version reads, "Behold, I have come, in the scroll of the book it is written concerning me; to do your will, O my God, is what I desire." The psalmist, in other words, expresses his *desire to do* God's will. He *wants* (or perhaps *intends*) to do the will of God. The speaker in Hebrews, by way of contrast, confidently declares that he *has come to do* God's will.

Once again we have the writer segmenting the biblical text. The words he has cited are almost certainly the precise words of the text as he knows it, *but he has not cited all the words* in the scriptural statement. He breaks the citation off just after the complementary infinitive. Thus Jesus, the new speaker of the words in the context of Hebrews, does not express a desire or intent to obey God. He claims to have come for the very purpose of doing God's will. In this way the author recontextualizes the wording of the psalm in order to emphasize that in the case of Jesus, God's will is fully and completely done. Jesus is the obedient Son (see Heb 5:8), and as such he can present to God that thing the psalmist teaches God's people to desire, that thing with which God is most pleased, a life in complete accord with God's will.

CONCLUSION

In this essay we have examined some of the critical issues concerning the form of the biblical text at the point that Hebrews was written and some of the key assumptions and methods that have informed the interpretive activity of the author. We also looked at a handful of biblical citations in Hebrews to see how knowledge of these issues and assumptions can help us understand how the writer argues from Scripture. For the author, Scripture is a repository of divine speech, but these divine words are living and active. Moreover, because he finds himself living in the last days, he and his audience are able (or should be able, Heb 5:11–12) to see how Scripture speaks about Jesus, the Son, and the community that confesses Jesus' name. He can, therefore, create biblically informed arguments that support and inform his understanding of Jesus using the methods, traditions, and logic of his cultural context. All of this means that, while he recasts scriptural words in new ways, the words themselves also place constraints on him. Accordingly, he pays careful attention to them, sometimes noting where they occur in other passages, sometimes examining them one by one, and sometimes citing just as many of them as seem to correlate with what he knows about Jesus.

Hebrews, Rhetoric, and the Future of Humanity

Craig R. Koester

Hebrews is one of the earliest extant Christian sermons. Although it has been traditionally called an "epistle," the idea that Hebrews is a sermon or speech has gained broad support, and many recognize that the work draws on the devices of classical rhetoric (Koester 1994, 123–46; Watson 1997, 175–207). What is disputed is whether the author of Hebrews follows standard rhetorical patterns when developing the argument of the speech. Interest in this question is not limited to specialists, since the way that interpreters perceive the book's structure reflects the way they understand its message. The traditional chapter divisions give the impression that Hebrews was written to show Christ's superiority to the institutions of Judaism: Christ's superiority to angels (Heb 1:1–14), to Moses (3:1–6), to Aaron (5:1–10), to Melchizedek (7:1–10), and so on. Those who divide the book into three parts usually hold that the book is a call to hold fast to the confession, while the division into five concentric parts fixes readers' attention on the priesthood of Christ, which appears at the center of the book.[1] Interpreters generally agree on where the paragraphs within Hebrews begin and end but are less certain about the way the paragraphs fit together to create a sustained argument. This basic question concerning the shape and message of Hebrews is our focus.

---

1. The call to hold fast the confession is found in Heb 4:14–16 and 10:19–31. Accordingly, some divide the book into three parts: 1:1–4:13; 4:14–10:25; 10:32–13:25 (Kümmel 1975, 389–92; Thompson 2008). The five-part division proposes that Hebrews is framed by an introduction and conclusion (1:1–4; 13:20–21). The main sections are 1:5–2:18; 3:1–5:10; 5:11–10:39; 11:1–12:13; 12:14–13:19 (Vanhoye 1989; Attridge 1989; Mitchell 2007). For a survey and discussion of proposals, see Koester 2001, 83–84. An alternative approach is to consider Hebrews a type of synagogue homily, as argued by Gabriella Gelardini in a monograph (2005) and the next essay in this volume.

Speeches from the Greco-Roman period are often described as judicial, deliberative, or epideictic types of rhetoric (Aristotle, *Rhet.* 3.1–9; *Rhet. Her.* 1.2 §2; Quintilian, *Inst.* 3.4.1–16). Interpreters have debated whether Hebrews might be a form of deliberative rhetoric, since it tries to persuade listeners to follow the course of faithfulness (Lindars 1989, 382–406; Löhr 2005, 210), or whether it might better be considered epideictic, since its examples praise those who have shown faithfulness and reprove those who are unfaithful (Attridge 1989, 14; Olbricht 1993, 375–87). Nevertheless, neatly categorizing Hebrews is not necessary, since deliberative and epideictic elements were often interwoven in speeches (Aristotle, *Rhet.* 1.9.36; *Rhet. Her.* 3.8 §15; Quintilian, *Inst.* 3.7.28; deSilva 2000, 46–58). More important, various types of speeches included standard elements, such as an introduction, arguments, and conclusion. Although speakers showed considerable freedom in adapting typical patterns to specific situations, the use of familiar components helped listeners follow the speaker's train of thought. Some interpreters have tried to identify sections of Hebrews according to the usual rhetorical patterns, but little consensus has emerged, and other interpreters question whether the classic categories can be applied to the structure (Watson 1997, 182–83). The proposal made here is that the categories provide a sense of clarity about the flow of the argument.

Major sections of the speech can be identified by considering the formal characteristics, the thematic content, and the rhetorical function of the material. Perhaps the best known of the formal characteristics of Hebrews is its use of catchwords and *inclusios* to mark the beginning and end of paragraphs. Similar *inclusios* may also mark larger sections of material (Vanhoye 1989, 19–22; Guthrie 1994, 76–111). Another formal characteristic is the period, which is a complex sentence that integrates a number of thoughts into a unified whole. Periods were often used to introduce and conclude sections of an argument by drawing together the speaker's main points (BDF §464; *Rhet. Her.* 4.19 §27; Quintilian, *Inst.* 9.4.128; Lausberg 1998, §947). Since periods could be used for various purposes, we will note ways in which periods seem to conclude a section by summarizing the points that preceded the sentence itself. Thematic coherence is another factor in identifying sections of an argument. A section should develop a given line of thought in a way that can be distinguished from what comes before and after it. Finally, asking about the rhetorical function of a section shows one's awareness that parts of a speech may work in different ways. The arguments appeal primarily to logic, but digressions and perorations (concluding parts of discourses) often appeal to emotion. The interplay among these elements enables us to discern the flow of the speech.

The salient features of the structure of Hebrews can be summarized as follows. First, the book's introduction, or *exordium*, extends from 1:1 to 2:4, which means that the opening section concerning the exalted Son of God is not part of the main argument but is preparatory to it. Second, many assume that the *exordium* should be followed by a *narratio*, which is a statement of the facts pertaining to the topic, but speakers in antiquity did not consider a *narratio* to be essential, and Hebrews omits it (Quintilian, *Inst.* 4.2.4–5; 5.preface.5). Instead, the author moves directly to the thesis, or *propositio*, in 2:5–9, where he affirms that in Jesus' death and exaltation listeners can see how God's designs for human beings are accomplished through the suffering and exaltation of Christ. Third, the body of the speech includes three main series of arguments, each of which draws on a different group of images: the generation of the exodus and the wilderness, priesthood and sacrifice, and the story of God's people that culminates in the heavenly city. Transitions between sections are created by digressions in which the author interrupts the flow of thought in order to appeal for attention and to warn about the dangers of spurning God's word (2:1–4; 5:11–6:20; 10:26–39; 12:25–27).[2] Fourth, the peroration or conclusion begins not at 13:1 but at 12:28, where the author makes an appeal for service that is pleasing to God (12:28–13:21). An epistolary conclusion comes after the peroration. Hebrews can be outlined in this way:

I. Exordium (1:1–2:4)
II. Proposition (2:5–9)
III. Arguments (2:10–12:27)
  A. First Series (2:10–6:20)
    1. Argument: Jesus received glory through faithful suffering—a way that others are called to follow (2:10–5:10)
    2. Transitional Digression: Warning and encouragement (5:11–6:20)
  B. Second Series (7:1–10:39)
    1. Argument: Jesus' suffering is the sacrifice that allows others to approach God (7:1–10:25)

---

2. Using digressions of different lengths was common (Lausberg 1998, §§340–42, 345). Hebrews 3:7–4:11 has the hortatory features of a digression but does not interrupt the argument.

I. The Exordium (Heb 1:1–2:4)

Hebrews begins with what can be called an *exordium* according to the canons of classical rhetoric. An important question concerns the length of the *exordium*, because knowing where the *exordium* ends helps us identify where the author presents the speech's central thesis. Interpreters often identify the *exordium* as the first sentence (1:1–4) because the style shifts from the elevated poetry of 1:1–4 to a series of biblical quotations in 1:5–13, and the content changes from God's revelation in the Son in 1:1–4 to the Son's superiority to the angels in 1:5–13 (Attridge 1989, 35; Lane 1991, 1:9; Mitchell 2007, 35).

There are, however, good reasons to think that the *exordium* encompasses all of 1:1–2:4. In style, the introduction is framed by periods that deal with God's mode of speaking in the past through prophets and angels and in the present through his Son (1:1–4; 2:2–4). In content, the first part of the *exordium* introduces the Son as the heir and creator of all things who is seated at God's right hand (1:1–4), and the second part provides a battery of Old Testament quotations concerning divine sonship, eternity, and exaltation to support these claims (1:5–14). The final part (2:1–4) brings what has been said into an appeal for attention. The author cautions that, if neglecting the message that was delivered of old had dire consequences, the result of neglecting the salvation proclaimed through Christ will be even more serious. Significantly, there is no major shift in subject matter after 1:4. Only after 2:4 does the author begin considering Jesus' suffering, the topic that will be developed in the remainder of the speech. Thus the *exordium* provides an *indirect* introduction to what follows it, as was common in the *exordia* crafted by ancient orators (Quintilian, *Inst.* 4.1.30). The depiction of the Son of God enthroned in heaven does not address the principal concern of the speech; instead, it has an important preparatory function. By reminding listeners that exaltation followed Jesus' crucifixion, it provides a perspective from which the meaning of Jesus' death can be comprehended.

Comparison with other speeches suggests that an *exordium* extending from 1:1 to 2:4 would have been appropriate for Hebrews. The length of an *exordium* depended on the issue being addressed; a few sentences might be sufficient for simple matters, while longer introductions were used for more complex issues (Quintilian, *Inst.* 9.4.125). An *exordium* might be as brief as Heb 1:1–4 (e.g., Demosthenes, *Exord.* 3 and 51), but speakers typically allowed themselves at least two to three hundred words of introduction—several minutes in delivery time—and they frequently went longer. Hebrews is a speech that would have taken about forty-five or fifty minutes to deliver, and an *exordium* lasting for three to four minutes—about three hundred and twenty words (1:1–2:4)—would have been appropriate for a speech of this scope and complexity.[3]

Exordia were usually designed to make listeners attentive and ready to receive instruction (*Rhet. Her.* 1.4 §§6–7; Quintilian, *Inst.* 4.1.5; Lausberg 1998, §270). Hebrews achieves this, in part, through the use of rhetorical conventions. The elevated style of the first sentence is reminiscent of the oratory of Isocrates (*Rhet. Her.* 3.12 §21; Moulton, Howard, and Turner 1906–1963, 4:106–13). Words beginning with the *p* sound catch the listener's ear: *polymerōs kai polytropōs palai ho theos lalēsas tois patrasin en tois prophētais* ("God, having spoken on many occasions and in many forms to the forebears of old by the prophets," Heb 1:1). In terms of content, a speaker could gain attention by announcing that he would address matters that were new or unusual or that pertained to the listeners or to God. This is what the author of Hebrews does in 1:1–2, which focuses on the word of God that came recently "to us." Attention could also be secured through an appeal to listen carefully. This is what the author does at the end of the *exordium* through a direct appeal to "attend all the more to what we have heard" (2:1). By using rhetorical questions at the conclusion of the *exordium*, the author also heightens the level of interaction with the listeners, helping to move them from being passive recipients of information to being more active participants in the thought process (Demosthenes, *Exord.* 35.4; 51; Dio Chrysostom, *Or.* 1.10).

---

3. Walters 1996, 59–70; Cockerill 1999, 31. Compare the opening of Romans (1:1–15), which begins with a period (1:1–6). The thesis follows the introduction in Rom 1:16–17, as in Heb 2:5–9.

The author also altered rhetorical conventions to suit the content of his speech. Writers often began by referring to the "many" (*poly-*) things that people had said previously about a subject. For example, Demosthenes began, "Many speeches are delivered, men of Athens, at almost every meeting of the Assembly" (*3 Philip.* 1). Dionysius of Halicarnassus said, "Many strange and paradoxical pronouncements has our age brought forth," and "this statement of yours seems to me to be one of them" (*1 Amm.* 1). In the same way, Jewish and Christian writers sometimes referred to what "many" of their predecessors had said on a given topic (Sirach prologue; Luke 1:1). Hebrews, however, shifts the level of discourse from human speech to divine speech by focusing on God, who spoke in times past through the prophets and who now spoke again through a Son (1:1–2). Presenting God as speaker was unconventional rhetorically and significant theologically. Some speeches opened with an appeal that God or the gods might help the speaker (Philo, *Ait.* 1; cf. Plato, *Tim.* 27bc; Demosthenes, *Cor.* 1.1; *Letters* 1.1), but Heb 1:1–4 identifies God *as* the speaker. The scriptural quotations in 1:5–13 maintain the focus on God as speaker, since the quotations are not prefaced with a formula such as "it is written," as is common in the New Testament, but declare what God "said" or "says" (1:5, 6, 7, 13). Old Testament passages are cited rapidly and virtually without comment, so that listeners are confronted not with the author's reflections about God but with God's words from the Scriptures.

Another distinctive element is the positive value given to what God has said in the present when compared to what he has said in the past. Speakers commonly considered their contemporaries to be inferior to previous generations in virtue and in the ability to speak: people "of the present day, apart from a small fraction of them, do not resemble those of former times in their aims and actions," for language "that was once healthy and robust they have turned into a jargon hopelessly depraved" (Philo, *Plant.* 156–57; cf. Kennedy 1972, 446–64). By emphasizing the superiority of what God said "in these final days" (1:2), the author reverses a widespread perception of decline. Many may have thought that human speech was degenerating, but God was not captive to the trend. Rather than dwelling on how things have declined since a past golden age, the author moves listeners to consider their situation with a view to the salvation that God had newly declared, seeking to draw them forward in the hope of its consummation.

The *exordium* also presented an opportunity to make listeners well-disposed toward the speaker. Often this involved establishing the speaker's integrity, since whatever was said was more persuasive when listeners were confident that the speaker was reliable (Quintilian, *Inst.* 4.1.7). The author assumes that listeners will grant that God is a speaker of the highest moral integrity (Heb 6:13). By quoting the Scriptures and by tracing the transmission of the divine message from Christ to the listeners in 1:1–2:4, the author assures the audience that they have been confronted with an authentic word of God. It was fitting to emphasize that God is the primary speaker, because the arguments made in the rest of the speech depend on the conviction that God will be faithful to the promises that he made. The proposition that will be put forward in the next section (2:5–9) is that God wills that people be crowned with glory and honor. Since this hope seems to be contradicted by experiences of conflict and loss (10:32–34; 13:13–14), affirming the integrity of the divine message in the *exordium* places listeners in a position to expect that God's integrity will be demonstrated through the speech.

The author depicts himself first as a listener rather than a speaker, including himself among those to whom the word of God has come (1:2; 2:3); nevertheless, the *exordium* does help to establish the author's credibility indirectly. The author's identity was already known to the intended audience, and it would appear that he already had some rapport with them (13:22–25). The *exordium* helps to confirm the author's integrity by including what is, in effect, a confession of faith concerning the exalted Christ. The opening lines emphasize aspects of the faith that cannot be seen, including the Son's exaltation and his activity in creation (1:1–4). Therefore, when the author later asks listeners to hold fast to their confession (4:14; 10:23) and their boldness (3:6; 4:16; 10:19), his appeal has integrity, for he does not ask them to do anything that he has not done already.

II. The Proposition (Heb 2:5–9)

The next section is the proposition (*propositio*), which identifies the principal issue to be addressed in the speech (2:5–9; cf. *Rhet. Her.* 1.10 §17; Cicero, *De or.* 1.22 §31; Quintilian, *Inst.* 4.4.1–9). The proposition is a discrete section consisting of a quotation of Ps 8:4–6 and a brief exposition of the text.[4] The author placed the proposition immediately after the

---

4. Some include 2:5–9 with 2:10–18 (e.g, Ellingworth 1993, 143). The arguments that begin in 2:10 are closely related to 2:5–9. Nevertheless, identifying 2:5–18 as a unit tends to separate this section too sharply from what follows in 3:1–6. See n. 5 below.

exordium, which is framed by periods concerning divine speech (1:1–4; 2:1–4), and just before the first series of arguments, which is framed by statements about the Son of God becoming complete through suffering (2:10; 5:8–10). Situated at the juncture between these two parts of the speech, the proposition marks the point at which attention turns from the glory of the exalted Christ to the significance of Christ's suffering. Therefore, the proposition sets a course for what is to come. (On the pivotal role of 2:5–9, see Hurst 1987, 151–64; Brawley 1993, 81–93.)

A proposition is effective to the extent that it frames a question in a way that contributes to its solution. The direction of the argument is established through the quotation of Ps 8:4–6, a text that speaks of glory, honor, and dominion. The passage is useful because its references to "man" and "son of man" can be taken broadly as a statement about God's intentions for humankind and more specifically as a statement about the exalted Christ. On one level, the references in Hebrews to human beings inheriting salvation from God (1:14; 2:3) move listeners to take the psalm as a statement about the glory, honor, and dominion that people will receive in God's kingdom in "the world to come" (2:5). On another level, the psalm can be applied to Christ, who is God's Son and heir of all things. Hebrews has already used language from Ps 110:1 to say that God promised to make the Son's "enemies a footstool" for his feet (Heb 1:13). Since Ps 8:7 uses similar language to declare that God had placed all things "under the feet" of the son of man, listeners might well apply both passages to Jesus. Hebrews will develop both senses, arguing that in Jesus listeners can see how God has fulfilled his purposes in a manner that anticipates and brings about the salvation of other people (Swetnam 1981, 137–41; Ellingworth 1993, 151–52; Lane 1991, 1:48). The question of God's purposes for humanity undergirds the speech. (Compare the approach of David M. Moffitt in the previous chapter.)

When defining an issue, speakers tried to distinguish the points of agreement from those that were disputed. The formulation of this crux or *stasis* was most widely developed in juridical cases, but it was a feature of other kinds of oratory as well (Quintilian, *Inst.* 3.6.1–104; Nadeau 1964, 361–424; Lausberg 1998, §§79–254). Hebrews formulates the issue in several steps. After quoting the psalm and repeating that God's intention is to bring all things into subjection (2:6–8b), the author raises an objection that, once stated, would be readily apparent to his listeners. Experience does not conform to what is stated in the psalm, since "at present we do not *see* all things" in subjection as God intends (2:8c). Hebrews was written for a community that had been persecuted in the past and continued to experience verbal harassment and internal malaise. Some members of the community remained in prison (10:32–34; 13:3, 13; cf. 5:11; 6:12). These experiences called into question the idea that God has placed all things in subjection to either Christ or his followers.

The author responds to the objection by interpreting the psalm in light of Jesus' death and exaltation. The *exordium* of Hebrews assumes that listeners have already come to believe that Jesus has been exalted to heavenly glory. Instead of using the *exordium* to persuade the listeners that Christ had been exalted, the author presupposes this belief, citing it in the *exordium* in order to establish common ground with the listeners. Given the conviction that Christ has been exalted, the author now points out that suffering and death preceded Christ's exaltation to glory, just as the subject of the psalm verse was made "lower than the angels" for a time before receiving glory, honor, and dominion (Heb 2:9). In the context of Ps 8, the statements about being made "lower than the angels" and being "crowned with glory and honor" are parallel and could be understood *synonymously*, but Hebrews takes them to be *opposites*, so being made "lower than the angels" means humiliation. When applied to the exalted Christ, the psalm describes his present glory; when applied to the beleaguered people of God, the psalm promises future glory (1:14; 2:10). For Jesus and his followers, glory does not come by exemption from suffering, but comes out of suffering.

The concluding lines of the proposition set the direction for the remainder of the speech. (1) One point is that Jesus was "crowned with glory and honor because he suffered death," opening the way for others to follow (2:9a). This idea is developed in the first series of arguments, which are framed by statements about Christ being made complete through suffering so that he brings salvation for others (2:10; 5:8–10) and which deal with questions of glory and honor (2:10; 3:3; 5:4–5).

(2) A second point accents the sacrificial aspect of Jesus' death, since Jesus suffered so that "by the grace of God he might taste death for everyone" (2:9c). The sacrificial quality of Jesus' death "for everyone" is most fully explored in the second series of arguments, which concerns Jesus' priesthood and self-offering (7:1–10:25).

(3) The third series of arguments returns to the contradiction between the hope of glory in God's kingdom and the inglorious experience of life in the world. The proposition acknowledges that Jesus' followers do not yet "see" all things subjected as God intends (2:8c), but the final series

of arguments shows that faith is bound to what is unseen (11:1–12:24). Since listeners do "see" that Jesus who suffered and died is now crowned with glory and honor (2:9), they can keep looking to him as they journey toward the heavenly city that is the consummation of their hope (12:1–2, 22–24).

III. Arguments and Digressions (Heb 2:10–12:27)

The body of the speech begins when the author declares that it was fitting that God, "in bringing many sons and daughters to glory, should make the pioneer of their salvation complete through suffering" (2:10). It concludes by showing the culmination of God's purposes in the heavenly Jerusalem, where, through the work of Jesus the pioneer, the righteous are made complete so that they can celebrate with the angels in glory (12:2, 22–24). Thus the broad movement of the speech shows how God brings people to the glory that he has promised them by means of the suffering and exaltation of Christ and that life along the way is lived by faith in this promise.

Within this large section are three major series of arguments, each showing listeners how Christ's suffering and exaltation open the way for them to come into the presence of God. In one sense, the arguments are progressive, so that the first series holds that Jesus received glory through faithful suffering, a way that others are called to follow; the second series argues that Jesus' suffering is the sacrifice that enables others to approach God; and the third series maintains that God's people persevere through suffering to glory by faith. In another sense, the internal movements of the three series are repetitive. Although they use different images, they send a constant message that faith is a journey that culminates in the fulfillment of God's promises. In the first series, listeners are like the generation in the wilderness, for they have experienced God's act of deliverance, but they still journey toward God's promised rest. In the second series, they are worshipers in the sanctuary who stand in the outer court and now have the prospect of entering the inner chamber, where God is present. In the third series, they are among the generations of Israel, sojourning on earth in the hope of finding a place in Zion, the city of God. Thus different images—the promised land, the sanctuary, Zion—work together to convey the same hope (Dunnill 1992, 134–38).

Transitional digressions separate the three series of arguments. These digressions do not move the larger argument forward in a direct way but allow the author to turn and address the listeners with words of warning and encouragement. The digressions resemble each other in that they admonish the listeners to pay attention and warn about the dangers of neglect, sluggishness, apostasy, and persistent sin, since divine judgment is inescapable (2:1–4; 5:11–6:20; 10:26–39; 12:25–27). Rather than trying to fit the digressions into the flow of the argument, as is common in outlines of Hebrews, we can better treat them as digressions that seek to retain the audience's attention during the transitions between sections. At the same time, the importance of the digressions in the author's rhetorical strategy should be recognized. The arguments appeal to logic, and the digressions speak more to the listeners' will and emotions, so that together the two phases of the discourse promote the goal of faithfulness. For convenience, we will consider the arguments and the digressions separately.

A. The Three Series of Arguments

1. First Series: Jesus received glory through faithful suffering—a way that others are called to follow (2:10–5:10).

The first series of arguments develops the point made in the proposition that Jesus is "crowned with glory and honor because he suffered death" (2:9a). The course of Jesus' life, death, and exaltation shows that suffering need not mean that God's purpose has failed, for in Jesus' case suffering was the way in which God's purpose was carried out. The arguments that develop this idea are framed by parallel statements that connect suffering with being "made complete," an expression that links suffering with entry into glory (Peterson 1982, 96–103; Attridge 1989, 87). The section begins with that statement that Christ was "made complete through suffering" (*dia pathēmatōn teleiōsai*) so that he has become the pioneer of "salvation" (*sōtēria*) for others (2:10). The section concludes with a period that recalls how, in the days of his flesh, Jesus "learned obedience by what he suffered" (*epathen*) and was "made complete" (*teleiōtheis*) so that he might be a "source of eternal salvation" (*sōtēria*) for others (5:8–10). A complete change in subject matter occurs afterward (5:11–6:20). If the *exordium* prepared for the arguments by focusing on the glory of the ascended Christ, the arguments themselves emphasize that suffering preceded and led to Christ's exaltation.

In content, these arguments emphasize the relationship of Christ's suffering to his glory. Two portrayals of Christ serve as bookends for the section. In the first, the glory of Christ is compared to that of Moses, and

Jesus' death and exaltation are recounted in terms taken from the exodus. If Moses left the Egyptian court to identify with and deliver an enslaved people, Christ also identified with people who were enslaved by oppressive powers in order to liberate them. Therefore, if Moses is rightly honored for his faithfulness as God's servant, Jesus is worthy of even greater glory for his faithfulness as God's Son (2:10–3:6).[5] In the second portrayal, the glory of Christ is compared to that of Aaron, Moses' brother, who did not seize the honor of high priesthood for himself but who was called to that position by God. Like Aaron, Jesus did not glorify himself by seeking the priesthood. Rather, he was exalted to that position by God, in order to raise up a "priest forever after the type of Melchizedek," as God said in Ps 110:4 that he would do (Heb 4:14–5:10).

Between the comparisons of Moses and Aaron to Jesus, who now rests in heavenly majesty, the author likens Jesus' followers to the generation that accompanied Moses and Aaron out of Egypt and into the wilderness in the hope of finding rest in the promised land. Like that generation, which was delivered from slavery in Egypt through the exodus, the followers of Jesus have been delivered from slavery to fear of death through Jesus' exaltation (2:10–18). Like that generation, too, Jesus' followers have received promises from God and live in the hope of entering God's promised rest (4:1–10). The people in the wilderness missed receiving what God had promised, not because God failed, but because they refused to trust God (3:7–19). The question is whether the followers of Jesus will also prove unfaithful or whether they will persevere in the hope of entering God's rest (4:11), as Jesus persevered and now sits at God's right hand.[6]

---

5. Interpreters sometimes treat 2:10–18 and 3:1–6 as separate sections, but the two passages can best be taken together. The word *hothen* ("because of this") in 3:1 shows that the author is in the middle of a section (cf. *hothen* in 2:17; 7:25; 8:3; 9:18; 11:19). Repetition of key words and ideas strengthens connections between 2:10–18 and 3:1–6: God is the Creator of all things (2:10; 3:4), Jesus' followers are the brothers and sisters who belong to God's household (2:11–12; 3:1, 6), and they can be called "holy" because Christ sanctifies them (2:11; 3:1). The portrayal of Christ as the one sent to deliver people (2:14–16) and as the priest who makes atonement (2:17–18) continues in 3:1, where he is called "apostle" (i.e., "sent one") and "high priest."

6. Some outlines of Hebrews include ch. 5 with what follows it because Christ's priesthood is a topic in 4:14–5:10 and again in 7:1–10:25. I link ch. 5 with what precedes it because 4:14–5:10 emphasizes the theme of glory, which is important in 2:10–5:10 but less so in chs. 7–10. Moreover, 4:14–5:10 emphasizes the similarities between

2. Second Series: Jesus' suffering is the sacrifice that enables others to approach God (7:1–10:25).[7]

After a digression in which the author reproves the listeners and exhorts them to perseverance, the second series of arguments takes up a second point that was made in the proposition: by the grace of God, Christ tasted death on behalf of everyone (2:9d). This section, which extends from 7:1 to 10:25, is bracketed by two major digressions (5:11–6:20; 10:26–39) and is unified by its content. The author introduces the section by speaking of Christ's passage through the curtain and into the inner chamber of the sanctuary, where he has gone as a high priest and a forerunner for others to follow (6:19–20). The arguments themselves show that Christ is a priest whose sacrifice enabled him to enter the heavenly sanctuary (7:1–10:18), and the conclusion reiterates that Christ the high priest has opened the way for others through the curtain and into the presence of God (10:19–25). Repeated references to Christ being seated at God's right hand (8:1–2; 10:11–15) and quotations from Jeremiah's oracle announcing the new covenant (8:8–12; 10:16–17) enhance the unity of this section.[8]

If the first series of arguments showed that Christ suffered *like people* before he was exalted to glory, the second series of arguments shows that Christ suffered *for people* in order to bring them glory. Biblical texts dealing with priesthood and sacrifice provide the author with a way to show how Christ's suffering and exaltation could benefit others. Initially, the author demonstrates that Christ's exaltation to eternal life makes him uniquely qualified to serve as a "priest forever after the type of Melchizedek" (Ps 110:4). Because Christ's priesthood is "forever," the author argues that it is superior to the Levitical priesthood. Next, he speaks of Christ's death and

---

Christ and Aaron, whereas 7:1–10:25 stresses the differences between Christ's priesthood and the Levitical priesthood.

7. Many interpreters identify 10:18 as the conclusion of the previous series of arguments and treat 10:19–39 as a block of hortatory material (e.g., Ellingworth 1993, 515; Lane 1991, 2:271). I include the exhortation to enter the sanctuary (10:19–25) with the arguments that precede it and treat 10:26–39 as a transition (cf. Attridge 1989, 283; Guthrie 1994, 144).

8. Although the topic of priesthood was already discussed in 4:14–5:10, that section belongs in the first series of arguments. In the previous series of arguments, the author showed the *similarities* between the priesthood of Aaron and Jesus, but here he stresses the *differences* between the Levitical priestly service and Christ's priestly service.

exaltation as a sacrifice that was made on behalf of others. Christ's sacrifice is the definitive source of the atonement that was foreshadowed by the law's provision for an annual atoning sacrifice. Because Christ's death is a definitive source of atonement, it fulfills God's promise to make a new covenant under which he would remember sins no more. The arguments move like footsteps along a path, alternating between comparing Jesus' ministry with Levitical ministry, on the one hand (8:1–6; 9:1–14; 10:1–10), and elaborating the meaning of the new covenant, on the other (8:7–13; 9:15–28; 10:11–18).

Formally, the period in 10:19–25 creates a peroration that closes the second cycle of arguments (see Quintilian, *Inst.* 6.1.1, 54–55; Lausberg 1998, §§431–42). The period draws together the main themes of the section and urges listeners to draw near to God as the Day of the Lord draws near to them. Perorations could help to refresh listeners' memories by drawing together ideas from previous arguments, so that even "though the facts may have made little impression" in detail, "their cumulative effect is considerable" (Quintilian, *Inst.* 6.1.1). This occurs here. The author has said that previously the "way" (9:8) into God's presence was closed and the "conscience" was not cleansed (9:9), even though the first covenant was "dedicated" (9:18) and people "sprinkled" their flesh according to Levitical ordinances (9:13, 19). Now Christ has "dedicated" a new and living "way" (10:19–20), so that Jesus' death provides a "sprinkling" not only for the body but also for the "conscience" (10:22).

3. Third Series: God's people persevere through suffering to glory by faith (11:1–12:24).

In this final series of arguments, the author returns to the problem raised in the proposition, namely, that the listeners do not yet "see" the realization of God's promises (2:8c). The author sounds the theme in the opening declaration, which stresses that "faith is the assurance of things hoped for, the proof of things unseen" (11:1). Repeated references to ways in which generations of God's people have acted "by faith" illustrate the claim. The author traces the journeys of the righteous who endured conflict, disappointment, and death on earth: Abraham lived as a foreigner on earth in the hope of life in God's city (11:10, 16); Moses gave up wealth in Egypt for a future reward (11:26–27); and the martyrs accepted death in the hope of resurrection (11:35). These heroes and heroines were not "made complete" during their lifetimes (11:39–40), but the author brings their story to its culmination in chapter 12, where the spirits of the righteous are finally "made complete" in God's heavenly city (12:22–24). Distinctive comments about the blood of Abel frame the section (11:4; 12:24).

The author brings the listeners into this epic story of faith by depicting them as athletes in a race who are called to persevere in the hope of receiving what God has promised. Faithful figures from the biblical world— Abraham, Sarah, Moses, Rahab, and the others in Heb 11—join the "great cloud of witnesses" in the stadium where the listeners run the race of faith by looking to Jesus, who completed the contest before them and is now seated at God's right hand (12:1–4). The followers of Jesus are to persevere in faith, despite its difficulties, just as athletes complete a contest and children receive discipline for the sake of a greater good (12:5–17). That greater and final good is life in the heavenly city of God, where the hope of celebrating in the presence of God and God's people will be fully realized (12:22–24). The courage to live faithfully in one's earthly city, despite experiences of conflict and loss, comes from the confidence that God will not abandon his people but will grant them a place in his eternal city, as he has promised.

B. The Digressions

The three series of arguments that were described above are separated by digressions (Quintilian, *Inst.* 4.3.1–17; 9.1.28; cf. Cicero, *Inv.* 1.51 §97; Lausberg 1998, §§340–45). Short digressions, which contrast the way that God spoke in the past at Sinai with the way God now addresses the listeners, make the transition from the *exordium* to the proposition (2:1–4) and from the final series of arguments to the peroration (12:25–27). Longer digressions create transitions between major sections of the argument by warning about apostasy, recalling the listeners' faithfulness, and encouraging perseverance (5:11–6:20; 10:26–39). Working together, the digressions and arguments promote perseverance in faith.

The digressions provide transitions between portions of the speech much as modulations in a musical composition provide transitions between sections that are written in different keys and tempos. This is most evident in the major digressions, which begin by elaborating a point made in the preceding arguments and end by introducing the next series of arguments. The first series of arguments concluded by telling how Jesus reached completeness and "learned obedience" by what he suffered (5:8–9). The digression that follows contrasts Jesus with the listeners, who instead of learning seem unresponsive to learning and instead of being complete seem immature (5:11–14). Following rhetorical convention (Cicero, *De or.* 2.77 §§311–312; 3.53 §203), the author signals the end of the digression by taking up the reference to Jesus' priesthood "after the manner of Melchizedek" (6:20) that was introduced just prior to the digression (5:10). Jesus' priesthood will be a focus in the next section (see 7:1). The reference to Melchizedek paraphrases Ps 110:4, and the idea that Melchizedek represents a priesthood that endures "forever" becomes the lens through which the account of Melchizedek in Gen 14 is read in Heb 7:1–10.

The next two digressions follow a similar pattern. The second series of arguments concludes with a carefully fashioned period that twice refers to faith or faithfulness (10:22, 23). Faith was not mentioned in the second series of arguments, but it becomes the focus of the third series. The period also mentions the "Day" of the Lord (10:25), and before taking up the theme of faith the author embarks on a digression that deals with divine judgment (10:26–39). The author signals the end of the digression by returning to the theme of faith, which was announced earlier, using words from Hab 2:3–4 to declare that the righteous live by faith (Heb 10:37–38). Just as Ps 110:4, which was paraphrased at the end of the earlier digression, provided the hermeneutical key to the next series of arguments, the quotation of Hab 2:3–4 in Heb 10:37–38 provides the lens through which Old Testament narrative is considered in Heb 11:1–40. The third series of arguments concludes with references to the way God and the sprinkled blood of Jesus speak (12:18–24), and the digression that follows urges listeners not to neglect the one who is speaking (12:25). The digression includes a quotation of Hag 2:6 warning that God will "shake" heaven and earth, and it concludes by saying that only what "cannot be shaken" will remain (12:26–27). The peroration that follows the digression calls Christians to the kind of "acceptable worship" or service that is a fitting response to the hope of receiving an "unshakable kingdom" (12:28–13:21).

The rhetorical function of such digressions was to prepare the audience to give their full attention to what would follow. Although modern interpreters who deal with Hebrews in written form might prefer a single sustained argument, speakers in antiquity often digressed to regain the attention of live audiences, who found it difficult to follow a sustained argument without occasional respites (Quintilian, *Inst.* 4.3.12–17; Cicero, *De or.* 3.53 §203; Lausberg 1998, §§340–42). Speakers were aware that people typically "dismiss their minds elsewhere," since they are preoccupied with business, politics, and home life. Therefore, when it comes to the subject of the discourse, "they are deaf, and while they are present in the body are absent in mind, and might as well be images or statues" (Philo, *Prelim. Studies* 64–65). The digressions, some of which would have taken several minutes to deliver, are designed to secure people's attention by addressing them with reproof, warning, and encouragement. Intensity was considered appropriate in a digression. Speakers might express indignation or pity, and they might rebuke or excuse someone; both praise and blame were common (Quintilian, *Inst.* 4.3.1–17; 9.1.28; cf. Cicero, *Inv.* 1.51 §97; Lausberg 1998, §§340–45).

The first digression warns listeners about the dangers of "drifting away" from the message that they received, for "neglecting" the message of salvation would bring inescapable consequences (2:1–4). The second digression occurs about fifteen minutes into the speech, where the author reproves those who are "sluggish," then warns of the devastating consequences of apostasy, before offering more assuring and encouraging words (5:11–6:20). Coupling reproof with assurance was common rhetorical practice. Speakers understood that cutting remarks were to proceed out of concern for the listeners and to be aimed at the listeners' improvement, just as a physician sometimes makes a painful incision in order to free a patient of some malady. Sharp remarks were also to be accompanied by more soothing comments, just as a physician uses ointment to soothe an incision that he has made (Plutarch, *Mor.* 74de; cf. Philo, *Migr.* 116; Dio Chrysostom, *Or.* 77/78.38). Through both warning and promise the author of Hebrews seeks to create a willingness to listen carefully to what he is about to say concerning the work of Christ.

About thirty or thirty-five minutes into the speech, the author of Hebrews digresses again after completing the second series of arguments (10:26–39). This digression was not designed to convey new information, since it deals with divine judgment and the history of the listeners' community—topics that were familiar to the audience (6:1–2; 10:26–34). Instead, the digression seeks to awaken uneasiness before a God who deals mercilessly with those who reject his grace. God's opponents are depicted starkly: they know what is right but willfully sin; they have been sanctified by Christ's blood but seek to defile it; God's Spirit is gracious, yet they are insolent. Listeners would presumably grant that such behaviors warrant divine wrath. Rhetorically speaking, this is *deinōsis*, or language that gives "additional force to things unjust, cruel, or hateful," so that the speaker not only brings the listener to a negative judgment on the matter but awakens emotions that are stronger than the case might otherwise warrant (Quintilian, *Inst.* 6.2.24; 8.3.88; Lausberg 1998, §257 [3c]). The final digression, which begins about forty-five minutes into the speech, leads into the peroration. It resembles the earlier digressions in its call for attention and its warning about the inescapable consequences of rejecting God's word, but also in the words that orient listeners toward the hope of receiving something of abiding value (12:25–27).

IV. The Peroration (Heb 12:28–13:21)

"Peroration" is the term for a conclusion, according to the canons of classical rhetoric (Aristotle, *Rhet.* 3.19.1–6; Cicero, *Part. Or.* 15 §§52–60; *Inv.* 1.52 §§98–109; *Rhet. Her.* 2.30 §47; Quintilian, *Inst.* 6.1.1–55; Lausberg 1998, §§431–42). Used in various types of speeches, the peroration gave the speaker a final opportunity to influence the listeners by reviewing key arguments and by appealing to the emotions. The strength of this section comes not from new arguments but from a creative fusion of themes and images from earlier portions of the speech, together with appeals for solidarity in community life. Modern readers might expect the peroration to begin at 13:1, since that is where the chapter division has been placed since the Middle Ages. The traditional division allows chapter 12 to end forcefully, with the contrasts between shakable and unshakable things running throughout 12:25–29, but it creates a thirteenth chapter that is so different from the rest of the speech that some have argued that it was tacked on to a completed composition in order to make Hebrews conform more closely to other early Christian letters.[9] It is better to recognize that the medieval chapter division obscures the natural section break—a phenomenon that occurs elsewhere in Hebrews.[10] Although the "unshakable kingdom" in 12:28 continues the idea of "shaking" from 12:25–27, it works well to place the reference to the unshakable kingdom at the beginning of a new section, since Hebrews regularly begins a new section with an idea cited at the end of the previous section.[11]

---

9. Some have argued that Heb 13 was added by someone other than the author (Buchanan 1972, 243–45, 267–68), but the more common view is that it was an epistolary appendix added by the author himself (Lane 1991, 2:495–98).

10. A section on Jesus' high priesthood begins not at 5:1 but several verses earlier in 4:14, and the next section begins not at 6:1 but several verses earlier in 5:11. Similarly, the peroration begins not in 13:1 but several verses earlier in 12:28.

11. The first series of arguments ended with what Jesus "learned" by suffering

Worship or service "pleasing" to God is the theme of the peroration (12:28–13:21). The idea of pleasing service (*euarestōs*) is introduced in 12:28–29 and is developed in 13:1–19 through exhortations to show brotherly love, hospitality, and compassion and to remain faithful in marriage and avoid avarice. The author repeats that offerings of praise and sharing one's possessions are sacrifices "pleasing" to God (*euaresteitai*, 13:15–16), and his benediction asks God to equip the listeners to do what is "pleasing" (*euareston*, 13:21). If the central part of Hebrews argued that Christ's death was a sacrifice for others, the peroration urges that those who receive the benefits of Christ's sacrifice offer their own sacrifices of praise and service as a response. These exhortations, when read as an explication of worship or service, form a coherent part of the speech and a compelling conclusion to the treatment of priesthood and sacrifice (Lane 1991, 2:497–98).

Internally, the peroration contains three movements of thought, of which the first and third are parallel:

A. Service to God (12:28–29)
Serving others (13:1–6)
Attention to leaders (13:7–9)

    B. Priestly Sacrifice (13:10–11)
    Christ's death for others (13:12)
    Attention to Christ's lead (13:13–14)

C. Service to God (13:15)
Serving others (13:16)
Attention to leaders (13:17–19)

Going over the same material at the beginning (12:28–13:9) and the end of the peroration (13:15–19) emphasizes that service to God involves service to others. In order to shape and support this view of Christian discipleship,

---

(5:7–10), while the ensuing digression considers the listeners' lack of learning (5:11–14). At the end of the digression there are references to the curtain of the tabernacle and the priest like Melchizedek (6:19–20), both of which are developed at length in 7:1–10:25. The second series of arguments concludes with a reference to the "Day" of the Lord (10:25), and the digression that follows explores the theme of judgment (10:25–39). That digression concludes by declaring that the righteous live by faith (10:38–39), and the next cycle explores the theme of faith (11:1–12:24).

the middle section (13:10–14) creatively fuses themes of Christ's priestly self-sacrifice and the hope of entering the city of God that were developed earlier in Hebrews. The benediction in 13:20–21 concludes the speech proper (Guthrie 1994, 134; Vanhoye 1989, 32). Personal greetings follow in 13:22–25.

One function of a peroration was to affect the listeners' commitments by influencing their emotions. Speakers often appealed to common values such as love for God, one's parents, and one's family and respect for virtues that promote generosity and human community (Cicero, *Part. or.* 16 §56). By calling for compassion, hospitality, faithfulness, and generosity (13:1–6), the author of Hebrews emphasizes community-building values that listeners would find hard to reject. A peroration also helped evoke sympathy for the speaker's case, and this speaker helps to generate sympathy by remembering afflicted Christians, faithful leaders of the past, and Christ's suffering on his people's behalf (13:3, 7, 12). The author also requests prayers for himself, implying that his integrity has been unfairly challenged (13:18–19). Such a request can reinforce bonds with the listeners. Finally, a peroration might seek to evoke indignation at opponents. Hebrews is remarkable for its lack of polemic against those who threaten the community (10:32–34; 13:13), but the author does warn against "those who serve the tabernacle" (13:10), and this helps to foster opposition to positions that differ from those of the author.

Another function of a peroration was to refresh the listeners' memory. Judicial perorations sometimes summarized the main points of a court case, but other kinds of speeches exhibited more variety (Cicero, *Part. or.* 17 §59). The peroration of Hebrews draws on the second series of arguments (7:1–10:39) when recalling how regulations about food and service in the tabernacle failed to benefit people, whereas Christ's death was an effective sacrifice for sins (10:9–12). The author also weaves in elements from the third series of arguments (11:1–12:27) by calling on listeners to endure reproach for Christ, knowing that they have no abiding city on earth but seek the one that is to come (13:13–14). In so doing, the author provides a "refreshing of the memory of the audience, rather than a repetition of the speech" (Cicero, *Inv.* 1.52 §100).

Stylistically, a good peroration was to be brief, and that of Hebrews would have taken perhaps four minutes to deliver. When composing a peroration, speakers were counseled to use a number of short sentences that were not linked by connectives: "I have spoken; you have heard; you know the facts; now give your decision" (Aristotle, *Rhet.* 3.19.6; cf. Cicero,

Part. or. 15 §53). This style, which is evident in Heb 13:1–6 and in the hortatory sections of other New Testament writings (e.g., 1 Pet 5:6–11; Phil 4:4–7), is useful because the author is not developing new arguments but calling for decision: "Let brotherly love abide.... Remember those in prison.... Let marriage be held in honor" (Heb 13:1, 3, 4). Using strong metaphors was encouraged (Cicero, *Part. or.* 15 §53), and our author follows this practice by comparing the taking of a sacrificial victim outside the Israelite camp on the Day of Atonement to Christ's death outside the gates of the city. The use of strong metaphors continues in the haunting summons to follow Christ outside the social setting of one's earthly city, enduring the kind of denunciation that Christ endured in the confidence that his followers have a place in God's abiding city (13:10–14).

CONCLUSIONS

Hebrews is addressed to a Christian community in decline. During its early period, the group experienced miracles and an outpouring of the Holy Spirit (2:3–4), but soon violence from non-Christians led to incidents where Christians were denounced before the authorities and were physically abused. Some were imprisoned and lost property. Nevertheless, members of the community remained in solidarity with one another during the crisis (10:32–34). Hebrews was written after some more time had passed, and the group exhibited signs of a malaise that was evident in tendencies to neglect the faith and the community (2:1–2; 5:11; 6:12; 10:25). The causes of decline were probably complex and may not have been fully apparent to the members of the community themselves. Therefore, the author of Hebrews had to define the issue that was plaguing the community in a manner that would enable him to address it.

The author focused his speech on the way that the hope of inheriting glory in God's kingdom seemed to be contradicted by the inglorious experience of Christian life in the world. He affirmed that God's intention is that people should be crowned with glory and honor, and he acknowledged that his listeners could not yet "see" the realization of God's promises in their own experience. Nevertheless, he declared, they could "see" in Jesus' death and exaltation the assurance that God will be faithful and bring his suffering people to the glory that has been promised to them. Jesus suffered with people and for people, so that they might come to the glory for which God created them, to the glorious rest that Christ has already entered. God's faithfulness is the basis for human faithfulness.

Since God has raised Christ to serve as "a priest forever" (Ps 110:4; Heb 5:6) and established a new covenant on the basis of Christ's death (Jer 31:31–34; Heb 10:16–17), the faithful can be confident that God will yet bring them to the inheritance that has been promised to them (Hab 2:3–4; Heb 10:37–38). In the meantime, the shape of faithfulness corresponds to the work of Christ, whose self-sacrifice is the basis for Christian sacrifices of praise to God and service to others.

Hebrews, Homiletics, and Liturgical Scripture Interpretation[*]

Gabriella Gelardini

The author of the book of Hebrews (hereafter *Auctor ad Hebraeos*) is widely recognized as a talented theologian. This is largely because he, like the authors of Matthew and Romans, knows how to draw abundantly on Holy Scripture and is skilled at weaving the many references smoothly into his sophisticated train of thought. One may rightly ask, however, just why this is so, and also why he incorporates as many as thirty-four explicit quotations identifiable by means of their formulaic introduction. The same question pertains to his insertion of two-thirds of these quotations into the first third of the text, with more than half of these from the Psalms. Why does he reiterate certain quotes and not others? Further, since the two longest are among those repeated, Ps 95 (LXX 94):7b–11 and Jer 31 (LXX 38):31–34, does a correlation perhaps exist between them? Finally, what kind of function does the first quotation from Ps 2:7 fulfill?

Many other questions could be added to these, all considering the author's use of Scripture. This subject already has a substantial history of research,[1] including study of the following subject areas: (1) the research

[*] I am sincerely grateful to the editors of this fine book project, Eric F. Mason and Kevin B. McCruden, for inviting me to contribute, to Mark Kyburz for proofreading this article, and to Brinthanan Puvaneswaran for his support in gathering the necessary literature.

1. The following representative commentators have attended to the author's Scripture references: Westcott 1889, 467–95; Buchanan 1972, xix–xxii, xxvii–xxx; 2006, 3–5, 22–24; Michel 1975, 151–65; Bruce 1990, 25–29; März 1990, 7–9; Lane 1991, 1:cxii–cxxiv; Ellingworth 1993, 37–42; Koester 2001, 115–18; and Karrer 2002–2008, 1:60–66.

history itself;[2] (2) the textual basis of quotations from the Septuagint;[3] (3) the statistics and prioritization of quotations and references;[4] (4) the analysis of quotations in relation to the text's structure, content,[5] as well as genre,[6] including numerous specialized studies;[7] (5) methods and intentions;[8] as well as (6) the hermeneutics and theology[9] of an author entrenched in (proto-)rabbinic exegesis; and, finally, (7) the social context and *Sitz im Leben* (life setting) of Hebrews.[10]

The question of the social context and *Sitz im Leben* of Hebrews is an important one. Obviously, the author teaches and interprets sections of Scripture for his audience and adapts it to their particular situation. This practice of teaching, interpreting, and adapting Scripture for a first-century

---

2. Representative and current overviews of research history are offered by Guthrie 2003, 271–94; Rascher 2007, 2–11; and Docherty 2009, 9–82.

3. Due to recent Septuagint research, the view is held today that the author of Hebrews faithfully followed his *Vorlage*, or particular copy, of the LXX. Surveys on this topic include those of McCullough 1980, 363–79; Karrer 2002–2008, 1:63–65; and Docherty 2009, 121–42. See also Steyn's many more specialized studies on this subject (e.g., 2008, 327–52).

4. See Taut 1998 and also Gelardini 2007; 2005, who has allotted a prominent emphasis to the quotations from Ps 95:7b–11 and Jer 31:31–34.

5. Lane (1991, 1:cxiii–cxv), Ellingworth (1993, 37), Taut (1998), and Gelardini (2007; 2005) have claimed a constitutive function of the quotes in regard to Hebrews' structure.

6. Schröger (1968, 271) and Buchanan (1972, xix–xxii; 2006, 3–5) were among the first to identify Hebrews as a homiletical midrash, whereas Bruce (1990, 25–26) identified Hebrews as a synagogue homily that interprets the synagogal readings. This insight has been concretized in that respect that Taut (1998, 108) as well as Gelardini (2007, 2005) see Hebrews as converging with the *petichta* type.

7. On Hebrews' reception of Deuteronomy, see, for example, Allen 2008.

8. Many have identified the author's exegetical methods in handling quotations as indebted to (proto-)rabbinic hermeneutics, including Caird 1959, 44–51; Schröger 1968, 269–87; März 1990, 8; Lane 1991, 1:cxix–cxxiv; Bateman 1997; and Docherty 2009, 83–120, 143–206.

9. Particular attention to the author's scriptural hermeneutics and theology has been given by Barth 1962, 53–78; Schröger 1968; Johnson 2003, 237–50; Kowalski 2005, 35–62; and Rascher 2007.

10. A synagogal *Sitz im Leben* for Hebrews has been described by many, including Bruce 1990, 25–26; März 1990, 7; 2006, 389–403; Lane 1991, 1:cxxiv; and Gelardini 2007; 2005. März and Stökl Ben Ezra, (2003, 180–97)—among many others—have done so in relation to the (eschatological) feast day Yom Kippur and Gelardini in relation to the correlated fast day Tisha be Av.

audience occurred in various places in antiquity, but first and foremost in the synagogue. This is attested not only by Flavius Josephus and Philo of Alexandria but also by the New Testament, which speaks about Jesus and Paul along with their followers customarily visiting local synagogues on Shabbat (the Sabbath). As authorities, they were granted the privilege of giving a word of exhortation that interpreted the previous readings in a relevant manner. The most explicit examples for this are found in Luke 4:16–30 and Acts 13:13–52. In Acts 13:15 we read that the synagogue officials send for Paul and his assistants after the reading from the Law and Prophets, asking them to give a "word of exhortation" for the people, whereupon Paul responds with a long sermon. Exactly this designation, "word of exhortation," is used by the *Auctor ad Hebraeos* when referring to his speech in Heb 13:22, leading scholars to understand this statement as the author's own classification of Hebrews as a sermon or synagogue homily. Should this designation of Hebrews as synagogue homily indeed apply, and the quotations from Scripture stand in relation to the readings from the Law and the Prophets, then the question about the function of these quotations in the text needs to be turned around. That is, one needs to ask how quoted Scripture contributes to understanding *Hebrews*, rather than how the interpretation of the text contributes to understanding the *quotations*. Seen this way, scriptural quotations help to constitute the text in both structure and content.

Since most research has neglected the constitutive role of scriptural quotations and has disregarded their relation to the text's logic, I shall emphasize the fourth subject area itemized above. I thus wish to unfold the rest of my argument by offering the basic data of the ancient synagogue and its liturgy and for the ancient synagogue homily, working out the underlying readings of Hebrews via its two central scriptural quotations. Then I will apply formal aspects of the ancient synagogue homily to Hebrews and contextualize the remaining quotations, then, finally, situate Hebrews in the context of the ancient synagogue liturgy.

THE ANCIENT SYNAGOGUE AND ITS LITURGY

As stated in the introduction, Hebrews has often been portrayed as a synagogue homily, yet only seldom has this been discussed in the broader context of ancient synagogue research. Therefore, it is helpful to consider basic information about the ancient synagogue, including its origins, legal status, distribution, nomenclature, architecture, sacred geography, organization, and sociocultural and religious-cultic functions. I shall limit this brief survey to what seems beneficial for the use of Scripture in general and Hebrews in particular. (For more detailed investigations and extensive bibliography, see Levine 2005; Gelardini 2007, 87–121.)

The origins of the ancient synagogue remain obscure. Whereas in earlier research a preexilic or exilic beginning was favored, recent research postulates instead a postexilic beginning, namely, in the context of the *ma'amadot*, the twenty-four groups of laymen who witnessed, by turns of one week each, the daily sacrifice in the Second Temple as representatives of the common people. The synagogue apparently allowed them to mimetically participate in temple services from a distance (m. Ta'an. 4:2–4).

Synagogues in the Roman Empire were classified by the authorities as associations. This awarded the congregations the right to assemble, to maintain a meeting place, and to adhere to a monotheistic cult with its laws (such as circumcision of males and observance of the Sabbath, purity, and dietary regulations). Nonetheless, synagogues were also places where ethnic tensions with their social and political environments were fought out, so that legal security and protection periodically had to be reclaimed. Thus, the *Auctor ad Hebraeos* speaks about the absence of citizenship (11:13–16), slavery (2:15), imprisonment and the plundering of possessions (10:34), and public exposure to abuse and afflictions (10:33).

The existence of the ancient synagogue is attested not only in literary sources but also in numerous inscriptions and archaeological excavations. The latter evidence comes both from the Diaspora, where remains as old as the third century B.C.E. have surfaced and the synagogue of Delos (88 B.C.E.) is among the most important examples, and from ancient Palestine, where first-century C.E. remains have been discovered, including the Jerusalem Theodotus Inscription and the Gamla synagogue (Golan).[11] (In contrast, explicitly Christian architecture is archaeologically substantiated only from the beginning of the fourth century C.E.) Linguistically, two designations are attested, more frequently "synagogue" (*synagōgē*) and less frequently "house of prayer" (*proseuchē*). Terms in Hebrews implying a synagogal context include "gathering" (*episynagōgē*, 10:25) and "assembly" (*ekklēsia*, 2:12; 12:23).

---

11. For a photograph, transcription, translation, and other information about the Theodotus Inscription, see http://www.kchanson.com/ancdocs/greek/theodotus.html.

As for synagogal architecture and interior design, it should be noted that Diaspora synagogues—as far as we know—were not only older than those in Palestine but also larger, and the design of synagogues also evolved: they were rather plain before the destruction of the Second Temple in 70 C.E. but incorporated temple elements after its destruction. In contrast to the designs of the tabernacle and temple, the older synagogues consisted of only one rectangular room, serving as a sacred area but lacking the square portion behind the veil, or the holy of holies, because the synagogue was not to compete with the Jerusalem temple. The precious scrolls were brought from outside the building into the Shabbat service in a mobile "ark of the covenant" (Exod 25:10–22; *kibōtos*, Heb 9:4). After the loss of the Second Temple, however, the synagogue underwent a change in design so that a quasi–holy of holies—corresponding to that in the tabernacle and the two temples (Exod 25–27; 37–39), from which God once had spoken in person to Moses—was added to the synagogue. The function of this quasi–holy of holies in various forms (as shrine, aedicula, or apsis) was to contain the scrolls, so that symbolically God's word—although no longer uttered in person—at least was accessible through the scrolls. The synagogue attendees listened to the reading of these words of God while sitting on stone benches along three walls. The scrolls were read in various portions by attendees, possibly translated and then interpreted by a preacher from the bema, which usually stood in the room's center. But before people could enter the synagogue, they had to undergo cultic purification, by means of immersion in a *miqvah*, or pool for ritual washings, annexed to nearly every ancient synagogue known to date, unless natural waters nearby could meet this requirement. The three-part division of the cultic and synagogal complex into a holy of holies, sacred area, and outdoor court is interpreted by Josephus in a sacred sense, with the holy of holies symbolizing heaven and the sacred area symbolizing earth (*Ant.* 3.123). The center of the main room, defined as sacred or holy, therefore symbolizes the earth's center, which Ezek 5:5 ascribes to Jerusalem, and correspondingly the center of the quasi–holy of holies stands for the heavenly Jerusalem. Obviously, the author of Hebrews makes use of various such references to sacred geography, particularly when he invites the audience to "approach the throne of grace" (4:16; 10:22) and by stating that Jesus "went as forerunner behind the curtain on our behalf" (6:19–20).

A functioning synagogue presupposed not only well-educated synagogal personnel but also an efficient synagogal organization. Such was primarily guaranteed by the synagogue leader(s), the synagogue assistant, the elders, and, of course, wealthy founders. Sabbath worship required further specialists. On the one hand, they read from the Law and the Prophets, provided that these assistants were male Israelites, Levites, or priests. On the other hand, they served as translators as well as (itinerant) preachers. The congregational structure in Hebrews testifies to the use of the term "leaders" (*hēgeomai*, 13:7, 17, 24) and indicates that the author planned to visit the assembly, hopefully along with Timothy, now free from prison (13:23); that plan to visit may qualify the author as an itinerant preacher.

Invested with this personnel, the ancient synagogue fulfilled two functions, according to the aforementioned Theodotus Inscription: a sociocultural function, providing "hostel, rooms, and water installation for lodging needy strangers" in Jerusalem; and a more important religious-cultic function: "the reading of Torah and teaching of the commandments." Aspects of both are mentioned by the *Auctor ad Hebraeos.* Sociocultural functions include, for example, legal practice (Heb 6:16; 10:28–31; 13:4), hospitality (13:2), charity (6:10; 10:24, 32–34; 13:3, 16), and finances (13:5). The religious-cultic functions that are mentioned include the synagogal assembly (10:25), Shabbat rest (4:1–11), teaching (in the form of quotations, interpretations, education, and discipline; 5:11–6:3; 12:4–17; 13:22) that the audience is exhorted to heed (3:7–8, 15; 4:7; 5:11; 10:24–25), cultic ablutions (6:2; 10:22), and, finally, prayer (13:18).

THE ANCIENT SYNAGOGUE HOMILY

The central religious-cultic function of the ancient synagogue was thus a weekly celebration on Shabbat modeled after the prototypical covenant-renewal ceremony as portrayed in Neh 8:1–8, which culminated in a sermon (see Gelardini 2007, 123–68 for further discussion). The function of this sermon was to interpret and apply the Scripture readings for the audience. That such readings from the Law and the Prophets existed is also attested—alongside the aforementioned passages from the New Testament (Luke 4:16–20; Acts 13:15) and the Theodotus Inscription—in Josephus (e.g., *Ag. Ap.* 2.175), Philo (*Somn.* 2.127), the Mishnah (m. Meg. 4:1, 4) and the Tosefta (t. Sukkah 4:6).

Of the two readings from Law and Prophets, the reading from the Torah (*sidrah*) seems to be the older one, which is mentioned for the first time in Deut 31:10–13. On this basis, an early Jewish and Christian tradition ascribed the introduction of the Torah-reading to Moses (e.g., Josephus, *Ag. Ap.* 2.175; Philo, *Hypoth.* 7.12; Acts 15:21; m. Meg. 3:6; y. Meg.

4:1:75a), and a later tradition, in line with Neh 8, credited Ezra (e.g., y. Meg. 1:2:70b; b. B. Qam. 82a). That is why Lee I. Levine considers the passage in Nehemiah as the *terminus post quem* for the beginnings of public Torah-reading, and he holds that such a practice was institutionalized by the third century B.C.E. (2005, 150–51). The Torah was—according to the Mishnah (m. Meg. 4:4), the Tosefta (t. Meg. 3:10), and the Talmud (b. Meg. 24a)—to be read both in portions and in *lectio continua* (sequentially through a complete book), whereby a distinctive reading tradition developed. With a reading period of three years, portions or sections (*sedarim*) numbering 141, 154 (in the Masoretic Text), 161, and 167 are attested, and with a reading period of three and a half years, 175 *sedarim*. (For comparison, today's synagogue readings usually follow a reading period of one year with 54 sections.) The different numbers of *sedarim* have been explained, on the one hand, as due to varying lengths of the ancient Jewish year and, on the other hand, to the introduction of special readings for feast and fast days (attested for the first time in m. Meg. 3:4–6). Such special readings would have required that the regular Shabbat readings be interrupted if one of these feast or fast days fell on a Shabbat, moving the regular reading to the next Shabbat.

A reading from the Prophets (*haftarah*) was later added alongside the Torah-reading. Reasons for its introduction lie in obscurity; according to a medieval legend, when Antiochus IV decreed in the second century B.C.E. that the Torah could no longer be read in public, Jews sought to bypass this devastating law by replacing the Torah-reading with matching readings from the Prophets. Levine also localizes the introduction of the new readings during the Maccabean crisis, not evoked by Antiochus's decree but rather by a new esteem for prophetic literature in the context of political-apocalyptic thinking. This led the prophetic texts to be dubbed "holy," thus elevating them to equal status with Torah (Sirach preamble; 2 Macc 2:13; 15:9). In view of these considerations, Levine dates this new institutionalization of readings from the Prophets to sometime in the first century C.E. (2005, 153). Supporting Levine's hypothesis is the fact that the New Testament, as mentioned earlier, gives evidence of readings from the Prophets (Luke 4:17; Acts 13:27), besides readings from the Torah (Acts 13:15). As illustrated by Luke 4:18–19, a reading from the Prophets comprises two verses, and the Tosefta stipulates three to five verses (t. Meg. 3:18). Unlike the Torah selection, the reading from the Prophets was not to be in *lectio continua* but instead paralleled the content of the Torah-reading (b. Meg. 29b). It was to conclude the act of reading on a positive, comforting note, requiring a first list of texts to be excluded from public reading (m. Meg. 4:10). Only later were feast- and fast-day readings determined (t. Meg. 3:1–9). What exactly was to be read from the Prophets can be identified only on the basis of reconstructed reading cycles, which reveal that selections from Isaiah (particularly Isa 40–66) were especially popular.

This institutionalization of readings from the Torah and the Prophets in a particular number of sections also included the understandable and desirable coordination of narrative with time, something that probably prompted the development of a reading cycle within the liturgical year. Therefore, it may not be coincidental that within the triennial cycle the reading from Exod 19 (–31), the giving of the first two tablets, and Exod 34, the giving of the second tablets, are separated by eighty days, in line with the biblical narrative in which Moses stayed on Mount Sinai twice for forty days and forty nights. The reading from Exod 19 then falls near Sivan 6, which is Shavuot (the Festival of Weeks), commemorating when the two tablets of the covenant were given to Moses. The fact that these connections between sacred narrative and calendar time could not always satisfactorily be established, along with the loss of the Second Temple, may have required the aforementioned introduction of special readings for feast and fast days.

Two reading cycles existed: a probably older Palestinian triennial cycle beginning in the month of Nisan (Exod 12:2), and a probably younger Babylonian annual cycle beginning in the month of Tishri. The existence of both cycles is attested for the first time in the Babylonian Talmud (b. Meg. 29b). According to Levine, the specific word choice allows one to presume that their existence as an inherent element of synagogal practice was already long established (2005, 151–52). This assumption is supported by the fact that the *sedarim* (Torah-readings) of the triennial cycle largely coincide with the segmentation of manuscripts dating before the turn of the era. Scribes did not segment texts by means of chapters and verses, a medieval invention at least for the New Testament (Aland and Aland 1989, 6) but rather by means of narrative units, to which they referred by a clever title or first words. The author of Mark therefore speaks in 12:26 about the "[the story] at the bush" in referring to Exod 3:1–4:17, or Paul speaks in Rom 11:2 about "what the Scripture says about Elijah" in referring to 1 Kgs 19:10–14 (see also m. Meg. 3:4–6). Further, because the Palestinian triennial cycle can be traced in many literary corpora, in the Pentateuch, in halakic, haggadic, and homiletic midrashim, in targumim, piyutim, in the tanchumoth and rabboth, and, as some have claimed, even in John, many scholars assume that this triennial cycle was already in force by 70 C.E. Reconstructions of the triennial cycle have been proposed, *inter alia*, by the *Encyclopaedia Judaica* (2007, 20:140–43), Jacob Mann (1971), and Charles Perrot (1988). Despite various differences in these reconstructions, one needs to be reminded of what Perrot wisely advocated in view of early versions and local diversity (1988, 139): "The readings of the TC [triennial cycle] are a little like the ancient Jewish prayers: freedom of formulation must be joined by the recurrence of motifs already established by custom. Synagogues were not at the mercy of their own fantasies."

In what way, then, was the synagogue homily required to relate to the readings? First and foremost, it had to interpret and apply the readings. Since synagogue preachers participated in the Hellenistic-Roman *humanitas*, that is, education, they also borrowed from ancient rhetoric, yet not exclusively from that. As a genre *sui generis*, the ancient synagogue homily had to fulfill particular functions, whose main one was, as mentioned, to interpret and adapt Scripture for everyone from the educated scholar to the small child. We are familiar with two types of homilies: rather spontaneous type with the name *yelammedenu*, the kind to which the sermons of Jesus and Paul in the aforementioned passages may have belonged (Luke 4:16–30; Acts 13:13–52); and an elaborate literary type with the name *petichta* (in Hebrew meaning "opened" but also "sermon"). The *petichta* usually consists of a tripartite structure: a single- or multipart introduction (also called *petichta*), a middle portion, and a single- or multipart end (*chatima*).

The exhortatory introduction had to refer to the *sidrah*, the reading from the Law, in an implicit manner; only the introductory verse of the *sidrah* had to be explicitly cited at the end of the introduction. From the beginning to the end of the introduction, the preacher had to work his way in associative leaps and by means of quotations—mostly from the Psalms—to the introductory verse of the *sidrah*. Sure enough, this rhetorical formula was greatly entertaining, since every attendee may have wondered how the preacher would manage to reach the introductory verse of the *sidrah* from a distant point of departure, while being instructive and also being exhortative. The basic structure of a *petichta* included three things: (1) one but usually multiple *petichta* quotations with associative references to the *sidrah*, (2) the interpretation of the *petichta* quotations, and (3) the introductory verse of the *sidrah*. As already noted, the introduction may have consisted of more than one part. Other than the exhorting introduction, the mainly comforting middle part quoted the *haftarah* (texts from the Prophets) explicitly at its center. The eschatological-resultative end, the *chatima*, was to resemble the introduction, although with more freedom in view of its structure. Ideally a *chatima* consisted of a quotation that resumed the theme of the *sidrah*, provided a *chatima* quotation (mainly an eschatological passage from the Prophets, which contrasted the earthly cosmos with the future one), and included the interpretation of the *chatima* quotation.

To be sure, the methods applied by the author were not constrained by any limits. Apart from the use of literal scriptural quotations and their haggadic interpretation, he could allude to Scripture; refer to scriptural narratives, topics, and heroes; and make use of rhetorical figures and tropes, wordplay, (humorous) anecdotes, fictive dialogues, and so on. So far, nearly two thousand *petichtot* have been identified in midrashic texts, and I am certain that more will be added in the future. With the description of the synagogal homily just provided, I have answered the first two questions posed initially, namely, why the author crowded two-thirds of the quotations into the first third of the text and why he extracted more the half of his quotations from the psalms.

The Two Readings Underlying Hebrews, or Its Two Central Scriptural Quotations

Before one can start to identify Hebrews as a *petichta* synagogue homily, the question needs to be raised whether Hebrews has a *sidrah* and *haftarah* underlying its structure in the sense described above. A careful analysis of the text reveals that the *Auctor ad Hebraeos* puts Scripture in a broader context. In his view, it was prompted by a first "covenant" (*diathēkē*, 8:9; 9:4, 15, 20), mediated through "Moses" (*Mōysēs*, 9:19; 10:28), preached through the "prophets" (*prophētai*, 1:1), "received" by the people (*nomotheteō*, 7:11), and enclosed in the "scroll" (*kephalidi bibliou*, 10:7). As a whole, the Scriptures are called the "word" (*logos*, 2:2) or "law" (*nomos*, 7:5, 12, 16, 19, 28; 8:4, 10; 9:19, 22; 10:1, 8, 16, 28), and sections of it "commandment(s)" (*entolē*, 7:5, 16, 18; 9:19) or "regulations" (*dikaiōmata*, 9:1, 10).

The introduction of the Scripture occurs in various ways. Most evidently, they enter as quotations (or catenas of quotations) with explicit introductory formulae. Usually, these introductory formulae, in contrast to other New Testament texts, consist of lexemes from the semantic field of speech, which awards immediacy and actuality to the quotations. Hence, "God himself says" (*legō*, 3:10; 4:3, 4; 10:30; 13:5; *phēmi*, 8:5) to the audience, or "God speaks through the prophets" or through "his Son" (1:1, 2; 4:8: *laleō*, 1:1, 2; 4:8), or "God speaks through the Holy Spirit," or simply "it is said in the Scriptures" (*legō*, 1:6, 7; 3:7, 15; 4:7; 5:6; 6:14; 7:21; 8:8, 9, 10, 13; 10:16; 12:26), and, finally, the author refers to things "said earlier" (2:3; 5:12; 13:7) or "heard in the past" (2:1). However, the author also refers to Scriptures in other ways, by weaving quotations into the running text without introductory formulae, as in 3:5 (from Num 12:7 LXX), 7:1–2, 4 (from Gen 14:17–20), 10:37–38 (from Hab 2:3–4 LXX), 11:21 (from Gen 47:31 LXX), 12:15 (from Deut 29:17 LXX), or, finally, 12:29 (from Deut 4:24; 9:3). Also, the author alludes to Scripture by paraphrasing biblical narratives (Melchizedek in Heb 7), listing biblical heroes (apart from Moses, the heroes of faith in Heb 11), or elaborating on biblical themes (apostasy, sin, faith, sacrifice, purity, obedience). But among all these various ways of referring to Scripture, those with an explicit introductory formula are the most important, of which I count thirty-four (based on the *New Testament: New English Translation–Novum Testamentum Graece* 2004, 563–87):

	Hebrews	Septuagint	Verses	Repetitions
1.	Heb 1:5a	Ps 2:7b	1	
2.	Heb 1:5b	2 Sam 7:14 (1 Chr 17:13)	1	
3.	Heb 1:6	Ps 96:7 (Deut 32:43)	1	
4.	Heb 1:7	Ps 103:4	1	
5.	Heb 1:8–9	Ps 44:7–8	2	
6.	Heb 1:10–12	Ps 101:26–28	3	
7.	Heb 1:13	Ps 109:1	1	
8.	Heb 2:6–8a	Ps 8:5–7	3	
9.	Heb 2:12	Ps 21:23	1	
10.	Heb 2:13	Isa 8:17–18 (Isa 12:2; 2 Sam 22:3)	2	
11.	Heb 3:7b–11	Ps 94:7b–11	5	
12.	Heb 3:15	Ps 94:7b–8	2	2x
13.	Heb 4:3b	Ps 94:11	1	3x
14.	Heb 4:4	Exod 31:17b; Gen 2:2	1	
15.	Heb 4:5	Ps 94:11	1	4x
16.	Heb 4:7b	Ps 94:7b–8	2	5x
17.	Heb 5:5b	Ps 2:7	1	

18.	Heb 5:6	Ps 109:4	1	2x
19.	Heb 6:14	Gen 22:17	1	
20.	Heb 7:17	Ps 109:4	1	3x
21.	Heb 7:21	Ps 109:4	1	4x
22.	Heb 8:5b	Exod 25:40	1	
23.	Heb 8:8–12	Jer 38:31–34	4	
24.	Heb 9:20	Exod 24:8	1	
25.	Heb 10:5–7	Ps 39:7–9	3	
26.	Heb 10:16–17	Jer 38:33–34	2	2x
27.	Heb 10:30a	Deut 32:35a	1	
28.	Heb 10:30b	Deut 32.36b	1	2x
29.	Heb 11:18	Gen 21:12	1	
30.	Heb 12:5b–6	Prov 3:11–12	2	
31.	Heb 12:21	Deut 9:19	1	
32.	Heb 12:26b	Hag 2:6	1	
33.	Heb 13:5b	Deut 31:6	1	
34.	Heb 13:6b	Ps 117:6	1	

The author thus quotes nineteen times from the Psalms, including five times from Ps 94 LXX (MT Ps 95) and four times from Ps 109 LXX (MT Ps 110). Elsewhere the author quotes four times from Deuteronomy (including twice from Deut 32); three times from Exodus; twice each from Genesis and Jeremiah (both from Jer 38 LXX [= MT Jer 31]); and once each from Isaiah, 2 Samuel, Haggai, and Proverbs. If one counts according to the ancient Jewish tripartite division of Scripture into Law, Prophets, and Hymns (along with books containing commandments in view of life conduct; Josephus, *Ag. Ap.* 1.38–42; Luke 24:44), the author quotes nine times from the Law, five times from the Prophets, and twenty times from hymns and other books.[12] The author quotes between one to five verses on each occasion. He quotes five verses from Ps 94:7b–11 LXX and four verses from Jer 38:31–34 LXX, but the latter (with 132 words) is the longer quotation, actually the longest in the entire New Testament. The quotation of 67 words from Ps 94:7b–11 LXX is the third longest quotation in the New

---

12. Ellis (1991, 7) arranges the twenty-two books in three groups into Pentateuch (5); Joshua, Judges-Ruth, Samuel, Kings, Chronicles, Ezra-Nehemiah, Esther, Isaiah, Jeremiah-Lamentations, Ezekiel, Daniel, Twelve Minor Prophets, Job (13); and Psalms, Proverbs, Ecclesiastes, Song of Songs (4).

Testament, following Acts 2:17–21 (according to the appendix "IV. Loci Citati Vel Allegati" in the *New Testament: New English Translation–Novum Testamentum Graece* 2004, 772–808).

If one summarizes and compares the length and recurrence of quotations, the latter two quotations, Ps 94:7b–11 LXX and Jer 38:31–34 LXX, must be accorded preeminence for the understanding of Hebrews. Is Jer 38:31–34 LXX (MT 31:31–34) then possibly the *haftarah*, the traditional reading from the Prophets? This possible *haftarah* is positioned in the middle of the main part, as it should be, and is partly repeated at the end of this middle part. Its length also meets the required two to five verses. Last but not least, a *haftarah* from Jer 31 is attested, not in the annual, but in the triennial reading cycle. Various scholarly reconstructions (including those of *Encyclopaedia Judaica*, Mann, and Perrot mentioned above) differ somewhat, however, with one claiming that the cycle includes a reading beginning in Jer 31:31, while another names 31:32–39 (or 36) and yet another 31:33–40. In confronting these variant suggestions, one needs to bear in mind that ancient Scripture references did not occur by means of chapter and verse divisions but by way of thematic titles or the first word of a passage. Thus, all these variants belong to one and the same stretch of the story from MT Jer 31:31–40, which in its short span accounts for covenant breaking, rejection, and covenant renewal and furthermore speaks of the reconstruction of the "city," namely, Jerusalem, and the concluding promise that it shall never again face destruction. Consequently, one may claim with something close to certainty that Hebrews constitutes one of the oldest text sources testifying to the existence of this comforting *haftarah*.

What about Ps 94:7b–11 LXX (MT Ps 95:7–11)? It was said that the *sidrah* was not to be quoted within the introduction at full length; only its introductory verse was to be quoted explicitly at the end of the introduction. Instead, reference to the *sidrah* was to be established by quotations from the Psalms that would associatively relate to the reading from the Law. Psalm 94:7b–11 LXX refers to the narrative in Num 13–14, which tells about the ultimate breaking of the Sinai covenant at Kadesh-barnea. If Ps 94:7b–11 LXX—while indirectly relating to the *sidrah*—speaks of covenant breaking, then the theme of the introduction fits the theme of the middle part, which was covenant renewal, in an antithetical manner. Prior to Num 13–14, there is only one other narrative about covenant breaking, Exod 32–33, which describes the idolatry of the people with the golden calf directly after God has entered covenant with them. As a matter of fact, the triennial cycle also knows readings from Exod 32–34, although

again variants have been reconstructed. Mann identified a series beginning in Exod 31:1, followed by 32:(7, 11, 13,) 15 and 34:27. Another series,
however, begins in Exod 30:11, followed by 31:18, 33:1(, 12), and 34:1.
According to Mann, only for the second series, in particular Exod 31:18
and 34:27, is a *haftarah* from Jer 31:32–(36,) 39 within the triennial cycle
attested (Mann 1971, 1:510–33). Hence, an introductory verse citing the
sidrah should stem either from the beginning of Exod 32 or the end of
Exod 34. What was said in regard to the *haftarah* variants applies also in
regard to the *sidrah* variants, since all variants belong to one and the same
narrative of covenant breaking and covenant renewal in Exod 32–34. I
have determined that the cited *sidrah* introductory verse comes from Heb
4:4. Although this quotation seems to refer to Gen 2:2, it even better suits
Exod 31:17b, since Exod 31:12–18 speaks as much as Hebrews does about
rest, that is, Shabbat rest as covenant sign and duty, because it honors
God as creator and resembles exactly the opposite of what takes place in
Exod 32, namely, idolatry. Thus one may conclude that Ps 94:7b–11 LXX
is the *petichta* quotation that strongly relates to the *sidrah* and that Heb
4:4 quoting Exod 31:17b is the *sidrah* introduction beginning in Exod
31:18. Hebrews is therefore not only one of the oldest text sources that
testifies to the existence of the established *haftarah*; it is also one of the
oldest testifying to the existence of the reading pair Exod 31:18–32:35 and
Jer 31:31–34, with the main theme of covenant breaking in opposition to
covenant renewal. With this said, I have answered the third and fourth
questions initially posed, as to why the two main quotations are repeated
and whether they are interrelated.

Hebrews, an Ancient Synagogue Homily and Its Remaining Scriptural Quotations

Since the main theme of Hebrews could be identified in the reading pair
Exod 31:18–32:35 and Jer 31:31–34 as apostasy from the living God
(*aphistēmi*, Heb 3:12), which is covenant breaking, followed by covenant
renewal, it still remains to analyze in what way the *Auctor ad Hebraeos*
interprets and applies this theme in his sermon and how the remaining
quotations fit his train of thought (for more detailed exegesis, see Gelardini 2007, 201–385). It is obvious that the author crafts his sermon in a
careful rather than spontaneous way, and I have argued above that he followed the rabbinic *petichta* or proto-*petichta* type. The numerous observations of scholars that the author's methods correspond to methods of

rabbinic exegesis thus need to be extended to the determination of genre for Hebrews. The *petichta* type of synagogue homily, as was said, follows a tripartite structure. This conforms to the basic scheme of Hebrews, whose cultic middle part 7:1–10:18 has often been isolated by commentators (including myself) from its introduction and end. The resulting structure comprises a hortatory introduction in Heb 1–6, a comforting middle part in 7:1–10:18, and an eschatological resolution in 10:19–13:25.

Insofar as the introduction is concerned, according to my understanding it consists of two *petichtot*: Heb 1–2 and 3–6. Both *petichtot* should contain one or more *petichta* quotations and their interpretation, and the second *petichta* should enclose the *sidrah* introductory verse. The first *petichta* Heb 1–2 includes ten explicit quotations with introductory formula, out of which eight—as usual for *petichtot*—are taken from the Psalms (the numbering corresponds to the chart above) .

(1) Heb 1:5a with Ps 2:7b LXX	Jesus is God's Son and begotten today.
(2) Heb 1:5b with 2 Sam 7:14 LXX	God will be the Son's Father, and he will be his Son.
(3) Heb 1:6 with Ps 96:7 LXX	All angels of God shall worship the Son.
(4) Heb 1:7 with Ps 103:4 LXX	God makes his angels winds and his servants flames of fire.
(5) Heb 1:8–9 with Ps 44:7–8 LXX	Jesus' throne is everlasting, his scepter righteous, so God anointed him.
(6) Heb 1:10–12 with Ps 101:26–28 LXX	Heaven and earth will perish, but the years of Jesus will not end.
(7) Heb 1:13 with Ps 109:1 LXX	God invites Jesus to sit at his right, and he will make his enemies a footstool for his feet.
(8) Heb 2:6–8a with Ps 8:5–7 LXX	God is mindful of his Son of Man, although subjected to angels for a little while he crowns him and subjects all things under his feet.
(9) Heb 2:12 with Ps 21:23 LXX	Jesus will proclaim God's name to his brothers.

(10) Heb 2:13 with Jes 8:17–18 LXX · Jesus puts his trust in God with the children God gave him.

From a formal point of view, I understand this catena of Psalm quotations to be the *petichta* quotations, which the author interprets in the sense that Heb 1 speaks of the elevation of the Son above the angels and at the right hand of God and Heb 2 of the Son's temporary subjection under the angels with the aim of saving the other "sons." How does this fit the theme of covenant breaking in the *sidrah*? In his analysis of homilies with the same reading pair as Hebrews, Mann was able to show that the motif of danger caused by avenging angels sent out to punish Israel for apostasy from God is a prominent one (Mann 1971, 1:510–33). The angels, just as in the biblical narrative in Exod 32:34 and 33:2–3, symbolize the absence of God due to covenant breaking. The author seems to conciliate the audience in view of this impending danger by saying that the power of the avenging angels is limited, and thus they are subject to the Son and controlled by him. But with that the sin does not simply disappear. Instead, Jesus takes this justified peril to life caused by the people's idolatry upon himself. For this reason, he is subject to the avenging angels, including Satan, yet only for a moment, in order to atone the audience before God, just as Moses did in the biblical narrative in Exod 32:30–32. Further, this salvation of countless lives through atoning intercession, grants him—like Moses—elevation next to God.

The second *petichta* includes nine explicit quotes with introductory formula, of which seven—again as usual for *petichtot*—are taken from the Psalms, particularly Ps 94 LXX.

(11) Heb 3:7b–11 with Ps 94:7b–11 LXX · The audience shall not harden their hearts as the desert generation did, which was denied entrance into God's rest.

(12) Heb 3:15 with Ps 94:7b–8 LXX · The audience shall not harden their hearts today as the people in the desert did.

(13) Heb 4:3b with Ps 95:11 LXX · God denied the desert generation entrance into his rest.

(14) Heb 4:4 with Ex 31:17b LXX	God rested on the seventh day from all his work.
(15) Heb 4:5 with Ps 94,11 LXX	God denied the desert generation entrance into his rest.
(16) Heb 4:7b with Ps 94:7b–8 LXX	The audience shall not harden their hearts today.
(17) Heb 5:5b with Ps 2:7 LXX	Jesus is God's Son and begotten today.
(18) Heb 5:6 with Ps 109:4 LXX	Jesus is priest forever according to the order of Melchizedek.
(19) Heb 6:14 with Gen 22:17	God will bless and multiply Abraham.

From a formal point of view, Ps 94:7b–11 LXX, which refers to Num 13–14, has been identified as the *petichta* quotation and Exod 31:17b in Heb 4:4 as the introductory verse of the *sidrah*. Since Num 13–14, just as Exod 32–33, speaks of covenant breaking, even the conclusive breaking of the Sinai covenant, its relation to the *sidrah* requires no further comment. The *petichta* quotation in Heb 3–4 is interpreted in the sense that the author warns his audience against breaking the covenant (again) just as their forefathers did, and since for them there remains a rest in the sense of heritage, by no means shall they fail to enter it. (See especially the excellent article by Randall Gleason [2000] for interpretation of Heb 3–4.) Hebrews 5–6 continues by stating that the audience, like the fathers at Sinai and Kadesh-barnea, is in existential need of a mediator similar to Moses (who essentially functioned as the high priest *avant la lettre*), and such a one is given to them in Jesus (Ps 109:4 LXX). Moses achieved atonement twice and thus saved the lives of the majority of the people (Exod 32:30–32; Num 14:19–20). The second time in Kadesh-barnea, however, the covenant was not renewed with the exodus generation except by a few, and so it was denied heritage, concretized in the prohibition of entry into the promised land. The very same thing might happen to the audience of Hebrews if they apostatize from God. Instead, they are invited to attend to the fact that God's oath with Abraham is still in effect and still has the power to provide for them what it was able to provide for Abraham, both offspring and heritage (Gen 22:17; see another fine article by Gleason [1998] on Heb 6).

The middle part, Heb 7:1–10:18, includes seven explicit quotations with introductory formulae, of which two—as usual for middle sections—are taken from the Prophets (Jer 31 [LXX 38]), three from the Psalms (109 LXX and 39 LXX), and two from the Pentateuch (both from Exodus).

(20) Heb 7:17 with Ps 109:4 LXX	Jesus is priest forever according to the order of Melchizedek.
(21) Heb 7:21 with Ps 109:4 LXX	Jesus is priest forever according to the order of Melchizedek.
(22) Heb 8:5b with Exod 25:40	Moses shall make in view of the tabernacle everything according to the pattern shown to him on the mountain.
(23) Heb 8:8–12 with Jer 38:31–34 LXX	The days are coming when God will establish a new covenant with the houses of Israel and Judah. He will put his laws in their minds and hearts, and they will know him, and he will remember their iniquities and sins no more.
(24) Heb 9:20 with Exod 24:8	Moses to the fathers: This is the blood of the covenant that God has ordained for you.
(25) Heb 10:5–7 with Ps 39:7–9 LXX	Jesus to God: You did not desire offerings, thus I have come to do your will.
(26) Heb 10:16–17 with Jer 38:33–34 LXX	He will put his laws in their mind and hearts, and he will remember their iniquities and sins no more.

On the basis of Exod 32–33 and Num 13–14, the introduction dealt with covenant breaking. Therefore, this comforting section accomplishes the announced atonement through the high priest. In the biblical narrative, Moses provided atonement prior to the enactment of the covenant law and cult, so here it is Jesus who atones on the basis of a divine oath according to the order of Melchizedek (Ps 109:4 LXX), likewise prior to the enactment of the new covenant. By means of this oath and the everlasting celestial cult, on which Moses had modeled the earthly desert cult

(Exod 25:40), Jesus is empowered to atone for the audience. Only now, precisely as Moses did, can Jesus mediate a new covenant inaugurated by God himself (Jer 38:31–34 LXX), whereas his blood—apart from atoning and cleansing—may also serve as the blood of the covenant (Exod 24:8). Further, since the laws of this covenant are not written on stone tablets but in the minds and hearts of the people, Jesus does what is also expected from them, namely, God's will (Ps 39:7–9 LXX). Because of this, God will remember their past iniquities and sins no more (Jer 38:33–34 LXX).

Next follows the eschatological-resultative—and at the same time comforting—ending, the *chatima* (Hebrew for end of sermon). I see this *chatima* as bipartite (in correspondence to the introductory *petichta*), similarly structured like the *petichta* yet less strictly. As expected, the *sidrah* theme resumes, possibly by a quotation, and specifically by an eschatological *chatima* quotation taken from the Prophets that contrasts the present world with the future one. The first part of the *chatima*, Heb 10:19–12:3, includes three quotations, all taken from the Pentateuch:

(27) Heb 10:30a with Deut 32:35a   God says that vengeance is his and that he will repay.

(28) Heb 10:30b with Deut 32:36a   God will judge his people.

(29) Heb 11:18 with Gen 21:12 LXX   God says to Abraham that through Isaac his descendants shall be named.

The first part of the *chatima* connects to the comforting middle part insofar as it warns the audience against sinning again after their cleansing and the inauguration of the new covenant. For those who fail, no sacrifice will be left, but only God's vengeance (Deut 32:35a, 36b). What is called for as appropriate conduct is faith(fulness). The *Auctor ad Hebraeos* spares no effort to call to mind for the audience the shining example of the heroes of faith(fulness) in Heb 11, in strong contrast to the apostatized fathers in Heb 3–6. But in view of the *sidrah*, the heroes of faith(fulness) fulfill another function: in his atoning intercession on behalf of the sinful people, Moses had reminded God of his faithful servants Abraham, Isaac, and Israel and his binding vow to them. It was this very argument that made God hold back from his decision to destroy the whole people (Exod 32:13–14). To conclude, then, the heroes of faith have the same atoning function *de jure*,

because in view of their faithfulness God is bound by his vow to them, and
their faithful deeds lighten the sinful deeds of the congregation. Therefore,
the author calls these heroes "witnesses," which is a legal *terminus techni-
cus* and in rabbinic homilies on Exod 32–33 a recurring motif.

The second part of the *chatima*, Heb 12:4–13:25, includes five quotes,
two from the Pentateuch and one each from the Prophets, Psalms, and
Proverbs.

(30) Heb 12:5b–6 with Prov 3:11–12	God says to the audience not to regard lightly his discipline and punishment, since he chastises those whom he loves.
(31) Heb 12:21 with Deut 9:19	Moses trembles with fear.
(32) Heb 12:26b with Hag 2:6	God will once more shake not only earth but also heaven.
(33) Heb 13:5b with Deut 31:6	God will never leave or forsake the audience.
(34) Heb 13:6b with Ps 117:6 LXX	God is my helper, says the audience, it will not be afraid, for what can anyone do to them?

The second part of the *chatima* ends in a way similar to Heb 1–2, in
an inverse abasement-exaltation scheme. Since the renewed acceptance by
God became concrete in a renewal of covenant, this fact entails a debasing
discipline for those whom he loves (Prov 3:11–12). But in the end it serves
the purpose of exalting his sons and heirs by granting them access to the
mountain. This is not access to Sinai, where in resumption of the *sidrah*
theme Moses trembled in fear of God's rage over the people's idolatrous
sin of worshiping the golden calf (Deut 9:19). Rather, access to Zion is
reinstituted, the heavenly Jerusalem, part of the promised inheritance as
well as the goal. There God the judge awaits them, and the sons are warned
not to reject him, because he will once again shake not only earth but also
heaven (Hag 2:6). There is no use in trying to escape it, since the outcome
is inevitable; instead, they had better accept God as their helper and be
saved in the assurance that no one will be able to harm them any longer
(Ps 117:6 LXX).

If the preceding exposition has been convincing, I have demonstrated
that, against the background of covenant breaking and covenant renewal,
which comprise the main themes in the two central quotations Ps 94:7b–

11 LXX and Jer 38:31–34 LXX, the remaining quotations fit well with the main theme and contribute to the establishment of a coherent sermon that interprets and applies the two identified scriptural readings to the contemporary audience. Further, since the author applies a considerable amount of motifs used in similar and subsequent homiletic midrashim interpreting these readings, I conclude that Hebrews is not only the oldest text source testifying to the existence of this reading pair but also that it may well be the oldest extant synagogue homily of the (proto-)*petichta* type that interprets these particular readings.

What relation do my claims have to the currently popular formal identification of Hebrews as ancient oratory conforming to Aristotelian rhetoric? Certainly the *Auctor ad Hebraeos* took part in Roman *humanitas* and its educational aims, and he even incorporates elements of ancient rhetoric into his homily, such as the rhetorical figure of anaphora in Heb 11. But I doubt whether deliberative, forensic, or epideictic oratory can do justice to a synagogal context, which must interpret scriptural readings and apply them to the circumstances of a diverse audience. Rabbinical oratory, and in particular a (proto-)*petichta*, is better equipped to do that. To presume that such a genre, or one of its early forms, existed already in New Testament times is historically reasonable for several reasons: (1) New Testament writers know readings from the Law and the Prophets; (2) they even include short synagogue homilies or sections based on them (Luke 4:16–30; John 6:26–59; Acts 13:13–41; 17:2–3); and (3) these extracts quote—just as Hebrews does—from Scripture (Acts 13:33 quotes Ps 2:7; Acts 13:34 quotes Isa 55:3; Acts 13:35 quotes Ps 16:10; and Acts 13:41 quotes Hab 1:5). This technique was most likely not applied at random. Also, (4) in the course of researching Qumran texts, scholars have found that countless rabbinic traditions need to be antedated, so that skepticism about the historical comparability of (early) rabbinic texts, concepts, and motifs with New Testament texts is currently being corrected (for a summary of this process, see Holtz 2009). Admittedly, my formal classification rests on arguments from what I trust are sound and better grounds, rather than on hard facts, but the proposed classification certainly holds its own with other formal classifications of Hebrews, including those based on Aristotelian rhetoric.

Hebrews in the Context of Ancient Synagogue Liturgy

Did Hebrews play a role in the context of ancient synagogue liturgy, and, if so, what kind of role? The underlying reading pair identified here, Exod 32 with Jer 31:31–34, falls in the reconstructed triennial reading cycle between the two fast days from Tammuz 17 and Av 9. In New Testament times, as mentioned earlier, the cyclic readings most likely were not yet interrupted for feast and fast days but rather fell on the weekday set for readings from the subsequent Shabbat. Thus, one could reliably expect that a preacher would establish interrelations between the theological contents of a particular feast or fast with readings from the following Shabbat.

The fast day of Tammuz 17, on the one hand, commemorates the destruction of the first covenant tablets by Moses due to the covenant breaking at Sinai (Exod 32:19; Deut 10:2; m. Taʿan. 4:6), which brings us back to the theme of Hebrews' *sidrah*. Moreover, this fast day is also related to the destruction of the First Temple (Jer 39:2 determines Tammuz 9 as the day in which a breach was blown into the city's defensive wall). The fast day of Av 9, on the other hand, is related to Num 14:29–35 in Kadesh-barnea, that is, the Hebrews *petichta* quotation from Ps 94:7b–11 LXX. Moreover, this fast day is also related to the destruction of the First Temple by the Babylonians in 586 B.C.E. (2 Kgs 25:8–9 fixes Av 7 as the date of the First Temple's destruction; Jer 52:12–13 sets it on Av 10), the destruction of the Second Temple by the Romans in 70 C.E., and, finally, the crushing of the Bar Kokhba revolt by the Romans in 135 C.E. Since the First Testament (Zech 7:3, 5; 8:19), together with Josephus (*J.W.* 6.250) and the Mishnah (m. Taʿan. 4:6; m. Roš. Haš. 1:3), is familiar with this fast day and relates it to the destruction of the Second Temple, I assume that the *Auctor ad Hebraeos* also did, just as his contemporary Josephus had. Both fast days, and particularly Av 9 (Tisha be-Av), mark the lowest point in the liturgical calendar, and they are shadow images of its highest point on Yom Kippur (the Day of Atonement). The tension-filled rapport between these two points is not accidental but stands within the context of determining, first, Tammuz 17 as the day when Moses broke the first covenant tablets and then eighty days later Tishri 10, which celebrates the atonement of this sin in the feast day Yom Kippur, which is reminiscent of the eighty days Moses tarried before God. That explains why the author of Hebrews constructs atonement within the symbolic frame of Yom Kippur.

In conclusion, one may claim that Hebrews is not only the oldest text that testifies to the identified reading pair and its interpretation in the genre of a (proto-)*petichta* but also testifies to the context of the triennial reading cycle by relating its genre, the exhortative synagogue homily, to both the fast day of Tisha be-Av (covenant breaking) and Yom Kippur (covenant renewal). Against this background, it therefore contextualizes the historical event of the temple destruction in the year 70 C.E. In the absence of an earthly temple, it is only natural that the author of Hebrews refers to the original, celestial one that remains.

I owe the reader one last answer to the questions that I initially posed: What possible function could the first Scripture quotation from Ps 2:7 in Heb 1:5a (and Heb 5:5b) have played in the context of what was been said? Obviously the *Auctor ad Hebraeos* concurs with rabbinic tradition that on Tisha be-Av the Messiah was born (y. Ber. 2:4:5a; Pesiq. Rab. 33:6; Midrash Tehillim on Ps 2:7).

JESUS THE BROKER IN HEBREWS: INSIGHTS FROM THE SOCIAL SCIENCES

Jerome H. Neyrey, S.J.

The Letter to the Hebrews ascribes to Jesus many different roles, most of which are traditional and commonplace: "Son" (1:5, 7; 3:6), "Son of God" (10:29), "ruler" (1:8), "pioneer" (2:10; 12:2), and "Christ" (3:14; 10:12). But in Hebrews the preferred, unique role of Jesus is that of "priest" (5:6; 7:21; 10:21) and "high priest" (2:17; 3:1; 4:15; 5:10; 6:20; 7:26 and 8:1). As we shall see, a "priest" is a bridge between God and mortals, a go-between, and thus a broker. Moreover, synonyms for "priest" as broker also occur in Hebrews, such as "apostle" (3:1), "guarantee" (*engyos*, 7:22), "minister" (*leitourgos*, 8:2, 6; 10:11), "mediator" (*mesitēs*, 8:6; 9:15; 12:24), and "source" (*aitios*, 5:9). The author also employs a variety of verbs that express the actions of a priest, whether those of Jesus or the Levitical high priesthood:

1. "to offer" himself (7:27; 9:14), "to offer sacrifices" (5:1; 7:27; 10:1), or "to offer gifts and sacrifices" (8:3; 9:9)
2. "to make purification" (1:3), "to purify" (9:14)
3. "to make intercession for them" (7:25)
4. "to save those who approach God through him" (7:25)
5. "to appear in the presence of God on our behalf" (9:24)
6. "to make a sacrifice of atonement" (2:17)
7. "to enter the sanctuary by the blood of Jesus" (9:12, 24; 10:19)
8. "he became the source of eternal salvation" (5:9)

Whether we label the role Jesus played as "priest," "mediator," "guarantee," "minister," or "source," all of these have something in common: they claim for Jesus the role of broker in the basic patron-client relationship between God and Jesus' disciples. A "broker" is a go-between, a bridge (*pontifex*), a mediator, and a priest. Brokers bring the client's needs to the attention of the patron, as well as the benefactions of the patron to the clients. "Broker," then, will be the focus of this study, synonyms for which are "priest" and "high priest."

In considering Jesus as a broker, our investigation includes the following. (1) We need to know about patron-client relations, which, according to the ancients, described the relationship of god as patron and mortals as clients. (2) We need clarity on the role of "broker." Where does a broker fit in terms of patron-client relations? (3) How does someone become a broker? What makes for a successful broker? What do brokers broker? Why a broker at all? Why this broker? What tariff do brokers receive? (4) In the course of the argument, we will present both the cultural theory of "broker" and provide pertinent illustrations from ancient literatures.

THE MAJOR MODEL: PATRON—BROKER—CLIENT

PATRONS AND BENEFACTORS, ESPECIALLY GOD

The ancients used a variety of terms to refer to the common role of patrons, which stems from their experience of earthly fathers, kings, saviors, benefactors, and the like. What follows can serve as the immediate cultural background for the interpretation of the role of God as patron in Hebrews. Although the Greek word *euergetēs* and cognates appear only four times in the New Testament (Luke 22:25; see Acts 4:9; 10:38), the term was widely used in the ancient Mediterranean world. Even if not formally used to describe God as "benefactor," we know of many names of God-as-patron found in Greco-Roman literature (Neyrey 2005).

1. *King*: Dio Chrysostom calls Zeus "king," referring to the positive results of his rule: "In like manner do the gods act, and especially the great King of kings, Zeus, who is the common protector and father of men and gods" (*Or.* 2.75). "King" and "father" are often found in combination, suggesting positive governance by a benefactor: "Yet all these poets … call the first and greatest god Father of the whole rational family collectively, yes, and King besides.… men erect altars to Zeus the King and, what is more, some do not hesitate even to call him Father in their prayers" (Dio Chrysostom, *Or.* 36.35–36).

2. *Father*: Greeks and Semites call god "Father," an example of which Dio provides: "At that time, the Creator and Father of the World, beholding the work of his hands" (*Or.* 36.60). Cicero comments: "the poets call him 'father of gods and men,' and our ancestors entitled him 'best and greatest,' putting the title 'best,' that is most beneficent, before that of 'greatest,' because universal beneficence is greater, or at least more loveable, than the possession of great wealth" (*Nat. d.* 1.64).

3. *Savior*: Studies of this word indicate that it enjoyed a wide range of meanings (Wendland 1904; Fohrer 1971; Bruce 1963). A savior is one who: (a) rescues another from danger, such as war, illness, judicial condemnation, floods, and famines; (b) protects and preserves the *polis* and its citizens; (c) inaugurates a golden age (Fohrer 1971, 1012); and (d) benefits others.[1] In this vein, Werner Foerster cites an inscription that tells how on the annual feast of Zeus *sōsipolis* the priests of Magnesia prayed for "the *sōtēria* of the city, country, citizens, wives, children and other residents, for peace, for wealth, for the growth of the grain and other fruits and cattle" (*SIG* 2:589, 26–31; Foerster 1971, 7:967).

4. *Benefactor*: Like "Savior," this term enjoys many meanings. One scholar noted that "Gods and heroes, kings and statesmen, philosophers, inventors and physicians are hailed as benefactors because of their contributions to the development of the race" (Bertram 1964, 2:654). Philo describes the benefaction characteristic of God:

> He [God] shall no longer exhibit toward me the masterfulness that characterizes the rule of an autocrat, but the readiness to bless that marks the power that is in every way kindly, and bent on the welfare of men. He shall do away with the fear we feel before Him as Master, and implant in the soul the loyalty and affection that goes out to Him as Benefactor. (*Plant.* 9).

Ethnic groups took various gods as patrons of different favors. The sun-god benefited the Egyptians; the God of Abraham promised both land and numerous sons to fill that land; Athena bestowed wisdom on Athens; Apollo dispensed a host of benefits on the Greeks assembling at his temple

---

1. Arthur Darby Nock notes that gods acted as saviors: "Zeus as father of men and gods, was strong to aid; Artemis protected women in childbirth; Athena guarded the Acropolis.... In fact, any deity was credited with powers which men lacked, and could aid as humanity could not" (Nock 1972, 2:721).

in Delphi. In the Roman pantheon, individual gods bestowed their own specific benefits on their clients:

> In the case of Jupiter, we extol his power as manifested in the governance of all things, with Mars we praise his power in war, with Neptune his power over the sea; as regards inventions, we celebrate Minerva's discovery of the arts, Mercury's discovery of letters, Apollo's of medicine, Ceres' of the fruits of the earth, Bacchus' of wine. (Quintilian, *Inst.* 3.7.6–9)[2]

In regard to the presentation of God in Hebrews, the familiar synonyms of "patron" seen above are used infrequently. God is "father" (1:5; 2:11; 12:9), "Lord" (1:10; 2:3; 7:21; 8:2), the one able to "save" (5:7), and "creator" (1:2). Nevertheless, we find a variety of benefactions bestowed by God, indicative of his role as patron. God bestows to his clients the following:

1. *wisdom and knowledge*: "God … has spoken to us by a Son" (1:1–2).[3]
2. *creation*: "Every house is built by someone, but the builder of all things is God" (3:4).
3. *kinship*: "The one who sanctifies and those who are sanctified have one Father" (2:11).
4. *grace and favor*: "Let us approach the throne of grace, so that we may receive mercy and find grace to help in time of need" (4:16; 12:15; 13:9).
5. *mercy*: "I will be merciful toward them and remember their sins no more" (8:12).

---

2. In his instructions on how to praise a benefactor deity, Alexander son of Numenius says: "You should consider his power, what it is and what works prove it; then the sovereignty of the god and the subjects of his rule, heavenly, marine, and earthly. Then his relation to art should be mentioned, as Athena is over all the arts, and Zeus and Apollo over divination. Then what discoveries the god has made. Then whatever works he has done among the gods or for the gods, as Zeus has primacy of power and Hermes heraldry. Then his philanthropy" (*Rhetores Graeci* 3:4–6; Grant 1953, 166–67).

3. Unless otherwise noted, all quotations of Scripture are from the NRSV (often with emphasis added).

6. *previous benefaction*: "It is impossible to restore those who have once been enlightened, have tasted the heavenly gift, shared in the Holy Spirit, and have tasted the goodness of the word of God" (6:4–5).

7. *promises*: "God made a promise to Abraham saying, 'I will surely bless you and multiply you.' Thus Abraham obtained the promise" (6:13–15; 11:6, 11, 13, 39–40).

8. *homeland*: "People who speak in this way ... are seeking a homeland ... [not] the land that they left behind, ... they desire a better country, that is, a heavenly one. Therefore God ... has prepared a city for them" (11:14–16).

9. *kingdom*: "Since we are receiving a kingdom that cannot be shaken..." (12:28).

10. *heavenly help*: "I will never leave you or forsake you. So we can say with confidence, 'The Lord is my helper; I will not be afraid. What can anyone do to me?'" (13:5–6).

11. *compendium of the patron's benefaction*: "You have come to Mount Zion, the city of God, the heavenly Jerusalem, to innumerable angels in festal gathering, to the assembly of the firstborn who are enrolled in heaven, to God the judge of all, to Jesus, the mediator of a new covenant, to the blood that speaks a better word than the blood of Abel" (12:22–24).

Whether the God of Hebrews is acclaimed by traditional names ascribed to patrons or not, there can be no doubt that God is structurally perceived as patron bestowing many, exceptional benefactions.

Clients in General

"Client" refers to the inferior partner in a patron-client relationship. Clients seek the patron's power (protection from bandits), generosity (food, seed, and animals), and loyalty and solidarity. For their part, clients are expected to sing the patron's praises and/or provide him with timely services (farming, harvesting, building, etc.). Clients may be mortals dependent upon gods, procurators seeking the favor of Caesar, and other such dependent relationships.

It goes without saying that the God of Abraham and of Moses acted as patron to Israel, his client. His good deeds to them included freedom from slavery, victory over their enemies, food and drink, and land and fertility; moreover, God kept his promises. In the Psalms we find a client's petitionary prayer. "But I am poor and needy; hasten to me, O God! You are my help and my deliverer; O LORD, do not delay!" (Ps 70:5). But after the patron provided the requested relief and rescue, the clients were wont to say: "Clap your hands, all you peoples; shout to God with loud songs of joy. For the LORD, the Most High, is awesome, a great king over all the earth. ... Sing praises to God; sing praises to our King, sing praises. For God is the king of all the earth; sing praises with a psalm" (Ps 47:1–2, 6–7).

In a patron-client relationship, both patrons and clients have duties. Above all, the patron must be trustworthy and loyal: "Let us hold fast to the confession of our hope without wavering, for he who has promised is faithful" (Heb 10:23; see 1 Cor 1:9; 1 Thess 5:24). The patron, so benevolent in past promises, must continue to do so: "By faith he received power of procreation, even though he was too old ... because he considered him faithful who had promised" (Heb 11:11). For Israel, the duty of the client was fidelity to the one and only benefactor. "Faithfulness" is expressed in many ways: (1) "by faith," whether belief in the patron's promise or endurance (11:8–10, 32–40); (2) "with reverence and awe": "Since we are receiving a kingdom that cannot be shaken, let us give thanks, by which we offer to God an acceptable worship with reverence and awe" (12:28); (3) "sharing his abuse": "Let us then go to him outside the camp and bear the abuse he endured" (13:13). Alternately, the author strongly censures the infidelity of some of the group, thereby affirming the duty of faithfulness to the patron. For example, the audience is exhorted thus: "We must pay greater attention to what we have heard, so that we do not drift away from it" (2:1); "[They] have tasted the goodness of the word of God and then have fallen away" (6:5–6); and "We are not among those who shrink back and so are lost, but among those who have faith and so are saved" (10:39).

In general, recipients of patronage understood that they were indebted to their patron; they owed some sort of recompense, such as praise or produce. Patrons gave so as to receive (*do ut des*; Dixon 1993b).[4] However, Romans and Israelites agreed that it was shameful to become a client and owe something to another. "They who consider themselves wealthy, hon-

---

4. Lucian (*Merc. cond.* 13) states that "no one does anything without pay." Cicero critiques this kind of patronage: "A great many people do many things that seem to be inspired more by a spirit of ostentation [*gloria*] than by heart-felt kindness; for such people are not really generous but are rather influenced by a sort of ambition to make a show of being open-handed" (*Off.* 1.44).

ored, the favorites of fortune, do not wish ever to be put under obligations by our kind services. They suspect that a claim is thereby set up against them or that something is expected in return. It is bitter death to them to have accepted a patron or to be called clients" (Cicero, *Off.* 2.20.69). Likewise Paul states, "Owe no one anything, except to love one another" (Rom 13:8). The failure of clients to show gratitude as payment for their debts was universally considered a grievous fault: "Homicides, tyrants, thieves, adulterers, robbers, sacrilegious men, and traitors there always will be; but worse than all these is the crime of ingratitude" (Seneca, *Ben.*1.10.4; Dixon 1993a).[5]

Clients in Hebrews

In Hebrews, the clients of the God of Israel can be identified in two ways. First, they are described as the recipients of many and varied benefactions from God: they are those who have been spoken to by God (1:1), have been given his word (2:3), have tasted the goodness of the word of God (6:5), and have received a promise confirmed by an oath (6:13, 17). Besides these verbal benefactions, God effects holiness in his clients: "It is by God's will that we have been sanctified" (10:10), and in their doxology to God the clients pray:

> Now may the God of peace, who brought back from the dead our Lord Jesus, the great shepherd of the sheep, by the blood of the eternal covenant, make you complete in everything good so that you may do his will, working among us that which is pleasing in his sight, through Jesus Christ, to whom be the glory forever and ever. Amen. (13:20–21)

The patron, who is the author of *peace*, has already *made a covenant* relationship with his clients *by the blood of our Lord Jesus*, and is petitioned to *make the clients complete* in goodness that they *do his will* and thus *he will work* among them what is *pleasing in his sight*.

Second, God's clients offer sacrifices of praise to their patron (13:15). Their sacrifices might take the form of service: "Do not neglect to do good and to share what you have, for such sacrifices are pleasing to God" (13:16). Similarly, they honor their patron by clinging in faith to the promises

---

5. Cicero says: "No duty is more imperative than that of proving one's gratitude" (*Off.* 1.15.47); see Seneca, *Ben.* 4.20.3; 7.31.1–3.

made ages ago (11:8–19) and manifesting perseverance and faithfulness to
God in distress (11:32–38). Most important, they praise their patron: "Let
us continually offer a sacrifice of praise to God, that is, the fruit of lips that
confess his name" (13:15).

Brokers in General

Brokers in the Heavenly World

The Greco-Roman world identifies many brokers, both heavenly and
earthly. As regards the former, the Greeks knew of two heavenly messengers, one male and the other female: Hermes and Iris. Of Iris Hesiod said:

> Rarely does the daughter of Thaumas, swift-footed Iris, come to her with
> a message ... but when strife and quarrel arise among the deathless gods,
> and when any of them who live in the house Olympus lies, then Zeus
> sends Iris to bring in a golden jug the great oath of the gods from far
> away. (*Theog.* 775–806)

Greece's famous oracles include a patron-god who gives illumination or
knowledge to clients through brokers. The brokers are the oracle herself
and then the interpreter of the oracle's messages, that is, a prophet: "The
voice is not that of a god, nor the utterance of it, nor the diction, nor the
meter, but all these are the woman's; he puts into her mind only the visions,
and creates a light in her soul in regard to the future; for inspiration is precisely this" (Plutarch, *E Delph.* 397c; Aune 1983, 23–48). Finally, a "priest"
in Rome was called a "ponti-fex," that is, a bridge-maker, linking gods-
patrons and mortals-clients (Schrenk 1965, 3:267).[6]

Philo describes God employing go-betweens, calling them lieutenants:

> There are others ... lieutenants of the Ruler of the universe, as though
> they were the eyes and ears of the great king, beholding and listening to
> everything. Philosophers are wont to call these demons, but the sacred
> scripture calls them angels, using a name more in accordance with
> nature. For indeed they do report *the injunction of the father* to his chil-
> dren, and *the necessities of the children* to the father. (*Somn.* 1.140–141,
> emphasis added)

---

6. See Gärtner 1978, especially the list of pontifices maximi on 346.

These "messengers," then, function as two-way agents: they bring God's injunctions to his clients and the clients' needs to God.

BROKERS IN THE WORLD OF MORTALS

Of course, the ancients did not use the technical term "broker," but they fully appreciated the function of this person in a patron-client relationship. They named this mediator/go-between by a rich variety of terms, indicative of their appreciation of his role in specific contexts, of which some of the most important examples are as follows:

angelos (messenger, envoy) (see Mitchell 1992, 644–51)
apostolos (ambassador)
diakonos (attendants, heralds)[7]
diallaktikos (conciliator, reconciler)
engyos (security)
entygkchanō (to appeal, obtain an audience)
exaitēsis (intercessor)
epitropos (agent, representative)
hierys (priest)
hiketēs (suppliant)
hypēretēs (petty official, attendant)
mesitēs (mediator)[8]
paraitētēs (intercessor)
paraklētos (a broker, a mediator)
presbeutēs (an ambassador)
prophētēs (one who speaks for God)

An intermediary (*mesitēs*) may be an arbiter in legal transactions, who is linked with a *kritēs* or appointed by one. An *engyos*, a type of intermediary, acts as the guarantor who accepts legal obligation for a bond or payment. He himself is the surety of the contract (Nash 1977, 114–15). Diviners, priests, oracles, prophets, and the like are also brokers.

---

7. Collins 1990 understands *diakonos* as more than a mere table-serving role. His data warrants calling the *diakonos* a "go-between" or middleman. Other *diakonoi* function as those who transmit messages, such as Hermes and Iris as well as earthly sibyls, prophets, interpreters of dreams, heralds, and couriers.

8. See Oepke 1967, 4:598–624; Becker 1975, 1:372–76; and Attridge 1989, 221.

Even rulers were considered brokers of the heavenly world in regard to the people of God's realm. "The king, regarded as god or the son of god, serves as a mediator of the people before the godhead, receiving divine laws and offering national sacrifices" (Oepke 1967, 4:609).[9] Some monarchs employed brokers because it was part of the royal mystique to be invisible to the crowds; the inaccessible Eastern potentates (patrons) used viziers to broker their plans to the world outside the palace and to gather information for him about the state of affairs of the empire.[10]

ISRAELITE BROKERS IN PRACTICE AND IN THEORY

Our abstract consideration of a "broker" can be clarified and confirmed by examining how brokers functioned in Israel's history. Abraham played the mediator for Sodom when God determined to destroy the city; we are all delighted in the way Abraham step by step persuaded God to withhold his wrath (Gen 18:22–33). In another instance, Abraham petitioned God for healing: "Abraham prayed to God; and God healed Abimelech, and also healed his wife and female slaves so that they bore children" (Gen 20:17). But Israel valued Moses as the consummate broker between God and the people by virtue of two episodes in his life: Israel's arrival at Sinai and its worship of the golden calf.[11] Upon arriving at Sinai, the people begged Moses to be their mediator with God: "You speak to us and we will hear; but let not God speak to us, lest we die" (Exod 20:19). Philo interprets this to mean that God respected human incapacity to receive "unmixed and exceedingly great" benefaction without a mediator or broker:

> It was our attainment of a conception of this that once made us address to one of those *mediators* [*mesitōn*] the entreaty "Speak to us and let not God speak to us, lest we die" (Exod 20:19). For if He, without *ministers* [*hypēretais*], holds out to us … benefits unmixed and exceeding great, we are incapable of receiving them. (*Somn.* 1.143, emphasis added; see also *Post.* 143)

---

9. Scharbert (1964, 21–67), in his comparative study of intercession in antiquity, listed kings and priests as the premiere mediators in the ancient Near East.

10. Greene (1989, xvi–xvii) distinguishes five types of messengers (ambassador, emissary-courier, envoy, herald, and harbinger). He argues that the concept of messenger was constant and did not change (40–41).

11. Abraham was also appreciated as an intercessor for the people with God (Nash 1977, 95).

Second, on the occasion of the golden calf, Moses played the role of intercessor between sinful Israel and the sinless God (Exod 32:32). Using a wide variety of synonyms, Philo articulated Moses's role as mediator/ broker between the offended deity and the offending people:

> Yet he took the part of *mediator* [*mesitēs*] and *reconciler* [*diallaktēs*] and did not hurry away at once, but first made prayers and supplications, begging that their sins might be forgiven. Then, when this *protector* [*kēdemōn*] and *intercessor* [*paraitētēs*] had softened the wrath of the Ruler, he wended his way back in mingled joy and dejection. (Philo, *Mos.* 2.166, emphasis added)

The Anatomy of a Broker in Social-Science Perspective

"Broker" is an abstract term that identifies the specific role of mediation between patrons and clients, in our case, between immortals and mortals (Boissevain 1974, 147–48). Mediator, bridge, go-between, messenger, and agent are types of brokers. The advantage in using "broker" lies in its suggestive power to contextualize its function in terms of patron-client relationships. What, then, do we mean by "broker"? As Bruce Malina notes, "A *social broker*, by definition, is a professional manipulator of people and information who brings about communication for personal benefit" (Malina 1996, 152; see also Davis 1994, 484–85). "Professional" means that the broker is not an ad hoc but an enduring role. "Manipulator" describes someone who is an "uniter," who brings together those who want something with those who have something. By "people and information," we understand that mediators do not themselves have what clients desire but *know* to *whom* to turn—potential patrons. "Communication" refers to the fact that through brokers patrons speak to clients and clients to patrons. "Personal benefit" refers to the tariff brokers receive for their services—brokers are rarely altruistic. Where should we locate a "broker" in the social dynamics of the ancient world? When viewed in terms of the patron-client model of social relations, the "broker" belongs in the middle, on the border, mediating the patron's benefactions to the clients and alternately presenting the client's needs and praise to the patron.

Although we noted above that Hebrews is unique in the New Testament in describing Jesus' primary role as that of "priest" or "high priest," the letters in the Christian Scriptures abundantly claim the role of broker for Jesus in the way they describe God's benefactions coming *through*

Jesus to believers and the prayers and praise of believers arriving before God *through* Jesus. We digress to consider the data that acclaim for Jesus the role of broker precisely because *through* him God blesses mortals and *through* him mortals approach God. All benefaction descends *through* Jesus, as all praise and petition ascends *through* him.

***

Excursus: Jesus as Broker in New Testament Letters[12]

John: All things were made *through him*, and without him nothing made (1:3).

Romans: I thank my God *through Jesus Christ* (1:8); on the day when God, *through Jesus Christ*, will judge (2:16); we have peace with God *through our Lord Jesus Christ* (5:1); *through him* we have obtained access to this grace (5:2); to eternal life *through Jesus Christ* (5:21); thanks be to God *through Jesus Christ* (7:25); to the only wise God be glory *through Jesus Christ*! (16:21).

1 Corinthians: For us there is one Lord, Jesus Christ, *through whom* are all things and *through whom* we exist (8:6); God gives us the victory *through our Lord Jesus Christ* (15:57).

2 Corinthians: the confidence we have *through Jesus Christ* toward God (3:4); all of this is from God who reconciled to himself *through Christ* (5:18).

Ephesians: he destined us for adoption as his children *through Jesus Christ* (1:5).

Titus: this Spirit he [God] poured on us richly *through Jesus Christ* our Savior (3:6).

1 Peter: to offer spiritual sacrifices *through Jesus Christ* (2:4); that God may be glorified in all things *through Jesus Christ* (4:11).

---

12. The same pattern can be observed in the way Jesus' followers are told to "pray in my name" (John 14:13, 14; 15:16; 16:26). Redemption and forgiveness come from being "baptized in the name of Jesus Christ" (Acts 2:38). Healings occur "in the name of Jesus Christ" (Acts 3:6; 4:10, 30) and "by faith in his name" (Acts 3:16). When asked "by what name did you do this," the disciples replied, "There is salvation in no one else, for there is no other name under heaven given among mortals by which we must be saved" (Acts 4:12).

Jude: to the only God *through Jesus Christ*, be glory, majesty, power and authority (25).

✶✶✶

Thus, the phrase *through him* describes the benefaction of God-Patron that descends to mortals *through Jesus* (Acts 10:36; 2 Cor 5:18; Titus 3:6) and the prayers and praise that ascend from God's clients to him *through Jesus*. All doxologies are addressed to God *through Jesus* (Rom 7:25; 16:27; 1 Pet 4:11; Jude 25), and all sacrifices are offered to God *through Jesus* (1 Pet 2:4), and whatever confidence mortals have is *through Christ Jesus* toward God (2 Cor 3:4). This, then, is the typical way that the New Testament describes the role of broker to Jesus.

Besides the definition provided above, we need to examine various aspects of this role, so we ask the following questions to guide our exposition. (1) How does a person become a broker? (2) What makes for a successful broker?[13] (3) What does a broker broker?[14] (4) Why brokers at all? Why this broker? (5) What do brokers receive for their services?

How Does a Broker Become a Broker?

A broker may be authorized, called, or appointed. "One does not presume to take this honor, until *called by God*, just as Aaron was" (Heb 5:4). So "Christ did not glorify himself in becoming a high priest, but *was appointed* by the one who said to him, 'You are my Son, today I have begotten you' … 'You are a priest forever, according to the order of Melchizedek'" (5:5–6); he is "*designated by* God a high priest" (5:10). Jesus is not a priest-broker because of his blood lines but because God explicitly designated him a priest by means of an oath:

---

13. The characteristics of a successful broker depend on the work of Boissevain 1974, 148–63.

14. For further discussion of first- and second-order goods, see Boissevain 1974, 147–48; Malina 1996, 151–54. Israel's great prophets, Moses and Elijah, did not themselves possess power, manna and quail, oil and flour, etc. that they delivered to God's clients; they were but channels or bridges through which these benefactions came from Israel's divine patron.

This was confirmed with an oath; for others who became priests took their office without an oath, but this one became a priest *with an oath*, because of the one who said to him, "You are a priest forever." ... The law appoints as high priests those who are subject to weakness, but the *word of the oath* appoints a Son made perfect forever. (7:20–21, 28)

WHAT MAKES A BROKER SUCCESSFUL?

Brokers are successful for several reasons. First, they belong to the worlds of both patron and clients and so represent fairly the interests of both. Second, they maintain loyal and faithful relationships with both.[15] Moses was a successful broker because he had a foot in both worlds, both that of the patron and that of the clients. While Moses evidently serves as the bridge between God-Patron and Israel-client, nothing was said about why and how he qualifies as a broker, much less a successful one. But Philo's description of the Logos provides this important information.

To His Word, His chief *messenger* [*presbeutatō*], the Father has given the special prerogative, to stand on the border and separate creature from the Creator. This same Word both pleads with the immortal as *suppliant* [*hiketēs*] for afflicted mortals and acts as *ambassador* [*presbeutēs*] of the ruler to the subject. He glories that "and I stood between the Lord and you" (Deut 5:5), *that is neither uncreated as God, nor created as you, but midway between the two extremes* [*mesos tōn akroō*], a surety to both sides [*amphoterois homēreuōn*]. (*Her.* 205–206, emphasis added)

He belongs to both worlds, "neither uncreated as God, nor created as you"; he is "midway" between both and acts as "a surity" to both. Thus he serves both faithfully and fairly.

Similarly, Philo locates Israel's high priest on the border line between the world of God and that of humans; because he is a being higher than humans and like to the Divine, he belongs to both worlds and serves both.

---

15. Plutarch remarks that Solon was an ideal mediator because he represented the interests of patrons and clients: "He was chosen an archon to succeed Philombrotus, and made mediator (*diallaktēs*) and legislator (*nomothetēs*) for the crisis, the rich accepting him readily because he was well-to-do, and the poor because he was honest" (*Sol.* 14.2).

The law desires him to be endued with a nature higher than the merely human and to approximate the Divine, *on the border line* [*methorion*], we may truly say, between the two, that men may have a *mediator* through whom they may propitiate God, a *servitor* whom God may employ in extending the abundance of his boons to men. (*Spec.* 1.116, emphasis added)

The services of this two-way broker are best explained with reference to the patron-client model. The high priest acts "as mediator" for mortals when they petition God for remission of sin and as "a servitor" who channels God's benefactions to them. Elsewhere Philo comes back to the high priest as a border figure:

He is a being *bordering* on God; inferior to him but superior to man. "When," the Scripture says, "when the high priest goes into the Holy of Holies he will not be a man" (Lev 16:17), what then will he be if he is not a man? Will he be God? I would not venture to say that, nor is he man, but he touches both of these extremes as if he touched the feet and the head. ... But if at that time he is not a man, it is clear that he is not God either, but a *minister* of God, *belonging as to his mortal nature to creation*, but *as to his immortal nature to the uncreated God*. And he is placed in the *middle class* until he goes forth among the things which belong to the body and to the flesh. (*Somn.* 2.188–89, 2.231–232, emphasis added)

It should be clear, then, that the ancients understood why a mediator or ambassador served as a successful broker: he was a "border" figure whose feet touch earth and whose head touches heaven; he belongs to the worlds of both patron and client. Philo cannot clearly call the Logos a deity, but as we saw in the citation from *Her.* 206, this figure "stood between the Lord and you (Deut 5:5), that is neither uncreated as God, nor created as you, but midway between the two extremes, a surety to both sides."

JESUS, A SUCCESSFUL BROKER: HE BELONGS TO BOTH WORLDS

Hebrews is replete with remarks about how Jesus belongs to the world of God. The document begins with a celebration of Jesus' role and status: "In these last days he has spoken to us by a Son, whom *he appointed heir of all things,* through whom he also created the worlds" (1:2). He is the "reflection of God's glory and the exact imprint of God's very being" (1:3). There follows a series of remarks affirming that Jesus belongs to the world of

God: "When he brings the firstborn into the world, he says, 'Let all God's angels worship him' " (1:6).

Jesus is said to enjoy an attribute unique to God, immortality: "Of the Son he says, 'Your throne, O God, is forever and ever, and the righteous scepter is the scepter of your kingdom.' 'In the beginning, Lord, you founded the earth, and the heavens are the work of your hands; they will perish, but you remain; they will all wear out like clothing. But you are the same, and your years will never end' " (1:10–12). This quality, which properly belongs only to the Immortal One, extends also to Jesus. When Melchizedek was declared to be "without father, without mother, without genealogy, having neither beginning of days nor end of life," he only "resembles the Son of God" (7:3); the converse is not true. It has been shown that this collection of predicates describes a topos for a true deity who has no beginning and no end (Neyrey 1991). This likeness to the immortal God indicates how completely Jesus belongs to the world of God.

In contrast, all of Israel's priests were born and died. They are "descendants of Levi" (7:5), who died; unlike Melchizedek, they qualify as priests "through a legal requirement concerning physical descent" (7:17). Moreover, they are numerous because they were prevented by death from continuing in office" (7:23). The Levitical priests, therefore, in no way belong to the world of the living God. Jesus, however, "is a priest forever … through the power of an indestructible life" (7:17), for it is attested of him, "You are a priest forever, according to the order of Melchizedek." Later the text says that "he holds his priesthood permanently, because he continues forever" (7:24). He belongs to the world of God because he shares God's immortality and imperishability.

Jesus the broker also shares the world of God's clients, namely, that of mortals on earth. The point is made early in the document that to be an effective broker with God, Jesus "had to become like his brothers and sisters in every respect" (2:17); in short, he had to belong to their world in a most meaningful way. Hence, he became mortal and died. "Since, therefore, the children share flesh and blood, he himself likewise shared the same things" (2:14). The purpose of sharing their world of "flesh and blood" was to die like all mortals, and the purpose of his dying was that "through death he might destroy the one who has the power of death, that is, the devil, and free those who all their lives were held in slavery by the fear of death" (2:14–15). His brokerage between the two worlds is interpreted as a sacrifice: "He had to become like his brothers and sisters in every respect, so that he might be a merciful and faithful high priest in the service of God, to make a sacrifice of atonement for the sins of the people" (2:17; 9:15–17).

Much more is said about how Jesus-the-broker belongs to the earthly world of mortals. He expresses human emotions such as sympathy: "We do not have a high priest who is unable to sympathize with our weaknesses, but one who in every respect has been tested as we are" (4:15). He also earnestly prayed to God: "In the days of his flesh, Jesus offered up prayers and supplications, with loud cries and tears, to the one who was able to save him from death" (5:7); in addition, like all mortal sons, he endured discipline from his father: "Although he was a Son, he learned obedience through what he suffered" (5:8; see 12:4–11).

Why a Broker? Why This Broker?

Is Jesus just one more in a line of priests? Is he unique and superior? The author argues for the absolute necessity of *this* broker by engaging in an extensive comparison between Jesus, "a priest according to the kind of Melchizedek," and Israel's priests. "Comparison" (*synkrisis*) was a standard compositional exercise learned in progymnastic studies; literate people knew how to compose one, and audiences readily recognized it. The topics of a comparison are the traditional loci of honor and praise that derive from the core structure of an honor and shame society (see *Rhet. Her.* 3.6.10; Quintilian, *Inst.* 3.7.16; Menander Rhetor 1.386.9–21; and Aelius Theon, *Progym.*). Because their instructions are remarkably similar, only one example needs to be examined, that of Aelius Theon.

> When we compare characters, we will first set side by side their noble birth, their education, their children, their public offices, their reputation, their bodily health, as well as their bodily good qualities and external good qualities. After these items, we will compare their actions by choosing: those which are more noble, more reliable, more enduring, those done at the proper time, those from which great harm results when they have not been done, those done with a motive rather than those done because of compulsion or chance, those which few have done rather than those that many have done, those done with effort rather than easily. (Butts 1987, 497)

Since comparisons were tailored to specific situations, they did not need to develop all the possible topics mentioned above. Thus, I report on the topics by which the author crafts this comparison.

Origins Compared

In terms of origins–generation, Israelite priests must come from the sons of Aaron and Levi (Heb 7:16); genealogies in Ezra and Nehemiah witness to the importance of pure and provable bloodlines. Jesus, however, is from "Judah" (7:14), suggesting a Davidic connection. But it is hardly accidental that Melchizedek is both "*priest* of the Most High God" and "*king* of righteousness, king of Salem" (7:1–2). Unlike the sons of Aaron and Levi, Melchizedek is "without father, without mother, *without genealogy*" (7:3). But this is hardly a slur on Jesus' origins. Tribal origins hardly exhaust Jesus' *generation,* because he is the Son of a heavenly Father. Twice Ps 2:7 is cited apropos of Jesus: "You are my Son. Today I have begotten you" (1:5; 5:5), as well as 2 Sam 7:14, which confirms the relationship: "I will be his Father, and he will be my Son" (1:5). Often Jesus is acclaimed the "Son" through whom God spoke (1:2) and of whom God spoke (1:8). His generation, then, is vastly more honorable than that of the priests.

When the topic origins–geography is discussed, remarks are typically made about the honor and fame of the city from which the person comes. The priests of Levi and Aaron come from Jerusalem, in particular its temple complex—very honorable indeed. But the author locates Jesus in the heavenly world, the realm of God. Remarks in 1:1–4 suggest Jesus' residence there prior to becoming like us in all things, as well as his abiding residence at "the right hand of God" when his task was completed. An aspect of comparative *geography* occurs when the temple of the sons of Levi is compared with that which Jesus enters. The Jerusalem temple is denied honor because it was made by human hands (9:11, 24) and is a mere shadow of the things to come (8:5; see 10:1); moreover, inasmuch as the high priest enters behind the veil but once a year, the author interprets this as a defect: "By this the Holy Spirit indicates that the way into the sanctuary has not yet been disclosed as long as the first tent is still standing" (9:8). Jesus, however, "did not enter a sanctuary made by human hands, a mere copy of the true one, but he entered into heaven itself" (9:24). "We have confidence to enter the sanctuary by the blood of Jesus, by the new and living way that he opened for us through the curtain (that is, through his flesh)" (10:19–20). In generation and geography, Jesus is superior to Israel's priests in honor and thus can perform his role more effectively. Nothing is said about the nurture, training, and education of these two kinds of priests. But the most developed areas of comparison are between their public offices and their respective reputations.

Roles and Statuses Compared

Unlike the priests of Israel, Jesus enjoys many roles, all of which indicate extraordinary honor. (1) He is *high priest* in the line of Melchizedek: "He had to become like his brothers and sisters in every respect so that he might be a merciful and faithful high priest" (2:17; 4:15); "For it was fitting that we should have such a high priest, holy, blameless, undefiled, separated from sinners, and exalted above the heavens" (7:26). (2) He is also *Son and Son of God*: "In these last days he has spoken to us by a Son, whom he appointed heir of all things, through whom he also created the worlds. He is the reflection of God's glory and the exact imprint of God's very being, and he sustains all things by his powerful word" (1:2–3). "To which of the angels did God ever say, 'You are my Son; today I have begotten you'? Or again, 'I will be his Father, and he will be my Son'?" (1:5–6; 4:14). Finally, he is a *pioneer, a forerunner*: "It was fitting that God should make the pioneer of their salvation perfect through sufferings" (2:10; 12:2). "We have this hope, a hope that enters the inner shrine behind the curtain, where Jesus, a forerunner on our behalf, has entered" (6:20).

In contrast, the priests of Israel enjoy only the role of priest, nor do they have another relationship with God (sonship), nor are they described as pioneers or forerunners. In terms of brokering, they have a role of modest significance.

Status is a vertical quality that ranks persons as higher/lower, first/last, best/worst. As such, status pertains to the ranking of a person in relationship to and thus expresses the honor of that person. In Hebrews, the two kinds of priests are contrasted in terms of eight categories: (1) oath versus bloodlines, (2) the quality of the blood offered, (3) the frequency of offering, (4) the duration of the priest's role and (5) the termination of it, (6) the efficacy of offerings, (7) perfect priests make others perfect, and (8) what is "better" and "distinctive."

1. *Oath versus bloodlines.* The priesthood of Jesus resulted from an *oath*, a direct act of God: "This one became a priest with an oath, because of the one who said to him, 'The Lord has sworn and will not change his mind, "You are a priest forever"'" (7:21, 28; on the significance of God's oath, see 6:16–17). But the priests of Israel qualify only because of a material factor, bloodlines. "He has become a priest, not through a legal requirement concerning physical descent" (7:16).

2. *Quality of blood offered.* The contents of Jesus' sacrifice are vastly superior to the offerings and gifts of Israel's priests. Jesus offers his own

blood, not that of goats and bulls; whereas Jesus offered his own blood, Israel's priests offered the blood of animals: "He [Jesus] entered once for all into the Holy Place, not with the blood of goats and calves, but with his own blood, thus obtaining eternal redemption. For if the blood of goats and bulls, with the sprinkling of the ashes of a heifer, sanctifies those who have been defiled so that their flesh is purified, how much more will the blood of Christ purify our conscience" (9:12–14). "Nor was it to offer himself again and again, as the high priest enters the Holy Place year after year with blood that is not his own" (9:25). "For it is impossible for the blood of bulls and goats to take away sins" (10:4–5).

3. *Frequency: once and for all versus daily and yearly.* "Nor was it to offer himself again and again, as the high priest enters the Holy Place year after year with blood that is not his own; for then he would have had to suffer *again and again* since the foundation of the world. But as it is, he has appeared *once for all* at the end of the age to remove sin by the sacrifice of himself" (9:25–26). "Unlike the other high priests, he has no need to offer sacrifices day after day, first for his own sins, and then for those of the people; this he did *once for all* when he offered himself" (7:27; 9:14). Not so Israel's priests: "Every priest stands *day after day* at his service, offering again and again the same sacrifices that can never take away sins" (10:11; see 9:13–14).

4. *Duration.* The duration of Jesus' priestly role lies in the fact that it never ceases. Repeatedly God swore with an oath, "You are a priest *forever*" (5:6, 10; 6:20; 7:17, 21); further, "he holds his priesthood permanently, because he continues *forever*. … consequently he is able for all time to save those who approach God through him, since he *always lives* to make intercession for them" (7:24–25). The same cannot be said for the priests of Aaron and Levi: "The former priests were many in number, because they were prevented by death from continuing in office" (7:23–24). Their role lasts only a lifetime.

5. *Effectiveness.* "He came as a high priest of the good things that have come, then through the greater and perfect tent … he entered once for all into the Holy Place … with his own blood, thus obtaining *eternal redemption*" (9:11–12); "how much more will the blood of Christ, who through the eternal Spirit offered himself without blemish to God, *purify* our conscience from dead works to worship the living God!" (9:14; 10:10, 14). "It is by God's will that we have been *sanctified* through the offering of the body of Jesus Christ once for all" (10:10). "For by a single offering he has *perfected* for all time those who are sanctified" (10:14). But about the sons

of Aaron and Levi, the author says: "Gifts and sacrifices are offered that cannot perfect the conscience of the worshiper" (9:9); "since the law has only a shadow of the good things to come and not the true form of these realities, it can never, by the same sacrifices that are continually offered year after year, make perfect those who approach" (10:1–2).

6. *Perfect versus imperfect priest.* Not only is Jesus the priest made perfect, but he actually perfects others: "The word of the oath appoints a Son who has been *made perfect* forever" (7:2; 2:10); "it was fitting that God, for whom and through whom all things exist, in bringing many children to glory, should *make* the pioneer of their salvation *perfect* through sufferings" (2:10). "Having been *made perfect*, he became the source of eternal salvation for all who obey him" (5:9). "For the law appoints as high priests those who are subject to weakness, but the word of the oath, which came later than the law, appoints a Son who has been *made perfect* forever" (7:28; 10:14).

But the sons of Aaron and Levi are imperfect priests who offer imperfect offerings: "Now if perfection had been attainable through the levitical priesthood, what further need would there have been to speak of another priest arising according to the order of Melchizedek?" (7:11; 9:9). "The law ... *can never*, by the same sacrifices that are continually offered year after year, *make perfect* those who approach" (10:1).

7. *Better and distinctive.* Besides establishing that the brokerage of Jesus as high priest is superior to the brokerage of Israel's priests, the author argues that he is "as much superior to angels as the name he has inherited is more excellent than theirs" (1:4). He is no mere messenger, like the angels, "For to which of the angels did God ever say, 'You are my Son; today I have begotten you'? Or again, 'I will be his Father, and he will be my Son'? And again, when he brings the firstborn into the world, he says, 'Let all God's angels worship him.' Of the angels he says, 'He makes his angels winds, and his servants flames of fire'" (1:5–7; see 2:9).

Moreover, it is not enough that Jesus be superior to Israel's broker-priests. He is acclaimed superior to Israel's greatest broker, Moses: "Jesus is worthy of more glory than Moses, just as the builder of a house has more honor than the house itself. ... Now Moses was faithful in all God's house as a servant. Christ, however, was faithful over God's house as a son" (3:3–6).

Eventually the author begins to compare elements of the old with the new system, labeling the new ones as "better." With Jesus we have "the introduction of a *better hope*" (7:19); "Jesus has also become the guarantee of a *better covenant*" (7:22); "Jesus has now obtained a *more excellent ministry*, and to that degree he is the mediator of *a better covenant*, which has been enacted through *better promises*" (8:6) and "through the *greater and more perfect* tent he entered once for all" (9:11–12).

What Does Jesus Broker?

Although some mediators and messengers in the ancient world functioned as one-way brokers (patron → broker → client), more commonly we read about two-way brokers (patron → broker → client and client → broker → patron). We noted earlier the benefactions that God bestows on the disciples of Jesus. God the patron, by means of an oath, authorized Jesus as priest for the very purpose of channeling the following benefactions: (1) purification and purification for sins (1:3; 5:9; 9:14); (2) a sacrifice of atonement (2:17); (3) a single sacrifice for sin (10:12, 14; 9:26); (4) redeem/ eternal redemption (2:15; 9:12, 15); and (5) perfection (10:14). Thus whatever benefactions God bestows will inevitably be brokered to the clients by Jesus—and they are not insignificant. But does Jesus broker the clients' prayers and praise to God? While Jesus' brokering of patronal benefits to the disciples is clearly dominant in the description of his role, we find some instances of his mediation of the clients' prayers to God. First, glory and honor are sung to the divine patron *through* Jesus: "Through him let us continually offer a sacrifice of praise to God, that is, the fruit of lips that confess his name" (13:15). Alternately, petitionary prayer describes the scene when "Jesus offered up prayers and supplications, with loud cries and tears, to the one who was able to save him from death" (5:6; see 2:17). This qualifies him to be a merciful high priest, one who is sympathetic to the clients' needs. Hence it is through Jesus, priest and broker, that his disciples "approach the throne of grace with boldness, to receive mercy and find grace in time of need" (4:16). This is clearly petitionary prayer because of the qualifier "in time of need." In another place Jesus' task is described as the eternal intercessor: "Consequently he is able for all time to save those who approach God through him, since he always lives to make intercession for them" (7:25; see 9:24). "Intercession" signals petitionary prayer.

What Tariff Does a Broker Receive?

In our world, brokers such as stock brokers, investment brokers, commodity brokers, marriage brokers, and real estate brokers receive a tariff from both buyer and seller in the form of the most valued thing in our world: money. A comparable recompense was true for the Levites who functioned in Israel's cult system as priestly brokers. Although the Levites did not receive a portion of land, they were supported by tithes and by fixed portions of the animals sacrificed. Sharing in tithes and sacrifices, then, was their tariff.

> You shall bring the fat with the breast, so that the breast may be raised as an elevation offering before the LORD. The priest shall turn the fat into smoke on the altar, but the breast shall belong to Aaron and his sons. And the right thigh from your sacrifices as well you shall give to the priest as an offering.... For I have taken the breast of the elevation offering, and the thigh that is offered, from the people of Israel, from their sacrifices of well being, and have given them to Aaron the priest and to his sons, as a perpetual due *from the people of Israel.* (Lev 7:30–34)

This includes nonanimal foods as well: "All the best of the oil and all the best of the wine and of the grain, the choice produce that *they give to the Lord, I have given to you.* The first fruits of all that is in their land, which they bring to the LORD, shall be yours" (Num 18:12–13).

One might ask who is awarding what portion of the priestly tariff: God? the people? both? Sometimes it is the Lord's portion, and other times it comes from the people's offering: "The Levitical priests, the whole tribe of Levi … may eat the sacrifices *that are the Lord's portion*" (Deut 18:1). It is the Lord who bestows this food: "I have given to you, together with your sons and daughters, as a perpetual due" (Num 18:19; see 18:12–13). Alternately, a portion comes from the people: "This shall be the priests' due *from the people*, from those offering a sacrifice, whether an ox or a sheep: *they shall give to the priest* the shoulder, the two jowls, and the stomach" (Deut 18:3).

The tariff of foods for the Levites is codified in Israel's law as their "due." "All the holy offerings that the Israelites present to the LORD I have given to you as *a perpetual due*" (Lev 6:18). "This shall be the *priests' due* from the people, from those offering a sacrifice, whether an ox or a sheep:

they shall give to the priest the shoulder, the two jowls, and the stomach" (Deut 18:3; see Lev 7:34; 10:13; Num 18:8, 11).[16]

Does Jesus receive a tariff? He does not need nourishment as did the Levites. Moreover, there is no possible repayment for his mediation. Yet there are suggestions that Jesus is awarded the most valuable commodity in antiquity: honor, glory, and respect. Hebrews states that, after completing his labor, God seated him at his right hand: "When he had made purification for sins, he sat down at the right hand of the Majesty on high" (1:3). "Right hand of God" is indeed the most honorable place possible, and like priesthood, one must be invited to sit there. This motif threads its way through the document, for example: "But when Christ had offered for all time a single sacrifice for sins, 'he sat down at the right hand of God'" (10:12; see 1:13; 8:1; 12:2). Considering that the basic Christology of Hebrews focuses on Jesus' death and exaltation, his sitting at God's right hand is a unique honor. God assigns Jesus this honor because of his obedience (5:8; 10:7, 9) and faithfulness: "Consider that Jesus, the apostle and high priest of our confession, was faithful to the one who appointed him, just as Moses also 'was faithful in all God's house.' Yet Jesus is worthy of more glory than Moses, just as the builder of a house has more honor than the house itself" (3:1–3).

In addition to the use of Ps 110:1 to declare Jesus' tariff from God, other psalms are used similarly. The author employs Ps 8:4–6 to explain the basic cultural pattern of shame and honor: "What are human beings that you are mindful of them, or mortals, that you care for them? You have made them for a little while lower than the angels; you have crowned them with glory and honor, subjecting all things under their feet" (2:6–8). The author quickly interprets the psalm in terms of Jesus: "We do see Jesus, who for a little while was made lower than the angels, *now crowned with glory and honor because of the suffering of death*" (2:9). God, of course, "crowns him with glory and honor," a most desirable tariff. We know that one party of the relationship bestowed a tariff to Jesus, namely, the honor and glory that accompanies his exaltation.

---

16. These materials stand behind Paul's claim that he has a "right" to be fed by the Corinthian church: "Do you not know that those who are employed in the temple service get their food from the temple, and those who serve at the altar share in what is sacrificed on the altar?" (1 Cor 9:13).

What Do We Know If We Know This?

1. We have been introduced to a significant social model, namely, "broker," which implies patron-client relationships. Although the articulation of this model is a product of the twentieth century, it was well known and appreciated in antiquity.

2. We are by no means the first or only persons to use the patron-client relationship to interpret the dynamics of the ancient world, but few, if any, scholars have given attention to the figure of a "broker," much less use it to interpret a New Testament document.[17]

3. "Broker" is a reliable model that quite adequately fits with the data from the ancient world. Philo's presentation of Moses and the Logos as "brokers" proves beyond a doubt that the model with all of its subtopics was known in times past. The modern model of "broker" makes salient in Philo and other ancient writers the essential and implied elements of the model. Let it never be said that this is an imposition of a modern model on an ancient text. I would go so far as to claim that a modern reader cannot adequately interpret Philo and Hebrews without such a model.

4. The focus of this study has been on the patron-client relation and the role of the broker as bridge between them. Many items from the ancient world appeared, which were basically taken from the exercises of the progymnasmata. These, too, describe aspects of the model of broker, especially "comparison," which argues that a new, better broker is needed.

5. Although we focused on the model of patron-broker-client, other social-science concepts and models are used to provide a thick interpretation of Hebrews. First and foremost, the ancient model of honor and shame gives native importance to the extended comparison (is a new broker needed?). It provides the proper appreciation of the tariff that God provides Jesus, namely, his session at the right hand of God. In consideration of why patrons give and why a tariff is appropriate to the broker, a theory of reciprocity is most helpful. Entering the cultural world of Hebrews, one comes to know that more and more social-science models are necessary.

6. Besides Hebrews, where might a reader go to interpret a text or test the model of patron-broker-client? First, one might consider the ubiquitous phrase "through Christ our Lord," which appears in benedictions, doxologies, and the like, in the New Testament. Is all New Testa-

---

17. Neyrey 2007 first developed a model of "broker" and applied it to the Fourth Gospel; it proved a most useful way of interpreting Jesus' role in the Fourth Gospel.

ment prayer addressed to God through Jesus? Second, what is claimed when Jesus presents himself as God's prophet, whom God made powerful in word and deed (see John 9:29–31)? Third, Paul often presents himself to various churches as their link to God and Christ. He styles himself as God's master-builder, judge, parent, teacher, and prophet. In one case he is the "minister of Jesus Christ to the Gentiles in the priestly service of the gospel of God so that the offering of the Gentiles may be acceptable" (Rom 15:16); he is a "servant of Christ and steward of the mysteries of Christ" (1 Cor 4:1; Eph 3:1–19). Often he presents himself as "apostle" of God (Rom 1:1; Gal 1:1). He also presents himself as an official in the collection of funds for the Jerusalem church.

HEBREWS AS THE RE-PRESENTATION OF A STORY: A NARRATIVE APPROACH TO HEBREWS

Kenneth Schenck

THE STORY SUBSTRUCTURE OF HEBREWS

Story is a fundamental human category. Few individuals and cultures define themselves primarily in terms of a set of propositions or truth claims about who they are. Rather, we tell our stories. Most cultures, families, and individuals have identity-expressing stories they tell when they get together or when they want to instill children with their values. They tell stories of their strengths, weaknesses, and most characteristic features. They tell stories of their heroes and enemies. They tell stories of the rewards of living according to their values and stories that forewarn the bad consequences of disregarding them. If these dynamics do not seem as prevalent in the Western world, it is only a sign of how atypical our atomistic and rationalistic individualism is in contrast to most peoples who have lived throughout history in most times and places.

Well over half the material in the Bible is in narrative form. A narrative, as I define it here, is a text or discourse that is in the explicit form of a story, a text whose "surface structure" is that of a story. You can, of course, tell the same "underlying" story in countless different ways. You can start *in medias res* ("in the middle of the matter") and flash back to earlier events. Indeed, you can start telling the story at the very end, just as it is virtually over. The same underlying *story*, therefore, can be told by way of countless different *narratives*, where a narrative is a "story-as-discoursed," a story that has been told in one particular way (Chatman 1978, 43).[1]

---

1. Some postmodern thinkers have rightly raised questions about what I am calling an "underlying story" here. Stephen Moore pointed out some time ago that you cannot ever really abstract a story from a rhetorical presentation. Your abstracted

However, we can argue over stories, too, not just tell them. More than anyone else, Richard Hays drew our attention some time ago to the fact that the apostle Paul in Galatians was arguing with his opponents *over a story* (2002, 7). In other words, even though Galatians is in the form of a letter, not a narrative, it has a kind of "narrative substructure" (hence the subtitle of Hays's book: *The Narrative Substructure of Galatians 3:1–4:11*). It references a number of stories from the Jewish Scriptures. The surface structure of Galatians is that of a letter, but it argues over, alludes to, and draws from stories Paul shares in common with his opponents. For example, many suggest that Paul's rather unique allegory about Sarah and Hagar in Gal 4:21–31 was his attempt to give a different interpretation to a passage in Gen 21 that his opponents had first raised themselves in argument against him (e.g., Barrett 1982, 154–70).

Those who have approached biblical texts from the standpoint of story have generally used one or more tools from broader literary criticism. For example, Richard Hays's work built off the structuralist model of A. J. Greimas (1966). Structuralism proceeded from the assumption that all stories have a basic, universal structure, even if not all stories fill in the details for us.[2] A story has an explicit or implied "initial sequence" in which some unfulfilled goal sets up the direction of the plot. A fulfilled "final sequence" would thus ideally see that goal accomplished. In between are any number of "topical sequences" in which the plot advances or at least moves.

It is perhaps not too surprising that structuralist approaches to biblical narratives were neither long-lived nor widely adopted. For one thing, this "actantial model" (conceptualized in terms of opposing forces such as subjects and objects, helpers and opponents, senders and receivers) involved a technical language of its own that was complex and often seemed quite removed from the explicit terms of the very narratives it was used to analyze. Even further, the rise of postmodernism quickly supplanted the structuralist model. Postmodernism eschews any absolute framework in which one might locate truth in general, and the structuralist model is

---

story will inevitably turn out to be another "narrative" of *your* creation (1989, 67). Nevertheless, the notion of an underlying story is a useful heuristic device that we all understand and that helps us say meaningful things about stories and narratives. I will continue to use this language under advisement.

2. Thus most versions of the Cinderella story do not tell much about how she came to live with her stepmother and stepsisters in the first place.

exactly such an approach to stories.[3] Structuralism thus soon yielded to *post*structuralism, an era in which absolute and universal structures are rejected on principle.

Nevertheless, the 1980s saw the rise of a much more user-friendly off-shoot of structuralism in biblical studies: narrative criticism (see Powell 1990). In the 1970s, biblical criticism had already begun to shift from interest in sources and traditions *behind* biblical narratives to the final product of the narratives themselves. If earlier source and form criticism had aimed to unearth hypothetical sources and layers in the development of a narrative, redaction criticism of the 1970s shifted its focus to how the *final product* reflected an editor's intended meaning. We witnessed a trend in the guild of biblical scholarship that seemed to say it was time to focus on the texts we have more than on hypothetical ones we generally do not have. Narrative criticism took this trajectory even one step further by generally ignoring sources altogether and treating biblical narratives as self-contained wholes. To do so, it used familiar language such as "events," "characters," "settings," "point of view," and so forth.

It is no surprise that those interpreters who have drawn on structuralism and narrative criticism have primarily focused on biblical narratives. Apart from generalities, few have followed Hays's example and explored the stories evoked by nonnarrative material. Probably the most notable scholar to use somewhat of a structuralist lens on the New Testament is N. T. Wright. In his multivolume, decades-long project, *Christian Origins and the Question of God*, he has used the actantial model both to propose an overall, underlying story to the New Testament and to analyze biblical stories of much smaller proportion (e.g., Wright 1992, 69–77). I have also used some of the lenses of structuralism and narrative criticism to examine Hebrews in both a monograph (Schenck 2007) and a less technical work (Schenck 2003).

At the same time, some have raised legitimate questions about the kind of use to which individuals such as Wright have put the notion of such underlying stories. For example, Francis Watson has countered that "the Pauline gospel is not in itself a 'story'" and that "what Paul does *not* do is to incorporate his gospel into a linear story of creation and Israel as the end and goal of that story" (2002, 234). He accepts that Paul's theology does

---

3. Thus Jean-François Lyotard defined postmodern as "incredulity toward meta-narratives" (1984, xxiv), by which he meant a rejection of absolute, overarching frameworks that identify fixed and unchanging truth about anything.

have a "narrative substructure" but asserts that "it consists in the scriptural narratives relating to Israel's history with God, whose significance Paul contests with Jewish or Jewish Christian opponents in Romans and Galatians" (232). This counterclaim, along with that of others in the volume *Narrative Dynamics in Paul* (Longenecker 2002), are worth some brief reflection.

On the one hand, we *are* safer to engage the "story world" presupposed by someone like Paul primarily in terms of smaller moments and components of the "plot" rather than on some continuous, all-encompassing story not clearly evoked by an author. One suspects that Wright does at times go too far in how much of his storied reconstructions are truly presupposed by the biblical texts and how much of them are ingenious organizations within his own consciousness. Nevertheless, Watson will almost certainly miss important aspects of Paul's thinking if he truly limits the story substructure of Paul's thoughts to the narratives of the Jewish Scriptures. A key feature of precritical interpretation is that someone like the author of Hebrews sees himself both as part of the world *within* the texts of the Jewish Scriptures at the same time that the world within those texts becomes part of *his* past (Schenck 2009, 323–24).[4] One result is that we will not be able to appreciate Hebrews fully unless we understand the way its author merges the stories within the individual narratives of the Jewish Scriptures with his own story. We must either implicitly or explicitly engage Hebrews with a sense that the situation of the author and audience is, in the author's mind, part of a story that also included Abraham, Moses, and, most importantly, Christ.

In this engagement, the categories of story can serve as very helpful heuristic devices. The core elements of a story are its events, characters, and settings. Together these components constitute a story's plot. Texts that are narrative in form have additional features, such as the "point of view" from which the story is told in the narrative and the distinction between "story time" and "real time."[5] These latter features are less helpful

---

4. I assume here that the author is male because of the masculine singular participle in 11:32.

5. The distinction between "story time" and "real time" has to do with how much time is given over to something in a specific narrative versus how long it would take in real life. Noticeable in the Gospels is the fact that a vastly disproportionate amount of story time is given to Jesus' passion, which only represents a week out of his entire life and ministry. Given our definitions, we might say it is the difference between "narrative time" and "story time."

for us than they might be if we were analyzing a text in the actual form of a narrative.[6] Nevertheless, the rest of this essay will demonstrate how much insight can come from an exploration of Hebrews as a rhetorical re-presentation of a story that the author holds in common with his audience to varying degrees. From one point of view, Hebrews is an argument over the significance of various characters, settings, and events in a common story.

THE RE-PRESENTATION OF EVENTS

The rhetoric of Hebrews references a number of "events" in the story its author presupposes. These range from events in the Jewish Scriptures to events relating to Jesus Christ to events in the life of the audience. As a pre-critical interpreter, the author often does not strongly distinguish between the content of scriptural narratives and the historical past.[7] When he is interpreting in one mode, they are one and the same.[8] Further, he can view a moment in time as an event (e.g., Jesus suffering outside the gate, 13:12), or he can treat a whole sequence of moments as a singular event (e.g., the crucifixion-ascension-entrance of Christ into heaven). Despite the author's flexibility in arguing from the story, these are storied-arguments.[9]

On the one hand, Hebrews is not concerned with a number of events in the plot, even though they would at least hypothetically be part of its story world. Its rhetorical situation—the situation that brought it into existence—did not give rise to extensive discussion of many events about which

---

6. Narrative criticism includes a number of other categories that are of little advantage when looking at stories in relation to nonnarrative material, such as those of narrator, narratee, implied author, and implied reader. For an overview, see Powell 1990.

7. As Hans Frei (1974, 1) put it, such interpretation is "strongly realistic, i.e. at once literal and historical."

8. The author of Hebrews can, of course, interpret in more than one mode. In Schenck 2009 I imply several: (1) uses based on taking biblical texts literally and historically (e.g., quotes from biblical characters, examples of biblical characters); (2) nonliteral interpretations of scriptural events and entities (shadowy exempla, parabolic witnesses); (3) pneumatic reinterpretations of scriptural words (prophetic scripts, words of the Holy Spirit).

9. Watson's objection (2002, 232–34) that Paul does not view the Christ-event from a straightforwardly linear perspective thus proves to have too simplistic a view of story, on the one hand, while overloading Paul's theological perspective with modern profundity, on the other.

the author may very well have had strong opinions. How did humanity come to be enslaved to the one holding the power of death, the devil (2:14)? Did God create the world out of preexisting materials, or did he create it out of nothing (11:3)? Does the future shaking (12:26–27) and rolling up (1:11–12) of the created realm refer to the transformation of the world or to its complete and irrevocable removal? The structuralist model raises these questions, but the text of Hebrews is not particularly concerned to answer them. All we have are hints here and there that seem insufficient in the end to give us definitive answers. Indeed, we cannot know for sure in many cases whether the author himself had thought such things through.

Nevertheless, Hebrews is strongly concerned with the "Christ-event" and with the events currently engaging the audience. Unfortunately, we are left once again with only hints of the audience's situation, not because the author was not interested in them but because they were common knowledge shared between him and his audience. The author had no need to detail them. Further, whatever the audience's uncertainty was about the Christ-event, it also involved a (re)interpretation of earlier events in the Jewish Scriptures. The author responded to the situation of the audience with a thoroughgoing contrast between the event of Christ's atonement, ultimately viewed as a singular event (e.g., 10:14), and all the amalgamated "events" of the Levitical system. The general contours of this contrast are clear, yet how one understands the precise connotations the author invested in these events will depend significantly on one's reconstruction of the audience's situation. Unfortunately, we cannot speak of anything close to a consensus on such matters.

One very common reconstruction of Hebrews' situation pictures a Jewish audience that is waning in its confidence in Jesus as the Son of God (see 3:1; 4:14; 10:23). The reason for their wavering is variously given as anything from incipient persecution to the fatigue of shame from prolonged alienation within society, to the delay of Christ's return. As a result, they are tempted to return to mainstream Judaism and its Levitical means of atonement. Although Hebrews never mentions the Jerusalem temple, the audience would almost certainly have connected Hebrews' use of the wilderness tabernacle to the temple. Many with the "return to mainstream Judaism" view date Hebrews prior to the temple's destruction, where its tabernacle rhetoric would be tantamount to a polemic against the temple. In this case Hebrews would reassure a Jewish audience that mainstream Judaism had nothing to offer them that was not more perfectly available through Christ.

I have a quite different reconstruction. If we date Hebrews to the time after the temple's destruction, it becomes less a polemic against the temple and more of a consolation in its absence. Acts seems to imply that many Jesus-followers did not understand his death to nullify participation in the Jerusalem temple (e.g., Acts 21:20–26). Whether the audience consisted of Christian Jews, Gentiles, or a mix, the destruction of the temple might easily have troubled the faith of such individuals. For Gentile believers whose very introduction to Judaism came by way of Christian Judaism, the temple's destruction might call into question their entire Christian-Jewish faith, which they would have experienced as of one piece. In this way, the temple's destruction might call into question not only their faith in Christ but their faith in the "living God" of the Jews himself (3:12). Hebrews would reassure them that the temple's destruction did not nullify their faith but that in fact Levitical atonement was never necessary in the first place.

Whichever of these—or some other reconstruction—is the correct backdrop to Hebrews' rhetoric, the author's perception of the audience's situation leads him to re-present the events of the story he holds in common with the audience. They, whatever the precise reasons, view the Levitical cultus as significant in the formula of their atonement. The author's response is sweeping and brilliant. It involves a radical reinterpretation of key events in the common Christian-Jewish story. In particular, the author took the Levitical cultus of the Jewish Scriptures, the sacrificial system of Israel, and transformed it from a perpetual institution into only the first "act" of a drama, with Christ's atonement as the key event of the second act.

The establishment of the Levitical cultus in the Jewish Scriptures was clearly an identity-expressing story for many Jews at the time of Christ. At the same time, it is quite possible that they experienced the Levitical cultus less as part of a story and more as an assumed institution. For Jews in Judea and Palestine, it served as an essential embodiment of their understanding of the world, of Yahweh's relationship with Israel and the Jews.[10] For Diaspora Jews, it probably played varying roles of prominence, with some valuing it just as much as those in Judea and others finding it relatively tangential to their existence. The Jewish thinker Philo, who lived

---

10. See Philo's description of the willingness of Jews in Palestine to die in defense of the temple in *Legat.* 212.

in the Egyptian city of Alexandria, provides a good test case because he clearly valued the Jerusalem temple personally at the same time that he considered its significance almost entirely symbolic.[11]

The author of Hebrews, however, undermines the given status of the temple as an institution by re-presenting the story of God's people. He heightens the narrative dimension of the temple's significance by linking it with a former time (Heb 1:1) and an age that has become outdated and near disappearance (8:13). He retells the story so that the earthly sanctuary of Israel was always symbolic and destined to be "removed" later in the story (9:8–9). It only foreshadowed the one-time "sacrifice" of Jesus (10:9, 14). The inauguration of the wilderness sanctuary was an event in Israel's story that, if invoked by Jews, gave the etiology of an institution they assumed as part of their identity (see Exod 40). For Hebrews, this event became only the inauguration of a *first* covenant, which in reality was never able to take away sins (e.g., Heb 10:11). It only anticipated in a shadowy, illustrative way that a later event would take place in which Jesus inaugurated the true tent in heaven (9:18–24; 8:2).[12] This rhetorical shift is a dramatic re-presentation of an event in Israel's story, and the author does so in order to move the audience in a particular direction.

The inauguration of the wilderness sanctuary, however, was not the only event the author thus re-presented. The author re-presented *all* the Levitical events of what had become for him the former age. It is all the different types of Levitical sacrifices *taken together as a whole* that correspond to the singular sacrifice of Jesus. The author contrasts with Christ not only the inauguration of the wilderness tabernacle but the Day of Atonement sacrifice once a year (e.g., Heb 9:7, 12); the use of the ashes of a red heifer, hyssop, and scarlet wool in skin cleansing (9:13, 19; cf. Num 19:6, 9); the daily sacrifices at morning and evening (Heb 9:6); and indeed *all* the sacrifices of the "first" covenant (see 10:1). For the author, the Jewish law was enacted on the basis of the Levitical system, with the result that a change in priesthood implied a change in the entire system (see 7:11–12).

---

11. For the tension in Philo's thought, compare *Somn.* 2.250 with his pilgrimage to the temple (*Prov.* 2.64) and his horror at the Roman emperor Caligula's attempt to set up a statue of himself there (*Legat.* 189–190).

12. I have argued elsewhere that the Platonic-sounding translation "copy and shadow" is almost certainly a mistranslation of Heb 8:5 and 9:23 (e.g., Schenck 2007, 165–68). "Shadowy illustration" is much more likely.

Without question, the most important event of all for the rhetoric of Hebrews is what we might call the "Christ-event" of atonement and exaltation. We can distinguish several moments in this "event" that can be viewed either separately or together in the author's argument. Although some have argued over the precise moment of atonement in Hebrews' thought, to do so is probably to miss the free-flowing movement from quasi-literal to metaphorical in the author's thinking. Is the event of atonement Jesus' death on the cross (e.g., 9:27–28), or is it his entrance into heaven itself (9:24)? The answer is probably both, but on different levels. The literal event that the earliest believers related to an atoning sacrifice was the death of Jesus on a cross (see Rom 3:25). However, the earliest Christians also believed that the resurrected Jesus had gone to God's right hand, implying in their cosmology an ascension through the various layers of sky to the highest heaven.

Hebrews ingeniously re-presents this sequence of moments/events with its metaphor of entrance into a heavenly sanctuary. Christ's death on the cross is variously the moment of atonement (as in the inherited traditions of author and audience) as well as something like the sacrifice in the courtyard of the sanctuary on earth, whose blood might then be taken into the innermost sanctum of the sanctuary proper in heaven.[13] Christ's ascension through the skies and sitting at God's right hand (e.g., Heb 4:14) becomes something like the passage of a high priest through the rooms of the sanctuary into its Most Holy Place (e.g., 9:24). It would be inappropriate to try to harmonize all these images into a single picture because they involve varying layers of metaphor that do not fit tidily together. The main point is to say that recent events relating to Christ's death and resurrection have once and for all fulfilled the intended purpose of the entire Levitical system.

The nature of Hebrews' argument thus accentuates the storied dimension of the Levitical system within the broader story of God's people. Events form the backbone of a plot, and the events of greatest import to Hebrews' rhetoric are the Christ-event of atonement and the amalgamated Levitical events of foreshadowing in Israel's past. The purpose of Hebrews' re-presenting of such events is to lead to an "event" of recommitment to the Christian confession in the present of the audience. This "word of

---

13. Although, reflective of the metaphorical nature of this argument, Hebrews never exactly says that Christ took his blood into heaven (see below).

exhortation" is not entirely clear about the situation of the audience, but it is quite possible that various events (or lack of events) in their environment are also currently under interpretation. Perhaps they are trying to interpret whether the destruction of the Jerusalem temple implies that the entire Christian-Jewish story is faulty, or perhaps they are concerned with the delay of Christ's return and vindication of the Christian message. Whatever the situation, Hebrews significantly involves the re-presentation of events in the story of God's people to address its context.

THE RE-PRESENTATION OF CHARACTERS

Just as Hebrews re-presents the events of the story the author and his audience hold in common, it also re-presents the characters in the plot of which they are a part. Once again, the focal point of the retelling has to do with Christ. The audience has believed that Jesus is the Son of God, the Messiah, for some time (e.g., 10:32–34). However, the author of Hebrews now introduces a new characterization of Christ: his identity as a priest and high priest. Indeed, Hebrews recasts him as the *only* truly effective high priest in their common story. It is possible that some other early Christian might have thought of Jesus in priestly terms (see Rom 8:34), but we have no other explicit statement to that effect in the rest of the New Testament and not even a potential allusion to Christ as *high* priest.

This additional characterization of Christ entails a re-presentation of all earlier priests in the story. In fact, it requires a fundamentally new category of priesthood, which the author ingeniously draws from the story of Melchizedek in Gen 14. All the earlier priests, the author argues, were ineffective not only because they were handicapped by their own sin (7:27–28) but because, perhaps as a consequence, they always died and were unable to continue in office (e.g., 7:23–24). Just as the sacrificial events they performed were not truly able to take away sins (e.g., 10:4), their priesthoods were not effective in what some assumed they accomplished. In the end, they were Levitical priests participating in the Levitical system, which was only a shadowy example meant to point toward the true priesthood of Christ (e.g., 8:5).

The author thus pits the Levitical priesthood against a different order of priesthood, a Melchizedekian priesthood modeled on the story of Melchizedek in Gen 14. Hebrews' engagement with Melchizedek does make recourse to the story of Genesis, but the author is arguably less interested in Melchizedek as a character in the overall story of God's people than in the way in which the text of Gen 14 might allegorically and exegetically shed light on what a "priest after the order of Melchizedek" might be in Ps 110:4. The earliest Christians took Ps 110:1 messianically, as a statement about the fact that God would exalt the Messiah and enthrone the Messiah on his right hand in heaven. The author of Hebrews pursued this interpretation on into Ps 110:4 and understood it to say that God would make the Messiah a "priest after the order of Melchizedek." What would such a priest be like? To answer this question, Hebrews turned to the only other text in the Jewish Scriptures to mention Melchizedek: Gen 14.

While Christian tradition often viewed Melchizedek as a christophany (a cameo of Jesus in the "Old Testament") and some modern interpreters see Melchizedek as an exalted, angel-like figure (as Eric F. Mason argues elsewhere in this volume), I think the best understanding of Heb 7 is to see the author making a *non in thora non in mundo* argument ("not in the Torah, not in the world"). This was a Jewish exegetical technique that, for interpretive purposes, treats the silence of a biblical text as an indication that something does not exist. So Gen 14 does not mention the father, mother, or priestly genealogy of Melchizedek (see Heb 7:4) or a time when Melchizedek became a priest or stopped being one. For interpretive purposes, therefore, the author of Hebrews could conclude that a priest after the order of Melchizedek was a priest who did not have a priestly genealogy and who continued in office forever. The author thus used the Genesis text to delineate exactly what a priest after the order of Melchizedek was like and thus to characterize Jesus as a priest. Jesus as Messiah did not need to have a priestly genealogy to be a priest because he belonged to a different, special kind of priesthood. He was a priest after the order of Melchizedek.

By placing Christ in a different order of priesthood from Levitical priests, the author was able to pit Christ against the entirety of the Levitical priesthood and all the Levitical priests from Aaron to his day. He suggests that the Jewish law was put into effect on the basis of the Levitical priesthood (7:11). The arrival of a priest after the order of Melchizedek thus implied a change in law and priestly system (7:12). Such is the case because the Melchizedekian priesthood is superior to the Levitical priesthood, a point the author argues from the story of Melchizedek in Gen 14. Abraham gave tithes to Melchizedek, and Melchizedek blessed Abraham (7:6–7). In both instances Melchizedek takes the role with superior status to Abraham. Since Levi, as it were, was in Abraham's loins at the time, we see that a priest like Melchizedek is superior to a priest like Levi. The author thus makes his rhetorical point in part based on the way he characterizes various individuals in the story of God's people. (See also the discussion of this passage in the essay by David M. Moffitt.)

As with the Christ-event, however, the author's characterization of Jesus is not limited to just one picture or metaphor. It does not end with the contrast between Levi and Melchizedek. Psalm 110:4 only says that Christ is a *priest* after the order of Melchizedek. Hebrews goes one step further to consider Christ a *high* priest. In Heb 5, Jesus' appointment as high priest is cast in terms analogous to the appointment of earthly high priests. Then in Heb 9 the entrance of the high priest once a year into the innermost sanctum of the earthly sanctuary is compared to Christ's one-time entrance into heaven itself. The Day of Atonement is clearly in view.

This characterization of Jesus as the reality to which all Levitical priests correspond extends to other characters in the story of the Jewish law as well. Moses, for example, was the mediator through whom the law was delivered to Israel on Mount Sinai. The author thus regularly contrasts Jesus and his covenant with Moses and his covenant. Those who disobeyed the law of Moses received a stern punishment. Those who rejected the law of Moses died without mercy (10:28). So how will the author and audience escape punishment if they ignore the message of Jesus (2:3)? What do you think, the author asks, will be the consequence for those who trample the Son of God (10:29)? In the end, Moses was only a *servant* in God's house (3:5). Jesus, on the other hand, is a *Son* (3:6). His prominence is as much greater than Moses as the builder of the house is greater than the house (3:3).

Angels were also associated with the giving of the law in Second Temple Judaism (see 2:2; elsewhere in the New Testament at Acts 7:53 and Gal 3:19). It is thus perhaps no surprise that Hebrews also contrasts Christ with them. If the angels are the heavenly administrators of the earth and Israel under the old covenant, then Christ has displaced them from this role. In the current age, they are "ministering spirits sent for ministry to those about to inherit salvation" (1:14). As Christ is enthroned at God's right hand, therefore, their role as administrators of the cosmos begins to decline and will eventually end, allowing them to dedicate their time to praising God (see 12:22). Jesus became lower than them for a little while (2:9) but has now been enthroned as divine Son, a title and role much greater than theirs (1:4). I have argued elsewhere that the entirety of Heb 1:5–14 should be read as a kind of celebration of the enthronement of Christ on his cosmic throne at the point of his exaltation (Schenck 2001).

Hebrews also invokes many other characters from scriptural stories it shares in common with the audience. The author's division of history into two ages, the one before Christ and the other inaugurated by Christ, connects these individual stories from the Jewish Scriptures into one overarching story with characters in the old age and characters in the new. In the old age are examples of faith and endurance, as well as examples of disbelief (Schenck 2003, 56–70). The wilderness generation and Esau constitute the key examples of disbelief the author presents. The audience does not want to model itself after them. The wilderness generation, which we can conceptualize as a single character in the plot, did not enter the promised land. Although they left Egypt, their corpses fell in the desert (3:16–17). The audience is also a character in the story. Even though they have embarked on the Christian journey, they will not arrive at their heavenly destination if they do not continue in faith (see 12:16).

Esau similarly represents someone who was a firstborn son, like the audience. Nevertheless, he sold his birthright for food (12:16). Later he was not able to find a place of repentance and did not inherit the blessing, even though he apparently desired to reverse his course (12:17). These two "characters" from the first age stand as poignant examples after which the audience must not model itself. They, too, have experienced the Holy Spirit (6:4) and have been sanctified, made pure by the blood of Christ (10:29). If they were to "trample the Son of God under foot" and insult the Spirit of grace by denying their confession and apostatizing (10:29), they would use up Christ's sacrifice (10:26) and fall away with no hope of repentance (6:4–6), just like Esau.

Other examples from the Jewish Scriptures model a more positive course of action. The "cloud of witnesses" in Heb 11 does not simply consist of random examples of faith and endurance. The author has chosen them carefully with a view to the kinds of character traits the audience should have in similar circumstances, and these exempla presumably contain clues to the audience's situation. Some of the examples have to do with alienation while living in a foreign country. Abraham continues in faith even though he is a stranger in the land (11:9). In the longest aside of the chapter, the author points to a heavenly homeland as the audience's true point of focus (11:14–16). Abraham's attitude in an earlier part of the story thus serves as a model for the audience, whether they are in a position of shame in their current location, are experiencing the shame of Jerusalem's recent destruction (see also 13:14), or both.

Some examples have to do with trusting God even though one cannot yet see the promise. So the author believes that God did not create the cosmos out of visible materials but out of things that our senses could not detect (11:3). Noah constructed an ark when no rain was in sight (11:7). Other examples have to do with impending persecution and even death, particularly at the hands of a hostile power. Moses is faithful despite the edict of the king (11:23). Abel was faithful even though it brought him death (11:4). Others, like Enoch, were rescued from death (11:5). These examples bespeak of a situation in which the audience fears impending persecution from the ruling powers in their location. They are based on the characterization of various key figures from the story of God's people.

One of the most intriguing characters in Hebrews' story world is none other than the earthly Jesus himself.[14] The author holds up the preexalted Jesus as an example of someone who faithfully endured suffering (e.g., 12:2) and of a son who learned obedience to his father through discipline (e.g., 5:8). This characterization of Jesus in particular was meant to show the audience that, even though they were the children of God, they would still have to endure the discipline of their father, God (see 12:7). God is, of course, the most central character of all in the plot, the one who binds the former age with the new one, the one who has spoken and continues to speak. He is the one who created the world "through" Christ (1:2) and the one who will finally shake the created realm (12:25–29).

What we see is that, even more so than Paul, the author of Hebrews connects its audience with the events and characters of the past in such a way that an overall story is created. Paul's Adam-Christ typology has this effect on a smaller scale, but the all-encompassing nature of Hebrews' contrast between old covenant and new has the effect of recasting all the individual stories of the Jewish Scripture into a narrative whose primary nature is to anticipate the Christ-event and its consequent age. With regard to the characters of Scripture, they all die in faithfulness without ever receiving the promise they were awaiting (11:39). Only after the Christ-event could they be "perfected" (11:40), truly cleansed of their sins (see 10:1–2).

---

14. Obviously, the author considered the earthly Jesus as the same individual as the exalted Christ, but it is fascinating that the characterization of each stage of Jesus' existence is somewhat distinct.

The Re-presentation of Settings

The settings of a plot can be both spatial and temporal, as well as abstract. The settings in time have to do with when events take place, and we have already discussed indirectly the author's re-presentation of time into two ages. His argument extensively divided the story of God's people into the period that preceded Christ and the age of the new covenant that Christ himself inaugurated. The audience had no doubt inherited this "before and after" distinction long before they first heard Hebrews read to them.[15] Nevertheless, the argument of Hebrews would have considerably sharpened the break and contrast between the former times and "these last days" (1:2), a phrase that echoed the new covenant promises of Jer 31 and signaled that the audience was living in the final age of the earthly story.

As far as settings in space, the author and audience shared in common a sense of many spatial settings in the story under discussion. They both lived on earth and had a concept of heaven, as well as locations such as the wilderness tabernacle, the cross, and the Jerusalem temple. Nevertheless, Hebrews re-presents the nature of these settings in ways that likely differed from the way the audience had previously understood them, perhaps quite significantly in some instances. Whether the Jerusalem temple was still standing or destroyed at the time of writing, the argument of Hebrews would have evoked it in thought and would have recast its significance in quite dramatic terms. The author of Hebrews also increased the scope of Jesus' death on the cross. The death of Jesus was no doubt quite significant to the audience prior to Hebrews, but in the argument of Hebrews it becomes the place of atonement for all time, past and present.[16]

I wonder, however, if the most striking re-presentation of the settings of the story has to do with the nature of heaven and earth for the author. For the apostle Paul, the creation is currently enslaved to the power of corruption but will be redeemed from its enslavement (e.g., Rom 8:20–21) at the same time that the bodies of believers are also redeemed and glorified (8:23). If the author of Hebrews had such a view, he nowhere makes it clear. Strikingly, he speaks rather in terms of the *removal* of the created

---

15. In an oral culture, most of the audience would be illiterate, and an author would write a document such as Hebrews with the expectation that it would be read aloud to an assembly of believers.

16. Although not clearly for all time future, since Jesus' sacrifice for sins does not seem limitless in scope to cover all the *future* sins of the audience (see 10:26).

realm (Heb 12:27) and God rolling it up like a piece of clothing (1:12). The heaven/earth, spirit/body contrast is much starker, much more dichotomous than in Paul, even though Paul also at times uses dualistic language. The homeland that the faithful are seeking is not a new earth but a *heavenly* homeland (11:16), while they are strangers on the earth (11:13).

Although the metaphor of Christ's high priesthood points toward him taking his blood into heaven, Hebrews always seems to fall just shy of saying so. True, 9:12 does speak of Christ entering into the heavenly holies "through his own blood," but the parallel is not one of location but of means. It was not "through the blood of goats and bulls but through his own blood." The author's point is not that Christ took his blood into heaven but that it was *by means of* his blood that atonement took place. Indeed, Christ's offering in 9:14 is said to be "through eternal spirit," which could refer to the Holy Spirit but might just as well be a reference to Christ's spirit. In my opinion, it would not really fit the author's cosmology to think of blood entering the heavenly realm, the realm of spirit.

A good number of interpreters have argued over the years that the author was in some way indebted to "Middle Platonism" and its view of reality (see Schenck 2002, 112–35, and the essay by James W. Thompson in this volume). In my opinion, however, such indebtedness is best seen not in terms of the author's use of terms such as *shadow* (8:5; 10:1) or *image* (10:1), let alone what I take to be the mistaken translation of "copy" in 8:5 and 9:23. Rather, it is in the stark dichotomy the author makes between heaven and earth, spirit and body. Heaven is the place of the "*spirits* of the perfected righteous" (12:23). God is the father of *spirits* (12:9). Angels are "ministering *spirits*" (1:14), and Christ makes his offering through an/the eternal *spirit* (9:14). Interestingly, Hebrews has almost nothing to say of the resurrection of Jesus proper and focuses instead on his exaltation to God's right hand. It uses curious wording when it actually alludes to the resurrection, using spatial language: God "brought up" the great shepherd of the sheep from the dead.[17]

In the end, Hebrews does not provide us with enough evidence to speak definitively of the precise nature of its re-presentation of heaven and earth as settings in the plot of salvation's story. It nevertheless has a unique flavor that hints of some reinterpretation. The author agrees with

---

17. The use of *nekros* for "dead," however, is often taken to imply the reembodiment of corpses (see also 6:1).

the audience's sense of alienation, whatever its precise cause. Yet his interpretation of the earthly setting is intrinsically as a place of alienation. Of
course one will feel like an alien and stranger on the earth, for we are
seeking a heavenly homeland and have no city here on earth that will
remain permanently (13:14), just as those priests who minister on earth
can have no permanent or effective priesthood (see 8:5).

HEBREWS' POINT OF VIEW

Hebrews' re-presentation of the story of God's people is sweeping and ingenious. We cannot know for sure the precise nature of the audience's situation, but they are clearly wavering to some degree in their commitment
to the Christian confession. They may perceive themselves to be facing
hardship of some kind, and they may be suffering from the fatigue of long-
term social disgrace and shame. In some way, the question of atonement
plays into their situation. The key point of Hebrews' teaching is the effectiveness of Christ's sacrifice and high priesthood (e.g., 8:1), and the point
that sparks off the most vigorous and direct critique from the author is the
Melchizedekian priesthood of Christ (see 5:10–11). These are the kinds of
factors that gave rise to the writing of Hebrews as a word of exhortation to
the audience.

In response, the author builds on the audience's current understanding and common Christian traditions and re-presents them in
striking terms. Earlier Christian tradition viewed Jesus' death as a sacrifice offered by God in atonement for God's people (e.g., Rom 3:25).
Earlier Christian tradition believed that God had enthroned Jesus at his
right hand as cosmic Lord at the point of his resurrection (e.g., Acts 2:32–
35; Rom 10:9). Also well known was the idea that the earthly sanctuary
symbolized and corresponded to a kind of heavenly sanctuary in whose
innermost sanctum God dwelt (e.g., Philo, *Mos.* 2.88; Josephus, *Ant.*
3.180–181). These, along with the scattered stories of God's people in the
Jewish Scriptures, provided the author with the building blocks he would
use to re-present the story as one overarching drama.

Christ, the hero of the story, has brought about the climax of the plot.
True, the story has not yet ended. As the audience recognized all too well,
they were still waiting on some key events that would play out the significance of the Christ-event. They also were characters in the plot, along with
characters from the first act of the drama, such as Abel, Abraham, Moses,
and David. Nevertheless, the Christ-event of atonement had brought

about a turning point in the story more sweeping than the audience had understood up to that point. He had divided the plot into two parts. The first part involved a "former" temporal setting (1:1). It was a time of anticipation. It was a time in which prophets looked forward and Moses witnessed to things "about to be spoken" (3:5). It was a time when priests in their earthly setting offered sacrifices that could not actually take away sins. They were only shadowy illustrations of what was to come.

Christ thus fulfilled all those expectations and inaugurated a new covenant and a new age. His sacrifice was a superior sacrifice to theirs, offered through an eternal spirit. He was a greater high priest than any prior priest, from a greater order of priests. He was a priest after the order of Melchizedek. With the arrival of a priest in this order, the order of Levi and Aaron was replaced. Finally, this superior priest offered his superior sacrifice in a superior sanctuary, in fact, the true tent that the wilderness tabernacle only symbolized. Christ's ascension through the skies/heavens to the throne of God in the highest sky/heaven was the entrance of this heavenly high priest into the true sanctuary and Most Holy Place, the highest heaven itself where God dwells. The author thus connected what might otherwise have been individual stories into a single, overarching story, and by making Christ's sacrifice, priesthood, and sanctuary the definitive ones, he rhetorically eliminated the need of the audience for any other earthly sacrifice, priest, or sanctuary.

THE THEOLOGY OF THE EPISTLE TO THE HEBREWS

Frank J. Matera

The task of New Testament theology is to provide a thick and rich description of the theology in the New Testament so that what was written in the past will have meaning and relevance for the future (Schnelle 2009, 25). This, of course, is a difficult task, since the diverse writings of the New Testament were not composed as theological treatises. Written by believers for believers, these writings primarily sought to strengthen and exhort the early Christian community to persevere in its faith. As we shall see, this is especially true for the Epistle to the Hebrews, which describes itself as a "word of exhortation" (13:22 NRSV).

Although their primary goal was to exhort and encourage, the writers of the New Testament also found it necessary to remind believers of the content of the faith they had embraced. Consequently, in addition to exhorting, they describe the person and work of Jesus, what theology calls Christology (the study of the person of Christ) and soteriology (the study of the salvation Christ brings). Moreover, since the New Testament writers sought to sustain believers in their faith, they reminded them of their identity in Christ and of the final salvation for which they were still striving, what theology calls ecclesiology (the study of the church) and eschatology (the study of the last things). Although the New Testament writers did not write theological essays, then, they did discuss issues that became the subject of theological discourse. This suggests that, even though the writings of the New Testament do not employ the terms Christology, soteriology, ecclesiology, and eschatology, these theological categories can be helpful for analyzing the religious thought of the New Testament, provided we remember the purpose and nature of the material we are studying.

GETTING AT THE THEOLOGY OF HEBREWS

Hebrews is an especially rich document for those engaged in New Testament theology, and those who embark upon a study of this great writing will do well to consult the ways in which monographs, introductions to the New Testament, and New Testament theologies have summarized its theology (Holladay 2005; Lindars 1991; Marshall 2004; Matera 2007; Schnelle 2009; Strecker 2000; Thielman 2005; Witherington 2009). Although anonymous, its author is one of the great religious thinkers of the New Testament, being on a par with Paul and John. Providing its audience with the most systematic presentation of the person and work of Jesus in the New Testament, Hebrews engages in a creative and insightful christological exegesis of Israel's Scriptures that allows us to see how it generates its theology.

The rich theology of Hebrews, however, is not without its problems. First, although it presents Christ as the Son of God, Hebrews is the only New Testament writing to portray him as a high priest according to the order of Melchizedek. Second, although Hebrews has a great deal to say about the death of Christ, apart from a few texts it rarely speaks of his resurrection (6:2; 7:16; 13:20) and parousia (9:28, 10:37). Finally, although Hebrews appears to be a sustained reflection on the person and work of Christ, it describes itself as a "word of exhortation" (13:22).

As a word of exhortation, Hebrews tends to alternate between "exposition" and "exhortation." In its exposition, it develops a theology of Jesus, the Son of God, a high priest according to the order of Melchizedek, whose self-sacrifice establishes a new covenant that results in the forgiveness of sins once and for all. In its exhortations, it calls upon its audience to pay careful attention to the word spoken through the Son and follow the faithful example of Jesus so that they may enter God's Sabbath rest. The manner in which Hebrews juxtaposes exposition and exhortation is illustrated in the diagram on page 191.

This simplified diagram is *not* an outline of Hebrews, nor does it pretend to uncover the deep structure of this complicated text, which has been thoroughly analyzed by Albert Vanhoye (1976), George H. Guthrie (1994), and others. Rather, its purpose is to highlight the rhetorical role that the juxtaposition of exposition and exhortation plays in this writing.

This juxtaposition can be interpreted in two ways: (1) Hebrews is primarily a doctrinal exposition of Christ's person and work that makes use of exhortation to relieve what would otherwise be a ponderous presentation;

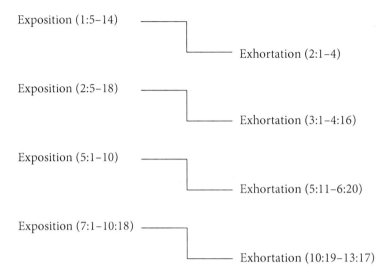

Exposition (1:5–14) ——— Exhortation (2:1–4)

Exposition (2:5–18) ——— Exhortation (3:1–4:16)

Exposition (5:1–10) ——— Exhortation (5:11–6:20)

Exposition (7:1–10:18) ——— Exhortation (10:19–13:17)

(2) Hebrews is primarily an exhortation that derives its power from its exposition of Christ's person and work. Although arguments have been made for both approaches, Hebrews' description of itself as a "word of exhortation" (13:22) indicates that its primary goal is moral exhortation. Consequently, its doctrinal exposition is at the service of its moral exhortation, thereby suggesting that Hebrews theologizes with a view to the needs of its audience.

The remainder of this essay proceeds in three steps. First, I will consider the doctrinal exposition of Hebrews in order to summarize what it says about the person and work of Christ. In doing so, my focus will be on Christology and soteriology. Second, I will turn to the moral exhortation of Hebrews in order to illustrate what it says about its audience and their hope for the future. Here I will concern myself with issues of ecclesiology and eschatology. Third, I will consider the significance of Hebrews' theology for contemporary Christian faith and theology.

Doctrinal Exposition

Christology and soteriology stand at the heart of New Testament theology. Without a vibrant Christology and soteriology, there would be no ecclesiology or eschatology. The church, after all, views itself as the community of those who confess Jesus Christ as their Lord and Savior, the one who rescued them from the powers of sin and death. Redeemed and sanctified by Christ, this community waits in hope for the fulfillment of the salvation Christ has inaugurated. Consequently, ecclesiology and eschatology begin with an understanding of Christ and the benefits of his saving death and resurrection. It is not surprising, then, that Hebrews devotes its doctrinal expositions to the person and work of Christ. What is surprising is the manner in which it presents Christ and his redemptive work (on the soteriology of Hebrews, see Koester 2005 and Marshall 2009).

Since this essay is concerned with the theology of Hebrews, it will be helpful to read its four doctrinal expositions apart from their intervening moral exhortations (as does Guthrie 1994, 116–27) in order to appreciate how it develops the Christology and soteriology that will support its moral exhortation.

The first two expositions explain why the Son, who is superior to the angels, was made lower than the angels in order to rescue humanity from death (1:5–14; 2:5–18). Here the focus is on what later theology calls the incarnation. The second two expositions explain how the Son was designated a priest and offered himself in sacrifice to establish a new covenant for the forgiveness of sins once and for all (5:1–10; 7:1–10:18). Here the focus is on what theology calls the redemption. Thus the overall movement of these two expositions can be summarized in this way: the eternal Son of God became lower than the angels (the incarnation) in order to become a high priest who could atone for the sins of his brothers and sisters once and for all (the redemption).

THE SON OF GOD WHO BECAME LOWER THAN THE ANGELS

Hebrews prefaces its presentation with a brief *exordium* (1:1–4) that introduces the central themes it will develop (see Webster 2009). First, whereas God previously spoke "in many and various ways" through the prophets, "in these last days" God has spoken through a Son. Second, the Son, who has inherited all things, is the one through whom God created the world. As the reflection of God's glory and the very imprint of God's being, the Son sustains the world. Third, the Son has made purification for sins and now sits at God's right hand. Fourth, the Son is as superior to the angels as the name he inherited is superior to their name. At the outset of Hebrews, then, there is no doubt about the exalted status of the Son and the new circumstances in which the audience finds itself. The audience is living in the final age of redemptive history, what Hebrews calls "these last days" (1:2). This has come about because the one whom they confess is the preexistent Son of God, who, having carried out the redemptive work of purification, now sits at God's right hand.

Superior to the Angels

The final words of the *exordium* announce the theme that Hebrews will develop in its exposition. Having explained the superiority of the Son to the angels, Hebrews employs a chain of scriptural quotations in 1:5–14 to confirm its claim. The manner in which it introduces these quotations ("For to which of the angels did God ever say" ... "Of the angels he says" ... "But of the Son he says" ... "But to which of the angels has he ever said...?" [NRSV]) indicates that the purpose of these citations is to establish the Son's superiority to the angels.

In these quotations Hebrews provides us with an important insight to its theological and exegetical method: it will read Israel's Scriptures christologically as the living Word of God. Accordingly, Hebrews portrays God as speaking to the Son, even though these quotations had a different meaning in their original historical setting. For example, Ps 2, from which the first quotation is taken, is a royal psalm in which God addresses the newly anointed Israelite king as his adopted son. Hebrews, however, reads the psalm christologically as God's word to the eternal Son: "For to which of the angels did God ever say, 'You are my Son: today I have begotten you?'" (1:5a). A similar phenomenon occurs in the second quotation, which is taken from Nathan's oracle to David (2 Sam 7:14). Originally addressed to David, Hebrews reads it as God's word about the Son: "Or again, 'I will be his Father, and he will be my Son'" (1:5b).

The boldest use of Scripture, however, occurs in the fifth and sixth quotations (1:8–9), which are taken from Pss 45 and 102, respectively. Although these texts were originally addressed to God, Hebrews reads them as God's word to the Son. In them, God addresses the Son as "God": "Your throne, O *God*, is forever and ever" (1:8), "therefore *God*, your God, has anointed you." In yet another quotation, God says of the Son, "In the beginning, *Lord*, you founded the earth, and the heavens are the work of your hand" (1:10). If we ask how Hebrews can read Scripture is such a bold and creative way, the answer is the Christology of its *exordium*. Since the Son is the reflection of God's glory and the exact imprint of God's being, Hebrews can portray God as addressing the Son as "God."

Lower Than the Angels

Having established the superiority of the Son through this christological exegesis, in the second exposition (2:5–18) Hebrews turns its attention to the abasement of the Son. The exposition begins with a quotation from Ps 8, which points to the destiny God envisions for humanity. According to the psalm, humanity will be crowned with glory and honor, and all things will be put under its feet. Although humanity has not yet attained this goal, one human being has: Jesus, "who for a little while was made lower than the angels" and is now "crowned with glory and honor" (2:9). It is at this point that Hebrews introduces its teaching on what later theology calls the incarnation. The Son who is greater than the angels was, for a little while, made lower than the angels, so that "he might taste death for everyone" (2:9). Because Jesus has cleared the path that humanity must trod and reached the goal that humanity must attain, he is "the pioneer of their salvation" (*archēgon tēs soterias autōn*, 2:10). This is why, having shared in the flesh and blood of human beings, he calls them his brothers and sisters (2:11–12).

Toward the end of this exposition, Hebrews explains the reason for the Son's abasement. In order for the Son to destroy the devil (who had the power of death) and to free humanity (which lived in slavery because of its fear of death), it was necessary for the Son to share in the human condition so that he could become "a merciful and faithful high priest … to make a sacrifice of atonement for the sins of the people" (*eis to hilaskesthai tas hamartias tou laou*, 2:17).

With these words Hebrews explicitly introduces the theme of priesthood for the first time. In doing so, it provides its audience with a way to understand the purpose of the incarnation: the Son of God became human in order to be a merciful and faithful high priest who could atone for the sins of the people. For, even though he was the Son of God, he could not be a priest until he shared in the flesh and blood of human beings. This is why it was necessary for the Son, who is superior to the angels, to be made lower than the angels.

The High Priest Who Sacrificed Himself

Having explained that it was necessary for the Son to share in the human situation so that he could become a merciful and faithful high priest, next Hebrews takes up the task of describing the nature of Jesus' priesthood and the significance of his redemptive work. To accomplish this, it provides its audience with two doctrinal expositions (5:1–10; 7:1–10:18). The first and the shortest (5:1–10) identifies Jesus as a "high priest according to the order of Melchizedek" (5:10). The second and longer one explains the superior nature of Jesus' priesthood to the Levitical priesthood (7:1–28) before considering the meaning and significance of the Son's priestly sacrifice (8:1–10:18).

Appointed a High Priest

Hebrews faces a seemingly insurmountable task. Although it has called Jesus a merciful and faithful high priest (2:17), and although it has affirmed that "we have a great high priest who has passed through the heavens" (4:14), Jesus was not qualified to be a priest according to the Mosaic law, since he was not a member of the tribe of Levi. Consequently, Hebrews must explain how and why it can call Jesus a high priest (5:1–11).

To address this problem, Hebrews reminds its audience that one must be called by God to be a high priest, as was Aaron (5:4). Next Hebrews makes its most creative exegetical move. Drawing upon Ps 110, which had already played a central role in the early church's understanding of Jesus' exaltation, Hebrews quotes the fourth verse of the psalm, "You are a priest forever, according to the order of Melchizedek." By extending the reading of this psalm to verse 4, Hebrews finds a way to call Jesus a high priest. According to this christological exegesis, the psalm speaks of Jesus' priesthood (Ps 110:4) as well as of his exaltation (110:1). Jesus is qualified to be a high priest because God called him to this office when he said, "You are a priest forever, according to the order of Melchizedek."

The Priesthood of Melchizedek

Identifying Jesus as a high priest according to the order of Melchizedek, however, raises further questions. Who was Melchizedek, and what was the nature of his priesthood? Hebrews addresses these questions in chapter 7. The discussion begins by recounting the story of Melchizedek and Abraham found in Gen 14. Noting that Scripture says nothing of Melchizedek's parents or genealogy, Hebrews concludes that Melchizedek is eternal like the Son of God and that his priesthood remains forever (7:3). Observing that Abraham paid tithes to Melchizedek, Hebrews identifies Melchizedek as the greater of the two. Finally, since Abraham is the ancestor of Levi,

Hebrews playfully asserts that Levi himself (the ancestor of the Levitical priesthood) paid tithes to Melchizedek through Abraham (7:9).

The appearance of this other priesthood (which had been dormant until the appearance of God's Son) calls into question the need for, and the effectiveness of, the Levitical priesthood. For if the Levitical priesthood could have brought its adherents to their goal, there would have been no need for a priesthood according to the order of Melchizedek. Contrasting these two priesthoods, Hebrews observes that, whereas the Levitical priests were designated priests through a law of physical descent, Jesus became a priest "through the power of an indestructible life" (7:16), namely, resurrection from the dead. Furthermore, whereas there were numerous priests because death prevented them from serving forever, Jesus' priesthood remains forever (7:23–24). Finally, whereas the law appoints priests who are subject to weakness, the word of God's oath in Ps 110:4 appoints a Son who is perfect forever (Heb 7:28). There is need for only one priest, then, a high priest according to the order of Melchizedek.[1]

The Son's Priestly Work

Having established that Jesus is a priest according to the order of Melchizedek, Hebrews embarks upon a still more difficult task: it must explain the nature of Jesus' priestly work (8:1–10:18). Aware that Jesus was not qualified to offer gifts as a priest in the earthly sanctuary, which is only "a sketch and a shadow of the heavenly one" (8:5), Hebrews affirms that Jesus has obtained "a more excellent ministry" and become the mediator of a "better covenant" with "better promises" (8:6). It then explains the significance of the Son's priestly work in terms of the new and better covenant that Jesus established by entering the heavenly sanctuary with the offering of his own blood.

Just as Hebrews drew a contrast in chapter 7 between the Levitical priesthood and the high priesthood of Jesus according to the order of Melchizedek, so it draws a contrast in chapter 9 between the earthly sanctuary in which the Levitical high priest ministered and the heavenly sanctuary in which Jesus ministers. Focusing on the ritual of the Day of Atonement (see Lev 16), Hebrews notes that the Levitical high priest entered the most sacred place of the tabernacle, the holy of holies, once a year, with blood, to atone for his sins and the sins of the people (9:7). Hebrews

---

1. For further discussion of the idea of "perfection" in Hebrews, see the essay by Kevin B. McCruden in this volume.

interprets this annual ritual as an indication, given by the Holy Spirit, that the way into the heavenly sanctuary had not yet been disclosed. Furthermore, it sees the repeated nature of this ritual as evidence that the sacrifices offered in the earthly tent could not adequately deal with sin (9:9–10).

In light of this interpretation of the Day of Atonement, Hebrews introduces its understanding of Christ's priestly work. Viewing Christ as a high priest according to the order of Melchizedek, Hebrews presents him as a high priest who entered with his own blood, "once for all into the Holy Place" (9:12), which is heaven itself. Thus whereas the high priest went into the holy of holies of the earthly sanctuary with the blood of animals year after year, Christ entered the heavenly sanctuary with his own blood once and for all. Because of this priestly work, he has become the mediator of a new and better covenant.

Playing on the meaning of *diathēkē*, which can mean "will" as well as "covenant," Hebrews notes that a "will" (*diathēkē*) only goes into effect when the person who made it dies (9:16–17). Thus it was necessary for Christ to die in order to inaugurate the new "covenant" (*diathēkē*). However, since he is a high priest according to the order of Melchizedek who has entered the heavenly sanctuary through his death, there is no need for him to offer sacrifice again and again, as do the high priests of the old covenant, who enter the holy of holies year after year. Having died once and received an indestructible life, this high priest cannot die again.

Before concluding its extended discussion of the Son's priestly work, Hebrews provides its audience with a final reflection on Christ's sacrifice. Engaging in christological exegesis once more, Hebrews reads Ps 40:6–8 as the words of the preexistent Son spoken to God upon entering the world: "Sacrifices and offerings you have not desired, but a body you have prepared for me; in burnt offerings and sin offerings, you have taken no pleasure. Then I said, 'See, God, I have come to do your will, O God'" (10:5–7). Hebrews interprets this quotation in two ways. First, Christ has done away with the need for further sacrifices. Second, by doing God's will, Christ has sanctified humanity once and for all by the sacrifice of himself (10:8–10).

Hebrews concludes its discussion of Christ's priesthood by contrasting Christ and the priests of Levi. Whereas they stand at the altar day by day offering sacrifices that cannot take away sins, Christ sits at the right hand of God, having offered one sacrifice that forever perfects those who are sanctified (10:11–14).

As my colleague John Heil has reminded me, Hebrews reveals its distinctive understanding of Christ's sacrifice and its benefits by explaining how his sacrifice of submitting himself to God's will (10:5–10) has interiorly purified the consciences of those who believe in him. Whereas the Levitical cult offered sacrifices that could not "perfect the conscience of the worshiper" (9:9; see also 10:22), the blood of Christ has purified the consciences of believers so that they can "worship the living God" (9:14). Consequently, Hebrews exhorts its audience to approach God with their "hearts sprinkled clean from an evil conscience" (10:22) so that they can offer "a sacrifice of praise to God, that is, the fruit of lips that confess his name" (13:15).

Summary

The Christology and soteriology of Hebrews can be summarized in this way. Jesus is the Son of God, a high priest according to the order of Melchizedek. As the Son of God, he is greater than the angels. But in order to rescue humanity from the fear of death and deal effectively with sin, it was necessary for the Son to share in the flesh and blood of humans so that he could become a merciful and faithful high priest. According to Heb 7:21, God appointed him high priest by an oath: "The Lord has sworn and will not change his mind, 'You are a priest forever.' " As a priest according to the order of Melchizedek, Jesus enjoys a superior priesthood that he exercised in a unique way through his death. By dying, he entered the holy of holies, the heavenly sanctuary, where he offered his blood—his very life—for the sins of his brothers and sisters once and for all. In Hebrews, then, Christology and soteriology are intimately related in the person of Jesus, who is both priest and victim.

Moral Exhortation

Having considered Hebrews' exposition of Christ's priesthood, I now turn to its moral exhortations. As I have already noted, these exhortations are intimately related to the doctrinal expositions with which they are juxtaposed, and it is on the strength of these expositions that Hebrews exhorts its audience to persevere in faith. For example, having identified Christ as a merciful and faithful high priest who has entered into the heavenly sanctuary, Hebrews encourages its audience to follow the example of Jesus, "the pioneer and perfecter" of their faith (12:2), so that they also may enter into God's presence. Consequently, whereas the expository sections focus on the identity and work of Christ (Christology and soteriology), the moral exhortations shed light on the identity and destiny of the audience (ecclesiology and eschatology). Thus Hebrews develops its ecclesiology and eschatology in light of its Christology and soteriology.

For the purpose of this essay, I have identified four passages where exhortation plays a prominent role in Hebrews. The first (2:1–4) occurs within the exposition of the Son of God and the angels (1:5–14; 2:5–18). The second (3:1–4:16) and the fourth (10:19–13:17) bracket the exposition of Christ's high priesthood (5:1–10; 7:1–10:18). The third (5:11–6:20) stands in the midst of this exposition.

The Son of God and the Angels (1:5–14)
   First Exhortation (2:1–4)
The Son of God and the Angels (2:5–18)
   Second Exhortation (3:1–4:16)
Christ's High Priesthood (5:1–10)
   Third Exhortation (5:11–6:20)
Christ's High Priesthood (7:1–10:18)
   Fourth Exhortation (10:19–13:17)

THE NEED TO PAY GREATER ATTENTION

The first exhortation (2:1–4) occurs immediately after Hebrews has established the superiority of the Son to the angels of God. Before explaining why the superior Son was made lower than the angels, Hebrews interrupts its doctrinal exposition to warn its audience that it must pay greater attention to what it has heard (2:1). Employing an argument that moves from the lesser to the greater, it asks its audience if those who disobeyed a message declared through angels were so severely punished, how can they expect to escape punishment if they disobey what they have heard though the Son.

Hebrews relates this brief exhortation to the preceding exposition by contrasting the message that was declared by angels with the greater salvation that the audience has received through the Son of God. In doing this, Hebrews echoes the *exordium* (1:1–4), which contrasted the manifold ways in which God spoke in the past with the way in which God has spoken "in these last days" by a Son (1:2).

In its first and briefest exhortation, Hebrews reminds its audience that it is an eschatological community living in the last days. Those who have heard this word stand in a different situation than their ancestors did, for they have heard God's final word. Should they reject this salvation, there will be no other offer of grace to take its place. The community that has heard this message is the eschatological people of God.

A PILGRIM PEOPLE IN SEARCH OF SABBATH REST

The second exhortation (3:1–4:16) occurs between the exposition of the Son's superiority to the angels and the exposition of Jesus' priesthood. Hebrews relates this exhortation to the surrounding material in several ways. First, it begins with a consideration of the faithfulness of Jesus (3:1–6), which builds upon the earlier description of Jesus as "a merciful and faithful high priest" (2:17). Second, it concludes with an exhortation that anticipates the theme of Jesus' priesthood that will be developed in the exposition that follows: "Since, then, we have a great high priest who has passed through the heavens … let us hold fast to our confession.… Let us therefore approach the throne of grace with boldness" (4:14–16). Between these two subunits (3:1–6; 4:14–16), Hebrews presents a christological exegesis of Ps 95 that identifies its audience as the pilgrim people of God, which is poised to enter God's Sabbath rest (3:7–4:11).

At the outset of this exhortation, Hebrews speaks of the audience as "partners in a heavenly calling" who confess Jesus as "their apostle and high priest" (3:1). Comparing the faithfulness of Moses and Jesus, it describes Jesus as one who "was faithful over God's house as a son," and it reminds its audience that they are his house (3:6). Hebrews will echo this statement later when it writes, "and since we have a great priest over the house of God" (10:21). At the outset of this exhortation, then, Hebrews identifies its audience in two ways: (1) as an eschatological community whose members are "partners in a heavenly calling" (*klēseōs epouraniou metochoi*); and (2) as a community that belongs to the household of God that Jesus has built and presides over as a faithful Son (3:3, 6).

Having identified its audience in this way, Hebrews provides the audience with a christological interpretation of Ps 95 that explains what it means to be partners in a "heavenly calling." In doing so, it equates this heavenly calling with God's Sabbath rest. Although Hebrews quotes extensively from Ps 95 (in Heb 3:7b–11), it is primarily concerned with two parts of that text: "Today, if you hear his voice, do not harden your hearts as in the rebellion," and "They shall not enter my rest" (see Heb 3:15, 18a; 4:3, 5b, 7b).

Hebrews reads the psalm as God's living word that contains a promise as well as a lesson from the past. But whereas the psalm originally understood God's rest as referring to the promised land of Canaan, Hebrews views this "rest" as an eschatological reality, the Sabbath rest of God that "still remains for the people of God" (4:9). Hebrews arrives at this interpretation in two ways. First, in 4:4 it construes the meaning of "rest" in Ps 95 in terms of God's rest as described in Gen 2:2 ("And God rested on the seventh day from all his works"). In light of this reading, it understands "rest" as an eschatological reality, God's own Sabbath rest. Second, in 4:8 Hebrews concludes that, if Joshua had brought the people into this rest when he led them into the promised land, God would not have spoken about another day when they would receive rest. For this reason, the living word of Ps 95 must refer to another rest: God's eschatological rest. The "heavenly calling" (3:1) to which Hebrews refers, then, is nothing less than God's Sabbath rest into which Jesus, the great high priest, has already entered by passing through the heavens (4:14).

To summarize, in this second and longer exhortation Hebrews presents its audience with an ecclesiology that is related to, and dependent upon, its eschatology. The community of the "last days" is the household of God whose members are partners with Christ (3:14) in a "heavenly calling" that will be attained when they enter God's Sabbath rest, which their high priest has already attained by passing through the heavens.

Better Things

The purpose of the third exhortation (5:11–6:20) is to prepare the audience for advanced teaching on Christ's priesthood. Complaining that its audience has not advanced to maturity (5:12–14), Hebrews states that it is time to move beyond "the basic teaching about Christ" (6:1). Accordingly, it warns its audience that there will be no second repentance for those who apostatize after having been "enlightened," "tasted the heavenly gift," "shared in the Holy Spirit," and "tasted the goodness of the word of God and the powers of the age of come" (6:4–5). Ultimately, however, Hebrews expresses its confidence in its audience by speaking of "better things" that pertain to their salvation (6:9). The exhortation concludes with a striking metaphor that portrays their hope as an anchor firmly set in "the shrine behind the inner curtain" that draws them forward (6:19).

Although brief, this exhortation continues to develop the ecclesiological and eschatological themes of the first two exhortations. By warning the audience that there is no second repentance for those who fall away after experiencing "the powers of the age to come" (10:5), it reminds its audience that they belong to the community of the "last days," the eschatological people of God. By employing the metaphor of the anchor, Hebrews directs the attention of its listeners to the eschatological hope that lies before them and makes them the pilgrim people of God: their hope of entering into the heavenly shrine that Jesus has already attained (6:21). By entering this shrine, the community will attain its heavenly calling, which is participation in God's Sabbath rest. The manner in which Hebrews relates this hope to Christ's high priesthood once more illustrates how ecclesiology and eschatology derive their meaning from Christology and soteriology.

MOUNT ZION, THE HEAVENLY CITY

Although I have designated the final part of Hebrews as a fourth exhortation (10:19–13:17), this part consists of several discrete units: an exhortation closely related to the great teaching on the priesthood of Christ (10:19–39), a call to faith based on several examples of faith (11:1–40), an exhortation that derives its power from the example of Jesus' faith (12:1–13), an exhortation that reminds the audience of the new situation in which it finds itself (12:14–29), and a concluding exhortation (13:1–17).

Echoing themes it developed earlier, Hebrews exhorts the community to persevere in its eschatological hope (10:19–39). This exhortation derives its power to persuade from the extended exposition of Christ's high priesthood that precedes it. In that exposition, Hebrews explained how Christ entered into the sanctuary of heaven as a high priest, with his own blood, in order to atone for the sins of his brothers and sisters. Since Christ has opened the way into the sanctuary through his death, those who confess him as their high priest can be confident of entering the sanctuary where they will attain God's Sabbath rest. Given this new situation, Hebrews reminds the community of the eschatological nature of the salvation it has received. Because of the unrepeatable nature of Christ's sacrifice, there is no further sacrifice for sins for those who willfully persist in sin (10:26). Thus Hebrews continues to develop its ecclesiology and eschatology in light of its Christology and soteriology.

Although Hebrews describes its eschatology in terms of entering the heavenly sanctuary, it is aware of more traditional notions about the parousia and the Day of Judgment. It warns its audience that "the Day" is approaching (10:25) and promises that "in a very little while, the one who is coming will come and will not delay" (10:37). How these more traditional notions of the parousia and Day of Judgment cohere with Hebrews' distinctive eschatology is not clear.

In a second unit Hebrews exhorts its audience to persevere in faith by presenting them with examples of men and women who persevered even though they did not attain that for which they hoped (11:1–40). Hebrews describes these heroes and heroines of faith as people who confessed that "they were strangers and foreigners on the earth" (13:13). What they were seeking was "a homeland," (11:14), "a better country, that is, a heavenly one" (13:16). Like Abraham, they were looking for the city "whose architect and builder is God" (13:10).

At the end of this powerful celebration of faith, Hebrews notes that, even though these people were commended for their faith, they did not receive the promise because God determined they would not be perfected "apart from us" (11:40). With this remarkable statement, Hebrews again highlights the unique situation of its audience. Its recipients are the eschatological people of God, the beneficiaries of God's salvation. Like their predecessors in faith, the eschatological people of God are a pilgrim people who find themselves as "strangers and foreigners" on the earth. But unlike their ancestors who did not enter into the heavenly city they were seeking, they are about to do so.

The extended praise of faithful men and women leads to a third unit that presents Jesus as the pioneer and perfecter of faith (12:1–13). Before the eschatological people of God can enter into the heavenly city, they must finish the course they have begun. Accordingly, Hebrews reminds its audience of Jesus who endured the cross, despite its shame, and now sits "at the right hand of the throne of God" (12:2). With this powerful reminder of Jesus' shameful death on the cross, Hebrews disabuses its audience of any triumphalistic notions. Although they are the people of God, they are not yet the church triumphant.

In a fourth unit Hebrews describes the situation in which the believing community finds itself (12:14–29). Unlike Israel, which stood in fear in the presence of God at Mount Sinai, the eschatological people of God have arrived at Mount Zion, the city of the living God, the heavenly Jerusalem, the dwelling place of innumerable angels and of Jesus the mediator of a new covenant. The community, of course, has not yet entered into this city, since it must still run the course that Jesus has completed. But since Jesus has finished the race, it is now possible for them—his brothers and sisters—to enter the heavenly city. The eschatological promise is no longer a distant and remote hope. Because Jesus has entered the heavenly sanctuary, entrance into that sanctuary has become a possibility for those who follow in the way of the pioneer and perfecter of faith.

The final unit of this exhortation functions like a letter-closing, providing the audience with a series of moral exhortations and repeating some of the central themes that it has heard (13:1–17). Reminding its audience that Jesus died outside of the city of Jerusalem in order to sanctify them by his blood, Hebrews encourages its listeners to "bear the abuse he endured" (13:13), since they have "no lasting city" here and are still looking "for the city that is to come" (13:14). With this exhortation, Hebrews highlights the intimate relationship between Christology and soteriology, on the one hand, and ecclesiology and eschatology, on the other. The church is the community of those who pattern their lives after the life of the one who suffered for its sake. Consequently, its destiny is the destiny of the One who entered God's Sabbath rest by enduring the shame of the cross.

Although Hebrews never explicitly refers to its audience as the "church" (*ekklēsia*), and although it has little to say about the parousia apart from 9:28 and 10:37, it presupposes a vibrant ecclesiology and eschatology that can be summarized in this way. The church is the eschatological people of God because it lives in the last days in which God has spoken through his Son. As the eschatological people of God, the church is a pilgrim people in search of a lasting city where it will find the eschatological rest into which Jesus, the "pioneer" of its salvation (2:10) and the "perfecter" of its faith (12:2), has entered. Accordingly, just as the soteriology of Hebrews presupposes a Christology that presents Jesus as the eternal Son of God, a high priest according to the order to Melchizedek, so its ecclesiology presupposes an eschatology that looks for an eternal city where the pilgrim people of God will enjoy God's Sabbath rest. This intimate relationship between Christology, soteriology, ecclesiology, and eschatology can be expressed in this way. Whereas the soteriology of Hebrews presupposes its Christology, and its ecclesiology presupposes its eschatology, the eschatology and ecclesiology of Hebrews presuppose the Christology and soteriology of Hebrews. This relationship can be diagrammed as follows:

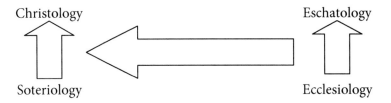

Christology   Eschatology

Soteriology   Ecclesiology

The Enduring Significance of Hebrews

Hebrews generates its theology by a creative and insightful reading of Scripture (see Schenck 2009 and his essay in this volume). Rereading Israel's Scriptures in the light of Christ, it provides its audience with new ways of understanding (1) the person and work of Christ and (2) the nature and destiny of the community that believes in him. In the final section of this essay, I highlight four ways in which the theology of the Epistle to the Hebrews has an enduring significance for faith and theology.

The Death of Christ

One of the most insightful contributions of Hebrews is the manner in which it rethinks the significance of Christ's death. If Jesus was the Messiah, the Son of God, why was he crucified as a political rebel and a common criminal? In light of Jesus' resurrection, whereby God vindicated Jesus by raising him from the dead, the first Christians concluded that Jesus' death was in accordance with God's will as revealed in the Scriptures (Luke 24:25–27, 44–46; 1 Cor 15:3). Furthermore, the early Christians began to understand that Jesus had died for their sins and for the sins of the world. Paul, more than any other writer of the New Testament, highlights the soteriological dimension of Jesus' death in terms of justification, reconciliation, and atonement for sins (Rom 3:21–26; 2 Cor 5:14–15, 19–21; Gal 1:4).

It is Hebrews, however, that provides a profound reflection on the meaning and significance of what (from a merely human point of view) was the shameful death of a criminal outside of the city gates. In light of its christological reading of Ps 110:4, Hebrews concludes that Jesus' ignominious death was the act of a high priest who, by his death, entered into the heavenly sanctuary. This understanding of death as entrance into the heavenly sanctuary is somewhat akin to the Johannine presentation of Jesus' death as departure and return to the Father. Like John, Hebrews appears to collapse the death and resurrection Christ into a single act whereby death *is* entrance into life. But whereas the Gospel of John presents Jesus' death as the hour of his glorification, Hebrews highlights the shame of the cross.

This presentation of Jesus' death as a priestly act challenges contemporary readers of Hebrews to reconsider their own understanding of death. As Jesus' death shows, death is not always what it appears to be. From the point of view of the world, Jesus died as a common criminal, but from the point of view of God (as revealed in Scripture) he died as a high priest according to the order of Melchizedek.

The Death of the Individual

The answer that the first Christians gave to the meaning and significance of Jesus' death provided them with a new insight to the meaning and significance of their own deaths. The death and resurrection of Jesus offered them hope that God would vindicate them just as God had vindicated Jesus. Paul, for example, views the resurrection of Jesus as the beginning of the general resurrection that will occur at the parousia (1 Cor 15:20–28). Hebrews does not discuss the general resurrection of the dead, and it has little to say about the parousia. Although this does not necessarily mean that it was unaware of these teachings, it does suggest that Hebrews preferred to express the mystery of the death and resurrection in another way. Portraying Jesus as the pioneer of salvation, it draws an analogy between the experience of Jesus and the experience of those who follow the path he trod; namely, just as Jesus entered the heavenly sanctuary through his death, so will those who follow him in the way of faith. For just as Jesus entered the heavenly sanctuary by offering himself in sacrifice to God, so those who believe in him will enter the heavenly sanctuary by offering their lives to God.

The Priest Who Is Victim

The way in which Hebrews understands the person and work of Christ results in a new understanding of priesthood whereby priest and victim are united in the same person. To arrive at this new understanding, Hebrews draws an elaborate comparison between the daily sacrifices that the Levitical priests offered and the singular sacrifice that Jesus offered by surrendering his life to God. By presenting Jesus' death as a willing sacrifice of himself, Hebrews redefines the nature of priesthood and sacrifice. Instead of offering sacrifices to God, the priest *is* the sacrifice he offers. In this view of priesthood, sacrifice is no longer the offering of something external to the priest but the free and internal offering of oneself to God.

For Hebrews, this understanding of priesthood and sacrifice means that there can only be one priest and one sacrifice. There is no need and no room for a multiplicity of priests or sacrifices because the Son of God offered himself as a perfect sacrifice for sin, once and for all. This understanding of priesthood is analogous to the Pauline notion of the church as the temple of God (1 Cor 3:16–17) and the Petrine understanding of the church as a "spiritual house" built of "living stones" whose people are a "holy priesthood" that offers "spiritual sacrifices acceptable to God" (1 Pet 2:5). But whereas the Pauline and Petrine traditions focus on the community as the new temple or spiritual house that offers a spiritual sacrifice, Hebrews focuses on Christ, the one in whom priest and victim have become so perfectly united that there is no further need for a cultic priesthood and sacrifice. This understanding of priesthood challenges contemporary theology to reflect upon the contemporary meaning of ministry and priesthood in terms of Christ, the high priest who sacrifices himself.

Redemption and Incarnation

Whereas Paul and the Synoptic Gospels view Christ from the perspective of his redemptive work on the cross, the Johannine tradition understands him from the perspective of the incarnation. Accordingly, while Paul and the Synoptic writers focus their attention on Christ's death and resurrection, the Johannine tradition presents Jesus as the incarnate Word of God who comes from the Father to reveal the Father to the world before returning to the one from whom he came. The theology of Hebrews, however, makes extensive use of *both* the incarnation and the redemption in its theology. Aware of Jesus' redemptive work on the cross, it understands that this redemptive work could not have occurred if the Son of God did not share in the flesh and blood of his brothers and sisters. Accordingly, before presenting the Son's redemptive work as a high priest, Hebrews explains why it was necessary for the Son who is superior to the angels to become lower than the angels so that he could be a merciful and faithful high priest.

By integrating a redemptive and incarnational approach, Hebrews cautions those who would focus on the cross to the detriment of the incarnation, and it warns those who would attend to the incarnation at the cost of neglecting the cross. Although every theology inevitably gives greater emphasis to one of these two dimensions, the best theology takes into considerations *both* the incarnation *and* the redemption.

Hebrews is one of the most remarkable writings of the New Testament. Although it presents itself as a "word of exhortation," it provides us with new ways to think about Christ, his benefits, the church, and its destiny. In doing so, it reminds us that a fruitful theology is always related to the needs and situation of the audience it addresses.

THE CONCEPT OF PERFECTION IN THE
EPISTLE TO THE HEBREWS

Kevin B. McCruden

Few texts in the New Testament offer a more theologically complex appraisal of the Christ-event than the Epistle to the Hebrews. Fewer still cultivate the concept of perfection as deliberately as does Hebrews in working out the implications of Christ's death for both the person of Jesus and the identity of the believer.[1] Nevertheless, it is difficult to arrive at a clear understanding of the idea of perfection in Hebrews for at least two reasons. First, although there is abundant comparative material from the ancient world that provides a broad range for the application of perfection terminology, it is doubtful that Hebrews adopts any of these usages in an arbitrary fashion (Attridge 1989, 86). Second, uncertainty about the precise occasion of Hebrews makes the interpretation of its Christology, as well as of specific passages containing the language of perfection, all the more challenging. For example, in 13:22 the author characterizes the main body of the letter as a "word of exhortation."[2] Does this classification lend support to the claim that Hebrews was written to encourage a socially marginalized group of early Christians (Koester 2001, 67–72; Thompson 2008, 20; Mitchell 2007, 12)? Or is it more accurate to conceive of the occasion of Hebrews in a less localized manner, in the sense that the letter envisions a more universal Christian audience, perhaps in a manner akin

---

1. Although sometimes obscured by English translations, perfection terminology appears in the following passages of Hebrews: 2:10; 3:14; 5:9, 14; 6:1, 8, 11; 7:3, 11, 19, 28; 9:9, 11; 10:1, 14; 11:40; 12:2, 23.

2. This same phrase appears in Acts 13:15 in the context of a synagogue homily delivered by Paul.

to the more generalized audience envisioned by the Letter to the Ephesians (Eisenbaum 2005b)?[3]

Although certainty concerning the occasion of Hebrews is impossible to attain, enough textual markers exist to suggest that Hebrews was motivated by a pastoral concern to comfort a community of discouraged first-century Christians (Lane 1991, 1:cxliii).[4] Hebrews 10:32–36 clearly envisions persecution in the form of societal scorn (10:32) as well as instances of social dislocation borne in the past (10:34). Such experiences threatened to corrode the confidence of the community's hope in its transcendent destiny (10:34–35). The pastoral intention of Hebrews is further demonstrated on the structural level by the twice-repeated summons to the community in 4:14 and 10:23 to hold firmly to the "confession" (*homologian*). Indeed, Heb 4:14–16 and 10:19–25 together function to frame the central section of the letter that deals with the high-priestly activity of Christ; such literary framing seems to indicate that communal exhortation is the author's principal concern (Thompson 2008, 15–16). The rhetorical artistry of the letter also suggests an essentially pastoral motivation. While Hebrews artfully blends elements of what Aristotle (d. ca. 322 B.C.E.) characterized as epideictic and deliberative oratory (*Rhet.* 1.3), Hebrews appears to approximate most closely the epideictic variety of ancient oratory. In contrast to deliberative speeches, whose purpose was to persuade an audience with reference to some future course of action, epideictic speeches functioned to praise persons or objects worthy of celebration in the present (Aune 1987, 35). The Christology of Hebrews is overwhelmingly celebratory, particularly in its estimation of Christ's exalted status (1:1–4; 4:14; 7:26; 8:1, 6; 10:19–21). In addition to eliciting a response of pride and pleasure from its ancient auditors, the celebratory Christology of Hebrews likely also addressed a communal issue of flagging commitment (6:11–12; 10:39; 12:12; Mitchell 2007, 27).

---

3. Significant early Greek manuscripts containing the Letter to the Ephesians lack the place name "Ephesus" in Eph 1:1. This could suggest that the book was originally intended to serve multiple Christian house-churches.

4. The location of the recipients of Hebrews is unknown. Hebrews 13:24 reads, "Those from Italy send you greetings." The Greek phrase *apo tēs Italias*, "from Italy," is attested in Acts 18:1, where it clearly indicates Rome. However, even if the phrase in Hebrews also indicates Rome, it remains unclear whether this should be taken to mean that Roman Christians are sending greetings back home to fellow Roman Christians or that Roman Christians are sending greetings to fellow non-Roman Christians residing somewhere else in the Mediterranean world.

Scholarly investigation of Hebrews has witnessed something of a reevaluation of traditional attempts at interpreting the letter. While much speculation in the past focused on locating a single conceptual back-ground to the letter, more recently there has emerged an appreciation for how Hebrews employs multiple conceptual models for the crafting of its Christology (Schenck 2007, 5). Particularly welcome of late has been the recognition of the narrative character of the theology contained in the writings of the New Testament (Schenck 2007, 13; Hays 1983). Such a turn to the text raises renewed possibilities for the task of drawing fruitful con-nections between the narrative world of Hebrews and its Christology of Christ perfected.

In this essay I intend to analyze the idea of perfection in Hebrews while guided by the methodological assumption that a larger narrative world or theological story informs this ancient sermon. James C. Miller defines the conceptual category of a narrative world as a "component" of a cultur-ally conceived symbolic universe. If one thinks of a symbolic universe as the aggregate of the conceptual lenses through which one interprets real-ity, then a narrative world refers more explicitly to the deepest personal assumptions, convictions, and aspirations associated with that symbolic world (Miller 2005, 246–47). While Hebrews could expect the majority of its auditors to find many of the aspects of its story world familiar (Schenck 2007, 15–16), this same narrative world will likely strike contemporary readers as profoundly alien. In this story world, for example, God appears as the transcendent source of life and the one for whom judgment will be reserved at the end of time (2:10; 4:13; 9:27; 10:30–31). Likewise, sin in the story world of Hebrews functions as a barrier impeding access to God and can only be removed through the act of sacrificial expiation (1:3; 9:14, 22, 26; 10:12, 14). Perhaps most alien of all is the epistle's valorization—quite typical of the ancient world—of unseen, eternal reality as fundamentally more real than perceptible reality (8:1–5; 9:11, 23–24; Johnson 2005, 2).

I do not intend to examine every facet of the theological story of Hebrews. Instead, this essay will focus largely on the human career of Jesus within the narrative world of Hebrews, in particular the role that per-fection occupies in that human career. I share the opinion that Hebrews evinces an affinity with the theological perspective taken on the shape of the Christ-event as depicted in the so called *kenōsis* hymn found in Paul's Letter to the Philippians (2:6–11; Miller 2005, 261). The frequent empha-sis one sees in Hebrews concerning the exaltation of Jesus into the pres-ence of God as a consequence of suffering and death (1:3; 5:8–10; 7:26–28;

10:12–13) conforms to the similar movement of humiliation followed by exaltation discernible in the *kenōsis* hymn contained in Philippians. In a manner reminiscent of the opening verse of that hymn (Phil 2:6), the *exordium* or formal introduction of Hebrews (1:1–4) begins by depicting the glorified Son in accordance with the category of Jewish wisdom (1:3). Echoing the description of personified wisdom found in Wis 7:25, Hebrews depicts the glorified Jesus as the "reflection" (*apaugausma*) of God's glory. Despite references in the opening part of the letter to what we might call the incarnation beginning in 2:14–18, much of the epistolary body of Hebrews focuses on what the *kenōsis* hymn in Philippians describes as Jesus' self-emptying (Phil 2:7), namely, Jesus' earthly career, in particular his high-priestly activity that culminates in his sacrificial death. In contrast to the *kenōsis* hymn, however, Hebrews eschews the metaphor of slavery (Phil 2:7) in favor of developing the theme of the radical solidarity that Jesus enters into with humanity (Heb 2:14, 18; 4:15), a solidarity that culminates in Hebrews' distinctive vision of Christ as both victim and priest (9:26). Lastly, the *kenōsis* hymn concludes on the triumphal note of Jesus' resurrection, conceived along the lines of cosmic exaltation (Phil 2:9–11). Similarly, throughout its extended theological exposition Hebrews celebrates a portrait of the glorified Jesus as the living and reigning Son who fulfills the scriptural vision of Ps 110:1: "The Lord says to my Lord, 'Sit at my right hand until I make your enemies your footstool' " (NRSV).

Hebrews' reflections concerning the perfection of Jesus relate essentially to the second and third stages of the human career of Jesus as outlined above. On the one hand, perfection for Jesus, as well as for the believer, involves the event of exaltation or glorification into the eternal presence of God. Hebrews describes this destiny with a variety of fresh metaphors that serve to nurture the eschatological hopes of its audience: participation in a heavenly calling (3:1); entering into Sabbath rest (4:9); approaching the "throne of grace" (4:16); arrival at the heavenly Jerusalem (12:22); and, perhaps most evocatively, stepping behind the curtain of the sanctuary to encounter God (6:19; 10:19). While the author of Hebrews is confident that Jesus has already attained the goal of entering into the presence of God (1:6; 10:12–13), for the faithful such communion with God is ultimately a heavenly destiny whose final fulfillment lies in the age to come (12:28; 13:14). As we will see, however, Hebrews can at the same time conceive of communion with God as a present reality that has been made possible through the sacrificial death of Jesus. On the other hand,

Jesus' perfection for Hebrews has as much to do with the response of personal faithfulness that Jesus demonstrated during his human life (3:1–2; 5:7–9; 10:5–9). The faithfulness of the Son, which was made complete through Jesus' acceptance of suffering and death on behalf of embodying God's kingdom, in turn models for the believer the faithfulness that is to characterize their own lives (12:2; 13:21).

THE PERFECTION OF JESUS

ENTERING THE PRESENCE OF GOD

Hebrews applies perfection terminology directly to Jesus three times (2:10; 5:9; 7:28). In each instance the author employs the same Greek verb, *teleioō*. At the most basic lexical level, *teleioō* denotes the formal concept of completion in the sense of attaining a goal (Koester 2001, 122–23; DuPlessis 1959, 77; Schenck 2007, 68). Since in practice, however, ancient writers made use of the verb in a variety of ways, one must examine the surrounding context to discern the specific nuance of completion that a given author has in view. For example, the verb appears in the writings of the Jewish philosopher Philo of Alexandria (d. ca. 50 C.E..) to describe both the maturation of a harvest (*Praem.* 128) and the completion of a specific task (*Opif.* 89). The verb could also be used metaphorically to refer to the termination of life, as when the author of 4 Maccabees praises the heroic death of the Jewish martyr Eleazar, who endured physical persecution for his refusal to eat ritually defiled food (4 Macc 7:15; see also Philo, *Leg.* 3.45). The author of the Third Gospel also seems to be conscious of this connection between death and perfection, since Luke can equate the goal of Jesus' ministry with his impending prophetic death in Jerusalem (Luke 13:32–33). In a similar way, John's Gospel uses a Greek verb derived from the same *tel-* root (*tetelestai*) to describe the moment preceding Jesus' death on the cross (John 19:30).

The verb *teleioō* could also convey more specifically religious associations, as when both Plato (d. ca. 348 B.C.E.) and Philo employ the verb in reference to the initiation rites of the mystery religions (Philo, *Mos.* 2.14; Plato, *Phaed.* 249c). Several passages in the Septuagint (the Greek translation of the Hebrew Bible) employ the verb in this specifically religious sense to describe persons who demonstrate faithfulness to God, especially through the display of ethical righteousness (Sir 31:10; Wis 4:13–14). In a more philosophical vein, Philo frequently employs perfection terminology in order to conceptualize the act of contemplation, as well as the life of virtue that promotes the contemplative ascent of the mind above the senses (*Leg.* 3.74; *Sacr.* 120). In the New Testament, Paul construes perfection in a religious sense when he describes the mystical goal of his life as a "straining forward" to live in conformity to the pattern of Christ's suffering and resurrection (Phil 3:10–13). Outside of Hebrews, *teleioō* appears most frequently in the New Testament in the Fourth Gospel (John 4:34; 5:36), where it is used to depict Jesus as the Son who brings to completion the will or commission of God (Peterson 2005, 35–37). Hebrews' use of the verb, however, is unique in the New Testament, since Hebrews consistently applies the concept of perfection to the actual person of Jesus. Thus the author writes:

> Now God did not subject the coming world, about which we are speaking, to angels. But someone has testified somewhere, "What are human beings that you are mindful of them, or mortals, that you care for them? You have made them for a little while lower than the angels; you have crowned them with glory and honor, subjecting all things under their feet." Now in subjecting all things to them, God left nothing outside their control. As it is, we do not yet see everything in subjection to them, but we do see Jesus, who for a little while was made lower than the angels, now crowned with glory and honor because of the suffering of death, so that he might taste death for everyone. It was fitting that God, for whom and through whom all things exist, in bringing many children to glory, should make the pioneer of their salvation perfect [*teleiōsai*] through sufferings. (Heb 2:5–10 NRSV)

Hebrews introduces the theme of Jesus' perfection by first recalling a portion of Ps 8. In its original context in the Jewish Bible, Ps 8 celebrated the position of honor and privilege that humanity presently occupies within creation. One of the ways in which Hebrews reinterprets the psalm is first by portraying Christ as the representative of collective humanity (2:9) and then by envisioning humanity's noble stature as the yet unfulfilled intention of God (2:8). The destiny of humanity in the age to come (2:5) consists in the participation of glory (2:7, 10), a glory that Hebrews elsewhere interprets metaphorically as entrance into the living presence of God (4:16; 6:19; 7:25; Scholer 1991, 196). Hebrews emphasizes that it was precisely through the experience of suffering and death that Jesus paradoxically entered into God's presence in the heavenly world (1:6; 2:9). In so doing, Jesus fulfills ahead of time and in a

representative manner the possibility for all of humanity to attain end-
time glory as well.

Few passages convey more keenly what Harold Attridge (2009, 99)
has described as Hebrews' implicit narrative attesting to God's beneficent
involvement with humanity. The divine intention is to lead humanity to
communion with God through the Son (1:2), who is described as the
archēgos, or "pioneer," of humanity's salvation (2:10). Central to this providential drama is the role that the suffering and death of Jesus plays in the
fulfillment of the divine intention. Hebrews 2:9 affirms boldly that Jesus
is "crowned" with "glory" (*doxa*) and "honor" (*timē*) as a consequence
of, and not despite, the apparently disgraceful experience of crucifixion.
Here, as elsewhere in the letter (12:2; 13:12–13), Hebrews takes care to
reevaluate for the reader the evident scandal of the cross by inverting the
core ancient categories of honor and shame (deSilva 2008). The theme of
Christ's present session at the right hand of God (10:12)—already celebrated in the honorific language of the *exordium* of the letter (1:1–4)—
serves to reconfigure the death of Jesus as a portal, not an obstacle, to the
realization of honor and glory (Koester 2001, 217). In all this theological
reflection, Hebrews' overriding motivation is undoubtedly pastoral. Since
the memory of the degradation endured by Jesus was likely part of the
public abuse endured by the audience at the hands of the dominant culture
(10:32–34), Hebrews assures the reader that the exaltation of Jesus into the
presence of God (9:24) vindicates the honor of his public ministry (deSilva
2008, 160). Such an appraisal likely also functioned to encourage community members to view their own personal struggles in a less shameful light.

Hebrews continues to emphasize the paradoxical honor attaching
to the suffering and death endured by Jesus by affirming that "it was fitting that God, for whom and through whom all things exist, in bringing many children to glory, should make the pioneer of their salvation
perfect through sufferings" (2:10). The proximity with which Hebrews
associates the death of Jesus with the divine intention to guide humanity to glory suggests that Jesus' perfection relates in the first instance to
his exaltation (Scholer 1991, 195–96; Isaacs 1992, 44; Koester 2001, 123;
Käsemann 1984, 140). To put this in slightly different terms, Jesus is made
complete or perfect when God "leads" (*eisagagē*) Jesus into the "heavenly
world" (*oikoumenēn*, 1:6) wherein the presence of God dwells (8:1; 9:24).
The explicit link that Hebrews draws between perfection and exaltation is
heightened by the ubiquitous presence of Ps 110 (LXX 109) seen throughout the letter (1:3, 13; 5:6, 10; 6:20; 7:3, 11, 15, 17, 21; 8:1; 10:12). The

psalm—in particular its first verse: "The Lord says to my lord, 'Sit at my right hand until I make your enemies your footstool'" (Ps 110:1)—was early and popularly employed by the first Christians as a scriptural lens through which to understand God's vindication of Jesus (Acts 2:32–33; 1 Cor 15:25; Mark 12:35–36). Psalm 110 is a royal psalm that in its original setting celebrated the divinely sanctioned strength of the Davidic monarch to conquer on behalf of God. Although Heb 2:10 does not explicitly quote Ps 110, a clear ascription to Jesus of royal status appears in the preceding verse: "but we do see Jesus, who for a little while was made lower than the angels, now crowned [estephanōmenon] with glory and honor because of the suffering of death, so that he might taste death for everyone" (2:9). Hebrews depicts Jesus' royalty, however, in paradoxical terms, since unlike the royal personage of the psalm who deals death to God's enemies (Ps 110:5–6), Jesus tastes death on behalf of everyone (2:9). Moreover, Hebrews proceeds to clarify that the vanquished enemy no longer refers to the foreign nations (Ps 110:6) but instead to the devil, who wields the cosmic power of death over all humankind (2:14; see also Wis 2:24).

Despite the fact that Hebrews will proceed in its argumentation to make innovative use of the figure of Melchizedek (Ps 110:4), it should not be missed that the turn itself to Ps 110 shows just how deeply Hebrews can be situated within a theological narrative that ranges broadly over a variety of New Testament texts. Hebrews reveals its immersion in such a narrative world by its preoccupation to reflect on, and to celebrate, the event of Jesus' victory over death through his resurrection (13:20). While the canonical Gospels for their part give literary and symbolic expression to the experience of God's vindication of Jesus through the vehicle of empty-tomb accounts (Mark 16:1–8; Matt 28:1–8; Luke 24:1–9; John 20:1–13) and appearance stories (Matt 28:9–20; Luke 24:10–53; John 20:14–21:24), Hebrews chooses to envision the divine vindication of Jesus more abstractly by construing Jesus' victory over death as a process of completion or perfection whereby the Son is elevated into God's presence (4:14) to serve a priestly role (4:15–16; 7:24–25).

The place where the connection between the idea of perfection and the exaltation of Jesus is perhaps most explicit is in Heb 7:26–28:

> For it was fitting that we should have such a high priest, holy, blameless, undefiled, separated from sinners, and exalted above the heavens. Unlike the other high priests he has no need to offer sacrifices day after day, first for his own sins, and then for those of the people; this he did once for

all when he offered himself. For the law appoints as high priests those who are subject to weakness, but the word of the oath, which came later than the law appoints a Son who has been made perfect [*teteleiōmenon*] forever.

Throughout chapter 7 Hebrews employs the rhetorical device of extended comparison in order to contrast the superior priesthood of the Son with what the author considers the imperfect institution of the Levitical priesthood. Hebrews' intention, however, is not to denigrate Jewish institutions. As described by Aristotle, the rhetorical device of *synkrisis* sought to amplify the honor of a person or object by comparing the subject to an object or person whose excellence was conceded by all (*Rhet.* 1.9.38–39). Hebrews employs the same device of *synkrisis* in 3:1–6, where the author contrasts the superior faithfulness of the Son to the faithfulness of God's greatest servant, Moses. Returning frequently to the mysterious figure of Melchizedek, who appears in Gen 14:17–20 and Ps 110:4, Hebrews posits in chapter 7 the superiority of Jesus' priestly status over the priests descended from Aaron on the basis of the everlasting life that Jesus shares with God (7:15–16, 23–25). The enigmatic figure of Melchizedek is important for the author's argument for two reasons. First, Ps 110:4 presents a scriptural precedent for the sanction of applying the title of priest to someone other than a descendant of Levi (Koester 2001, 345–46). Second, in the only other extended scriptural account of Melchizedek (Gen 14:17–20), nothing is said concerning the lineage of the mysterious priest king of Salem. Working on the dual assumption that Scripture points to Jesus and that even the silences of Scripture hold hidden meaning, Hebrews discerns in the genealogically challenged Melchizedek the foreshadowing of the eternal life Christ has as a consequence of his exaltation (7:15; Koester 2001, 317, 348).

Central also to the author's argument in chapter 7 is the theme of the binding oath that the author gleans from the beginning of Ps 110:4: "The Lord has sworn and will not change his mind." Mindful that Jesus' lineage in the tribe of Judah (7:14) technically disqualified him from the hereditary office of the Jewish priesthood, Hebrews applies this verse to the subsequent oath that God addresses to the Son on the occasion of Jesus' resurrection from the dead (7:20–21). The idea of an oath is important, since it functions rhetorically to picture God, and indeed God alone, as the one who directly and authoritatively confers this priestly status upon Jesus (Koester 2001, 359). Hebrews 7:26–28 provides a fitting summation to these themes by linking the concept of Jesus' completion or perfection (7:26) to the idea of qualification for priestly activity, since it is ultimately Jesus' exaltation above the heavens (7:26) that enables the Son to execute a more perfect/complete mediatorial role than the one performed by human priests: "but he holds his priesthood permanently, because he continues forever. Consequently he is able for all time to save those who approach God through him, since he always lives to make intercession for them" (7:23–25).

It is legitimate, therefore, to see Hebrews making a connection not only between the concepts of perfection and exaltation but between the concepts of perfection and priesthood as well (5:9–10; 2:10–17; 7:26–28). Since in the estimation of the author the sons of Aaron neither live forever nor have obtained the office of the priesthood through a divine oath, this confirms that Jesus alone is the authentic high priest who ful-fills adequately the salient role of a priest to remove the barrier of sin that separates persons from God (Koester 2001, 123). Of potential interpretive significance here is the fact that the Greek translation of the Jewish Bible employs *teleioō* as a part of a fuller technical phrase—"to fill the hands" (*teleioun tas cheiras*)—for describing the formal installation of the Jewish high priest (Exod 29:9; Lev 4:5; 16:32; Num 3:3). Given the textual evidence for this technical expression, some commentators have wondered if Jesus' perfection in Hebrews therefore amounts to the notion of consecration for priestly duty (Windisch 1931, 44–46). While it is accurate to say that perfection terminology as applied to Jesus carries cultic overtones in Hebrews (Johnson 2005, 96–97), the specific claim that Jesus' perfection is tantamount to consecration misses the mark (Attridge 1986, 85). While the entire expression *teleioun tas cheiras* does indeed denote the technical act of consecration, the verb *teleioō* by itself does not convey this technical sense (Ellingworth 1993, 397; Attridge 1989, 85).

THE FAITHFULNESS OF THE SON

While the idea of exaltation to glory constitutes one aspect of what it means for the Son to be perfected, perfection in Hebrews also encom-passes the earthly career of Jesus. In an important study on the concept of perfection in Hebrews, David Peterson proposed a vocational under-standing of the concept. According to Peterson, Jesus' perfection entailed "a whole sequence of events" that, while including Jesus' exaltation, was not limited to the Son's entry into the heavenly sphere (2005, 73). Crucial to Peterson's argument is his insistence that the event of the suffering and death of Jesus (2:10; 5:7–10) functions in Hebrews as something more than just a preliminary stage for Jesus' subsequent glorification. Instead, the experience of suffering and death serves as part of a larger experiential process that culminates in the exaltation of the Son (2005, 68). While it would be incorrect to say that Hebrews thinks of such an experiential process along the lines of moral development within the person of Jesus (Matera 1999, 199), it is appropriate to affirm that Hebrews thinks of the human Jesus as growing or maturing in some way in the context of his human career (Johnson 2005, 151). An adequate interpretation, then, of what Jesus' perfection amounts to in Hebrews must necessarily address the role that suffering and death play in the perfecting of Jesus (Peterson 2005, 68–69).

Peterson's insight that there exists for the author of Hebrews an experiential, vocational dimension to Jesus' perfection is supported by passages such as Heb 5:7–10:

> In the days of his flesh, Jesus offered up prayers and supplications, with loud cries and tears, to the one who was able to save him from death, and he was heard because of his reverent submission. Although he was a Son, he learned obedience through what he suffered; and having been made perfect [*teleiōtheis*], he became the source of eternal salvation for all who obey him, having been designated by God a high priest according to the order of Melchizedek.

Significantly, Hebrews associates Jesus' perfection in this passage not with the event of the Son's exaltation but with the quality of obedience that the Son is said to have learned through the experience of suffering. Before attempting to interpret this passage, it is important to contextualize it within its larger literary context. Hebrews 5:7–10 appears in the second major section of Hebrews, which begins in 4:14 and extends through 10:18. It is in this part of the letter where the theme of Christ's high priesthood, first announced in 2:17, is now developed at length. Tellingly, the first thing we encounter in this section concerning the character of Jesus' priestly status pertains to the human Jesus' stance toward humanity: "For we do not have a high priest who is unable to sympathize with our weaknesses, but we have one who in every way has been tested as we are, yet without sin" (4:15). To say that Jesus "sympathizes" (*sumpathēsai*) with human weaknesses is to confirm the essentially familial bond of solidarity that Jesus shares with humanity (Sobrino 2001, 137–38). This same high priest who has passed through the heavens (4:14) is also the Son who has drawn near to humanity in a radical gesture of self-commitment (2:11–13):

> Therefore he had to become like his brothers and sisters in every respect so that he might become a merciful and faithful high priest in the service of God, to make a sacrifice of atonement for the sins of the people. Because he himself was tested by what he suffered, he is able to help those who are being tested. (2:17–18)

The reference above to the theme of the testing of Jesus returns us to the topic of the obedience that Hebrews maintains Jesus learned through the experience of suffering (5:8). The portrait of an anguished Jesus in prayer in 5:7–10 bears some resemblance to the passion accounts found especially in the Gospels of Mark and Matthew (Mark 14:32–42; Matt 26:36–46). However, there are enough differences between the latter and Heb 5:7–10 to suggest that Hebrews is not simply supplying here a variant of the Gethsemane tradition (Attridge 1989, 148; Johnson 2005, 146).[5] Whatever may have been the specific source for this passage, a deeply human portrayal of Jesus is immediately apparent to the reader. In contrast to ordinary high priests, who offer external gifts and sacrifices (5:1; 8:3–4; 9:12), Jesus offers to God personal prayers and supplications accompanied by intense emotional investment over the prospect of facing his death (5:7). The notice in 5:7 to "the days of his flesh" suggests that Hebrews has in view here the entire period of Jesus' incarnation and not simply the specific moments before his execution (Thompson 2008, 115). But what could it mean for Jesus to have demonstrated such personal investment throughout his entire life? For that matter, what could it mean to say that Jesus learned obedience? Hebrews is likely working here—as Paul seems to be as well (see Gal 2:15–16)—from a larger theological assumption that takes for granted the response of faithfulness demonstrated by the Son throughout his human career. While it is easier to recognize the response of faithfulness on the part of Jesus in the narrative context of the canonical Gospels (Mark 14:36; Matt 4:1–11; Luke 4:1–13), numerous passages in Hebrews make the same point, although in a more compressed manner. As early in the letter as 1:9 and 2:13, respectively, Hebrews employs Ps 45 to designate Jesus as someone who "loved righteousness" and placed his trust in God. In addi-

---

5. For example, Hebrews does not supply a setting for Jesus' prayer, nor do the Synoptic passion accounts make any reference to Jesus weeping.

tion to evincing the qualities of mercy (2:17) and sympathy (4:15), Jesus is twice described as "faithful" (2:17; 3:2). Most significant of all, Hebrews depicts Jesus as the Son who discerns God's will and is committed to putting the divine will into practice (10:7, 9). When we hear, therefore, of the "reverent submission" of Jesus in 5:7, the author's point seems to be that Jesus was obedient in the sense that he was completely open to the will of God throughout his entire life. More important, Jesus' conformity to the divine will entailed human struggle and development, as evidenced by the reference to the "loud cries and tears" (5:7) of Jesus. According to Hebrews, therefore, it was such ever-deepening conformity to the divine will that both constituted the heart of Jesus' education into obedience and accounted for the sinlessness of Jesus (4:15; 7:26; 9:14). On this issue, Luke Timothy Johnson makes the point that although the preexistent Son was the "reflection of the divine glory" (1:3), Jesus still needed to grow into the status of sonship throughout his earthly career (Johnson 2005, 151). Jon Sobrino offers a similar observation when he states that Jesus' "faithfulness is also characterized by process, by having to journey in history" (2001, 136). For the author of Hebrews, then, the repeated references to the sinlessness of Jesus (4:15; 7:26) seem to refer to the idea of the experiential struggle of Jesus to live a life of fidelity to, and openness before, God. Jesus is perfected, therefore, in the sense that his continual response of faithfulness to God both matures into, and brings to realization, the faithfulness that God desires in every human being (13:21). When viewed with these observations in mind, the event of the exaltation of Jesus becomes an integral dimension—but only one dimension—of a more inclusive process of perfection that begins in the incarnation, extends through Jesus' earthly existence and death, and culminates in the heavenly glorification of the preexistent Son (9:11–12).

If one goes on to inquire concerning the specific shape of God's will for Jesus, Heb 1:8–9 offers at least a partial answer: "But of the Son he says, 'Your throne, O God, is forever and ever, and the righteous scepter is the scepter of your kingdom. You have loved righteousness and hated wickedness.' " The specific quote comes from Ps 45:6–7, a royal psalm whose original function was to praise the Jewish king. Weaving together an assortment of scriptural passages beginning in 1:5, the author continues a pattern in 1:8–9 whereby the reader is privileged to overhear God's address to the Son on the occasion of the Son's exaltation. The passage is noteworthy, first of all, for the clear ascription of divine status accorded to the Son, a clarity that is rare in the New Testament (Attridge 1989, 58). Of

significance also is the mention of the Son's kingdom and the righteousness that defines Jesus' royal authority. Given what we have seen regarding Hebrews' emphasis on the human career of Jesus, it is possible that
this passage demonstrates the author's interest in the memory preserved
in the canonical Gospels concerning how Jesus embodied in his ministry
the reality of the kingdom of God. For Hebrews, as for the Synoptic Gospels in particular, it appears that one of the ways in which God's kingdom
becomes concrete in the world is through a life of countercultural commitment to other persons. One of the places in the letter where Hebrews
seems to give expression to this notion of God's kingdom is in the section
that deals with the incarnation of the Son:

> Since, therefore, the children share flesh and blood, he himself likewise
> shared the same things, so that through death he might destroy the one
> who has the power of death, that is, the devil, and free those who all
> their lives were held in slavery by the fear of death. For it is clear that he
> did not come to help angels, but the descendants of Abraham. (2:14–16)

This passage follows closely on the heels of Heb 2:10. In that passage we
saw how Hebrews links the first occurrence in the letter of the theme of
the perfection of Jesus with the heavenly goal of leading humanity to glory
conceived as communion with God. Immediately prior to 2:14–18 we
read that Jesus was not ashamed to call the children destined for glory his
"brothers" (2:11). Now in 2:14–16 we see that the depth of God's involvement with humanity is characterized by radical solidarity in the person of
the Son.[6] Repeating a highly traditional connection that linked the agency
of the devil with the reality and bondage of death (Mitchell, 2007, 75),
Hebrews construes the purpose of the incarnation as liberation from the
existential fear of death for the benefit of "the descendants of Abraham,"
by which Hebrews likely means both the Jewish and Gentile recipients
of the letter. The path to communion with God begins, therefore, with
the Son drawing radically near in solidarity with fellow human beings.
Further, since the Son participates fully in human existence (2:14, 17),

---

6. It is probably significant that Hebrews employs two different Greek verbs in
2:14 to describe the incarnation. Whereas the "children shared [*kekoinōnēken*] blood
and flesh," Jesus "participated" (*meteschen*) in the same things. Nonetheless, the persuasive force of the verse has to do with the clear emphasis on the Son's thoroughgoing
solidarity with humans.

he necessarily struggles, as all persons do, to live a life of authentic faith before God (2:18; 12:1–2). For Hebrews, this struggle equips, even qualifies, Jesus to be a certain kind of high priest. As the presently exalted high priest in the heavenly sanctuary, Jesus is a source of eternal salvation (7:25). But at the same time Jesus is a merciful high priest (2:17) who can help persons because of the personal quality of the sacrifice he made during his earthly career.

Jesus' commitment to serve others, especially the most vulnerable of persons, for the sake of embodying the kingdom results in the injustice of his suffering and death on the cross, according to the canonical Gospels. The extensive treatment of the nature of Christ's sacrificial activity in Heb 9:11–10:18 relates in an abstract mode what the canonical Gospels present in a more narrative form. A central concern for the author of Hebrews in this section of the letter consists in highlighting the personal nature of the sacrificial offering that Jesus makes:

> But when Christ came as a high priest of the good things that have come, then through the greater and perfect tent (not made with hands, that is, not of this creation), he entered once for all into the Holy Place, not with the blood of goats and calves, but with his own blood, thus obtaining an eternal redemption. For if the blood of goats and bulls, with the sprinkling of the ashes of a heifer, sanctifies those who have been defiled so that their flesh is purified, how much more will the blood of Christ, who through the eternal Spirit offered himself without blemish to God, purify our conscience from dead works to worship the living God. (9:11–14)

If Heb 7:1–28 focuses on the superior high-priestly status of Christ in comparison to the Levitical priesthood, then beginning in chapter 8 the author establishes a new focus that relates more to the character of the sacrificial activity of Christ (Koester 2001, 375). Hebrews 9:11–14 is an important passage in this regard, since it encapsulates two major themes that recur frequently throughout the section 8:1–10:18. The first of these themes relates to the unique location of Christ's sacrifice, while the second relates to the unique quality of the sacrifice that Hebrews envisions Jesus as offering. Christ's sacrificial activity proves superior to the sacrificial activity of ordinary priests since it takes place in what Hebrews describes as an authentic tent or sanctuary located in heaven (8:1; 9:11–12), as opposed to an earthly tent or sanctuary (8:5; 9:1, 11). The basis for the author's reflections here stem from the scriptural account of the portable sanctuary that accompanied the Israelites during their wanderings in the wilderness

(Exod 25–27). In terms of the specifics of the biblical story, Hebrews shows particular interest in God's command to Moses to construct the sanctuary in accordance with the pattern or example revealed to him on the mountain (Exod 25:40). There is much scholarly debate concerning the particular conceptual background that might be influencing Hebrews in this section of the letter. Some point to texts such as Heb 8:5 as evidence that Hebrews here borrows the Platonic emphasis on transcendent reality that alone is fully real in comparison to the perceptible world. Others wonder if depictions of heavenly temples in various Second Temple Jewish texts provide a better conceptual fit (Mitchell 2007, 164). Whatever the appropriate background, it seems clear that Hebrews means to depict Christ as entering into the transcendent presence of God conceived metaphorically as a heavenly sanctuary (8:2; 9:11–12, 24; Schenck 2007, 181). Since in the thought world of Hebrews transcendent realities are better than earthly realities (9:23–24; 12:27), the heavenly location of Christ' sacrificial ministry (8:1–2) makes his offering superior to the sacrificial offerings that take place in earthly sanctuaries (8:5).

At the same time, however, Hebrews understands the superior nature of Jesus' sacrifice as arising out of its radically personal quality: Jesus is a priest who is at once also a victim. Much earlier in the letter Hebrews recounts the qualifications for the human priesthood. Among these qualifications was included the responsibility "to offer gifts and sacrifices for sins" (5:1). Hebrews shows Jesus as someone who also makes an offering, but his particular offering is decidedly more experiential, namely, prayers and supplications accompanied by emotional distress (5:7). In 8:3 there is once again a reference to the offerings made by human priests, and the same emphasis is placed on the external character of these priestly offerings. In place of external gifts, Jesus offers, according to Hebrews, the gift of his own life (8:3; 9:14). Much the same thought is captured by the repeated references one finds in Hebrews to the image of Jesus' blood, which likely functions as a metaphor for Jesus' life. No less than five times in the space of two chapters Hebrews makes the point that the blood offered by priests and even Moses was not their own, in contrast to Jesus, who gave his own blood (9:7, 12, 19, 25; 10:4). This emphasis on the personal nature of Jesus' sacrifice seems to bear some kind of connection to the idea of Jesus' response of faithfulness to God that was addressed above. For if solidarity with, and self-giving toward, others is part of God's will for humanity, then we perhaps see in Heb 9:11–10:18 the human struggle of Jesus to perfect that divine intention even to the point of suffering and death (9:14; Sobrino 2001, 137).

THE PERFECTION OF THE FAITHFUL

The Greek verb *teleioō* appears a total of nine times in Hebrews (2:10; 5:9; 7:19, 28; 9:9; 10:1, 14; 11:40; 12:23). In three of these instances Hebrews reflects directly on what perfection means for the life of the faithful (9:9; 10:1, 14). In the broadest sense believers experience perfection in the age to come when they inherit a kingdom that transcends all manner of corporeal existence (12:26–27; 13:14) and enter fully into the glory of God's transcendent presence. Perfection for others refers ultimately, then, to the completion of the divine plan of salvation when God endows humanity with honor and glory (2:5–10; Lindars 1991, 44). As experienced in the lives of the faithful, however, perfection also has a present dimension in Hebrews, since those who participate in Christ (3:1, 6) are pictured as already enjoying access to God in their earthly existence (4:16; 6:19; 7:19; 10:19–22; 12:22–24; Scholer 1991, 199).

In keeping with its strongly sacrificial assessment of the death of Jesus, Hebrews tends to relate the perfection of the faithful to the idea of sanctification (10:10, 14). To sanctify implies the notion of setting someone or something apart for a sacred or holy use. Christ's death is understood by Hebrews to effect sanctification in the lives of believers, since it accomplishes not only the forgiveness of sin (9:22) but even its abolition (9:26), and with the removal of sin authentic access to God becomes a present reality for the faithful:

> Therefore, my friends, since we have confidence to enter the sanctuary by the blood of Jesus, by the new and living way that he opened for us through the curtain (that is, through his flesh), and since we have a great priest over the house of God, let us approach with a true heart in full assurance of faith, with our hearts sprinkled clean from an evil conscience and our bodies washed with pure water. (10:19–22)

Earlier Hebrews described the entrance of the Son into the heavenly sanctuary that is superior to any transient sanctuary on earth (9:24). Within that sanctuary Jesus appears before the presence of God (9:24). The somewhat misleading translation "to enter," which is found in the NRSV, is a translation of a single Greek noun, *eisodon*, which means literally a "door" or "portal." Strikingly, Hebrews encourages the believer to proceed through the portal opened through Jesus' death to encounter God on the other side. Here Hebrews is concerned to place before the community the present dimension of salvation that stems from Christ's own deeply personal act of faithfulness (9:14; 10:9). Hence, the experiential dimension that characterized Jesus' own perfection through his living out of God's will (5:7–9) engenders within the lives of believers the experiential "confidence" (*parrēsian*) of communion with God in the present (4:16). For the author of Hebrews, it is this lived experience of direct access to God that constitutes what perfection means for the believer this side of the age to come.

The same weight given to the experiential dimension of salvation appears also in the letter's frequent references to the purification of the conscience (*suneidēsin*) of the faithful (9:9, 14; 10:2, 22). The author of Hebrews writes:

> This is a symbol of the present time, during which gifts and sacrifices are offered that cannot perfect the conscience [*suneidēsin*] of the worshiper.… For if the blood of goats and bulls, with the sprinkling of the ashes of a heifer, sanctifies those who have been defiled so that their flesh is purified, how much more will the blood of Christ, who through the eternal Spirit offered himself without blemish to God, purify our conscience [*suneidēsin*] from dead works to worship the living God! (9:9–14)

The term "conscience," which appears frequently in the letters of Paul, conveys the basic idea of awareness and frequently suggests the nuance of moral awareness (Attridge 1989, 242). Hebrews employs the term to draw attention to that which is most inward within a human being. For the believer, the sacrificial death of the Son engenders the experiential conviction of purification, by which Hebrews means the act of expiation or the cleansing of sin (Attridge 1989, 251–52). Such cleansing reaches far into the depths of the personality in the sense that even the consciousness of sin is understood to be removed (10:2). Since Hebrews perceives sin to be an obstacle that separates God from human beings, the purification of the conscience through the sacrificial death of Jesus enables the believer to draw inwardly near to the transcendent presence of God. Hebrews connects this notion of internal cleansing of the conscience with the scriptural expectation of God's renewal of the covenant that is found in Jer 31:31–34:

> The days are surely coming, says the Lord, when I will establish a new covenant with the house of Israel and with the house of Judah.… This is the covenant that I will make with the house of Israel after those days,

says the Lord: I will put my laws in their minds, and write them on their hearts, and I will be their God, and they shall be my people. (Heb 8:8–10)

The importance that the prophecy from Jeremiah has for Hebrews is borne out by the fact that Hebrews quotes Jeremiah twice (8:8–12; 10:16–17). The idea of a renewed covenant made possible through the death of Jesus likely appealed to the author because the idea of covenant implies relationship. In 9:18–21 Hebrews recalls the covenant-ratification ritual found in Exod 24:3–8. Central to the scriptural account is the focus on the commitment of the ancient Israelites to obey the commandments of the Lord and thus become God's holy or sanctified people (Exod 24:3, 7). Put another way, the promise made by the Israelites to live in obedience to the laws of the covenant functions as a way to honor God's loving decision to live in relationship with the Jewish people. Moreover, the commitment of the Israelites to live lives of obedience is pictured as being confirmed through the sacrificial rite of animal sacrifice (Exod 24:5–8). Working with such a communal understanding of the idea of covenant, Hebrews sees the promise of a renewed and deeper relationship with God fulfilled in the personal shedding of the blood of Jesus (9:13–14; 10:14).

This understanding of perfection conceived as both direct access to God and renewed relationship with God bears a direct connection to the author's criticism of the cultic activity that took place under what Hebrews characterizes as the first covenant (8:7, 13; 9:1). While in the central section of the letter Hebrews actually refers to three separate sacrificial rituals, it is clear that the ritual of the Day of Atonement as described in Lev 16:1–34 is foremost in the author's mind.[7] Hebrews' treatment of the ritual, however, is highly selective:

Such preparations having been made, the priests go continually into the first tent to carry out their ritual duties; but only the high priest goes into the second, and he but once a year, and not without taking the blood that he offers for himself and for the sins committed unintentionally by the people. (9:6–7)

---

7. The Day of Atonement ritual in 9:6–7, 25; 10:3–4 (Lev 16:1–19); the Sinai covenant ratification ritual in 9:18–21 (Exod 24:1–8); and the ritual of the red heifer in 9:13 (Num 19:1–13).

In Heb 9:1–5 the author supplies a selective synopsis of the layout of the wilderness sanctuary in accordance with the scriptural account found in Exod 25–27. While the description of the sanctuary in Hebrews is ambiguous at points, there appears to be a clear motivation on the part of the author to make a distinction between an interior compartment of the sanctuary in contrast to an outer vestibule (Mitchell 2007, 178–79). With this visualization of the sanctuary in mind, 9:6–7 depicts the dramatic movement of the high priest behind the curtain within the sanctuary. Once behind the curtain, the high priest proceeds to sprinkle the sacrificial blood of a bull and a goat upon the so-called mercy seat, where it was believed that the presence of God invisibly dwelled (Lev 16:2). The entire ritual was understood to effect the expiation or cleansing away of sin that served as a barrier separating God from the covenant people (Lev 16:11–16).

Hebrews is keenly interested in the link between the wilderness sanctuary and the presence of God. According to the biblical account, once the sanctuary was completed the "glory" (*kābôd*) or presence of God filled the portable tabernacle in order to accompany the Israelites on their journey (Exod 40:34–38). With the faith commitment already in place that the death of Jesus provided expiation for sin, Hebrews interprets the selectively chosen features of the Day of Atonement ritual as indicative of an overall pattern of imperfection hinted at long ago (9:8–9). On the one hand, the very repetition of sacrifices under the first covenant signals imperfection for Hebrews (10:1–3, 11–12), since lasting purification from the consciousness of sin was never achieved (10:2–3). On the other hand, Hebrews links the deeper imperfection of previous sacrificial rites to their failure to secure the goal of gaining access to God. Ultimately, it is this experiential conviction (10:22) of dwelling in the presence of God that is the real issue for Hebrews. Thus, while Hebrews grants that God's presence dwelled within the wilderness sanctuary, the author at the same time believes that the divine glory was shielded by a curtain that restricted access to all but the high priest, and even he could only enter behind the curtain once a year (9:7, 25). The connections that Hebrews makes between the concepts of perfection, purification of conscience, and communion with God are nicely brought together in the author's own words:

> Since the law has only a shadow of the good things to come and not the true form of these realities, it can never, by the same sacrifices that are continually offered year after year, make perfect those who approach. Otherwise, would they not have ceased being offered, since the worshipers,

cleansed once for all, would no longer have consciousness of sin? But in these sacrifices there is a reminder of sin year after year. For it is impossible for the blood of bulls and goats to take away sins. (10:1–4)

CONCLUSION

In this essay I have explored the concept of perfection in the Epistle to the Hebrews in relation to the person of Jesus and the life of the believer. We have seen that, while the event of Jesus' exaltation comprises one aspect of what Jesus' perfection means for the author of Hebrews, the personal faithfulness of Jesus also plays a significant role in the perfecting of the Son as eternal high priest. According to Hebrews, Jesus was perfected in the sense that he personally embodied God's kingdom of service to others, even to the point of giving his own life for the values of the kingdom, not the least of which is the value of solidarity with others. Hebrews also uses perfection terminology to reflect on the experience of the sermon's recipients. For the believer, perfection has both a future and a present dimension. The faithful ultimately experience perfection in the age to come when they inherit an abiding existence in the transcendent glory of God's presence. Even now, however, perfection understood as communion with God is an experiential reality that has been made possible through the personal sacrifice of Jesus that cleanses the believer from within.

The Jesus of Hebrews and the Christ of Chalcedon

Rowan A. Greer

There are many ways of studying how writers in the early church inter-preted Scripture (Grant 1984; Simonetti 1994; Young 1997). Important questions include: What canon do particular writers presuppose? To what degree and how do they employ the methods and conventions of the rhe-torical handbooks available to them? Are they influenced by the way texts were interpreted by other traditions, including the approaches taken by the Jewish rabbis, by Philo, and by the pagan allegorists of Homer? It is surely important to keep all these questions in mind, but my interest will be not so much in method or in the various cultural forces at work as in the theological results of ancient attempts to make sense of the Christian Bible. Of course, in one way or another all the early Christian interpreters assume that Scripture has been divinely inspired and somehow counts as the word of God. Nevertheless, most of them appear to recognize that this word has been accommodated to the conditions of those receiving it and that God's message is often obscure and not easily intelligible. They tend to focus their interpretations upon the difficulties of Scripture and, at their best, would have agreed with the rabbinic claim that its puzzles are like the grit in an oyster; they produce the great pearls of exegesis.

At the same time, early Christian interpreters approach the Bible with two fundamental assumptions. First, contradictions in it must be merely apparent; problems attach to interpreters, not to the texts themselves. Thus it proves necessary to press beyond the surface of Scripture to its unified meaning. This need not betray a failure to recognize the particu-larities of the writings bound together in the Bible, but even in the surviv-ing commentaries on specific books there is a clear attempt to locate the particular meaning in the context of the whole of Scripture. Assessing patristic exegesis, then, requires an examination not only of commentaries but also of the use made of texts in other writings. The second basic assumption that informs early Christian interpretation is the conviction that every detail of the biblical text is significant. There is a clear warrant for this assumption in Gal 3:16: "Now the promises were made to Abraham and to his seed [Gen 22:18]; it does not say, 'and to seeds,' as of many; but it says, 'and to your seed,' that is, to one person, who is Christ."[1] Here Paul employs a common rabbinic convention. For example, in Midrash Sifra on Leviticus the comment on Lev 26:42 finds a difficulty in the Hebrew text: "I will remember my covenant with Jacob, and my covenant with Isaac, and I will remember my covenant with Abraham." The difficulty is why "remember" is associated with Jacob and Abraham but not with Isaac. Why? The explanation depends upon a rabbinic tradition that Isaac was actually sacrificed (Gen 22; Spiegel 1967, 4–8), so that God had no need to be reminded of Isaac, since he always saw his ashes piled up. Needless to say, these are extreme examples of attention to detail, but it is clear enough that the early Christian interpreters read the texts the way only lawyers and poets read texts in our culture.

The two assumptions I have tried to describe have one limitation: they can obviously lead to a range of differing interpretations. For example, in his *Confessions* (12.18.27) Augustine lists a number of varying interpretations of passages from Genesis. Up to a point they are harmless disagreements, since one can argue that the opposite of an incorrect interpretation is not a single correct meaning. Instead, there can be a range of valid meanings. Indeed, unlike what are probably assumptions held by many historical critics as well as by fundamentalists, the early Christian interpreters left open the possibility of multiple meanings for a single text. Nevertheless, their approach raised the question of where to find the limits of validity, particularly at the level of Christian doctrines of God and of Christ. Since interpretation was not a private task, but one designed to inform the corporate church, the rule of faith, a summary of Christian beliefs somewhat vaguely defined but almost certainly embodied in baptismal creeds and later in the Nicene Creed, placed an increasingly strict limitation on validity. Augustine in *On Christian Instruction* added "the

---

1. Biblical citations are from the NRSV but sometimes follow the more literal translations indicated in its notes and sometimes are altered. For example, the NRSV of Lev 26:42 fails to supply a literal translation of the Hebrew.

rule of charity." Any interpretation failing to build up the love of God and neighbor is to be rejected.

Since Hebrews was largely neglected in the West until the fifth century, most of the evidence for its use appears in the writings of the Greek fathers. From at least the time of Origen in the early third century the Eastern churches accepted the Pauline authorship of Hebrews despite the letter's Greek style and the omission of Paul's name (Attridge 1989, 1–3; Bruce 1990, 14–17; Koester 2001, 19–27). Two central theological problems that texts from Hebrews are adduced to solve emerge in this evidence. The first involves the relationship of the Old to the New Testament, and it focuses not only upon the use Hebrews makes of Old Testament texts dealing with Abraham, Melchizedek, and Moses but also upon its interpretations of Pss 95, 8, and 110, as well as Jeremiah's prophecy of the new covenant. The Old Testament sanctuary was "a sketch and shadow of the heavenly one" (Heb 8:5), and "the law has only a shadow of the good things to come and not the true form of these realities" (10:1). These texts and others raise the central problem of whether we are to regard the relationship of the two Testaments in the light of a past hope fulfilled by Christ in the present and for the age to come, or from the perspective of something eternal and heavenly that has been dimly instantiated in the old covenant and is now to be seen perfectly in the new dispensation. There are, of course, differing ways of giving coherence to the apparently conflicting perspectives of Hebrews. It is this issue that primarily engages Origen's interest in the third century (Wiles 1967, 66 n. 1).

In what follows, however, I wish to pursue what I take to be the second major theological puzzle raised by Hebrews: how we are to understand the letter's assessment of Christ. It is by no means difficult to see that the New Testament as a whole makes a double judgment about Christ. Thomas calls him "my Lord and my God" (John 20:28), yet this God has died on the cross. The double judgment that Christ is both one of us and at the same time somehow identical with God finds one of its sharpest expressions in Hebrews. Christ is "the reflection of God's glory and the exact imprint of God's very being" (Heb 1:3). He is the one "through whom" God "created the worlds" (1:2). But, as well, he "offered up prayers and supplications, with loud cries and tears, to the one who was able to save him from death.... Although he was a Son, he learned obedience through what he suffered" (5:7–8). These and other texts make it extremely difficult to find a way of giving coherence to Hebrews' account of Christ's identity. If Christ is "the exact imprint of God's very being," does this mean that he is divine in such a way as not to compromise monotheism? Further, if Christ is divine, why would he need to "learn obedience by what he suffered"? Indeed, how could a divine being possibly suffer at all?

The first of these two questions was the concern of the Arian controversy (318–381 C.E.) and was resolved at the Council of Constantinople in 381 by the formulation of what we call the Nicene Creed. But this Trinitarian solution raised more sharply the second question of explaining how the divine Christ, the second person of the Trinity, could have lived and died as one of us. Hence, the Nestorian controversy (428–451) was, so to speak, engendered by the new Nicene solution of the earlier debate. In what follows I wish primarily to examine in what is admittedly a selective way the use made of Hebrews during the Arian controversy. I shall restrict consideration to Athanasius of Alexandria and Theodore of Mopsuestia, since their views are not only quite different but also set the stage for the Nestorian controversy (428–451). Here Cyril of Alexandria builds upon Athanasius's theology and adapts it to the question of Christ's person, while Nestorius does the same thing with Theodore's Antiochene theology. All four figures agree in their belief in Christ's divine nature, though Athanasius's treatment of the Trinity is sharpened by the new Nicene insistence upon the distinction of three persons (Greek, *hypostaseis*; Latin, *personae*). But Athanasius and Cyril focus upon the second person of the Trinity, the divine Word, as the sole subject in the incarnation, distinguishing his divine nature from the humanity that belongs to him not by nature but in virtue of the incarnation, often called the *economy*, that is, God's final providential dispensation. In contrast, Theodore and Nestorius insist upon two natures in Christ that nonetheless are joined together in the one Christ. The Alexandrians run the risk of implying that the two aspects of Christ are confused with one another, but their aim is primarily to honor a doctrine of salvation that insists upon the closest possible union of God and humanity in Christ. The problem for the Antiochenes is how to prevent their distinction from dividing Christ's two natures, but their aim is to honor the doctrine of God that requires a full distinction between uncreated and created nature. These presuppositions help explain the differing ways in which they interpret Hebrews.

ATHANASIUS OF ALEXANDRIA (CA. 300–373)

The fullest use of Hebrews to be found in Athanasius's writings appears in his *Orations against the Arians*. Most of the work involves the refutation of the chief scriptural proofs used by the Arians to support their claim that Christ was a creature. The Arian argument presupposed that all references in Scripture to Christ, by whatever name, refer to the Word of God. Thus, since texts referring to Christ's human operations and suffering must be applied to the Word by nature, it follows that the Word is limited and affected by these changes and is, consequently, a creature. Athanasius, then, is obliged to refute this basic argument and to find an alternative interpretation of the texts used by the Arians. After a fairly lengthy introduction, the first oration deals with Phil 2:9–10, Ps 45:7 (cited in Heb 1:9), and Heb 1:4. The second oration treats Heb 3:2, Acts 2:36, and—at great length—Prov 8:22. The third oration considers a number of texts taken from the Gospels. The fourth oration is an Apollinarian forgery.

The standard by which Athanasius judges the Arian interpretation of these texts is the theological framework he takes to be the church's faith and that he identifies with the creed ratified at Nicaea in 325. However much Athanasius's articulation of that faith is shaped and sharpened by the debate with the Arians, he is convinced that it has been constructed from Scripture. Early in the first oration he says that "we are made confident concerning the faith of true religion on the basis of the divine Scripture" (*C. Ar.* 1.9).[2] That faith is a lamp set upon the lampstand of Scripture, and it affirms the Father's Son as true and genuine, "belonging as his own to the Father's essence." The Only Begotten Wisdom and Word of God "is true God, existing as one in essence [*homoousios*] with the true Father." The passage continues by citing the expressions found in Heb 1:3: the Son or Word is "the exact imprint" (*charaktēr*) of the Father's being (*hypostaseōs*) and is "light from light." This last creedal phrase almost certainly alludes to the other expression found in Heb 1:3, "the reflection of glory." Similarly, the Son says, "Whoever has seen me has seen the Father" (John 14:9). Athanasius cites the verses from Hebrews and John's Gospel with some frequency throughout the orations.

The second of the phrases in Heb 1:3 employs the Greek word *hypostasis* (NRSV "very being"), which was already becoming a technical term in Christian theology. But the council of 325 condemned those claiming that the Son's *hypostasis* or *ousia* (essence) differed from the Father's, thereby identifying the two terms (Attridge 1989, 44–45; Koester 2001, 180). Atha-

---

2. For the text of *Orations against the Arians* (*C. Ar.*), see Bright 1873. The translations here are mine, but see also the translation in *NPNF* 2/4:306–477. Here chapter numbers, missing in Bright, have been added.

nasius surely has this identification in mind. The *hypostasis* of Heb 1:3 is the Father's, and just as the Son is "from the essence" of the Father, so he must be thought to be "from the *hypostasis*" of the Father. Athanasius treats the two expressions in Heb 1:3 as making the same point about the identity of Father and Son with respect to being, and he has no term by which to express their distinction from one another. For this reason the majority of the conservative Eastern bishops supposed that Athanasius was a covert "Sabellian," that is, someone who thought that the titles Father, Son, and Spirit were no more than verbal distinctions corresponding to the different modes in which the one God appeared. The charge is not fair, since in the third oration (*C. Ar.* 3.36) Athanasius disavows Sabellius and insists upon the distinct identity of the Son. One of the texts he uses to support this view is Heb 1:2, where the Son is described as the "heir of all things." This phrase refers to "the Son alone even though he is the Father's own according to essence."

In the introductory part of the first oration Athanasius gives a summary of his view of Christ (*C. Ar.* 1.16):

> [The Son] is the Wisdom and Word of the Father, by whom and through whom he creates and makes all things. He is the Father's reflection [*apaugasma*, Heb 1:3] by whom he enlightens all things and is revealed to whomever he wishes. This is the one who is the Father's exact imprint [*charaktēr*, Heb 1:3] and image, by which he is contemplated and known, since he and the Father are one [John 10:30]. Indeed, the one who looks at him looks also at the Father [cf. John 14:9]. This is the one who is Christ by whom all things have been redeemed and who has worked out again the new creation [cf. 2 Cor 5:17].

Here Athanasius has moved from the eternal, consubstantial Word of God to the Christ of the incarnation. But it is clear that he makes no distinction between the two. The Word is the agent of both creations. As we learn from Athanasius's treatise *On the Incarnation*, redemption consists of two gifts, the knowledge of God and the incorruptibility of the resurrection body, both of which represent Christ's victory over Satan, sin, and death, a victory achieved by the Son who became human so that humans might be divinized.

Athanasius recognizes that throughout Hebrews the apostle is speaking of the incarnation and Christ's redeeming work. He also realizes that many texts in the letter appear to compromise the Son's divinity. He tries to solve the problem by arguing that the interpreter must pay close attention to the "time, person, and matter" to which the scriptural text refers (*C. Ar.* 1.54). The *person* (*prosōpon*) is the same both apart from and in the incarnation. Hebrews 13:8 supports the idea: "Jesus Christ is the same yesterday and today and forever" (*C. Ar.* 1.48, 2.10). The *time*, however, can refer either to the Son in his eternal nature or to the same Son in his incarnation. These two times explain the double judgment of Scripture. The simplest way of clarifying what this means is to use as an analogy the story of the prince and the pauper. At a particular time the prince takes on a pauper's existence. The pauper's clothes and the situation in which the prince finds himself are real, but in no way do they affect the prince's identity as the prince. The Word's human operations and sufferings are truly human and are his, but they do not affect the Word's divine nature. With this in mind, Athanasius interprets the three Arian prooftexts taken from Hebrews so as to deny the Arian conclusion and to show that, while the texts must be referred to the incarnation, in one way or another they are at pains to demonstrate that the divine Word is the person of whom the texts speak. Despite the two times, there is only one and the same person.

The Arians argued that Heb 1:4 ("having become as much better than [*kreittōn*; NRSV "superior to"] angels") compares the Word to angels and proves that he and they share a created nature (*C. Ar.* 1.46–52). Athanasius begins his refutation by appealing to Heb 1:5 and 1:7 to demonstrate that the contrast between Son and servant proves that the comparison is not one of likeness but of unlikeness. As opposed to the angels, the Son, who is the agent of creation, remains forever (Heb 1:10–12) and is the eternal king (1:8). "Better," then, refers to the contrast between the uncreated nature of the Word and the created nature of the angels. But "having become" in 1:4 refers to the time when the Word was made flesh, and his *economy*, that is, his redeeming work, is also *better* than the previous economies exercised by servants. Hebrews 2:1–3 makes the point by contrasting "the message declared through angels" (the law) with "so great a salvation"; Heb 7:19 supports this interpretation by stating that the law "made nothing perfect." Other texts from Hebrews use the adjective "better" to refer to the Word's redeeming work: the "better covenant" (8:6; 7:22), "better" sacrifices (9:23), and a "better hope" (7:19).

The same pattern appears in Athanasius's refutation of the Arian use of Ps 45:7, cited in Heb 1:9 (*C. Ar.* 1.46–52). According to the Arians, Christ's anointing is a reward for his having loved righteousness and hated wickedness. "Therefore" is the key to this interpretation. But Athanasius can appeal to the preceding verse ("Your throne, O God, is forever and ever") to show that the person in the text is the *eternal* Word. The Arians fail to see that loving righteousness and hating wickedness refer to the fact that the Word's divine nature is immutably good. Consequently, "therefore" in the text means that it was because of this that the Word was anointed with the Spirit at the time of his incarnation. Changeless good appeared at the human level by the Word's appropriation of a human body, "so that humans might have the changelessness of the Word's righteousness as an image and type for virtue" (*C. Ar.* 1.51). As well, the last phrase of the psalm cited in Heb 1:8–9 is "beyond your companions." The Greek word for companions (*metochoi*) can also mean "partakers," so the Word is "beyond" or above those who partake of him and are thereby sanctified by him. But in the text Christ is himself sanctified by being anointed, and Athanasius appeals to Christ's citation of Isa 61:1 at the synagogue in Nazareth (Luke 4:18). Here Christ alludes to his baptism in the Jordan when the Word sanctified the body he had appropriated, and this is what he means when he says "I sanctify myself" (John 17:19). "Therefore, it is not the Lord as Word and Wisdom who is anointed with the Spirit given from him [John 16:7, 14 and 20:22], but it is the flesh assumed by him that is anointed in him and from him, so that the sanctification, as it came to the Lord as human, might come from him to all humans" (*C. Ar.* 1.47). What explains the references to "body" and "flesh" is that Athanasius, like Arius and Apollinaris, repeats the common Alexandrian view that in the Christ of the incarnation the Word takes the place of a human rational soul in governing the body he has appropriated as an instrument for his saving purpose. Only when Apollinaris develops this view will its full implications be seen, and later in his career Athanasius will at least recognize that the incarnate Word possessed a human soul.

The third text from Hebrews employed by the Arians to prove that the Word is a creature is Heb 3:1–2, especially the phrase "faithful to the one who *made* [NRSV "appointed"] him" (*C. Ar.* 2.1–11). Athanasius begins his refutation by noting that the *time* to which the text refers is when the Word became "the apostle and high priest of our confession." The text does not "indicate the essence of the Word or his natural generation from the Father." Instead, it speaks of how the Word clothed himself with a human body "to offer himself to the Father, cleanse us all from sin by his own blood, and rise from the dead" (*C. Ar.* 2.7). Statements in Scripture about Christ that include an indication of cause or purpose apply to the economy and not to the essence of the Word. Athanasius appeals to the context of Heb 3:1–2 to make the point, and he cites the whole of Heb 2:14–3:2, underlining Christ's sharing in blood and flesh (2:14) and his becoming like his brothers and sisters (2:17). Despite its reference to the time of the economy, Heb 3:1–2 does make it clear that the *person* is the Word of God. Terms such as "made," "created," and "becoming" are not decisive, since their meaning is ambiguous and must be determined by the nature of the one to whom they refer (*C. Ar.* 2.4). More decisively, the word "faithful" in the text is used by Scripture in two different meanings: "believing" or "to be believed." Here the second meaning must be chosen. The Word is by nature trustworthy, and "faithful" alludes to the divine immutability of the Word. Athanasius proves the point by appealing to Heb 3:2–6. The passage begins by comparing the faithfulness of Christ with that of Moses, but it goes on to contrast "over God's house" with "in God's house." The contrast is between Moses as a servant and Christ as the Son, the builder of the house, and "the builder of all things is God."

A final example of the way Athanasius interprets Hebrews occurs in the context of his refutation of the Arian use of Prov 8:22: "The LORD created me as the beginning of his ways [NRSV "work"], the first of his acts of long ago." The verse does not refer to the eternal generation of the Word from the Father but to the economy by which the new creation is inaugurated. As usual, Athanasius makes the point by appealing not only to the immediate context of the verse but also to its wider context in the entire aim (*skopos*) of Scripture. The time of Prov 8:22 is "when the Word clothed himself with what was created and became like us in body." For this reason he is rightly called "brother" and "firstborn" (*C. Ar.* 2.61–64). The two titles belong together; the Only Begotten has no brothers or sisters and is "firstborn" only because of the incarnation. Athanasius adduces the four passages in the Pauline letters that employ the term "firstborn" (Col 1:15; Rom 8:29; Col 1:18; Heb 1:6). The text from Hebrews ("when he brings the firstborn into the world") establishes the meaning of the other instances, and it also explains "the beginning of his ways" in Prov 8:22. Adam lost the first way by introducing death into the world through his sin, but the Word, as "firstborn," overcame death and "opened for us a new and living way through the veil, that is, through his flesh" (cf. Heb 10:20). This is the new creation (2 Cor 5:17) of which the Word made flesh is the firstborn. The striking feature of Athanasius's exegesis is his insistence upon identifying the person of all the texts he discusses with the eternal Word or Son of God, despite his necessary distinction of the two times of which the texts speak.

Theodore of Mopsuestia (ca. 350–428)

Theodore's approach to refuting Arian views is in sharp contrast to that of Athanasius, thereby foreshadowing the controversy between Nestorius and Cyril of Alexandria. He was clearly indebted to Diodore and, as far as we can tell, followed the fundamental lines of his teacher's theology and exegesis. Diodore had attacked the Arians not only because of their denial of the Word's divinity but also for their failure to acknowledge a human rational soul in their account of the incarnation. Apollinaris of Laodicea took exception to what he regarded as Diodore's two-Sons Christology, arguing that, since the human soul is prone to sin, its inclusion in an account of Christ's person would render the union of divinity and humanity in Christ unstable. As a result, both Diodore and Theodore were obliged to refute the Apollinarians as well as the Arians. Theodore's main claim to fame, however, was as an exegete of Scripture. After his death, his writings became the chief standard of orthodoxy for East Syrian or Nestorian Christianity, where he was known as "the Interpreter." Despite the fragmentary state of his writings, enough is available to give us a clear understanding of the main lines of his interpretation of Hebrews. His basic perspective concerning the double word of Scripture concerning Christ is not, as for Athanasius, a distinction between the Word's essence and his economy but rather one between two natures, or indeed between two subjects: the assuming Word and the assumed Man. His concern is with the necessity of preserving even at the level of an account of the incarnate Lord the theological distinction between the uncreated Word and the created Man. His problem is to avoid the implication that the two natures mean that there are two Christs, and his fundamental difficulty is how to explain the union of the two natures.

Theodore's account of Christ's divinity is, however, in complete accord with the new Nicene formula of three persons (*hypostaseis*) in one essence. His interpretation of Heb 1:3 reflects this agreement. A fragment from his commentary on Hebrews cites the first part of the verse, taking its two expressions as describing the relationship of the Son to the Father.[3] The apostle was right to call the Word the "reflection," not of God, but "of glory." This "striking" expression teaches us that we should not "busy ourselves" with defining the divine nature, "since it ought only to be glorified

---

3. The Greek text may be found in Staab 1933, 201.

by us." Nevertheless, the second phrase resolves "the obscurity of the comparison." The "reflection" preserves the "exact imprint" (*akribē charaktēra*) of the divine nature, "so that whatever you would suppose that *hypostasis* to be, suppose this one to be the same, since it bears the exact imprint of that one because this one differs in no way from that one." What Theodore appears to mean is that "reflection of glory" refers to the single and incomprehensible essence of God, while "exact imprint of *hypostasis*" must be interpreted by the hypostatic distinctions within the Godhead. This understanding also appears in Theodore's commentary on the prologue to John's Gospel.[4] Just as John 1:1 speaks of the Word as both "with God" and as "God," so Heb 1:3 refers both to the perfect likeness of Father and Son and to their distinction from one another. The contrast with Athanasius's equation of the two expressions is really one between the old Nicene and the new Nicene views of the Trinity.

The contrast with Athanasius is more striking in the way Theodore handles the incarnation of the Word by his divisive Christology. In another fragment from his commentary on Hebrews Theodore defends a textual variant in Heb 2:9 (Staab 1933, 204). There are many who read the last phrase "so that *by the grace of God* [*chariti theou*] he might taste death for everyone." But, says Theodore, this reading violates the logic (*akolouthia*) of the passage, as well as Paul's usual use of "grace" to speak of God's beneficence (1 Cor 15:10; Eph 2:8–9). Here, however, the apostle in his interpretation of Ps 8 is speaking of Christ's difference from the angels and of why he seems to be less than they because of his death. Theodore's text reads, "so that *apart from God*" (*chōris theou*) he might taste death for everyone" (Koester 2001, 217–18). That is, the text makes it clear that the divine nature did not undergo death. It was the Man who died and not the Word of God. (Origen had adopted the same variant reading but interpreted it to mean that Christ died for all, that is, for angels and demons as well as humans, with the one exception of the Father.) What Theodore goes on to say qualifies his interpretation. That the Word did not taste death does not mean that the indwelling Word abandoned the Man. The next verse in Hebrews (2:10) precludes this idea by saying that the Word ("he for whom and through whom all things exist") perfected "the pioneer [*archēgon*] of their salvation" (the Man) through sufferings. A parallel passage in *Cat-*

4. The Syriac text may be found in Vosté 1940, 62:24, and a Latin translation in 63:16.

echetical Homily 8.9 argues that, though the divine nature cannot die, the Word was present to the Man in his death "by careful attention."[5]

Theodore's argument makes two points. First, many if not most of the passages in Scripture concerning Christ must be referred either to the assuming Word or to the assumed Man; it is easy to see why this understanding exposed Theodore to the accusation that he was teaching two Christs. But, second, this analysis of the texts should not obscure the fact that Scripture speaks of a single Christ, nor may we deny the perfect unity of Word and Man in one Christ. Theodore frequently disavows the charge made against him. In his commentary on Colossians he notes the last phrase of Col 1:16, "all things were created through him and in him" (Swete 1880–1882, 1:272; Greer 2010, 385–87). "Through him" must apply to the Word as the agent of the first creation, while "in him" refers to the Man as the beginning of the new creation. But that honor is the Man's only "because of the indwelling nature through which all things were made." Continuing with the next verses in the hymn from Colossians, Theodore notes the common habit of Paul to alternate teaching about the Man with references to the divinity. One example is the passage beginning with Phil 2:6, where Paul turned from divine things to human "and yet said everything as though of one and the same." The alternation also occurs in the first chapter of Hebrews, where it is possible to understand differing parts of it as references either to the Word or to the Man. But in the first chapter of Hebrews, Paul "says everything in this part of the letter as if of one."

Several specific examples of what Theodore means occur in his interpretations of texts from Hebrews. As already noted, Heb 2:10 ("It was fitting that he for whom and through whom all things exist, in bringing many children to glory, should make the pioneer of their salvation perfect through sufferings") means that the Word perfected the Man, yet the single verse implies a single person. Similarly, Heb 7:3 ("without father, without mother") refers both to the fatherless virgin birth and to the motherless eternal generation of the Word.[6] Psalm 45 as cited in Heb 1:8–9 "marvelously both distinguished the natures and demonstrated the

---

5. The Syriac text and a French translation may be found in Tonneau 1949, 198–99, indicated hereafter as *Cat. hom.* See also the ancient Latin translation of this passage in the dogmatic fragments assembled by Swete 1880–1882, 2:235.

6. Dogmatic fragments in Swete 1880–1882, 2:314.

unity of person [*prosōpon*]."[7] Despite Theodore's emphasis on the *prosōpon* of union as a way of dispelling the objection that he is dividing Christ's person, the term is more exegetical than theological. His fullest account of the union appears in the fragments of book 7 of *On the Incarnation*.[8] Here he pulls together three biblical expressions into a formula designed to articulate the unity of the incarnate Lord: indwelling (John 1:14) by good pleasure (Matt 3:17) as in a Son (Heb 1:2). The indwelling of the Word in the assumed Man was not by nature or active operation but by good pleasure, and the basic analogy has to do with the interaction of God's grace and human free choice. But the formula needs further specification so as to avoid the implication that the Man is no more than a prophet or someone specially gifted by God. Thus, the indwelling by good pleasure is "as in a Son." Theodore cites Heb 1:2 ("he has spoken to us by a Son [*en huiōi*]"), noticing the absence of an article before "Son." This means that Paul by the indefinite term was able to make "no separation" and "to signify both by a single expression," that is, both the Word who is Son by nature and the Man who is Son by grace.[9] To be sure, the text from Hebrews means that God spoke through the Man, but the apostle in this part of the letter "tries to show in what way he is a sharer in divine honor and that he enjoys it not on account of his own nature, but on account of the nature which indwells him."[10] "Son," then, is a term that includes both natures and also articulates the unique and complete grace to be found in the Man. It is obviously possible to doubt the sufficiency of Theodore's Christology, based as it is primarily on the analogy of grace, but what he means is that the christological union represents the unique and perfect coincidence of two activities: God's grace and the perfect response of human freedom. Theodore is not entirely consistent in repudiating the body-soul analogy that dominates Alexandrian Christology, but his tendency is to regard an ontological definition of the christological union as less persuasive than the view he proposes.

Theodore finds the same juxtaposition of the divine and the human in the baptismal creed he explains in his catechetical homilies. The second clause of that creed reads, "[We believe] in one Lord Jesus Christ, the Only

---

7. The Greek text is from Devreesse 1939. Hill (2006, 578–79) translates: "he both separated the natures and gave a glimpse of the unity of the person."

8. Dogmatic fragments in Swete 1880–1882, 2:293–98.

9. Dogmatic fragments in Swete 1880–1882, 2:303.

10. Dogmatic fragments in Swete 1880–1882, 2:305.

Begotten Son of God, the firstborn of all creation." He notes the incompatibility of "Only Begotten" and "firstborn" and draws his usual distinction between the Word and the Man. But both terms are governed by "one Lord Jesus Christ." Moreover, the creation of which the Man is firstborn (Col 1:15) is the new creation in which the Man is "the first of many brothers" (*Cat. hom.* 3.6–7). Theodore alludes not only to Rom 8:29 but also to Heb 2:17 ("like his brothers and sisters"). In this sense the Man is the proximate agent of salvation, an agency made possible by the indwelling Word and effected by the Man's death and resurrection. Theodore makes frequent use of the interpretation of Ps 8 given in Heb 2:5–9 (e.g., *Cat. hom.* 6.10, citing also Heb 2:16). He also treats the Man as the high priest, citing numerous texts from Hebrews (e.g., *Cat. hom.* 15.15–19). It is, of course, the Man's resurrection that inaugurates the new creation and gives Christians their hope of salvation. But since this "perfection" was accomplished "through sufferings" in order to "lead many children to glory," Theodore has no difficulty taking seriously Christ's suffering and death. On the cross the Man cites the first verse of Ps 22 ("My God, my God, why have you forsaken me"), not because it prophesied his death, but because he used it as religious people would to bear testimony to his suffering, the scourgings and beatings, the nails and the cross (Hill 2006, 242–43). Even before the cross "we see him suffer hunger, and we know he thirsted, and we learn he was afraid, and we find him ignorant."[11] I can find only one reference to the passage that begins with Heb 5:7. Commenting on Rom 7:5, Theodore discusses the various meanings Paul gives to the word "flesh." "In the days of his flesh" (Heb 5:7) means "in the time of his suffering," when he was about to die (Staab 1933, 124). The Man's suffering and death are obviously the prelude to his resurrection, but they are more easily explained by Theodore and the Antiochenes than by the unitive Christology of Athanasius and Cyril, who must somehow explain how the divine Word suffers and dies. Cyril's expression "he suffered without suffering" (*apathōs pathei*) may express a mystery, but it scarcely explains it.

The Nestorian Controversy (428–451)

Both Athanasius and Theodore were dead by the time the Nestorian controversy began not long after Nestorius, a monk from Antioch, became

---

11. Dogmatic fragments in Swete 1880–1882, 2:297.

bishop of Constantinople in the spring of 428. But, as I have suggested, their theologies and interpretations of Scripture are the implicit basis of the debate that became explicit throughout the Christian world in the fifth century and continued beyond the Council of Chalcedon in 451 because of the monophysite and Nestorian churches that refused to accept its solution. What I am suggesting is that the possible contradiction between interpretations of Hebrews given by Athanasius and Theodore became actual when Cyril of Alexandria condemned Nestorius. One of Nestorius's sermons that provoked Cyril was an exposition of Heb 3:1–2. Cyril's refutation of the sermon dominates the third book of his *Against Nestorius*. Thus, in these two writings we can see the lines of battle drawn up on the basis of Hebrews at least a year before the Council of Ephesus in 431.

Nestorius's sermon, while it purports to be an attack against "the heirs of Arius," fails to address the phrase in Heb 3:2 where Christ is said to be "faithful to the one who *made* him" and that had supported the Arian claim that the Word was a creature.[12] Instead, Nestorius's concern is to define "the apostle and high priest of our confession" as the human Jesus rather than the divine Word. While he wishes to insist upon Christ's full humanity, the real issue has to do with his conviction that the distinction between God as uncreated and humans as created must be drawn even at the level of an account of Christ's person. "For upon learning of the title 'apostle,' who would not immediately know that this meant the Man? And upon hearing the name 'high priest,' who would think that the high priest was the essence of divinity?" (Loofs 1905, 232). After pointing out that if the high priest were the Word, there would be no one to whom the priestly offering could be made, he appeals to texts from Hebrews related to 3:1. Hebrews 5:1–3 defines the priest as "taken from humans" and "ordained on behalf of humans." This can only refer to "the possessor [*ktētōr*] of divinity," not to the divine Word (Loofs 1905, 232–33).

Nestorius then cites the whole of Heb 2:16–3:2, omitting only the last phrase of 2:17. He assumes that the passage makes the distinction to be found in John 2:19, where the Word of God distinguishes himself from the temple of his body. The temple is destroyed, while the Word raises it up on the third day. In other words, we must distinguish the assumed Man, who dies, from the Word, who raises him from the dead. Similarly, the "seed of

---

12. The Greek text of the sermon may be found in Loofs 1905, 230–42. Citations for passages I have translated will be given in parentheses.

Abraham" (Heb 2:16) is "yesterday and today" (Heb 13:8) as opposed to
the Word, who is "before Abraham" (John 8:58). As well, the Man, who is
"like his brothers in all respects, sharing in blood and flesh" (Heb 2:17, 14),
is not the same as the Word, who says, "whoever has seen me has seen the
Father" (John 14:9). Moreover, the one who *became* high priest (Heb 2:17)
"did not eternally preexist." Nestorius then appeals to Heb 5:7–10 with its
reference to "the days of his flesh" and to his "having been made perfect"
through sufferings (5:9; cf. 2:10). We must not contradict Paul "by confus-
ing the impassible Word of God with the earthly likeness and by making
him the passible high priest" (Loofs 1905, 236).

The "seed [NRSV "descendants"] of Abraham" (Heb 2:16) calls to mind
for Nestorius God's promise to Abraham that the Gentiles would be blessed
in his seed (Gen 22:18), thereby prompting a discussion of the Man as the
agent of salvation. "Who should be the mediator of so great a promise?"
Moses, Aaron, and Elijah are weighed in the balance and found wanting.
The mediator must be sinless and yet of the same nature and subject to the
same sufferings as humans. It is the Man, who, "having demonstrated in
himself the *prosōpon* of the nature without sin," has "reconciled our nature
to God through his sinless conduct in that nature" (Loofs 1905, 239). The
mediator fulfills the type of Moses (Heb 3:2–3), but Jesus excels Moses
because of his union with divinity (Loofs 1905, 241). Nestorius concludes
his sermon with an exhortation: "Let us not include as incorporeal the
humanity with the incorporeal divinity, and let us not confuse the divinity with the sufferings of the humanity. Separating the characteristics of
the natures, let us join them together in a worthy kind of unity. Let us not
preach God the Word as the temple instead of the indweller, and let us not
name the temple the indweller instead of the indwelt" (Loofs 1905, 242).

Cyril's response to the sermon is essentially a rejection of Nestorius's
view by arguing that the sharp distinction he makes is tantamount to dividing Christ's person. It presupposes his assumption that salvation depends
upon the closest possible union of the Word with humanity. Immediately
before his first citation of a passage from Nestorius's sermon, Cyril summarizes his own view:[13]

> Therefore, we say that it is the Word from God the Father, when he is
> said to have been emptied for our sake by taking the form of a servant

---

13. The Greek text may be found in Pusey 1875. References in parentheses (*Adv. Nest.*) refer to the book, section, and page number in Pusey's edition.

[Phil 2:7], who is then also said to have lowered himself to the limits of humanity. To these limits most certainly are suitable both seeming to be sent [as apostle] and reckoning the priestly ministry of the highest honor. ... Why is it strange or incompatible with the rationale of the economy that he has been made high priest, since he has offered himself as a sweet-smelling savor for us and has offered us to God the Father through himself and in himself? (*Adv. Nest.* 3.1, 136)

Cyril is addressing the two titles of Christ in Heb 3:1 but is doing so by appealing to the hymn of Phil 2 and by focusing upon the saving work of the Word in his incarnation. Throughout his writings Cyril employs the language of Phil 2 in a formulaic way. The "emptying" (*kenōsis*) of the Word is his appropriation of the form of a servant and his lowering himself to human limitations. While it is not clear what this means with respect to the divine nature of the Word or how the formulation should be related to technical terms such as "essence," "nature," and "*hypostasis*," Cyril does agree with Nestorius that Christ's high priesthood belongs in the context of the incarnation and does not affect the essence of the Lord. But the high priesthood is not to be attributed to "the man born of a woman as someone other than the Word and having only a mere conjunction [*synapheia*] with the Word" (*Adv. Nest.* 3.1, 137). Such a view amounts to saying "that the Word of God was not sent into this world."

The Word remains the same in his divine nature despite his economic appropriation of humanity to become apostle and high priest. The Word "has come down in the form of a servant, that is, by taking the form of a servant, even though he exists as the exact imprint and reflection of the Father's glory" (*Adv. Nest.* 3.1, 140). Cyril conflates the two expressions in Heb 1:3, even though he treats them as making the hypostatic distinction between Father and Son. He is reasonably consistent throughout his writings in this interpretation. Here, however, his aim is to insist that the Word is one and the same both apart from and in the incarnation. Cyril also mocks Nestorius's designation of the Man as "the possessor of divinity," failing to note that the expression probably reflects Nestorius's metaphor of the temple indwelt by the Word. Cyril argues that the seed of Abraham cannot be the possessor of divinity, since it was the divinity that possessed it by appropriating the form of a servant. Following Athanasius, he employs the term "faithful" in Heb 3:2 ("faithful to the one who made him") as a designation of the Word's essence in order to prove that the Word remains what he always is even in the incarnation. Similarly, Heb

2:17 speaks of Christ as "a merciful and faithful high priest." The divine Word "was and is God, good by nature, both compassionate and always merciful, and did not become this in time; rather, he was shown to be such to us" (*Adv. Nest.* 3.2, 149). Cyril repeatedly rejects Nestorius's oppositions (the temple and the indweller, the seed of Abraham and the one before Abraham, the brother and the one in whom the Father is seen) on the grounds that the Word's existence as God was preserved "when he also became son of man" (*Adv. Nest.* 3.3, 151–54).

The contrast between these two views of Christ as high priest is striking. For Nestorius it is the man Jesus who is high priest, and his nature must be distinguished from that of God the Word. Cyril, however, identifies the high priest as the Word, distinguishing his incarnate existence from his nature. Nevertheless, deeper reflection suggests that the two interpretations of Hebrews need not be irreconcilable. Nestorius is concerned to say that the Man is the Savior, but he recognizes that this is true only because of the indwelling Word. Cyril insists that it is the divine Word who has saved us, but he also understands that this was possible only because the Word appropriated humanity. The course of the conflict after 430 illustrates the tension between conflict and compromise (Russell 2000, 31–58; McGuckin 2004, 1–243). It also reveals developments both in the Alexandrian position and in that of the Antiochenes, now under the leadership of Theodoret of Cyrus, developments that led to the Definition of Chalcedon in 451 (Pásztori-Kupán 2006, 7–27). This document, meant to explain but not to replace the Nicene Creed, accepted both the Antiochene insistence upon Christ's two natures and the Alexandrian view of his single *hypostasis*. It can be read as a compromise, placing boundaries around differing but valid interpretations of Christ. It affirms that Christ is "perfect in divinity" (against Arius), "perfect in humanity" (against Apollinaris), "acknowledged *in* two natures" without confusion (against Eutyches) and without division (against Nestorius). These four grammatical rules, as it were, are to be observed in any valid doctrine of Christ, and the council accepted as "orthodox" the rather different Christologies of Cyril (apart from the one-nature formula), of Theodoret, and of Pope Leo of Rome. The compromise proved unacceptable in Egypt and in much of Syria, largely because it had rejected the one-nature formula and had affirmed the continued existence of two natures after the incarnation by using the preposition "in" rather than "out of." Moreover, how to draw the line between moderate and extreme articulations of the two chief Christologies was not entirely clear, and for the schismatic monophysites, the chief defenders of Chalcedon, Theodoret and Leo, were both tainted with Nestorianism. Thus, Chalcedon is the end of one story and the beginning of another one that takes us to the fifth general Council of Constantinople in 553 and beyond.

A BRIEF CONCLUSION

Describing some of the interpretations of Hebrews put forth during the period of the first four general councils underlines the importance of the theological frameworks that shape them. Nevertheless, all the interpreters claim that their presupposed frameworks spring from Scripture. If we take these claims seriously, there is a circularity or reciprocity binding exegesis and theology together. In our time, I suggest, a similar circularity attaches to the largely historical interpretations of the New Testament with which we are familiar. Reconstructions of the historical contexts of the New Testament writings are presuppositions that shape interpretations. Yet the claim is made that these historical constructs derive from the texts themselves. Perhaps the reason patristic exegesis often seems quite foreign to us is the replacement of theology by history that is the legacy of the Enlightenment and the historical-critical method. At the same time, if the New Testament, and in particular Hebrews, are to be the basis for a theological interpretation of Christian faith and not merely evidence for the reconstruction of early Christianity, the church fathers have much to teach us. Surely we cannot ignore the conclusions of the historians, and they must be allowed to inform Christian theology. But, however difficult it may be to explain, it is equally clear to me that history, while necessary, is not sufficient for articulating the meaning of Christ for believers—or perhaps I should say meanings, since in my view there need to be multiple but valid ways of articulating what faith in Christ is and requires.

"A Sacrifice of Praise":
Does Hebrews Promote Supersessionism?

Alan C. Mitchell

Introduction

The challenge of reading Hebrews in the post-Holocaust era is magnified in the history of its interpretation by the fact that, from the second century C.E., Christians have used it to promote the view that Christianity, according to God's plan, has replaced Judaism. A further complication arises from the fact that the language of Hebrews and its author's style lend themselves to this kind of interpretation, so that well beyond the second century this view has, unfortunately, prevailed. The comparisons of Jesus' atoning death to the sacrifices of the Levitical cult, as well as the focus on the superiority of his priesthood and the emphasis on a new covenant, often punctuated by the use of the adjective "better," easily lead an unwary reader to conclude that Christianity has superseded Judaism in important ways. In theological terms, this way of thinking is called supersessionism, the belief that Israel's election by God was transferred to Christianity, which is a new Israel with a new covenant. The development over time of an exclusivist understanding of Christ and Christianity has abetted supersessionism and validated it in the eyes of its promoters.

Since much supersessionist thought rests on the belief that God has rejected Israel, it has served as a basis for anti-Semitism. Certainly, after the Jewish Holocaust, reading the New Testament through the lens of supersessionism seems like an irresponsible thing to do. Fortunately, there is a growing consensus among New Testament scholars that it is not necessary to continue reading Hebrews in this manner. When polemical New Testament texts are properly understood in the milieus in which they originated, alternatives to supersessionist readings become available. This certainly is the case regarding Hebrews.

My thesis is that Hebrews itself is not inherently supersessionist, but its theology is so rendered because of the customary way it has been interpreted since the second century C.E. In this essay, then, I will offer a brief treatment of what supersessionism is, examine three critical texts from Hebrews that have been invoked to promote supersessionism (7:1–12; 8:8–13; and 10:1–10), and then discuss a new direction in the interpretation of Hebrews that shows why it is unnecessary and undesirable to read Hebrews from that vantage point any longer.

The title of this chapter is taken from Heb 13:15, where the author exhorts his readers to offer their own sacrifice to God, a sacrifice of praise. The expression itself is taken from the LXX version of Ps 50 (LXX 49):14, and in the context of Hebrews when sacrifice at the Jerusalem temple had ceased, it speaks to the question of continuity with the past that concerns the author greatly. It also joins the readers of Hebrews to those traditions of Hellenistic Judaism that promoted praise and worship of God over animal sacrifice, thus locating Hebrews within a milieu that could hardly be supersessionist.

WHAT IS SUPERSESSIONISM?

The term *supersessionism* derives from the Latin *super,* "above" or "on," and *sedere,* "to sit." The original meaning of the compound *supersedere* was "to postpone" or "to defer." In the seventeenth century, the verb "supersede" took on the meaning of "to render void," "to annul," and "to replace," where the replacement was thought to be superior to what preceded it (*Oxford English Dictionary,* s.v.). This last definition captures the original sense of the two Latin words, *super* and *sedere,* with the meaning "*to place* something *above* something else." The theological term *supersessionism* carries this meaning with the result that, when applied to Christianity, Judaism is annulled or rendered useless because Christianity is placed above it and takes its place. Perhaps a few examples of supersessionist interpretations of Hebrews by early Christian authors will help to make the above given definition more concrete.

(1) The Epistle of Barnabas (Barn. 14) refers to Moses as a servant in God's house, which is an ostensible reference to Num 12:7 but could also refer to Heb 3:5, where Moses as servant is compared to Christ as Son. The text of Barnabas is ambiguous regarding the source of this comparison. Clearer is its purpose: to answer the question whether Christians are heirs to God's covenant with Israel. Barnabas concludes that, as servant, Moses

received the covenant, but, as Son, Christ gave it to Christians in order to show that they are its true heirs.

(2) Commenting on the Levitical priesthood in Heb 7:11–12, Theodoret of Cyrus (*Interpretation of Hebrews* 70) claimed that, not only was it replaced by the priesthood of Christ, but that it was also transformed by his priesthood, since through Christ the priestly lineage passed from the tribe of Levi to the tribe of Judah (Heen and Krey 2005, 111). There is no evidence for this claim in Judaism itself.

(3) When discussing Heb 8:5, a reference to the tabernacle as a shadow of the heavenly sanctuary, Irenaeus (*Haer.* 4.19.1) writes that gifts, oblations, and sacrifices were shown to Moses according to a heavenly pattern. These, he says, are types, and those who fixate on them will find only types and not the real God (*ANF* 1:486–87).

(4) In his explanation of the new covenant in Heb 8:8–12, Chrysostom (*Hom. Heb.* 14.5) writes that Jews could not claim that a law written on the heart was ever given to them; rather, the apostles, with whom God never made a written covenant, received the new covenant in their hearts through the action of the Holy Spirit (Heen and Krey 2005, 127).

(5) Likewise, Tertullian (*Marc.* 5.11.4) proclaims the new covenant as superior to the old because it is permanent, whereas the old was destined to be done away with. Thus God exalts the gospel over the law (Evans 1972, 2:579).

TYPES OF SUPERSESSIONISM

Whereas each of the above examples attests to supersessionism, altogether they witness to different kinds of supersessionism. In his excellent study on the topic, R. Kendall Soulen isolates three kinds of supersessionism, which date back to the earliest centuries of Christianity. (1) *Economic supersessionism* holds the view that Israel's role in the history of salvation was solely to prefigure Christ. Consequently, with the coming of Christ, Israel became obsolete in God's plan of salvation (examples 2 and 5 above). (2) *Punitive supersessionism* is even stronger as it stresses the idea that God has rejected Israel for refusing to accept Christ (examples 1 and 4 above). The element of hostility introduced into punitive supersessionism distinguishes it from economic supersessionism and inevitably contributes to anti-Semitism. (3) Soulen calls a third type *structural supersessionism*. According to it, the canon of Scripture structures the narrative of salvation so that Hebrew Scripture has meaning only in the way its narrative plot is fulfilled in the New Testament (example 3 above). Consequently, Hebrew Scripture has no independent valid role of its own as the sacred writ of Jews (Soulen 1996, 29–31).

All forms of supersessionism deprive Judaism of its inherent integrity and challenge the veracity of God's promises to Israel, but there is a serious consequence for Christianity as well. Supersessionism calls into question the basic claims of Christian theology. As long as Christian theologians maintain supersessionist views, what confidence can they have in the veracity and reliability of God's promises for Christianity (Soulen 1996, 4–5)?

Supersessionism contributes to anti-Semitism, but they are two distinct entities. Anti-Semitism is prejudice directed toward Jews themselves, individually and as a people, precisely because they are Jews, whereas supersessionism promotes Christianity as a replacement for Judaism (Kim 2006, 2–7). Neither position is tenable, so it is incumbent upon New Testament scholars to promote nonsupersessionist readings of polemical texts. One of the most viable ways of doing this is to locate New Testament authors and books within the sociohistorical background of their day.

The New Testament was composed before Christianity split definitively from Judaism. When one understands the rich variegation of Judaism in the first century c.e. and the processes of self-definition each of the various Jewish sects undertook, texts that appear polemical need not be seen as anti-Semitic or supersessionist. Rather, they can be viewed as part of an intra-Jewish debate about particular interpretations of Scripture, or differences over ritual and practice, and even the role of the law itself. This can be true if the audience of a given New Testament book is dominantly Gentile, because its interest in maintaining its Jewish heritage.

HEBREWS AND SUPERSESSIONISM

THE PURPOSE OF HEBREWS

Before we examine the question of whether Hebrews is inherently supersessionist, a brief overview of the book may help to set the stage. Rather than a letter, Hebrews is a sermon or homily composed by an anonymous Christian author for a Roman community of Christians some time after 70 c.e., when the temple in Jerusalem was destroyed. The author composed his sermon for a largely Gentile audience who suffered some social dislocation after the Jewish war with Rome (66–73 c.e.). The pressures and tensions they faced in the wake of the Roman victory may have caused them to doubt and waver in their faith. Perhaps they feared that the Romans would associate them with the Jews they had vanquished—and that they themselves would suffer because they would not be distinguished from Jews in Rome. Whatever feelings of loss they had experienced after the Roman victory in Judea were doubtless magnified by living among the victors in their capital city. Even though they were mostly Gentiles, they had not lost touch with their Jewish heritage and certainly counted Jewish Christians, and perhaps non-Christian Jews, among their friends. In search of a solution to the dilemma of this community, its leaders may have solicited the help of the author to support and encourage this community shaken by the circumstances under which it was forced to live.

In an effort to bolster the faith of the community and to emphasize positive things rather than negative, the author of Hebrews chose to speak about what this community still *had* rather than what it had lost. The catalogue of their spiritual possessions is impressive: hope (6:19), a great priest (8:1; 10:21), an altar (10:13), and confidence (10:19). What they lack is a lasting city on earth (13:14), so Hebrews directs its audience's attention to the eschatological future, where they will enter into God's rest (4:1, 9–11) in a heavenly Jerusalem (12:22) and will receive a kingdom that cannot be shaken (12:28; Mitchell 2007, 1–34).

THE CHALLENGE OF HEBREWS

As New Testament books go, Hebrews is perhaps the most difficult to understand. Although its Greek is sophisticated and polished, its language is challenging because of the number of words that occur only in it, such as "blood shedding" (9:22) and "perfecter" (12:2). Some of these words appear to have been coined by its author. Furthermore, the argument of Hebrews is difficult to follow, presenting the interpreter with serious challenges, as it alternates between exposition and exhortation.

The author's preference for several forms of comparison brings a measure of precision to his elucidation of what his readers have in Christ, yet some of the terms of the comparisons may confuse the reader unfamiliar with the rhetorical techniques the author employs. For example, he uses Greek rhetorical comparison, or *synkrisis*, in Heb 7:18–25. In speaking of Christ's priesthood arising from the order of Melchizedek rather than the order of Aaron, he notes that, since the Levitical priesthood was established on the basis of the law, a change in the priesthood brought about a change in the law (7:11–12). In his conclusion, however, he does not speak simply of a change in the law but juxtaposes the abrogation of a commandment with the introduction of a better hope in the priesthood of Christ (7:18). The reader may surmise that the purpose of the comparison is to show how the priesthood of Christ is inherently better than the Levitical priesthood and has effectively replaced it.

When *synkrisis* is properly understood, one need not arrive at this conclusion. Ancient rhetoricians advise that comparison is stronger when the two things being compared are in themselves excellent (Aristotle, *Rhet.* 1.9.39–41; Isocrates, *Hel. enc.* 22; Theon, *Progym.* 10.8–24; see Seid 1996, 52–55, 61–62, 68–69; 2007, 5; deSilva 2000, 262–63; Mason 2010a, 10–14). So, when drawing comparisons, it is possible for each of the terms of the comparison to constitute a good in itself. It is not necessary always to place one term over the other as superior to it. The comparative adjective "better" in this instance may not refer to something in itself but rather to its end. In other words, the Levitical priesthood had its purpose as long as it was in existence, and it accomplished the purpose for which it was ordained. For Christians, the priesthood of Christ has its own purpose in bringing them to salvation, and it accomplishes its purpose in a way other than the Levitical priesthood achieved its. There need be no denigration of the former by the latter.

Similarly, when the author of Hebrews employs *a fortiori* methods of Jewish exegesis, the reader can draw the conclusion that the terms of the arguments necessarily point to the superiority of Christianity over Judaism. One such method is called *qal wahomer,* meaning from the "light to the heavy." An example of this technique is found in Heb 9:11–14. In the last two verses, the author compares the blood of sacrificial animals with the blood of Christ. Whereas sacrificial blood was able to purify the flesh, the blood of Christ can purify the conscience from sin. The greater weight is given to the blood of Christ because the author is especially interested in showing his readers that Christ's atoning sacrifice was like the atoning sacrifices under the Levitical system but was also different in its effect: it was able to purify the conscience from sin (see 9:9; 10:22). Again we see that, in the author's view, animal sacrifices were in themselves good for the purpose for which they were instituted. Now that sacrifice has come to an end with the destruction of the Jerusalem temple, the atoning effect of Christ's blood is ordered to a different goal, the purification of the conscience.

Another Jewish exegetical method the author uses is *gezerah shawah,* meaning "equal category," where a catchword links two texts so that one interprets the other, rendering a new meaning of the linking word itself. An example is the use of Ps 95 (LXX 94):11 in Heb 4:1–11 to arrive at a new understanding of God's rest. There are three uses of "rest" in this text. There is the rest quoted in the psalm verse (Heb 4:3, 5) that the wilderness generation failed to enter into because of their disobedience (4:6), God's Sabbath rest from Gen 2:2, quoted by the author in Heb 4:4, and the rest that those who remain faithful may yet enter (4:6, 9, 11). The author moves among those three types of rest to apply the second meaning of rest to the third, thus redefining the first. The important transition comes in placing the citation of Gen 2:2 between the two citations of Ps 95 (LXX 94):11, so that when the author repeats the psalm verse in Heb 4:5, the reader now thinks of God's Sabbath rest, not the entrance into the promised land. He referred to that first instance of "rest" in order to provide the negative example of those who, through disobedience, were denied entrance into it. How can there still exist a hope for a later entrance? Psalm 95 (LXX 94):7–8 also exhorts the reader to take advantage of "today." Why would it do that if there was no possibility of a future entrance into God's rest? Thus the author shifts the focus to the present opportunity for his readers, which makes possible the entrance into God's rest through their obedience (Heb 4:11). Now, however, the rest is a Sabbath rest, as is clear from verse 9. Through the *gezerah shawah* method the author effectively equates the rest denied the wilderness generation with God's Sabbath rest, in order to offer a warning and a hope for his readers (see Johnson 2006, 126–28).[1]

An uninformed reading of this text may lead the reader simply to think that the Christian recipients of Hebrews are better off than their Jewish forebears because they have the possibility of entering God's rest that Jews no longer have (Montefiore 1964, 81–85; Johnson 2008, 28). To draw this conclusion misses the point of the midrashic method, *gezerah shawah,* that the author has employed in the text. In fact, his readers can suffer the same fate as the wilderness generation should they fail in obedience. They do not have an advantage simply because they are Christians.

The complexity of the argument of Hebrews as well as the peculiarities of the author's diction and style present challenges to an easy interpretation of the sermon. At times the author's use of comparison and *a fortiori* reasoning, when discussing the benefits of Christ for his readers, seems to

---

1. For additional discussion of the author's use of Jewish exegetical methods, see the essays by David M. Moffitt and Gabriella Gelardini in this volume.

support the view that God's covenant with Israel ended with the inauguration of the new covenant in Christ. Exposition and exhortation to embrace
and hold on to the Christian confession has also been read to mean that it
has superseded God's promises to Israel, of which Christianity is now the
rightful heir. A look at three texts of Hebrews in the next section will show
that, whatever difficulties arise from problems interpreters usually meet in
Hebrews, the book need not be read in a supersessionist way.

Problematic Texts in Hebrews

An underlying issue in the supersessionist interpretation of Hebrews is the
problem of continuity and discontinuity: how the past relates to the present and the future. The author of Hebrews understands how well-situated
the community for which he wrote is within the milieu of post-70 Judaism and how his audience shares the concerns of other Jews for the loss
of the city of Jerusalem, the temple, the priesthood, and the Jewish ritual
system. Although he does not reference any particular form of Judaism in
his day, he is thoroughly conversant with the Septuagint and Jewish ritual
tradition. He appeals to the past to shed light on the present and future
and engages issues of continuity and discontinuity between those periods
of time.

From the very outset of his sermon in the *exordium* (Heb 1:1–4), the
author locates God's revelation within the past and the future. Having
spoken in the past through the prophets "in these last days," God now is
speaking through the Son. What is continuous is God's revelation; what
is discontinuous is the form it now takes. There is no mention of the nul-
lification of past revelation or of its replacement. The author is careful to
distinguish the ancestors from his audience, among whom he includes
himself by using the word "us." There is no hint that, if God is using a different form to speak to a particular audience, God does not continue to
speak to others at the same time. The audience of Hebrews is not the only
one receiving God's revelation. That concern is one of a later time and
appears not to have occurred to the author of Hebrews.

We now turn to three texts that address the question of continuity
and discontinuity with the past, present, and future in relation to the
priesthood of Christ (Heb 7:1–12) and the covenant (Heb 8:8–13; 10:1–
10). They are also texts that have in the past been interpreted to resolve
the tensions between these time periods by resorting to a supersessionist
interpretation.

HEBREWS 7:1–12

In particular, when not properly understood, the comparison of the priesthood of Jesus with that of the Levitical cult can lead one to the conclusion that Christianity had indeed replaced Judaism, that is, to supersessionism.

The discussion of the mysterious figure of Melchizedek in Heb 7:1–12 facilitates the author's transition to his consideration of the priesthood of Christ. Melchizedek is the prototype of the eternal priest, as he is "without father, without mother, without genealogy, having neither beginning of days nor end of life" (Heb 7:3). Moreover, since Abraham paid him tithes (Gen 14:20), he honored him as someone higher in rank than he. The author even claims that, since Levi was an heir to Abraham, he was already in the latter's loins and therefore proleptically paid tithes to Melchizedek through Abraham. Levi, too, acknowledged Melchizedek's higher status as king and priest (Heb 7:8–9).

The author knows that an objection may be raised to the priesthood of Christ because the earthly Jesus was not from the tribe of Levi (Heb 7:14). Therefore, he must establish a change in the priesthood in order to present the basis for Christ's priesthood. He does this by invoking Ps 110 (LXX 109):4, "You are a priest forever according to the order of Melchizedek." Treating the psalm verse as a prophecy, he shows its fulfillment in the priesthood of Christ (Heb 7:20–26). In the author's view, a change in the priesthood requires a change in the law (Heb 7:12). The change in the priesthood was needed because Christ could not have been a priest on earth. Rather, he is a priest of a heavenly order, that of Melchizedek. The contrast, then, is not between two types of earthly priesthoods but between one earthly and one heavenly. As the priesthood was instituted under the law, the author believes any change in the priesthood necessarily changes the law. This is a curious argument, because the law only governed the earthly priesthood. The author does not say how a change in the law would govern a heavenly priesthood. In fact, the heavenly priesthood falls outside of the purview of the law, since it is not based on legal descent but on the "power of an indestructible life" (Heb 7:15). Thus it is not entirely clear how the change from an earthly priesthood to a heavenly priesthood requires a change in the law. Some, however, have understood the change to be rather sweeping, so that what changed was the entire covenant, both its cultic/ritual laws as well as its moral laws (Ellingworth 1993, 374; Hagner 1990, 107; Montefiore 1964, 124).

As already shown in the discussion of supersessionism in Hebrews, the author of Hebrews is concerned only with the cultic law of the Sinai covenant and the prescriptions governing the Levitical priesthood (Johnson 2006, 184; Thompson 2008, 155). Therefore, the change in the law mentioned in 7:13 pertains to the change of cultic law only. Thus, without distinguishing between different objects of the law, the law itself is reduced merely to cultic law. Whereas the covenant contains both moral and cultic laws, it is difficult to see how a change in cultic law would then result in a change in the law as a whole.

We should read Heb 7:12 to apply only to a change in ritual law, not to the entire covenant itself. The problem is only complicated by the fact that, having noted a change in the priesthood, the author of Hebrews does not argue for a new line of priests from the order of Melchizedek, since in his estimation the priesthood of Christ exhausts the line (Mitchell 2007, 150). Indeed, he is using the Levitical priesthood as a foil for what he wants to say about the priesthood of Christ, so we ought not to understand his rhetoric to support a supersessionist interpretation of this verse (Thompson 2008, 155–56).

HEBREWS 8:7–13

The central argument of Hebrews runs from 8:1 to 10:18. In the first six verses of chapter 8, the author presents his main thought, that the recipients have a high priest in Jesus Christ. He concludes the section with the claim that Jesus is a "mediator of a better covenant" (Heb 8:6). In the section that follows (8:7–13) the author continues to develop the exposition of a "better covenant," and it becomes clear that he is speaking of the fulfillment of Jer 31 (LXX 38):31–34, "the new covenant." The focus on the "new covenant" has often been taken to mean that the Sinai covenant was somehow nullified and is no longer in effect after the death of Christ (Johnson 2008, 41–42; Marshall 2009, 267–68; Montefiore 1964, 142; Schenck 2003, 73–74).

Perhaps the most critical verse in this section in Heb 8:13: "In speaking of a 'new covenant' he has made the first one obsolete. And what is obsolete and growing old will soon disappear" (NRSV). A plain reading of the verse may lead one quickly to a supersessionist interpretation of it. After all, the author says that the first covenant is obsolete, growing old, and soon to pass away. Yet, despite the way these words sound, one need not read them to say that God intended to put an end to the first covenant in order to replace it with the second or to replace Judaism with Christianity. "Obsolete" in this verse means simply "to make old." According to Harold Attridge, the word choice here may simply be an exegetical inference: if there is a new covenant, there has to be an old one (Attridge 1989, 221). When "new" and "old" are understood as temporal markers, they need not be interpreted to compare the validity of one covenant over another. Thus in speaking of a "new covenant," Jeremiah could have been referring to a further determination of the Sinai covenant, which was then seen to be the "old covenant."

It is important to remember in this context that the author of Hebrews saw himself and his audience as "children of Abraham" (Heb 2:16) living under God's promises to him; these could not be abrogated because God guaranteed them with an oath (6:13–18). We have here yet another example of how the author of Hebrews wrestles with the question of continuity and discontinuity. It is clear in the citation from Jeremiah that the change he speaks of takes place, at first, in the people of the covenant. Now it is internalized, placed in their minds, and written on their hearts (8:10). The people will not need external instruction under this covenant (8:11). The way the covenant is now actualized is what the author of Hebrews seems most to be interested in (Mitchell 2007, 170). There is nothing in the way he uses the text of Jer 31:31–34 to suggest that the "new" covenant amounts to a replacement of Judaism with Christianity.

Within Judaism itself, the term "new covenant" does not imply the rejection of the old. Luke Timothy Johnson has shown that the covenanters at Qumran saw themselves to be living under a new covenant without making a definitive break with the old. They speak of the "new covenant" that God established in Damascus (CD 6:19; 8:21; 19:33; 20:12) and also use the terms "covenant of conversion" (CD 19:16), "covenant of mercy" (1QS 1:8), and "covenant of judgment" (1QS 8:9). In so doing they are following an interpretation of the covenant that rejects the interpretation given to it by the Jerusalem priesthood, without rejecting their own Jewish identity. This understanding of the "new covenant" shows that "a Jewish community could claim absolute loyalty to the God of the Abrahamic covenant while negotiating change in the Sinai covenant" (Johnson 2006, 213–14; see also Thompson 2008, 170).

Despite the fact that the author of Hebrews cited Jer 31 (LXX 38):31–34 in Heb 8:7–13 and 10:15–18, we are unable to say whether he understood what Jeremiah meant by the term "new covenant." It is very likely that Jeremiah thought there was something new and different about the covenant he prophesied and that it was not just a renewal of the Sinai covenant, as we have in the case of Deuteronomy. Jack Lundbom shows how Jeremiah's "new covenant" is continuous with the Sinai covenant by isolating three things that he believes renders the covenant "new": (1) its unconditional nature; (2) the internalization of it; and (3) the way it grounds a new understanding of divine grace (Lundbom 2004, 466). Later he adds a fourth characteristic, that this covenant will be an eternal covenant (2004, 519). Seen in this way, Jeremiah's "new covenant" would have been very attractive to the author of Hebrews as he began the central argument of his sermon, with its focus on the priesthood of Christ and his once-for-all sacrifice (Heb 8:1–10:18). Having already addressed changes in the cultic aspects of the old covenant, the "new covenant" is now interiorized. Since he restricts his critique of the old covenant to its cultic aspects, the new covenant of Jeremiah—written on the heart, interiorized, and marked by the forgiveness of sins—would suit well the conditions of covenant observance that necessarily had to change after the destruction of the Jerusalem temple and the end of the sacrificial cult.

One further observation about Heb 8:13 may alleviate the need to interpret it in a supersessionist way. When the author says that the covenant is "growing old and will soon disappear," it is clear that the author does not think that this disappearance has already occurred (Johnson 2006, 209). He makes no prediction about when that might happen, if at all. Rather, he leaves the matter open-ended. This seems to indicate that he did not himself hold a supersessionist interpretation of the "new covenant."

Hebrews 10:1–10

The final text we will consider is Heb 10:1–10. An ambiguity in the text at 10:9, "he abolishes the first in order to establish the second," has led some commentators to refer the word "first" to the Sinai covenant and "second" to the "new covenant" (Attridge 1989, 276; Bruce 1990, 242). The verse itself concludes the first of a four-part larger unit, 10:1–18, whose purpose is to continue the comparison of the efficacy of the Levitical sacrifices with the sacrificial death of Christ. I would first like to note that the Greek verb *aneirein,* often translated as "abolishes," in its usual sense means simply "to take away" (Mitchell 2007, 202).

The word "covenant" is not present in the Greek text; the author speaks only of the "first" and the "second." In its context, the word "first" refers to the sacrificial cult and "second" refers to the obedience of Christ, who in his sacrificial death offered himself to God (Johnson 2006, 252). Thus the comparison is not between two covenants, "old" and "new," but rather between "sacrifices" and "obedience."

This language recalls similar language among the prophets (Isa 1:11–15; Jer. 6:20; Amos 5:21–25; Hos 6:6), who proclaim God's preference for obedience over sacrifice (Mitchell 2007, 201–2). The author of Hebrews is not addressing in this text the replacement of the entire covenant but rather seems to be joining the discussion about the efficacy of sacrifices, a discussion that was occurring within Judaism itself. In a post-70 C.E. era, when sacrifices ceased with the destruction of the Jerusalem temple, the author of Hebrews may be encouraging his audience to see how Christ's death could now be interpreted after the cessation of the sacrificial cult in Jerusalem.

Such a reading is not implausible, since the larger unit concludes with the words "there is no longer any offering for sin" (Heb 10:18), which can be taken in two ways, one theological and the other historical. In the theological sense, there is no longer an offering for sin because the once-for-all sacrifice of Christ has effected the forgiveness of sin. In the historical sense, the author may simply be acknowledging that sacrifices are no longer offered at the Jerusalem temple (Mitchell 2007, 206).

A New Approach

In recent years the tide has turned as more and more scholars have challenged the view that Hebrews itself promotes supersessionism (Johnson 2006, 210–15; Lincoln 2006, 114–20; Mitchell 2007, 25–28; Thompson 2008, 177). I will discuss two approaches to resolving the problem of supersessionist reading of Hebrews.

Pamela Eisenbaum has made a strong case against supersessionism in Hebrews (Eisenbaum 2005a). She raises an important question regarding the date of Hebrews and whether it is plausible to think that the author of Hebrews may actually be addressing the situation of Jews and Christians who were distressed over the loss of essential institutions of Second Temple Judaism such as the priesthood and sacrifice (Eisenbaum 2005a, 1; see Isaacs 2002, 12–14). A post-70 C.E. date for Hebrews would preclude the Levitical system as a viable alternative competing with Jesus. It would also exonerate the author of Hebrews from relegating the Jerusalem temple to obsolescence, since the circumstances of history brought that about. If one accepts a post-70 C.E. date for Hebrews, Eisenbaum asks whether the Levitical ritual system could be a viable alternative in competition with Jesus. Consequently, one could see the exposition of Jesus' priesthood in Hebrews as a response to the loss of the temple rather than "an attempt to write it out of existence" (Eisenbaum 2005a, 2). I am in full agreement with Eisenbaum on these points; in fact, I myself have argued that it may not have been possible for a Christian author to portray Jesus as a high priest as long as the temple was standing (Mitchell 2007, 26).

Another cogent point in Eisenbaum's argument concerns the way scholars reduce the cultic language in Hebrews to metaphor. The result of this reduction is the association of everything that is important, such as Christ, God, and heaven, with Christianity, whereas the metaphorical correlates, such as the temple, sacrifice, and blood, are associated with Judaism. One can incorrectly conclude, then, that Judaism confuses metaphor for reality and empties the meaning from Jewish rituals, because Judaism fails to see the spiritual significance of ritual actions, thereby focusing on the cultic things themselves (Eisenbaum 2005a, 3).

Perhaps the most important point in Eisenbaum's argument is that supersessionist interpretations of Hebrews do not identify exactly what form of living Judaism is superseded in the sermon. The author of Hebrews is concerned only with the ancient Levitical cult. Hebrews never discusses actual Jewish ritual practice and confines itself to the ancient Levitical system as described in Scripture. When Hebrews was written, Judaism was changing, as rabbinic Judaism was emerging after the destruction of the temple. The absence of a comparison with an identifiable form of Judaism contemporaneous with Hebrews impedes an easy understanding of what its author sees as being superseded by Christ. Since most Jews were not preoccupied with the temple cult, which was a matter pertaining only to priests, Eisenbaum cautions both Jews and Christians not to "confuse or conflate the religion of Israel—particularly the cultic expression of Israelite religion—with Judaism then (late first/early second century), with Judaism now, or with Judaism in general" (Eisenbaum 2005a, 5).

Richard Hays has recently proposed a way of avoiding a necessary supersessionist reading of Hebrews by introducing the category of "new covenantalism" as a framework for locating the thought of Hebrews within the context of sectarian Judaism in the first century C.E. In his approach Hebrews does not represent a distinct form of Christianity opposed to Judaism. Drawing on the author of Hebrews' interest in continuity and discontinuity, new covenantalism "*carr[ies] forward the legacy of Israel*" while it also "*transforms* Israel's identity" (Hays 2009, 155, emphasis original).

The basis for new covenantalism is found in the eight exegetical arguments that form the overall exposition of Hebrews. They are exegetical because each interprets Scripture in order to demonstrate how the past and the present point to an eschatological future in which the transformation of Israel will occur. The eight arguments deal with: the revelatory role of the Son, the Sabbath rest that remains for the people of God, the priesthood of Jesus, the heavenly sanctuary, the new covenant itself, Jesus' once-for-all sacrifice, the great heroes of faith, and the identification of the readers/listeners with the wilderness generation of Israelites. Each of the arguments attends to the past and to the future in the way it recalls the scriptural tradition but renders it anew for the readers of Hebrews (Hays 2009, 156–64). The author's comparisons of "old" and "new" do not constitute a break with the past. What is "new" is actually an eschatological transformation of the "old," as it continues to hand on the tradition in changed circumstances. Christianity, then, does not represent something "new" that has replaced something "old," Judaism.

Hays supports his understanding of new covenantalism by showing that none of the scriptural texts examined in the sermon's eight exegetical arguments is anti-Jewish. Also, none supports the view that God has rejected Jews in favor of Gentiles who believe in Jesus Christ. Rather, he finds precedents for the language of those texts in the book of Deuteronomy and in the prophetic literature. Hays also believes that the comparison of the old and new covenants in Hebrews restricts itself only to the ancient sacrificial cult as a means of atonement for sins and does not have the entirety of the Sinai covenant in view (Hays 2009, 165).

Locating Hebrews within a still-developing narrative that originated in Jewish Scripture, Hays sees the unfolding story terminating in the future salvation of Jews and Christians alike. Like others before him, he invokes the metaphor of a pilgrimage on the basis of Heb 13:14, "For here we have no lasting city, but we are looking for the city that is to come." Thus, for Hays, the story of Christianity and Judaism is unfinished, as both are on a similar journey that has yet to reach its destination.

Finally, Hays discusses three strategies used by the author of Hebrews that support a nonsupersessionist reading of the sermon. First, Hebrews makes its readers confront the actual sacrificial death of Christ, which results in atonement on their behalf. Second, Hebrews assures its readers that they have a sympathetic high priest who mediates between them and

God in a way that does not denigrate the Sinai covenant. Third, Hebrews asks its readers to think of ways that they, together with Jews, might carry forward the story of Israel (Hays 2009, 171–72).

The overall effect of these three strategies is to move the interpretation of Hebrews in a direction other than supersessionism. The sermon is an antidote for a triumphalist attitude about Christianity because it does not allow its audience to see itself as radically separate from Judaism. On the contrary, it invites its readers to imagine themselves on a similar journey as their Jewish confreres, a journey that awaits a future fulfillment. As Hebrews reminds its readers that they have "no lasting city," it presents God's rest as a goal that has not yet been attained (Hays 2009, 166–67). The warnings to stay the course and the exhortations "to hold on to the confession" prevent the readers from self-assured superiority because they have yet to reach their goal.

Pamela Eisenbaum and Richard Hays are representative of scholars who are reexamining Hebrews in an effort to reinterpret the sermon in a new way, one that does not support a supersessionist reading of it. The common threads of this approach are evident in their work: (1) a preference for a later dating of Hebrews to a time after the destruction of the Jerusalem temple; (2) the recognition that Hebrews itself does not promote the view that Christianity has replaced Judaism, because it never identifies a viable form of first-century Judaism that is being replaced; (3) a fuller understanding of the way Hebrews employs metaphor in a way that is not derogatory to Judaism; and (4) the contextualization of the comparative arguments of Hebrews within the scriptural tradition of Judaism and not against it. Their findings as well as those of other scholars of Hebrews demonstrate that, in the matter of supersessionism, Hebrews is not the source of this replacement theology. Once that burden is removed from Hebrews, one can more easily understand its purpose in supporting a community disheartened by the destruction of Jerusalem and the loss of the temple and the priesthood. The author's stress on what the recipients of Hebrews have in the wake of these losses need not add to the tragedy that Jews suffered in the last third of the first century C.E. by taking even more from them—their place in salvation history and their covenant with God—and transferring it to Christians. On the contrary, Hebrews witnesses to the fact that Jews and Christians alike await a common future goal. The text of Heb 11:39–40 suggests as much: "Yet all these, though they were commended for their faith, did not receive what was promised, since God had provided something better so that they would not, apart from us, be made perfect." The author intends to show in these words that the great heroes of faith will ultimately receive what God had promised them, as will his readers. When they complete their pilgrimage in the eschatological future, they will be made perfect together and not apart. Writing to this particular audience to assure them of what they have, the author naturally frames the ultimate goal in terms of them when he writes "they would not, apart from us, be made perfect." He could have easily said that his readers would not be made perfect "apart from them" and still retain the same meaning that they will all receive the fulfillment of God's promises together.

Conclusion

The purpose of this essay has been to revisit the question of whether Hebrews is inherently supersessionist. After a brief treatment of supersessionism itself, and why it unfortunately and unnecessarily drives a wedge between Jews and Christians, we looked at the author's use of comparison and *a fortiori* arguments that have been appealed to as evidence for Hebrews' supersessionism. In that discussion we tried to show how that conclusion is incorrect. Then we examined three texts of Hebrews that are invoked to promote a theology of replacement. Our discussion demonstrated that Heb 7:1–12; 8:7–13; and 10:1–10 need not be used to foster supersessionism because this purpose was not intended by the author of Hebrews. The last section discussed a promising new direction among scholars of Hebrews, who more and more are finding new and creative ways of resolving the problem of the supersessionist interpretation of Hebrews. One hopes that their efforts at reading Hebrews anew will not only reverse the centuries of supersessionist interpretation of Hebrews but will also repair the tremendous damage those interpretation have caused to the relationship between Jews and Christians.

Hebrews in the Worship Life of the Church: A Historical Survey

Mark A. Torgerson

Introduction

Scripture has been a central source of inspiration, guidance, and content for the worship life of the church. Scripture represents the revelation of God for the people of God. Scripture for Christians is rooted in the texts of Judaism. Sacred writings have emerged through time in the midst of the Hebrew people that helped them understand their identity, who God is, and how God would have them live in the world. The Mosaic covenant is a rich source of revelation that has guided the worship of God's people. Instruction for rituals, festivals, and creating places for worship are outlined in this covenant. The Epistle to the Hebrews represents the intersection of this ancient covenant with an emerging, first-century sect of Judaism that would come to be called Christianity. Hebrews represents a selective, creative recollection of covenant instruction that finds Jesus Christ as its ultimate fulfillment.

Hebrews has not had a large role to play in the theological development and practice of Christian worship, but it has occupied a unique niche. In this essay a window will be provided that outlines numerous ways in which the book of Hebrews has impacted preaching, baptism, Eucharist, ordered ministry, the lectionary, hymnody, service books, and visual art. The influence of Hebrews will be illustrated by examples drawn from Eastern and Western Christian traditions and from a variety of time periods. The examples that follow are not exhaustive but touch on primary ways in which the content of Hebrews has been incorporated into Christian worship.[1]

---

1. A comprehensive outline of the history of interpretation and influence of Hebrews in the life of the church can be found in Koester 2001, 19–63.

Theological Affirmations and Worship

Central affirmations of faith that pertain to worship are included in Hebrews. The church historically has found support for the doctrines of the preexistence of Christ, his participation in creation, and his fully divine and fully human nature in Heb 1–2.[2] The full identity of Jesus helps us understand the one whom Christians worship and his role in the Trinity (the activity of God the Father and the Holy Spirit are both referenced in Hebrews as well). Jesus' unique activity in fulfilling the role of ultimate worship leader (high priest) and ultimate sacrifice for reconciling God and God's people (the final offering, once and for all) is explored in Heb 5–10. The author establishes the intimate connection of Christ to the worship of God. There is even an admonition to meet for worship regularly in community (10:25), a long-standing tradition among God's people. Continuity in worship is maintained between the Jewish and Christian Testaments, with the fulfillment of the sacrificial expectations achieved in the person and work of Christ. Understandings of sin, guilt, alienation, offering, and reconciliation are all included in this vision of Jesus as high priest and sacrifice. The importance of enduring faith (even in the face of suffering), confidence in approaching the throne of God, encouragement to seek Sabbath rest, and remembering the faithful witness of those who have gone before us are all important themes found in Hebrews that pertain to worship. The affirmations of faith found here serve to initiate the believer into the Christian faith, provide beliefs important to the confession of faith (many of these themes can be found in the historical creeds of the church), and facilitate ongoing spiritual formation.

Preaching and *the* Homily

According to Heb 3:12, the word of God is alive and active among the faithful. The Epistle to the Hebrews itself exemplifies this understanding. Its literary composition is itself an act of worship. Contemporary scholars tend to agree that this New Testament composition is a homily more than a letter. The author develops multiple theological themes using biblical references from the Septuagint to compose an eloquent proclamation con-

---

2. See the essay in this volume by Rowan A. Greer for discussion of this kind of interpretation.

cerning the person and work of Jesus Christ. Though the author understands Jesus as God's ultimate revelation, continuity in God's revelation
between the ancient Jewish Scriptures and early Christian interpretation
of Jesus Christ is emphasized. The author uses Middle Platonic thinking
when imagining the priestly offerings of the ancient tabernacle to be a
foreshadowing of the ultimate offering of Jesus Christ. In the history of
the church, this has often led to a supersessionist reading of Hebrews (as
discussed elsewhere in this volume by Alan C. Mitchell). While the ongoing Jewish tabernacle offerings were commanded, the offering cycle came
to fullness in the final sacrificial offering of Christ himself. The power of
the rhetoric in the composition and the association of this writing with the
apostle Paul helped Hebrews find its way into the New Testament canon,
and the interpretive and rhetorical techniques of the author would be
emulated in Christian preaching through the ages.

One of the most significant extant early collections of sermons on
Hebrews consists of thirty-four homilies from John Chrysostom (347–
407 c.e.). Chrysostom was a renowned preacher in Antioch prior to his
appointment to become bishop of Constantinople in 397 c.e. Chrysostom
assumed Pauline authorship of Hebrews, a position generally affirmed in
the Eastern church from the earliest days. At least one homily is based on
each of the thirteen chapters in Hebrews. Chapters 10–12 are the focus of
fifteen of the homilies (four for ch. 10, six for ch. 11, and five for ch. 12).
Twenty-four of the homilies are focused on the exegesis of three or fewer
verses in a given chapter. Topics of the homilies are varied: ten homilies
address sin, confession, and/or temptations; seven address wealth, poverty,
and/or simplicity; two address heaven; and Scripture reading, prayer, baptism, and communion are addressed in a single homily each. In Homily
17, Chrysostom makes a claim that will underscore an existing interpretation of eucharistic celebrations. Preaching on Heb 9:24–26, he states in
section 6 of the homily:

> He is our High Priest, who offered the sacrifice that cleanses us. That
> we offer now also, which was then offered, which cannot be exhausted.
> This is done in remembrance of what was then done. For (saith He) "do
> this in remembrance of Me." (Luke xxii.19) It is not another sacrifice, as
> the High Priest, but we offer always the same, or rather we perform a
> remembrance of a Sacrifice. (*NPNF* 1/14:449)

Chrysostom's interpretation of the ritual remembrance of Christ's offering as a sacrifice in each celebration of the Eucharist would become normative for the church up to the time of the Reformation in spite of the assertion of Hebrews that sacrifices have now come to an end (Koester 2001, 26, 32). Chrysostom authored a eucharistic celebration, "The Divine Liturgy of St. John Chrysostom," that continues to be the primary liturgy for the Eastern Orthodox tradition as well. The adoption of Chrysostom's theological understanding so widely is a testimony to the power of his preaching on Hebrews and an indication of how treasured sermons continued to circulate widely in the church.

Baptism and Hebrews

Baptism is not a topic of significance in Hebrews, though it is acknowledged as an initial reality for the journey of the Christian. Explicit references to baptism are found in chapters 6 and 10. Repentance from sin and having faith in God are mentioned in Heb 6:1, while 6:2 pairs baptism with the laying on of hands. These activities are noted as part of an admonition to mature in the faith. The author is encouraging readers to move beyond their initial steps into the faith to seek completeness or perfection. No specific directions concerning the performance of baptism are noted. It seems likely that this mention of baptism is a reference to the ritual act of cleansing from sin accompanied by the impartation of the Holy Spirit (Koester 2001, 311). New Testament instances of baptism usually involved the confession of sin, cleansing with water, and the gift of the Holy Spirit. The Spirit is recorded in Scripture as arriving prior to baptism (Acts 10:44–48), at the time of baptism (2:38; 19:5–6), and after baptism (8:12–17). The writer of Hebrews appears to be acknowledging this initial step of faith and the connection between baptism and the receiving of the Holy Spirit. Receiving the gift of the Holy Spirit following baptism came to be called confirmation in early Christian communities of faith. Bestowing of the Spirit via the laying on of the hands of the bishop is found in the Western church by at least the mid-fourth century in the early church order, *The Apostolic Tradition* (in ch. 21, "Concerning the Tradition of Holy Baptism," verse 21; Bradshaw, Johnson, and Phillips 2002, 14–16, 118–19, 127–28).

In Heb 10:22 another reference is made to the act of baptism. Baptism is linked to faith here, as it was in 6:1–2. Internal and external cleansing appear to both be important for the believer. Reference is made to a clean conscience and a body washed with pure water. Again, there is no explanation of the baptismal rite nor particular understanding of its meaning offered. Rather, the physical act is affirmed as important for identifying the person with the community of the faithful (Koester 2001, 449).

References to passages from Hebrews are found in some fourth-century baptismal homilies. Catechetical homilies concerning the sacraments, particularly baptism and Eucharist, were shared with the catechumens shortly before or after baptism. The homilies of John Chrysostom and Theodore of Mopsuestia would be shared during the season of Lent in preparation for initiation at the Easter vigil. Both bishops reference Hebrews. In Baptismal Homily 2, Chrysostom includes a quote from Heb 11:1: "Now faith is the assurance of things hope for, the conviction of things not seen" (Yarnold 1994, 155). Chrysostom is accenting the necessity of having faith in this section of the sermon. Confidence and courage are needed to affirm and embrace invisible realities. Chrysostom is encouraging the candidates to trust in the activity of the Holy Spirit of God at work in the physical water in their lives.

Theodore of Mopsuestia (350–428/429 c.e.) was active in the exegetical school of Antioch. He was appointed bishop of Mopsuestia (a town about 100 miles from Antioch) in 392. In Baptismal Homily 2 Theodore quotes from Heb 2:10 under the section entitled "Renunciation of Sin" (Yarnold 1994, 169). Here he is talking to the candidates about the need for kneeling in the baptismal rite. The kneeling is a sign of humanity's fallen nature and the need to adore God in humility. The one to whom this adoration is directed is Jesus Christ, the "pioneer of our salvation." Later in the homily under the section entitled "Profession of Faith" there is a reference to Heb 11:6 (Yarnold 1994, 176). Theodore attributes the passage to Paul and emphasizes that in order to approach God a person must truly believe that God exists. The fact that Paul is mentioned as the source of the passage from Hebrews doubtless added authority to the teaching.

EUCHARIST AND HEBREWS

Eucharistic themes in light of an ordered (ordained) ministry have been discerned and denied in the Epistle to the Hebrews by interpreters through the ages.[3] Until the time of the Reformation the churches in the East and

---

3. Contemporary biblical scholars recognize the lack of explicit eucharistic refer-

West tended to interpret passages in Hebrews as authoritative reflections that supported a sacrificial understanding of the Eucharist, the offering of which was performed on behalf of the people only by ordained clergy. The symbolic interpretations that exist in the book itself encouraged the development of analogies and typological associations. While it is true that Hebrews does not explicitly mention Eucharist nor attribute the title of priest to any Christian minister, such observations did not deter theologians and preachers prior to the Reformation from linking Hebrews to both Eucharist and a Christian understanding of the priesthood.

Eucharist was read into texts such as Heb 6:4 ("tasted the heavenly gift") and 9:2 ("the table and the bread of the Presence"). The comparison of Jesus to Melchizedek and his fulfillment of the high-priestly duties provided the soil for developing a rationale for eucharistic sacrifice. In Gen 14:18–20, Melchizedek, high priest of God's people at Salem, made an offering of bread and wine to God. Although Hebrews does not mention the offering of bread and wine explicitly, interpreters of Hebrews imagined Jesus offering the bread and wine of his own body and blood at the altar in the heavenly sanctuary.

Clement of Alexandria (150–211/215 C.E.) considered the Melchizedek offering to be a type of eucharistic offering: "For Salem is, by interpretation, peace; of which our Saviour is enrolled King, as Moses says, Melchizedek king of Salem, priest of the most high God, who gave bread and wine, furnishing consecrated food for a type of the Eucharist" (*Strom.* 4.25, ANF 2:439).

Clergy were understood to be the primary human representatives of Christ on earth. It was not difficult to imagine the priests presiding at eucharistic celebrations as offering the wine and bread in his stead. A mysterious connection was affirmed between the heavenly offering of Christ and the earthly offerings of his priests. Cyprian (d. 258 C.E.), bishop of Carthage, made this association in his Epistle 62, "Caecilius, on the Sacrament of the Cup of the Lord." Following mention of the identification of Jesus as priest according to the order of Melchizedek, he states:

ences in Hebrews and often find it problematic to glean insights about the meaning of Eucharist from this epistle (see Williamson 1975; Koester 2001, 127–29). In spite of this consensus, there are some who continue to seek to find meaningful links to Eucharist in Hebrews (see Swetnam 1989).

For if Jesus Christ, our Lord and God, is Himself the chief priest of God the Father, and has first offered Himself a sacrifice to the Father, and has commanded this to be done in commemoration of Himself, certainly that priest truly discharges the office of Christ, who imitates that which Christ did; and he then offers a true and full sacrifice in the Church to God the Father, when he proceeds to offer it according to what he sees Christ Himself to have offered. (*ANF* 5:362)

The priestly offering of bread and wine itself took on a special role in fulfilling the representation of Christ's atoning work. Theodore of Mopsuestia in Antioch affirmed this understanding, as did the liturgy of St. Basil (authored by Basil the Great, 329–379 C.E., bishop of Caesarea in Cappadocia; Koester 2001, 25).

The Western church appreciated the eucharistic imagery connected to Melchizedek as well. Melchizedek and his offering have been explicitly mentioned in the Mass of the Roman Rite from at least the eighth century:

Vouchsafe to look upon them [the holy bread of eternal life and the cup of everlasting salvation] with a favourable and kindly countenance, and accept them as you vouchsafed to accept the gifts of your righteous servant Abel, and the sacrifice of our patriarch Abraham, and that which your high-priest Melchizedek offered to you, a holy sacrifice, an unblemished victim. (Jasper and Cumming 1980, 122)

Abel, Abraham, and Melchizedek were remembered for the excellence of their offerings to God. They became prototypes to be emulated by the Christian priests as they offer up the bread and wine. Even the visual art of some early basilicas underscored the central role of these three models (more is said of this in the visual art section below).

The Melchizedek reference has endured in the Roman Rite. Four eucharistic prayers are present in the current *Roman Missal* for celebrations. Eucharistic Prayer 1 reflects the inclusion of the offering of Melchizedek: "Look with favor on these offerings and accept them as once you accepted the gifts of your servant Abel, the sacrifice of Abraham, our father in faith, and the bread and wine offered by your priest Melchisedech" (*Roman Missal*, 1970). In the forthcoming third edition of the *Roman Missal*, the reference is retained in Eucharistic Prayer 1:

93. Be pleased to look upon these offerings with a serene and kindly countenance, and to accept them, as once you were pleased to accept the

gifts of your servant Abel the just, the sacrifice of Abraham, our father in faith, and the offering of your high priest Melchizedek, a holy sacrifice, a spotless victim. (*Roman Missal*, third edition, released for celebration in 2011; see www.nccbuscc.org/romanmissal)

A certain continuity has been maintained in the practice of Eucharist through the retention of this imagery. While this prayer is not the only option in the Missal today, it does provide a tangible link to a long-standing interpretation of Hebrews.

The Liturgy of St. James, a eucharistic celebration that emerged from a combination of materials from Antioch and Jerusalem in the third and fourth centuries, includes multiple references to Hebrews. In a section entitled "Prayer of the Veil," the following references can be found:

We thank Thee, O Lord our God, that Thou hast given us boldness for the entrance of Thy holy places, which Thou has renewed to us as a new and living way through the veil of the flesh of Thy Christ. [Heb 10:20] We therefore, being counted worthy to enter into the place of the tabernacle of Thy glory, and to be within the veil, and to behold the Holy of Holies, cast ourselves down before Thy goodness:

Lord, have mercy on us: since we are full of fear and trembling, when about to stand at Thy holy altar, and to offer this dread and bloodless sacrifice for our own sins and for the error of the people [Heb 5:1–3]: send forth, O God, Thy good grace, and sanctify our souls, and bodies, and spirits; and turn our thoughts to holiness, that with a pure conscience [Heb 9:14] we may bring to Thee a peace-offering, the sacrifice of praise [Heb 13:15]. (*ANF* 7:543)

The fullness of the tabernacle metaphor is present in this passage. The Christian priest takes the role of the ancient priest in confidently presenting the offerings of the people. The sacrifice of praise has become the bread and the wine, the once and forever offering of the sacrifice of Christ. Although this language will not necessarily be used in eucharistic liturgies that follow, the general understanding of Eucharist as the priestly offering that is to be made to God will endure. John Chrysostom can be credited with inspiring this particular understanding through his many sermons on Hebrews.

An interesting use of Hebrews occurred in the ninth century. A confrontation emerged in the West between two monks, Ratramnus of Corbie (d. 868 C.E.) and Paschasius Radbertus (d. 865 C.E.), over *how* Jesus was present in the Eucharist. Ratramnus did not believe it was helpful to equate the bread and wine literally with the body and blood of Jesus. He preferred a more mystical, symbolic understanding of Christ in the sacrament. He used Heb 11:1 to support his position. Paschasius insisted on a literal physical interpretation. A mid-ninth century exegete, Haimo of Halberstadt, used Heb 10:2–3 to defend Paschasius's position (Koester 2001, 32). The literal interpretation of real presence ultimately prevailed in the Western church.

The Reformation provided an intense context within which to interpret Hebrews. Martin Luther and others were concerned with an understanding of eucharistic sacrifice that seemed to emphasize the ritual act of the priest autonomously offering up the death of Christ again and again. The danger perceived was that the clergy were adding merit to the once and forever sacrifice of Christ through their own human efforts. As such, some people were afraid that the sacrifice of the Mass was being understood in a way that diminished the accomplished sufficiency of Christ's atoning work. Luther sought to reform theological understandings of the Eucharist and practices associated with it. In developing his response, he made use of the Epistle to the Hebrews at times.

In 1517 and 1518 Luther lectured on Hebrews; his lecture notes addressed select verses from chapters 1–11 (translated in *LW* 29:107–241). The homilies of Chrysostom are frequently referenced in Luther's notes, and it is interesting to see that Luther recognized their significance. Luther is generally quite appreciative of Chrysostom's insights, but he adds his own emphasis through his predisposition of accenting grace over works. For example, in Luther's notes on Heb 9:24 he recognizes the value of performing external ceremonies "to the extent that there is occasion to practice faith and love, and to curb sins more effectively," but is clear about the fact that performing external rituals alone does not yield salvation (*LW* 29:218–19). In quoting from section 6 of Homily 17, Luther emphasizes the remembrance of the sacrifice of Christ in the Mass celebration rather than the merit of the physical ritual act itself (*LW* 29:219–20). In other writings Luther is found to shift the theological meaning of the Mass from a sacrifice the people offer to God to a celebration of a promise Christ makes to the people (Koester 2001, 36). The way in which the sacrificial imagery of Hebrews is interpreted changes with the theological tenor of the historical period.

ORDERED MINISTRY AND HEBREWS

The unique role of the priesthood is related to the issue of Eucharist. Most of the church today continues to affirm the necessity of clergy presiding at eucharistic celebrations. A part of the justification for the unique duties of the priesthood relies on passages from Hebrews. Leadership for Christian communities emerged in the apostolic period. Various New Testament passages note the establishment of distinctive roles for its leaders (e.g., Acts 6:1–6; Phil 1:1; 1 Tim 3:1–13). Determination of the precise duties of the presbyters or priests evolved over time. An example of an emerging understanding of the priesthood that refers to Hebrews is found in *Apostolic Constitutions*, a late fourth-century C.E. compilation that seeks to provide order in the church. The exclusive domain of the priesthood is addressed in book 2, section 27, "That It Is a Horrible Thing for a Man to Thrust Himself into Any Sacerdotal Office, as Did Corah and His Company, Saul and Uzziah." This section mentions that laity may not perform the duties of a priest, and Heb 5:5 is cited as a scriptural reference to substantiate this claim:

> And as Uzziah the king, who was not a priest, and yet would exercise the functions of the priests, was smitten with leprosy for his transgression; so every lay person shall not be unpunished who despises God, and is so mad as to affront His priests, and unjustly to snatch that honour to himself: not imitating Christ, "who glorified not Himself to be made an high priest" [Heb 5:5]; but waited till He heard from His Father, "The Lord sware, and will not repent, Thou art a priest for ever, after the order of Melchizedek." [Ps 110:4 cited in the text, but also reflected in Heb 5:6] If, therefore, Christ did not glorify Himself without the Father, how dare any man thrust himself into the priesthood who has not received that dignity from his superior, and do such things which it is lawful only for the priests to do? (*ANF* 7:410)

The special call and role given to Christ to be a high priest in the order of Melchizedek is extended to apply to the entire earthly priesthood here. Duties peculiar to the clergy are clearly off limits to the laity. The prohibition is articulated again in book 3, section 10, "That a Layman Ought Not to Do Any Office of the Priesthood: He Ought Neither to Baptize, Nor Offer, Nor Lay on Hands, Nor Give the Blessing." It is true that the context of the passage quoted in Heb 5 cites the special calling of Aaron to be high priest. *Apostolic Constitution* expands the analogy to include the calling and authority of the entire priesthood. Precedent in a church document such as this tended to be reinforced in later guidelines.

The special domain of church leadership and its development with bishops, priests, and deacons continued to be observed throughout the centuries in both Eastern and Western churches. Texts from Hebrews continued to be cited as one source (among many) to substantiate this leadership development. Alan Mitchell summarizes references to passages from Hebrews for grounding ministerial priesthood at the Council of Trent (nineteenth ecumenical council of the Roman Catholic Church, 1545–1563) and the Second Vatican Council (twenty-first ecumenical council of the Roman Catholic Church, 1962–1965) in this way:

> The Council of Trent cited Heb. 7:12 as the foundation for a new eternal priesthood, a change from the old (*De Sacramento Ordinis*, 1). The Second Vatican Council made an explicit connection between the eternal priesthood of Christ (Heb. 5:1–10; 7:24; 9:11–28) and the ministerial priesthood of those who are consecrated in his image in the sacrament of Orders (*Lumen gentium*, 28). Elsewhere Vatican II alluded to Hebrews in support of the ministerial priesthood (*Presbyterorum ordinis*, 3) and the priesthood shared by all the baptized (*Lumen gentium*, 10). (Mitchell 2007, 24–25)

The Council of Trent was convened to develop a comprehensive response to the activities of the Reformers in challenging the Catholic church. Hebrews 7:12 helped to substantiate the need for retaining the existing priesthood in light of the claims of the Reformers, who sought to revise the traditional roles of the clergy and laity. From the Catholic perspective, to abandon the historical priestly role of the clergy would be tantamount to Israel abandoning the role of its priests. With Jesus as the designated high priest, the need for earthly priests in the church was not negated but transformed and made complete. The earthly priesthood remains necessary for mediation, at least until Christ's return. The Second Vatican Council reiterated the necessity of the earthly priesthood through its use of Hebrews but exhibits justification from a wider range of passages. The expanded use of Scripture was an important theme of Vatican II and will be seen again in relation to the inclusion of readings from Hebrews in the discussion of the lectionary below.

Lectionary Use and Hebrews

Selecting readings from Scripture for use in worship celebrations became systematized in the evolution of the liturgy. Precedents for recurring biblical readings in worship are found in the New Testament. In Acts 15:21 one reads that the books of Moses were read every Sabbath in the synagogues. The Law and the Prophets were read regularly in the context of synagogue worship, according to Acts 13:14–15 and Luke 4:16–17. The standardization of readings in the church corresponded to the development of a calendar that celebrated particular moments in the life of Christ (the church year). By the mid-third century, churches were celebrating events such as the death and resurrection of Christ annually. Scripture texts relevant to those events would be read in worship. A cycle of celebrations and readings began to emerge over time. Evidence from the fourth century indicates this association of certain texts with particular annual services. Some homilies that we have from Ambrose, Chrysostom, and Theodore of Mopsuestia imply the use of expected, preselected texts for certain festivals. Another source is the diary of a Spanish nun, Egeria, recounting her experiences of worship services in Jerusalem about 380 c.e. (see Wilkinson 1971 for translation and notes). Egeria indicates that the readings of the celebrations she attended were used annually. Major centers of faith such as Jerusalem, Rome, Constantinople, Antioch, and Alexandria attracted pilgrims from remote areas. The pilgrims would attend the elaborate services in the major cities and sometimes replicate portions of the celebrations they witnessed—the texts, prayers, songs, and rituals—in their home churches, and Egeria's diary appears to have functioned in this way. Such replication contributed to the use of a standardized set of Scripture lessons for worship (although variety remained between regions and among churches, too).

"Lectionary" is the term given to a schedule of preselected Scripture readings for worship. A fifth-century example is preserved in the Armenian lectionary (Renoux 1969–1971). The Armenian lectionary reflects the worship practices of the church in Jerusalem. Readings from Hebrews appear as follows:

Text	Celebration
Heb 1:1–12	Third day of the celebration of the Feast of the Epiphany

Heb 12:18–27	Fifth day of the celebration of the Feast of the Epiphany
Heb 11:32–40	Commemoration of Saint Anthony (17 January)
Heb 11:1–31 is reading 5 Heb 1:1–2:1 is reading 11	Commemoration of John, Bishop of Jerusalem (29 March)
Heb 2:11–18 is reading 10 Heb 9:11–28 is reading 12 Heb 10:19–31 is reading 14	Good Friday
Heb 2:14–18	Remembering the infants killed by King Herod (9 May).
Heb 11:32–40	Commemoration of the Prophet Elisha (14 June)
Heb 9:1–10	Commemoration of the Ark of the Covenant (2 July)
Heb 11:32–12:13	Commemoration of the Maccabees

Readings from Hebrews are designated for nine days of the church year and are taken from five chapters. The divine and human nature of Christ, his preexistence, and his high-priestly role and sacrifice are remembered in relation to his birth and death. Hebrews 11 is used for remembering the departed faithful, inclusive of those who preceded the death and resurrection of Christ.

Differing sets of readings developed in the Carolingian period in the various geographical regions of the church, Western and Eastern. Multiple readings from Scripture were included, especially Gospel and Epistle texts. Sometimes Old Testament readings were included, but they usually featured texts that were interpreted as pointing to Christ. At first lists of readings were developed in relation to the observance of the church year. In time these lists were turned into books that contained the readings for each eucharistic celebration. Sharing of lists and books of readings occurred as people visited churches in different geographical areas. Materials from Rome and Constantinople were especially influential by virtue of the leadership located in each city. Over time the leadership of the Western and Eastern churches sought to unify the worship life of their churches through sharing similar readings in the liturgy.

Ultimately the church formulated a single-year lectionary. The Western lectionary followed a general cycle of beginning with the anticipation of the nativity of Christ and concluded with the anticipation of his return. Two usual readings occurred: Heb 9:11–15 was read on the fifth Sunday of Lent, and Heb 1:1–12 was read on Christmas Day. This pattern of reading is preserved in the *Missale Romanum* promulgated by Pope Pius V in 1570. An additional reading of Heb 9:2–12 was included on the Ember Saturday in September in *Missale Romanum* as well. Saints' days could include additional readings from Hebrews (especially from Heb 11 and 12), but the Sunday celebrations reflected minimal inclusion of readings from Hebrews.

The Eastern Orthodox church lectionary was oriented around a single-year plan as well. It followed a general cycle of beginning with Pascha (Easter Sunday) and concluded with Holy Saturday. Two readings, a Gospel and Epistle lesson, were included for each Sunday and weekday celebration of The Divine Liturgy (the Orthodox name for Mass or The Lord's Supper). The Orthodox calendar celebrated many of the same events and festivals reflected in the Western calendar. The frequency of readings from Hebrews was much higher, however, than in the West. Each Sunday in the season of Lent, Good Friday, the eve of the Nativity, and numerous major and minor feasts had readings from Hebrews.

For a thousand years or so prior to the twenty-first ecumenical council of the Roman Catholic Church (Vatican II) in the 1960s, a one-year lectionary format was observed. Anglican (Episcopal) and Lutheran churches tended to maintain a very similar lectionary, with some modifications. In the twentieth century special attention was given to the reading of Scripture in worship celebrations. It was observed that only a relatively small number of biblical texts could be included in Mass celebrations on Sundays in a single-year rotation. A willingness to reform long-standing patterns of worship in the Catholic Church emerged through the Vatican II meetings. A three-year cycle was established in 1969 instead of a single-year cycle in an effort to expand the number and variety of readings in worship (Old Testament readings were added, too). The three years were designated A, B, and C. A two-year cycle, designated by Year I and II, was developed for weekday celebrations. Protestant churches were inspired by the three-year lectionary cycle of the Catholic Church. In the 1970s multiple denominations pursued a multiyear cycle of readings for Sunday and major feasts, including Episcopalians, Lutherans, Presbyterians, and United Methodists.

The Consultation on Common Texts, an ecumenical group of Catholic and Protestant scholars established in 1969, began work on an ecumenical lectionary in 1978. In 1983 the Common Lectionary was released. Continuing work on the Common Lectionary proceeded even as many denominations adopted it. The Revised Common Lectionary (RCL), released in 1992, is used in many Protestant traditions, including the Evangelical Lutheran Church in America, United Methodist Church, Presbyterian Church (U.S.A.), Cumberland Presbyterian Church, Christian Church (Disciples of Christ), American Baptist Churches USA, United Church of Christ, and Christian Reformed Church in North America. The Church of England and Anglican churches of Canada, Australia, and South Africa have also adopted the Revised Common Lectionary, but the American Episcopal Church has chosen to maintain its own three-year lectionary. Significant overlap occurs between the RCL and American Episcopal lectionaries.

The following table notes the designated readings for Sunday and major feasts from Hebrews in three current lectionaries that affect much of the church: the *Lectionary for Mass* (1998 American edition) serves the Roman Catholic Church;[4] the American *Book of Common Prayer* (1979) contains the lectionary for the Episcopal Church; and the Revised Common Lectionary (1992) serves multiple Protestant denominations.[5] Each designated celebration is found in the left-hand column below. The celebrations follow the church-year calendar and note the year for the reading (cycle A, B, or C). The three right-hand columns identify the readings from Hebrews for the different lectionaries. The entries are organized to show the scope of coverage that occurs with respect to the thirteen chapters of Hebrews.

Celebration	*Lectionary for Mass* (1981 Latin/1998)	*Book of Common Prayer* (1979)	*Revised Common Lectionary* (1992)
Christmas Day, Years A, B, C	Heb 1:1–6	Heb 1:1–12	Heb 1:1–4 (5–12)

---

4. Various editions of the lectionary can be found on the Internet at www.catholic-resources.org/Lectionary/.

5. An online edition of the Revised Common Lectionary with a Scripture text search function can be found at http://lectionary.library.vanderbilt.edu/.

27th Sunday in Ord. Time (Proper 22), Yr. B	Heb 2:9–11	Heb 2:(1–8) 9–18	Heb 1:1–4; 2:5–12
First Sunday after Christmas Day, Yr. A			Heb 2:10–18
Presentation of Jesus in the Temple, Years A, B, C (February 2)	Heb 2:14–18	Heb 2:14–18	Heb 2:14–18
28th Sunday in Ord. Time (Proper 23), Yr. B	Heb 4:12–13	Heb 3:1–6	Heb 4:12–16
29th Sunday in Ord. Time (Proper 24), Yr. B	Heb 4:14–16	Heb 4:12–16	Heb 5:1–10
Good Friday, Years A, B, C	Heb 4:14–16; 5:7–9	Heb 10:1–25	Heb 10:16–25 or 4:14–16; 5:7–9
30th Sunday in Ord. Time (Proper 25), Yr. B	Heb 5:1–6	Heb 5:12; 6:1; 9–12	Heb 7:23–28
5th Sunday in Lent, Yr. B	Heb 5:7–9	Heb 5:(1–4) 5–10	Heb 5:5–10
31st Sunday in Ord. Time (Proper 26), Yr. B	Heb 7:23–28	Heb 7:23–28	Heb 9:11–14
Sunday after Trinity Sunday: Blood and Body of Christ, Yr. B	Heb 9:11–15		

Wednesday of Holy Week, Years A, B, C		Heb 9:11–15, 24–28	Heb 12:1–3
32nd Sunday in Ord. Time (Proper 27), Yr. B	Heb 9:24–28	Heb 9:24–28	Heb 9:24–28
Ascension of the Lord, Yr. C	Heb 9:24–28; 10:19–23 (optional reading)		
Annunciation to Mary, Years A, B, C (March 25)	Heb 10:4–10	Heb 10:5–10	Heb 10:4–10
4th Sunday in Advent, Yr. C	Heb 10:5–10	Heb 10:5–10	Heb 10:5–10
33rd Sunday in Ord. Time (Proper 28), Yr. B	Heb 10:11–14, 18	Heb 10:31–39	Heb 10:11–14 (15–18, 19–25
19th Sunday in Ord. Time (Proper 14), Yr. C	Heb 11:1–2, 8–19 or 11:1–2, 8–12	Heb 11:1–3 (4–7), 8–16	Heb 11:1–3, 8–16
First Sunday after Christmas Day, Yr. B	Heb 11:8, 11–12, 17–19 (optional reading)		
Monday of Holy Week, Years A, B, C		Heb 11:39–12:3	Heb 9:11–15
20th Sunday in Ord. Time (Proper 15), Yr. C	Heb 12:1–4	Heb 12:1–7 (8–10), 11–14	Heb 11:29–12:2

21st Sunday in Ord. Time (Proper 16), Yr. C	Heb 12:5–7, 11–13	Heb 12:18–19, 22–29	Heb 12:18–29
22nd Sunday in Ord. Time (Proper 17), Yr. C	Heb 12:18–19, 22–24a	Heb 13:1–8	Heb 13:1–8, 15–16

In contrast to the single-year lectionary used in the church for hundreds of years that included two primary readings from Hebrews, the three-year sequence yields the two previous readings and at least a dozen more passages. Whereas only two chapters of Hebrews were touched on the single-year lectionary, seven or more are now utilized in the three-year cycle. Two readings remain constant for every year in the reading cycle. Years B and C have extended, continuous readings from Hebrews.

A two-year cycle of daily Catholic Mass readings has been developed as well. In Year 1 readings from Hebrews are assigned for Monday to Saturday during the first four weeks of Ordinary Time. Readings from Heb 1–4 appear in week 1, from Heb 5–9 in week 2, from Heb 9–11 in week 3, and from Heb 11–13 in week 4. In this way exposure to most of the book is achieved.

The Presbyterian Church (U.S.A.) and Cumberland Presbyterian Church incorporate a two-year daily lectionary in their denominational book of worship (Presbyterian Church [U.S.A.] 1993, 1050–1095). The whole cycle provides for reading through the entire New Testament twice and the Old Testament once. A Psalter, Old Testament, Epistle, and Gospel lesson is noted for each day. The Episcopal Church has a two-year daily office lectionary in the *Book of Common Prayer* (Episcopal Church 1979, 933–1001), and the Evangelical Lutheran Church in America has a three-year daily lectionary in its book of worship (Evangelical Lutheran Church in America 2006, 1121–1153). Between the Sunday/major festival and daily lectionaries developed in the last forty years, excellent coverage of the content of Hebrews can now be achieved in the worship and devotional life of the church.

The lectionary for the Orthodox Church remains a single-year cycle.[6]

---

6. The lectionary is reproduced in *The Orthodox Study Bible* 1993, 771–780, and

Pascha is the initiation point for the cycle of readings. Two sets of readings, Gospel and Epistle texts, for eucharistic celebrations for each day of the week are included. Texts from Hebrews are well-represented in the cycle. Readings from Heb 1, 2, and 11 are included in remembering the birth of Christ. The season of Lent has readings from Heb 1, 2, 3, 4, 6, 9, 10, 11, and 12. During the twenty-ninth, thirtieth, and thirty-first weeks after Pentecost, readings from chapters 3, 4, 5, 7, 8, 9, 10, 11, 12, and 13 are achieved. On the Sunday of All Saints, Heb 11:33–12:2 is read. Eleven additional feast days include readings from Heb 2, 5, 6, 7, 9, and 13. The volume of scripture that is incorporated into Orthodox eucharistic celebrations is impressive. The attention that St. John Chrysostom lauded on Hebrews is reflected in the wide range and frequency of readings from Hebrews in the Orthodox lectionary.

Hymns and Hebrews

Hymnic fragments have been identified in multiple New Testament documents (e.g., Phil 2:6–11; Col 1:15–18; John 1:1–18; 1 Tim 3:16; 1 Pet 3:18–19, 22). The structure of Heb 1:3 suggests that it, too, may be derived from an early Christian hymn (Attridge 1989, 41–42). Music has been used in the church throughout its history to share the content of the faith and to express confessional belief. By creating compositions that contain themes or even quotes from the Bible, the church has developed an effective tool for both celebration and spiritual formation. Hebrews has been a source for inspiring songs and hymns. A sampling of hymns and songs connected to themes or verses from Hebrews will be explored to illustrate another way in which the epistle has impacted worship through the ages.[7]

---

can be found online at the Greek Orthodox Archdiocese of America (www.goarch.org) or the Orthodox Church in America (www.oca.org) websites.

7. An excellent website for locating hymns and songs in relation to specific biblical texts is www.hymnary.org. The Hymnary is a joint effort of the Christian Classics Ethereal Library and the Calvin Institute of Christian Worship.

Hymn Title/ Author (Date)	Text	Example of Stanza(s)
"O Savior of Our Fallen Race," Latin (ca. sixth century)	Heb 1:1–3	1 O Savior of our fallen race, O brightness of the Father's face, O Son who shared the Father's might before the world knew day or night. 2 O Jesus, very Light of light, our constant star in sin's deep night; now hear the prayers your people pray throughout the world this holy day.
"O Splendor of God's Glory Bright," Ambrose of Milan (fourth century)	Heb 1:3	1 O splendor of God's glory bright, O thou that bringest light from light, O Light of Light, light's living spring, O Day, all days illumining. 2 O thou true Sun of heavenly love, pour down thy radiance from above: the Spirit's sanctifying beam upon our earthly senses stream.
"The Head That Once Was Crowned with Thorns," Thomas Kelly (1820)	Heb 2:9	1 The Head that once was crowned with thorns, is crowned with glory now; a royal diadem adorns the mighty Victor's brow. 6 The cross He bore is life and health, though shame and death to Him: His people's hope, His people's wealth, their everlasting theme.
"Meekness and Majesty (This Is Your God)," Graham Kendrick (1986)	Heb 1:3; 5:8	See hymn lyrics for stanzas 1 and 2 on the Internet.

"Join All the Glorious Names," Isaac Watts (1674–1748)	Heb 7:23–28	1 Join all the glorious names of wisdom, love, and power, that ever mortals knew, that angels ever bore: all are too mean to speak his worth, too mean to set my Savior forth. 3 Jesus, my great High Priest, offered his blood, and died; my guilty conscience seeks no sacrifice beside: His powerful blood did once atone, and now it pleads before the throne.
"At the Lamb's High Feast," Latin (1632)	Heb 9:11–12	1 At the Lamb's high feast we sing praise to our victorious King, who has washed us in the tide flowing from his pierced side, Alleluia! 2 Praise we him, whose love divine gives his sacred blood for wine, gives his body for the feast—Christ the victim, Christ the priest. Alleluia!
"For All the Saints," William W. How (1864)	Heb 11:13–16; 12:1–2	1 For all the saints, who from their labors rest, who Thee by faith before the world confessed, Thy Name, O Jesu, be forever blest. Alleluia! Alleluia! 3 O may Thy soldiers, faithful, true, and bold, fight as the saints who nobly fought of old, and win, with them, the victor's crown of gold. Alleluia! Alleluia! 4 O blest communion, fellowship divine! We feebly struggle, they in glory shine; yet all are one in Thee, for all are Thine. Alleluia! Alleluia!

"Take Time to be Holy," William D. Longstaff (ca. 1882)	Heb 12:14	1. Take time to be holy, speak oft with thy Lord; abide in him always, and feed on his word. Make friends of God's children, help those who are weak, forgetting in nothing his blessing to seek.
		3. Take time to be holy, let him be thy guide, and run not before him, whatever betide. In joy or in sorrow, still follow the Lord, and looking to Jesus, still trust in his word.
"In the Sweet By and By," Sanford F. Bennett (1868)	Heb 13:14–15	1. There's a land that is fairer than day, and by faith we can see it afar; for the Father waits over the way, to prepare us a dwelling place there.
		Refrain: In the sweet by and by, we shall meet on that beautiful shore; in the sweet by and by, we shall meet on that beautiful shore.
		3. To our bountiful Father above, we will offer the tribute of praise, for the glorious gift of his love, and the blessings that hallow our days! [Refrain]

Some of the hymns noted here quote lines from Hebrews, but many do not. Themes associated with these hymns can be found in Hebrews, but they can often be found in other New Testament passages as well. Some hymns even cite a number of scriptural sources. Many hymnals have a Scripture index as an appendix in the back of the hymnal to help locate hymns or songs that might correspond to particular verses. For example, in the *African American Heritage Hymnal* one finds twelve different hymns identified with particular verses in Hebrews (Carpenter and Williams 2001, 689). Hymnals often include Scripture passages in and amidst the songs and hymns or in sections toward the back of the hymnal. A responsive-reading index in the back of the *African American Heritage Hymnal* indicates that there are eleven texts from Hebrews that are included for corporate readings (Carpenter and Williams 2001, 690). Hebrews 1:8–9 is included in a responsive reading on the topic of anointing, Heb 6:11–12, 19–20 is included in a reading on hope, and Heb 4:1, 9–10 is included in a reading on the promises of God (other texts are woven into the readings as well; Carpenter and Williams 2001, 1, 24, 42).

In *The Covenant Hymnal: A Worshipbook* (the denominational hymnal of The Evangelical Covenant Church), two passages from Hebrews are included for unison congregational reading: 12:28–13:8 is included as a responsive reading under a section heading of "discipleship" (*The Covenant Hymnal* 1996, selection 960); 13:20–21 is included as a corporate blessing for concluding a worship gathering (selection 982). In the non-denominational resource *The Celebration Hymnal: Songs and Hymns for Worship*, eleven texts from Hebrews are found in congregational readings (Fettke 1997, 825). Four sets of verses from Heb 3, 4, 7, and 10 are joined under the title "Christ's Priesthood" (Fettke 1997, 381). Parts are arranged for "worship leader," "solo," and "everyone." Including Scripture passages in these types of formats is intended to encourage creative engagement in biblical content. These are just a few examples of how Hebrews finds an active role to play in contemporary hymnals.

Worship Books and Hebrews

The text of Hebrews continues to surface in worship resources developed for congregational ministry. Service books for worship often recommend specific Scripture texts for a whole variety of worship events and ministry situations. Hebrews finds an active place for facilitating worship across traditions in and through these ritual guides. An examination of the *Book of Common Worship* (Presbyterian Church U.S.A./Cumberland Presbyterian Church) yields the following examples:

Hebrews Text	Application (all are noted as optional for use)	Page Citation
4:16, combined with Rom 5:8	Service for the Lord's Day: Call to confession (said by the leader to prepare the people for the confession of sin)	52
4:14–16	Service for the Lord's Day: Call to confession (paraphrase of the passage as a preparation for the confession of sin)	53

13:16	Service for the Lord's Day: Preparatory statement for receiving the offering	67, 79
13:20–21	Blessing (often said at the end of a worship event)	161
4:12	Sentence of scripture for the 8th Sunday in Ordinary Time, Year A, B, C (an option for use as appropriate for focus or transition)	213
4:14, 16	Sentence of scripture for Ascension of the Lord or the 7th Sunday of Easter, Year A, B, C	332
4:12	Sentence of scripture for the 20th Sunday in Ordinary Time, Year A, B, C	368
12:1, 2b	Sentence of scripture for the 20th Sunday in Ordinary Time, Year C	368
8:10	Sentence of scripture for the 28th Sunday in Ordinary Time, Year A, B, C	379
4:12	Sentence of scripture for the 29th Sunday in Ordinary Time, Year A, B, C	380
12:1	Sentence of scripture for All Saints' Day, Year B	385
10:22	Call to confession for the Lord's Day when including reaffirmation of the baptismal covenant for a congregation	473
13:20–21	Blessing for the funeral: a service of witness to the Resurrection	926, 937
13:20–21	Blessing for the committal service	946
2:14–18 11:1–3, 13–16; 12:1–2	Scripture readings for services on the occasions of death (in a list of suggested readings)	949
2:14–18 4:14–16; 5:7–9	Scripture readings for ministry to the sick	973, 986–87

Eight of the thirteen chapters of Hebrews are drawn upon in the above suggestions, with quite a bit of repetition of short passages (two entries for 2:14–18; three for 4:12; four for 4:14–16/4:16; three for 12:1/12:1–2; and three for 13:20–21). Three times Hebrews is suggested for use with confession, three times for blessing, once for offering, seven times as an appropriate brief Scripture addition for focus or transition, and four times as readings for ministering to the sick or grieving. The *Book of Common Worship* uses the Revised Common Lectionary as well, which means that many other sections of Hebrews are potentially being introduced in various celebrations over the three-year cycle. It is good to keep in mind that the particularity of the Christian tradition will influence the frequency and range of the use of Hebrews in worship (e.g., more is done with the high-priestly and implicit eucharistic imagery in Catholic and Orthodox materials). It is encouraging, though, to see this level of use of a non-Gospel, non-Pauline New Testament text in a Protestant worship manual.

VISUAL ART AND HEBREWS

The four Gospels are the primary New Testament books that inspire the bulk of the visual art work used in the life of the church. Hebrews, however, does have a small role to play in providing material that artists have used for generating images for use in worship settings. Two examples are commonly derived from the reflections found in Hebrews. The first is the depiction of the story of King Melchizedek's offering of bread and wine following the rescue of Lot by Abraham (Gen 14:18–20). The reference is brief and contains many mysteries. It seems unlikely that Christian communities would have focused on this obscure account were it not for the attention that the author of Hebrews brings to it. It is the designation of Jesus as high priest in the order of Melchizedek that provoked multiple depictions of this scene in Christian communities throughout the ages.

In Santa Maria Maggiore, a fifth-century basilica in Rome, a mosaic in the nave depicts Melchizedek, a figure in the clouds, and Abraham.[8] The mosaic is located near the triumphal arch above the chancel area (the location of the main altar). The Melchizedek image functions as a link between images that depict the story of Abraham in the nave and those that remem-

---

8. See http://www.vatican.va/various/basiliche/sm_maggiore/en/storia/popup_storia/popup_interno12.html.

ber the infancy of Christ in the arch. In the mosaic scene Melchizedek is pictured on the left with an offering of bread, and below the bread is a vessel for wine. Abraham (wearing a Roman toga and standing before an array of horses and soldiers) is on the right, gesturing toward Melchizedek. Hovering in the center above the two figures (in the clouds) is a Christ figure gesturing toward the offering. The association here is thought to be that of Abraham meeting the Divine Word in the form of the ancient priest/king (Jensen 2005, 119). The location of the mosaic near the main altar accentuates the eucharistic interpretation of the Genesis account and reminds the faithful of the roles of priest and king that Christ fulfills (even from of old).

In San Vitale, a sixth-century basilica (completed in 548 c.e.) in Ravenna, Italy, a mosaic depiction of Abel and Melchizedek is located in the presbytery (sanctuary or chancel area) just above and near the main altar (in a lunette on the right wall).[9] On the opposite wall, in the lunette, is a depiction of two scenes from the life of Abraham: the visitation of the three mysterious guests (Gen 18:1–15; often interpreted as a representation of the Holy Trinity) and the sacrifice of Isaac (Gen 22:1–19; often interpreted as a foreshadowing of the sacrifice of Christ). Abel (to the left of a central altar in the mosaic) is depicted as looking up and offering a spotless lamb. Melchizedek (on the right side of the altar) is looking up and offering bread. The altar in the mosaic is similar in appearance to the main altar of the church below. Bread and a vessel for wine are on the altar. Directly above the altar is a hand pointing toward the altar and gesturing with a blessing. With the location of this mosaic just above the church altar, the eucharistic associations of spotless lamb, bread, and wine with the sacrifice of Christ are reinforced.

In Sant Apollinare in Classe, Ravenna, a third variation on the Melchizedek offering appears.[10] This basilica was consecrated in 549 c.e. A mosaic featuring Abel, Abraham and Isaac, and Melchizedek is located on the right wall of the presbytery. All three figures surround a central altar that resembles the main church altar. Two loaves of bread (with the sign of the cross on them) and a vessel for wine sit on the altar in the mosaic. Abel is looking forward on the left and offering a spotless lamb. Abraham is looking forward on the right and offering his son (Isaac is also holding

---

9. See http://www.artbible.net/1T/Gen1417_Melchizedeck_blessing/pages/07%20 RAVENNA%20ABEL%20AND%20MELCHIZEDEK%20SACRIFICING.htm.

10. See http://www.sacred-destinations.com/italy/ravenna-sant-apollinare-classe-photos/slides/xti_7368p.htm.

his hands out in an offering gesture). Melchizedek is directly behind the altar, between Abel and Abraham (and Isaac). Melchizedek is holding an offering of bread. Above and to the left of Melchizedek is a hand emerging from clouds, a representation of God accepting the offering. Again, the altar and offerings in the mosaic and its proximity to the main church altar accentuate the sacrificial associations of these Old Testament stories in relation to the sacrificial nature of the Eucharist.

Many other depictions of the story of Melchizedek and his offering have been generated by painters, illustrators, and sculptors throughout the history of the church.[11] Some paintings and illustrations omit any altar and simply show the meeting of Abraham and Melchizedek with his offering. The mosaics mentioned here are particularly significant in that their material composition and integration into the visual program of each chancel is integral to their interpretation.

The second primary visual expression that has emerged from Hebrews is a rendering of Jesus Christ as a priest. Icons have been used in the life of the Eastern Orthodox church from its earliest days. Icons provide a visual representation of the faith, reminding the faithful of the content of their beliefs and the faithfulness of earlier witnesses. Icons are central to the worship life of the Orthodox faith. The rich symbolism of the Old Testament tabernacle and temple provide a pattern and rationale for making use of visual artifacts in the life of Orthodox worship environments and function as a source for typological inspiration. The person and life of Jesus Christ constitute a significant portion of the visual repertoire of iconography. The designation of Jesus as the high priest of the church has yielded its own depiction. Different renderings of the icon exist. One primary expression depicts Jesus on a throne dressed in the vestments and crown of a bishop. His right hand gestures a blessing to the viewer; his left hand holds an open Gospel book. The text on the open pages states, "I am the Good Shepherd. The Good Shepherd lays down his life for the sheep" (John 10:11).

A contemporary iconographic rendering of Jesus as the high priest was recently selected for use by the Roman Catholic Church in promot-

---

11. A good starting point for exploring visual representations is the eight-volume *Lexicon der christlichen Ikonographie* (Freiburg: Herder, 1968–1976). The first four volumes explore various Christian themes. The last four volumes address the saints of the church, both Western and Eastern. References to works from the third to the nineteenth centuries are included. Melchizedek has an entry in volume 7.

ing the "Year for Priests" (19 June 2009–19 June 2010).[12] The icon was painted by iconographer Marek Czarnecki and is based on a fifteenth-century Greek prototype. Jesus is depicted in Latin rite vestments. He has an image of a pelican over his chest (an ancient Christian symbol for Christ based on the tradition that a mother pelican feeds her chicks her own blood if necessary). His right hand is held up in a gesture of blessing; his left hand holds open a Gospel book that reads: "I am the Good Shepherd. I know my sheep and they know my voice. The Good Shepherd lays down his life for his sheep." The words "eternal" and "high priest" are near his shoulders. Incorporated into the border of the icon are the figure of Melchizedek (on the left), St. Jean-Baptiste Vianney (on the right), and an altar set for Eucharist flanked by grapevines (on the bottom). St. John Vianney was declared the universal patron of priests by Pope Benedict XVI. The patristic interpretations of priesthood and Eucharist derived from Hebrews continue to be present in the worship life of the church through the use of this icon.

Conclusions

Although the Epistle to the Hebrews has not had a large role to play in the development and practice of Christian worship, it has remained an enduring source of inspiration and theological interpretation. As an excellent example of early Christian preaching, the epistle has invited homilies that have sought to understand the fullness of Christ in light of God's covenant with the Jews. Implications for Eucharist and ordered ministry have been found in Hebrews that shaped an understanding of how Christians can offer appropriate sacrifices of praise in corporate settings. Readings from the book of Hebrews have increasingly been incorporated into the services of the church. Passages continue to illuminate our celebrations of Christ's birth, work, and death and the lives of those who have gone before us. Hymns have been written with texts from Hebrews in mind, blessings emerge from its pages, and visual expressions of faith occasionally draw upon its imagery. Hebrews remains an integral part of the worship life of Christian communities, enriching the faith expressions of the community in a multitude of ways.

---

12. See http://www.seraphicrestorations.com/gallery/index.php?gallery=.&image=Christ_the_Great_High_Priest.jpg.

Epilogue

Harold W. Attridge

During the last quarter century, the Epistle to the Hebrews has experienced a resurgence of interest among scholars of the New Testament. The essays in this collection provide a useful window onto the contemporary discussion of this fascinating text. Each brings to the task of interpreting Hebrews a set of conceptual tools and potential intertexts. Their use of these various lenses through which to read Hebrews is a marvelous illustration of the challenges inherent in making sense of this biblical book. They also display the allure that many scholars have found in this work of the anonymous but enormously talented theological and literary talent that his given us this "word of exhortation."

Patrick Gray, in an effort to situate Hebrews in its larger cultural context, insists that the author of Hebrews engages with Hellenic culture, whether he is addressing Gentiles, Jews, or some combination of both. Gray notes some of the familiar points of contact between Hebrews and Greco-Roman rhetoric and philosophy. On the latter point he agrees with James W. Thompson on the importance of allusions to Platonism, territory that Thompson covers in greater detail. Gray's more original contribution is to focus on the themes of discipline (*paideia*) and brotherly love (*philadelphia*), important for the hortatory program of Hebrews, for which he finds interesting parallels from Greek and Roman sources. In developing the theme of brotherhood, he appeals to Greek and Roman conventions about legitimate and illegitimate sons, which he sees as an underlying issue in Hebrews. Gray also usefully explores the themes of athletics and political discourse and, echoing Ellen Aitken, finds in the text an implicit critique of the Roman political order. Hebrews' critique of the sacrificial cult of the temple is also seen to echo themes in the critique of traditional religious practice found in Greek and Roman sources. Whatever other resources it uses, Hebrews clearly is an integral part of the Greco-Roman world.

Issues of context and content arise in the essay by James W. Thompson, which reads Hebrews alongside contemporary Middle Platonic philosophy, with its stark dichotomy between this transient, phenomenal world and the eternal realm of unchanging truth. Thompson is careful to defend himself against the charge that he is involved in a reductionist reading of Hebrews as a philosophical text. No, he avers, Hebrews clearly displays elements of Jewish apocalyptic eschatology, but these have been framed and understood within a framework indebted to Platonic presuppositions.

Thompson's essay is instructive for all of the parallels that it draws between vocabulary and conceptual structures in Hebrews and contemporary Middle Platonism, and his admission that the work is not a philosophical text is appropriate. Yet I am not sure he has provided a roadmap to the way in which the apparently philosophical elements of the text relate to dimensions of the text that are not readily reconciled with a philosophical stance. Several options are possible. The author may have casually adopted philosophical phrases and concepts, perhaps imperfectly understood, as part of his homiletic effort. Anyone who has heard a homily lately can probably provide modern parallels. Or the author may have consciously appropriated philosophical terms/concepts and used them perhaps with a hint of irony or with the aim of teasing his listeners into new insight.[1] The point may be subtle, but it is important for understanding what is afoot in Hebrews. This is not a text interested in conceptual analysis or charting metaphysical or epistemological principles. It is a work of rhetoric that can exploit language and conceptual schemes for their effect on the audience. Hebrews does, in my estimation, gesture toward Platonic language and concept, only to subvert it in the interest of a new definition of where "ultimate reality" is to be found: in the footsteps of Jesus.

The essays in this collection display diverse perspectives, and Eric F. Mason's offers a dramatic contrast to the approach of Gray or Thompson. His intertexts come from the Dead Sea Scrolls, which he uses to illuminate the cosmology of Hebrews with its notion of a heavenly sanctuary and its priestly messianism, both of which have intriguing parallels in the works of the Qumran sectarians. Mason finally treats the figures of Melchizedek, emphasizing the role of Melchizedek as a heavenly, angelic figure especially in 11QMelchizedek.

---

1. I have argued that something like the latter situation obtains in Hebrews. See now the essays in Attridge 2010.

The evidence from Qumran on all these parallels is complex. Mason does an admirable job of explicating the texts and treading through several scholarly minefields. He is certainly correct that the literature of Second Temple Judaism casts important light on the contexts of Hebrews. He is at the same time careful to argue that Hebrews ought not be confined into a single cultural background. It obviously draws on a variety of traditions. Mason's work, brought into dialogue with that of Gray and Thompson, raises a question that future scholars will need to address: How does our learned and savvy author draw on these various cultural traditions without explicitly committing himself to any? For example, for all the ways that the Melchizedek tradition provides parallels to Hebrews, our author remains deftly reticent about the precise relationship between Melchizedek and Jesus. The old priest-king is never explicitly said to be an angel or an eschatological figure. He remains a figure in Scripture, though a penumbra of speculation about him derived from Jewish sources seems to loom offstage. What kind of literary play is at work here in the glancing gesture toward traditions that remain in the background?

David M. Moffitt's intertext is primarily the Greek Bible, set within the context of biblical interpretation in the Second Temple period. Moffitt argues that Hebrews' use of the biblical texts attends carefully to the precise words of Scripture. Nonetheless, our author can be selective in the words he chooses to cite, as in his quotation of Ps 40 in Heb 10:5–10. Moffitt covers generally familiar territory in noting the use of techniques familiar in rabbinic literature such as *gezerah shawah* and *qal wahomer*, which serve larger argumentative aims, such as showing the superiority of Christ to angels or demonstrating how his high priesthood should be understood. The essay is a useful reminder of what many commentators have pointed out about Hebrews. One point that deserves further study is the way in which the author attends to the personae of the speakers in the biblical text. How Hebrews construes innerbiblical dialogue and uses it as a device for engaging his audience is a topic that merits further attention.[2]

While other interpreters in this collection give some attention to the realm of ancient rhetoric, Craig R. Koester adopts oratorical practice as the chief lens for his reading of Hebrews. His major exegetical focus is to trace the flow of the argument in Hebrews. He acknowledges that most interpreters recognize the same paragraph units within the text but

---

2. See my attempt to explore some of this territory in Attridge 2002.

construe the relationships among those paragraphs differently. Koester makes a persuasive argument for finding a classical rhetorical structure in Hebrews that engages listeners with an *exordium*, states a proposition, then makes arguments for that proposition punctuated by hortatory excursuses. To support his reading of the text, he regularly calls on examples of Greco-Roman rhetorical theory and practice. His most valuable contribution is the effort to trace the flow of the argumentative logic of the text, and much of his treatment is highly useful for tracing that flow. I suspect that were I to do another commentary on Hebrews, I would want to revise the somewhat rigid formal view of the structure of Hebrews that I once defended. Nonetheless, there are points at which I hesitate to follow wholeheartedly Koester's reading of the flow of Hebrews. The designation of 2:5–9 as the "proposition" of the address, the section that lays out the thesis to be defended in the whole, does not do justice to what is happening in the first chapters of Hebrews. The rest of chapter 2, it seems to me, articulates a fundamental concern of our author to relate the Christ-event to the lives of his listeners. It is not so much substantiating argument as a foretaste of the whole appeal that is to follow. My quibble may be a matter of emphasis and nuance, but my larger point is to recognize that appropriation of the lens of ancient rhetorical theory and practice for interpreting Hebrews is much more art than science. Our author was clearly a skilled rhetorician, but like other such professionals, he adapted the canonical paradigms to the specific rhetorical situation that confronted him.

Issues of form and background arise in Gabriella Gelardini's paper, which offers an ingenious analysis of the Epistle to the Hebrews as an example of a particular type of Jewish homily. Like Mason, her approach differs from those who find their interlocutors in Greek and Roman culture. Her intertexts are primarily the formal homilies of rabbinic Judaism, well attested in later midrashic sources. She correctly notes that application of the principles of classical rhetoric is not sufficient to explain the literary form of Hebrews (I made a similar point in Attridge 1990), although her characterization of Aristotelian rhetoric simply in terms of figures of speech such as anaphora ignores important figures of thought, such as that abound in the homily.[3] Yes, Hebrews is certainly to be understood within

---

3. Several essays (Neyrey, McCruden, Mitchell) call attention to the importance of *synkrisis* in Hebrews.

the context of Jewish exegetical and hortatory practices, which revolve around the interpretation and application of scripture.

Gelardini argues (as she did in her longer monograph, Gelardini 2007) that there is a more specific and detailed parallel: the *petichta* form of rabbinic homily that interrelates two scriptural texts, from Torah and the Prophets, which would have been part of the synagogue lectionary cycle. Much is uncertain about the development of rabbinic homiletical styles, but for the sake of argument, we might assume with Gelardini that the forms and patterns of fourth-century rabbinic literature do indeed have roots in Second Temple Judaism. But is the pattern in evidence here? Her analysis suggests that the two biblical texts at play in the tripartite homily are Exod 31:17b and Jer 31. If the two were indeed involved, she would have an interesting case. Jeremiah certainly dominates the central expository section of Hebrews, 8–10, and citation at 10:16–17 of a portion of the passage initially cited at 8:8–12 constitutes a defining *inclusio*. But where is the citation of the Torah? She finds it hidden in the citation at Heb 4:4, which most commentators have identified as a citation of Gen 2:2.[4] The homilist's comment on his citation refers quite explicitly to the story line of Genesis, of God entering his "rest" when his works were done, and the allusion to Genesis is essential to making the immediate argumentative point that the divine "rest" is not simply the land of Canaan but is something available to the addressees now as they approach a heavenly Mount Zion (Heb 12:18–24). Hence, the attempt to connect Heb 4:4 to Exodus seems strained indeed, a very weak reed on which to build a major hypothesis.

There are, of course, allusions to Numbers all through the exegesis of Ps 95 in Heb 3 and 4, but Gelardini believes it important to find an allusion to the story of breach of covenant in Exodus.

Although her formal analysis remains unconvincing, the larger thematic suggestion that it supports is insightful. There is a balance in the overall economy of the text between the notions of failure to heed God's word in the history of Israel and the possibility of listening to that word, enunciated by the Son, who inaugurates a new covenant and invites other sons and daughters to follow him on the road to heavenly glory.

---

4. Heb 4:4, *kai katepausen ho Theos en tē hēmera tē hebdomē apo pantōn tōn ergōn autou*, is quite close to Gen 2:2: *kai katepausen tē hēmera tē hebdomē apo pantōn tōn ergōn autou*. Exod 31:17b, *tē hēmera tē hebdomē epausato kai katepausen*, refers to the same notion, but not in the precise words of Genesis.

The application of insights from the social sciences has been a feature of New Testament criticism for the last generation. Jerome H. Neyrey's essay well exemplifies this approach, reading Jesus in Hebrews in the light of sociological theory and ancient social practice. That theory focuses on the role of a "broker" in a social system dominated by patron-client relationships. The analysis is "etic" rather than "emic," that is, focusing on the structural pattern of behaviors implied by the various terms that are applied to Jesus, including mediator and guarantor, as well as priest, leader, and the like. The argument is sound at that level of analysis, but I wonder if a bit more attention might be paid to the "emic" components that Neyrey uses to make his case. The author of Hebrews might well take for granted the kind of structural relationship that the generic category "broker" connotes, but he does not have that category as an explicit part of his mental apparatus. In exploring the specifics of the kinds of "brokering" images that the author uses, there may be specific features of particular forms of the relationship that contribute to the picture of mediation that he wants to paint. The commercial function of a guarantor (*engyos*), as of a loan, is, it seems to me, different from that of a negotiator (*mesitēs*), who helps two parties determine the details of their pact. Further, neither is doing exactly what a priest or high priest is usually thought to do, and the kind of "brokering" that they do does not necessarily involve the patron-client relationship that seems to dominate much of the text. The next stage of analysis of the use of "brokering" image would be to attend to those subtle differences in social roles that are somehow attributed to Jesus. In the process, we might find that the author is consciously using, and subtly manipulating, the social categories at his disposal, just as he plays with philosophical categories.

Another attempt to provide new insight on Hebrews from a specialized methodological perspective appears in the essay by Kenneth Schenck, which, like his earlier monographs (Schenck 2003, 2007), explores the role of "narrative" in assessing Hebrews. His "intertext" comes not so much from other literary sources as from a reconstruction of the sequential narrative about the history of salvation and the role of Jesus in it implied in the argument and exhortation of Hebrews. Sensitive to criticisms of this kind of approach, he nonetheless argues that Hebrews assumes and projects the underlying "stories" of the history of Israel and the history of Jesus, in which the latter reshapes the former. Much that he has to say along the way, often in critical dialogue with some of the other contributors to this volume, is sensible and on target, however loosely it may be related to the organizing methodological concept of his essay. The most important insight in his approach is the notion that there is tension between the "narrative" assumed by the audience of Hebrews and the "narrative" that he is purveying. A simple narratological approach, with whatever theoretical framework, will not be useful unless it also attends to that "rhetorical" dimension of the text, its interaction with its hearers. Schenck realizes the importance of the rhetorical situation and sketches his own overall understanding of Hebrews as a work written after the destruction of the temple in an effort to offer consolation to those who lamented the destruction of the old center of worship. His analysis has much to recommend it, though the structuralist foundation, the search for an underlying "story" that Hebrews presupposes, may not allow for quite enough attention to the rhetorical dynamics of this complex and playful text.

Frank J. Matera's essay does not rely on reading Hebrews in connection with an "intertext" but reviews the overall argument of Hebrews and its combination of exposition and exhortation. That review grounds a reflection on the contemporary significance of the text's theology. The first point that he scores in this, the most creative, part of his essay is that Hebrews redefines the nature of priesthood in terms of self-sacrifice. That redefinition has implications for those who would follow in the footsteps of the Great High Priest, but it also has implications for what "priesthood" might mean in the setting of the contemporary church. He notes that Hebrews presents a challenge but makes no suggestions for how to answer the challenge. The point is interesting but begs for an engagement with the history of interpretation of the text. Catholic and Protestant readings of Hebrews since the time of the Reformation divided precisely on this crucial issue of understanding Christ's priesthood. The second point that Matera makes about the enduring value of Hebrews is that it balances incarnational and redemptive perspectives on the significance of Christ, combining, in effect, what he takes as the essential thrusts of John and Paul. Matera is certainly correct about the combination, but exactly how it is distinctive over against the other two major theologians of the New Testament is not clear. The dichotomy of Johannine/incarnation and Paul/redemption usefully captures something about the emphases of the two other great theologians, but it ignores important parts of their respective construals of the gospel.

Kevin B. McCruden's essay uses as one of its "intertexts" the Christ-hymn of Phil 2, but, like Schenck, he is interested in the implicit grand narrative implied by Hebrews. He finds the keystone of that narrative arch in the event of Christ's resurrection, equated with his exaltation and installation at God's right hand. It is that installation that constitutes Christ's essential "perfection" (see esp. 7:26–28). McCruden qualifies that judgment, following the important study of the theme of perfection by David Peterson, by noting the ways in which Christ's human experiences, including his suffering, "perfect" him and qualify him to be a faithful and merciful high priest (see esp. 5:7–10). From the central exposition of the significance of the sacrifice of Jesus in chapters 8–10 emerges the insight that the complex "perfection" of Christ arises from the intensely personal nature of his self-sacrifice.

"Perfection" in Hebrews is a concept that applies also to Christ's followers. McCruden's explanation of Christian perfection focuses on the lived experience of the living God made possible for believers by the "entry" to the divine presence that Christ's death made possible. Such entry to sacred space is possible because the most intimate part of the believer's self, the conscience, has been cleansed by the expiatory effects of Christ's shed and sprinkled blood.

McCruden's analysis thus captures an important part of what Hebrews is trying to convey through its rather elaborate imagery, the experience of personal, interior transformation effected by the sacrificial death of the Great High Priest.

Rowan A. Greer, who has made significant contributions to the history of interpretation of Hebrews in the fathers, returns to that territory in his essay. His intertexts are the theological polemics of the fourth and fifth centuries, in which several sections of Hebrews were critical points of contention. Debates first raged between Nicenes, especially Athanasius of Alexandria, and their Arian opponents about the status of the Word as truly divine. The solution to those debates, the Nicene Creed reformulated at the Council of Constantinople in 381, set the stage for the next round of controversy, the understanding of the relationship between the divine and human in Christ. Greer deftly sketches the different positions of the Alexandrians (Cyril) and the Antiochenes (Theodore of Mospsuestia) and the ways in which they played out in the Nestorian controversy (428–451) that culminated in the Council of Chalcedon.

Greer's treatment notes that the readings and controversies of the patristic period seem quite foreign to us, steeped as we are in the historical approach to Scripture characteristic of most post-Enlightenment biblical scholarship. He finally appeals for the possibility of having theology as well as history serve as the framework within which to engage in scriptural interpretation. He is, of course, not alone in launching such an appeal, although it is difficult to discern what exactly a theological reading of Scripture would be on the basis of the patristic controversies, however interesting they may be. A part of such an approach would certainly be a sensitivity to the kinds of claims that Christians make these days about God and Christ, and there would at least be a family resemblance between many of these claims and what the fathers affirmed. Yet there would be differences as well, in part occasioned by those very impulses of the Enlightenment that generated the enterprise of historical-critical study of Scripture. Whatever it will look like, theological "reading" of Scripture will be an increasingly important part of the world of biblical interpretation in the years ahead.[5]

Alan C. Mitchell takes as his context for reading Hebrews not an ancient body of literature but the situation of believers in the post-Holocaust period, which has prompted many Christian theologians to reflect on the elements of Scripture that have been interpreted in a "supersessionist" manner. That reading of the New Testament in general, and Hebrews in particular, suggests that a divine covenant with Christians has displaced the divine covenant with Israel.

Mitchell draws a distinction between the supersessionist rhetoric that came to dominate the discourse of the early church from the Epistle of Barnabas onward with the inner Jewish polemic of the first century, of which early Christians were very much a part. To make the distinction work, he needs to deal with several critical texts, including Heb 8:13. The "obsolescence" of the old covenant read out of the prophecy of Jeremiah has to do not with the covenant itself but with the mode of its implementation. The ancient covenant is thus renewed, not supplanted, in a way analogous to that envisioned by the sectarians of the Dead Sea Scrolls. The change from exterior to interior worship constitutes an adaptation of Judaism responding to the realities of the post-70 period, when the temple cult was no more. Similarly in Heb 10:9, the removal of the "first" and installation of the "the second" refers not so much to covenants as to the means by which the covenant relationship is effected, sacrifices on the one hand, obedience on the other.

---

5. For some recent attempts from two different perspectives, see Martin 2008 and Volf 2010.

Mitchell thus aligns himself with other recent scholars of Hebrews, such as Richard Hays and Pamela Eisenbaum, who have resisted a "super-sessionist" reading of the text in favor of one that stresses the continuity between "old" and "new." This approach is a welcome antidote to a superficial assimilation of Hebrews to the polemics of later generations and somewhat of a comfort to modern Christians uncomfortable with the history of anti-Semitism rooted in early Christian affirmations. Most important, the text clearly does not envision a replacement of one covenant people by another. Instead, as Mitchell notes, it forcefully insists on the shared fate of the faithful of old with the faithful followers of the heavenly high priest (11:39–40). It remains sobering to reflect on how easy it seems to have been for a shift in rhetoric to occur, from a position that said "A new form of covenant observance is available to us in these difficult times" to "A new covenant people has been created, supplanting the old." Seeds of that rhetorical shift are certainly present in Hebrews, in passages such as 13:10, distinguishing "us" from those who do not have a proper "table" but busy themselves with external regulations. To impose a later conceptuality on Hebrews is anachronistic. To ignore those elements of its rhetoric that push in what appears to us a negative direction does not do justice to the history of its reception.

Mark A. Torgerson focuses on the ways in which Hebrews has contributed to the worship life of Christians. Like Greer, he finds his most important intertexts in patristic interpretations of Hebrews (Chrysostom, Cyprian, *Apostolic Tradition*) and liturgical prayers that allude to passages on the priesthood of Melchizedek or the sacrifice of Christ as ways of explaining what is happening at the eucharistic table. Torgerson's intertexts range even more widely, through the writings of Martin Luther, who insists on the once-for-all character of Christ's sacrifice, and the documents of Trent and Vatican II, which cite Hebrews in favor of a Catholic understanding of the ordained priesthood.

Of particular interest is Torgerson's exploration of the impact of Hebrews outside the commentary tradition. He offers a summary of the role of Hebrews in the development of the lectionary cycle, including its traditional one-year cycle still used by Orthodox churches or modern instantiations in the analogous triennial or biennial cycles of Catholics, Episcopalians, and many Protestants. He provides a handy summary of various appearances of Hebrews in hymns and books of worship, and he compiles a roster of visual representations of Hebrews, usually having to do with Melchizedek or with Jesus as priest, in Christian art from antiquity through twenty-first-century icons. Torgerson's essay demonstrates the influence of Hebrews in a variety of venues and usefully suggests areas for further research.

In conclusion, let me congratulate Eric F. Mason and Kevin B. McCruden for bringing together this excellent collection of essays that should certainly serve to engage a new generation of students of my favorite early Christian homilist.

BIBLIOGRAPHY

Abegg, Martin G., Jr. 1995. The Messiah at Qumran: Are We Still Seeing Double? *Dead Sea Discoveries* 2:125–44.

———. 2003. 1QSb and the Elusive High Priest. Pages 3–13 in *Emanuel: Studies in Hebrew Bible, Septuagint, and Dead Sea Scrolls in Honor of Emanuel Tov*. Edited by S. M. Paul, R. A. Kraft, L. H. Schiffman, and W. W. Fields. Leiden: Brill.

Aitken, Ellen Bradshaw. 2005. Portraying the Temple in Stone and Text: The Arch of Titus and the Epistle to the Hebrews. Pages 131–48 in *Hebrews: Contemporary Methods—New Insights*. Edited by G. Gelardini. Biblical Interpretation Series 75. Leiden: Brill. Repr., Atlanta: Society of Biblical Literature, 2008.

Aland, Kurt, and Barbara Aland. 1989. *The Text of the New Testament: An Introduction to the Critical Editions and to the Theory and Practice of Modern Textual Criticism*. 2nd ed. Translated by E. F. Rhodes. Grand Rapids: Eerdmans.

Allen, David L. 2010. *Lukan Authorship of Hebrews*. NAC Studies in Bible and Theology. Nashville: Broadman & Holman.

Allen, David M. 2008. *Deuteronomy and Exhortation in Hebrews: A Study in Narrative Re-presentation*. WUNT 2/238. Tübingen: Mohr Siebeck.

Allen, Joseph, Michel Najim, Jack Norman Sparks, and Theodore Stylianopoulos, eds. 1993. *The Orthodox Study Bible: New Testament and Psalms (New King James Version)*. Nashville: Thomas Nelson.

Allen, Leslie C. 2002. *Psalms 101–50, Revised*. Word Biblical Commentary 21. Nashville: Nelson.

Anderson, Gary A. 2000. The Exaltation of Adam and the Fall of Satan. Pages 83–100 in *Literature on Adam and Eve: Collected Essays*. Edited by G. A. Anderson et al. Studia in Veteris Testamenti Pseudepigraphica 15. Leiden: Brill.

Andresen, Carl. 1953. Justin und der mittlere Platonismus. *Zeitschrift für die neutestamentliche Wissenschaft und die Kunde der älteren Kirche* 44:159–95.

———. 1978. Antike und Christentum. Pages 50–99 in vol. 3 of *Theologische Realenzyklopädia*. 36 vols. Edited by G. Krause and G. Müller. Berlin: de Gruyer.

The Ante-Nicene Fathers. 1885–1887. Edited by Alexander Roberts and James Donaldson. 10 vols. Repr. Peabody, Mass.: Hendrickson, 1994.

Aristotle. 1926–2011. Translated by H. Rackham et al. 23 vols. LCL. Cambridge: Harvard University Press.

Attridge, Harold W. 1989. *The Epistle to the Hebrews: A Commentary on the Epistle to the Hebrews*. Hermeneia. Philadelphia: Fortress.

———. 1990. Paraenesis in a Homily: The Possible Location of, and Socialization in, the "Epistle to the Hebrews." *Semeia* 50:211–26.

———. 2002. God in Hebrews: Urging Children to Heavenly Glory. Pages 197–210 in *The Forgotten God: Perspectives in Biblical Theology*. Edited by A. A. Das and F. J. Matera. Louisville: Westminster John Knox.

———. 2004. The Epistle to the Hebrews and the Scrolls. Pages 315–42 in vol. 2 of *When Judaism and Christianity Began: Essays in Memory of Anthony J. Saldarini*. Edited by A. J. Avery-Peck, D. Harrington, and J. Neusner. 2 vols. Supplements to the Journal for the Study of Judaism 85. Leiden: Brill.

———. 2006. How the Scrolls Impacted Scholarship on Hebrews. Pages 203–30 in vol. 3 of *The Bible and the Dead Sea Scrolls*. Edited by J. H. Charlesworth. 3 vols. Waco, Tex.: Baylor University Press.

———. 2009. God in Hebrews. Pages 95–110 in *The Epistle to The Hebrews and Christian Theology*. Edited by R. Bauckham et al. Grand Rapids: Eerdmans.

———. 2010. *Essays on John and Hebrews*. WUNT 264. Tübingen: Mohr Siebeck.

Aune, David E. 1983. *Prophecy in Early Christianity and the Ancient Mediterranean World*. Grand Rapids: Eerdmans.

———. 1987. *The New Testament in Its Literary Environment*. Library of Early Christianity. Philadelphia: Westminster.

———. 1990. Heracles and Christ: Heracles Imagery in the Christology of Early Christianity. Pages 3–19 in *Greeks, Romans, and Christians: Essays in Honor of Abraham J. Malherbe*. Edited by D. L. Balch, E. Ferguson, and W. A. Meeks. Minneapolis: Fortress.

Backhaus, Knut. 1996. Per Christum in Deum. Zur theozentrischen Funktion der Christologie im Hebräerbrief. Pages 258–84 in *Der lebendige Gott: Studien zur Theologie des Neuen Testaments*. Edited by T. Söding. Münster: Aschendorff.

———. 2001. Das Land der Verheißung: Die Heimat der Glaubenden im Hebräerbrief. *New Testament Studies* 47:171–88.

———. 2009. *Der Hebräerbrief*. Regensburger Neues Testament. Regensburg: Pustet.

Bannon, Cynthia J. 1997. *The Brothers of Romulus: Fraternal Pietas in Roman Law, Literature, and Society*. Princeton: Princeton University Press.

Barrett, C. K. 1956. The Eschatology of the Epistle to the Hebrews. Pages 363–93 in *The Background of the New Testament and Its Eschatology*. Edited by W. D. Davies and D. Daube. Cambridge: Cambridge University Press.

———. 1982. *Essays on Paul*. Philadelphia: Westminster.

Barth, Markus. 1962. Old Testament in Hebrews: An Essay in Biblical Hermeneutics. Pages 53–78 in *Current Issues in New Testament Interpretation: Essays in Honor of Otto A. Piper*. Edited by W. Klassen and G. F. Snyder. The Preacher's Library. London: SCM.

Bateman, Herbert W. 1997. *Early Jewish Hermeneutics and Hebrews 1:5–13: The Impact of Early Jewish Exegesis on the Interpretation of a Significant New Testament Passage*. American University Studies: Series 7, Theology and Religion 193. New York: Lang.

Bauckham, Richard, Daniel R. Driver, Trevor A. Hart, and Nathan MacDonald, eds.

2009a. *A Cloud of Witnesses: The Theology of Hebrews in Its Ancient Contexts.* Library of New Testament Studies 387. London: T&T Clark.

———, eds. 2009b. *The Epistle to The Hebrews and Christian Theology.* Grand Rapids: Eerdmans.

Baumgarten, Joseph M., ed. 1996. *Qumran Cave 4.XIII: The Damascus Document (4Q266–273).* Discoveries in the Judaean Desert XVIII. Oxford: Clarendon.

———. 1999. Yom Kippur in the Qumran Scrolls and Second Temple Sources. *Dead Sea Discoveries* 6:184–91.

———. 2000. Damascus Document. Pages 166–70 in vol. 1 of *Encyclopedia of the Dead Sea Scrolls.* Edited by L. H. Schiffman and J. C. VanderKam. 2 vols. Oxford: Oxford University Press.

Becker, O. 1975. "μεσίτης." Pages 372–76 in vol. 1 of *New International Dictionary of New Testament Theology.* Edited by C. Brown. 4 vols. Grand Rapids: Eerdmans, 1975–1985.

Bertram, Georg. 1964. "ἔργον, κτλ." *TDNT* 2:635–55.

Boissevain, Jeremy. 1974. *Friends of Friends: Networks, Manipulators, and Coalitions.* New York: St. Martin's Press.

Bradshaw, Paul, Maxwell E. Johnson, and L. Edward Phillips. 2002. *The Apostolic Tradition: A Commentary.* Hermeneia. Minneapolis: Fortress.

Braun, Herbert. 1984. *An die Hebräer.* Handbuch zum Neuen Testament 14. Tübingen: Mohr Siebeck.

Brawley, Robert L. 1993. Discoursive Structure and the Unseen in Hebrews 2:8 and 11:1: A Neglected Aspect of the Context. *Catholic Biblical Quarterly* 55:81–98.

Bright, William, ed. 1873. *The Orations of St. Athanasius against the Arians.* Oxford: Oxford University Press.

Brooke, George J. 1999. The Scrolls and the Study of the New Testament. Pages 61–76 in *The Dead Sea Scrolls at Fifty: Proceedings of the 1997 Society of Biblical Literature Qumran Section Meetings.* Edited by R. A. Kugler and E. M. Schuller. Society of Biblical Literature Early Judaism and Its Literature 15. Atlanta: Scholars Press.

Bruce, F. F. 1963. "Our God and Saviour": A Recurring Biblical Pattern. Pages 51–66 in *The Saviour God: Comparative Studies in the Concept of Salvation Presented to Professor Edwin Oliver James Professor Emeritus in the University of London by Colleagues and Friends.* Edited by S. G. B. Brandon. Manchester: Manchester University Press.

———. 1990. *The Epistle to the Hebrews.* New International Commentary on the New Testament. Rev. ed. Grand Rapids: Eerdmans.

Buchanan, George Wesley. 1972. *To the Hebrews: Translation, Comment and Conclusions.* Anchor Bible 36. Garden City, N.Y.: Doubleday.

———. 2006. *The Book of Hebrews: Its Challenge from Zion.* Intertextual Bible Commentary. Eugene, Oreg.: Wipf & Stock.

Bultmann, Rudolf. 1955. *Theology of the New Testament.* Translated by Kendrick Grobel. 2 vols. New York: Scribner's.

Burkert, Walter. 1985. *Greek Religion.* Translated by John Raffan. Cambridge: Harvard University Press.

Busch, Peter, 2000. Der mitleidende Hohepriester: Zur Rezeption der mittelplatonischen Dämonologie in Hebr 4,14f. Pages 19–30 in *Religionsgeschichte des Neuen Testaments: Festschrift für Klaus Berger zum 60. Geburtstag*. Edited by A. von Dobbeler, K. Erlemann, and R. Heiligenthal. Tübingen: Francke.

Butts, James. 1987. The "Progymnasmata" of Theon: A New Text with Translation and Commentary. Ph.D. diss., Claremont Graduate School.

Caird, George B. 1959. The Exegetical Method of the Epistle to the Hebrews. *Canadian Journal of Theology* 5/1:44–51.

Campbell, Jonathan G. 2004. *The Exegetical Texts*. Companion to the Qumran Scrolls 4. London: T&T Clark.

Carpenter, Delores, and Nolan E. Williams Jr., eds. 2001. *African American Heritage Hymnal*. Chicago: GIA.

Chatman, Seymour. 1978. *Story and Discourse: Narrative Structure in Fiction and Film*. Ithaca, N.Y.: Cornell University Press.

Cicero. 1913–2010. Translated by W. Miller et al. 30 vols. LCL. Cambridge: Harvard University Press.

Cockerill, Gareth L. 1999. *Hebrews: A Bible Commentary in the Wesleyan Tradition*. Indianapolis: Wesleyan.

Collins, John J. 1997. *Apocalypticism in the Dead Sea Scrolls*. Literature of the Dead Sea Scrolls. London: Routledge.

———. 2010. *The Scepter and the Star: Messianism in Light of the Dead Sea Scrolls*. 2nd ed. Grand Rapids: Eerdmans.

Collins, John N. 1990. *Diakonia: Re-interpreting the Ancient Sources*. Oxford: Oxford University Press.

Cox, Ronald. 2007. *By the Same Word: Creation and Salvation in Hellenistic Judaism and Early Christianity*. Behefte zur Zeitschrift für die neutestamentliche Wissenschaft und die Kunde der älteren Kirche 145. Berlin: de Gruyter.

Crook, J. A. 1967. *Patria Potestas. Classical Quarterly* 17:113–22.

Croy, N. Clayton. 1998. *Endurance in Suffering: Hebrews 12:1–13 in Its Rhetorical, Religious, and Philosophical Context*. Society for New Testament Studies Monograph Series 98. Cambridge: Cambridge University Press.

Daley, Brian E. 2003. *The Hope of the Early Church*. Peabody, Mass.: Hendrickson.

Davidson, Maxwell J. 1992. *Angels at Qumran: A Comparative Study of 1 Enoch 1–36, 72–108 and Sectarian Writings from Qumran*. Journal for the Study of the Pseudepigrapha Supplement Series 11. Sheffield: JSOT Press.

Davies, Philip R. 2000. War of the Sons of Light against the Sons of Darkness. Pages 965–68 in vol. 2 of *Encyclopedia of the Dead Sea Scrolls*. Edited by L. H. Schiffman and J. C. VanderKam. 2 vols. Oxford: Oxford University Press.

Davila, James R. 2000. *Liturgical Works*. Eerdmans Commentary on the Dead Sea Scrolls. Grand Rapids: Eerdmans.

Davis, P. G. 1994. Divine Agents, Mediators, and New Testament Christology. *Journal of Theological Studies* 45:479–503.

Demosthenes. 1926–49. Translated by C. A. Vince et al. 7 vols. LCL. Cambridge: Harvard University Press.

deSilva, David A. 2000. *Perseverance in Gratitude: A Socio-rhetorical Commentary on the Epistle "to the Hebrews."* Grand Rapids: Eerdmans.

———. 2008. *Despising Shame: Honor Discourse and Community Maintenance in the Epistle to the Hebrews.* 2nd ed. Atlanta: Society of Biblical Literature.

Devreesse, Robert, ed. 1939. *Le commentaire de Théodore de Mopsueste sur les Psaumes (I–LXXX).* Studi e Testi 93. Vatican City: Vaticana.

Dillon, John. 1993. *Alcinous: The Handbook of Platonism.* Clarendon Later Ancient Philosophers. Oxford: Clarendon.

———. 1996. *The Middle Platonists.* Rev. ed. Ithaca, N.Y.: Cornell University Press.

Dio Chrysostom. 1932–1951. Translated by J. W. Cohoon and H. L. Crosby. 5 vols. LCL. Cambridge: Harvard University Press.

Dionysius of Halicarnassus. 1937–1985. Translated by Earnest Cary et al. 9 vols. Cambridge: Harvard University Press.

Dixon, Suzanne. 1992. *The Roman Family.* Baltimore: Johns Hopkins University Press.

———. 1993a. "A Lousy Ingrate": Honour and Patronage in the American Mafia and Ancient Rome. *International Journal of Moral and Social Studies* 8:61–72.

———. 1993b. The Meaning of Gift and Debt in the Roman Elite. *Echos du Monde Classique/Classical Views* 12:451–64.

Docherty, Susan E. 2009. *The Use of the Old Testament in Hebrews: A Case Study in Early Jewish Bible Interpretation.* WUNT 2/260. Tübingen: Mohr Siebeck.

Drawnel, Henryk. 2004. *An Aramaic Wisdom Text from Qumran: A New Interpretation of the Levi Document.* Supplements to the Journal for the Study of Judaism 86. Leiden: Brill.

Duhaime, Jean. 1994. War Scroll. Pages 80–141 in vol. 2 of *The Dead Sea Scrolls: Hebrew, Aramaic, and Greek Texts with English Translations.* Edited by J. H. Charlesworth et al. Louisville: Westminster John Knox.

Dunnill, John. 1992. *Covenant and Sacrifice in the Letter to the Hebrews.* Society for New Testament Studies Monograph Series 75. Cambridge: Cambridge University Press.

DuPlessis, P. J. 1959. *ΤΕΛΕΙΟΣ: The Idea of Perfection in the New Testament.* Kampen: J. H. Kok.

Edwards, M. J. 1991. On the Platonic Schooling of Justin Martyr. *Journal of Theological Studies* NS 42:17–34.

Ehrman, Bart D. 2000. *The New Testament: A Historical Introduction to the Early Christian Writings.* 2nd ed. Oxford: Oxford University Press.

Eisele, Wilfried. 2003. *Ein unerschütterliches Reich: Die mittelplatonische Umformung des Parusiegedankens im Hebräerbrief.* Beihefte zur Zeitschrift für die neutestamentliche Wissenschaft und die Kunde der älteren Kirche 116. Berlin: de Gruyter.

Eisenbaum, Pamela M. 2005a. Hebrews, Supersessionism and Jewish-Christian Relations. Paper presented at the Annual Meeting of the Society of Biblical Literature. Online: http://www.hebrews.unibas.ch/documents/2005Eisenbaum.pdf.

———. 2005b. Locating Hebrews within the Literary Landscape of Christian Origins. Pages 213–37 in *Hebrews: Contemporary Methods—New Insights.* Edited by G. Gelardini. Biblical Interpretation Series 75. Leiden: Brill. Repr., Atlanta: Society of Biblical Literature, 2008.

Ellingworth, Paul. 1993. *The Epistle to the Hebrews: A Commentary on the Greek Text*. New International Greek Testament Commentary. Grand Rapids: Eerdmans.

Ellis, E. Earle. 1991. *The Old Testament in Early Christianity: Canon and Interpretation in the Light of Modern Research*. WUNT 54. Tübingen: Mohr Siebeck.

Episcopal Church. 1979. *The Book of Common Prayer*. New York: Seabury.

Evangelical Covenant Church. 1996. *The Covenant Hymnal: A Worshipbook*. Chicago: Covenant Publications.

Evangelical Lutheran Church in America. 2006. *Evangelical Lutheran Worship*. Minneapolis: Augsburg Fortress.

Evans, Ernest, ed. 1972. *Irenaeus of Lyons: Adversos Marcionem*. 2 vols. Oxford: Clarendon.

Eyben, E. 1991. Fathers and Sons. Pages 114–43 in *Marriage, Divorce, and Children in Ancient Rome*. Edited by B. Rawson. Oxford: Clarendon.

Feldmeier, R. 1992. *Die Christen als Fremde: Die Metapher der Fremde in der antiken Welt, im Urchristentum und im 1. Petrusbrief*. WUNT 2/212. Tübingen: Mohr Siebeck.

Ferguson, Everett. 1980. Spiritual Sacrifice in Early Christianity and Its Environment. Pages 1151–89 in vol. 23.2 of *Aufstieg und Niedergang der römischen Welt*. Part 2, *Principat*. Edited by H. Temporini and W. Haase. New York: de Gruyter.

Fettke, Tom, ed. 1997. *The Celebration Hymnal: Songs and Hymns for Worship*. N.p.: Word Music/Integrity Music.

Fitzmyer, Joseph A. 2000. Melchizedek in the MT, LXX, and the NT. *Biblica* 81:63–69.

———. 2004. *The Genesis Apocryphon of Qumran Cave I*. 3rd ed. Biblica et orientalia 18B. Rome: Pontifical Biblical Institute.

Fletcher-Louis, Crispin H. T. 2002. *All the Glory of Adam: Liturgical Anthropology in the Dead Sea Scrolls*. Studies on the Texts of the Desert of Judah 42. Leiden: Brill.

Flusser, David. 1966. Melchizedek and the Son of Man. *Christian News from Israel* April:23–29.

Foerster, Werner. 1971. "σώζω, κτλ." *TDNT* 7:965–69.

Fohrer, Georg. 1971. σωτήρ. *TDNT* 7:1003–21.

Frei, Hans W. 1974. *The Eclipse of Biblical Narrative: A Study in Eighteenth and Nineteenth Century Hermeneutics*. New Haven: Yale University Press.

Gäbel, Georg. 2006. *Die Kulttheologie des Hebräerbriefes: Eine exegetisch-religionsgeschichtliche Studie*. WUNT 2/212. Tübingen: Mohr Siebeck.

García Martínez, Florentino, Eibert J. C. Tigchelaar, and Adam S. van der Woude, eds. 1997. *Manuscripts from Qumran Cave 11 (11Q2–18, 11Q20–30)*. Discoveries in the Judaean Desert XXIII. Oxford: Clarendon.

Gärtner, Hans. 1978. Pontifex. Pages 331–96 in vol. 15 Supplement of *Paulys Realencyclopädie der Classischen Altertumswissenschaft*. Edited by G. Wissowa and W. Kroll. 50 vols. in 84 parts. Stuttgart: Metzler and Druckenmüller, 1894–1980.

Gelardini, Gabriella. 2005. Hebrews, an Ancient Synagogue Homily for *Tisha be-Av*: Its Function, Its Basis, Its Theological Interpretation. Pages 107–27 in *Hebrews: Contemporary Methods—New Insights*. Edited by G. Gelardini. Biblical Interpretation Series 75. Leiden: Brill. Repr., Atlanta: Society of Biblical Literature, 2008.

———. 2007. *"Verhärtet eure Herzen nicht": Der Hebräer, eine Synagogenhomilie zu Tischa be-Aw.* Biblical Interpretation Series 83. Leiden: Brill.

Gleason, Randall C. 1998. The Old Testament Background of the Warning in Hebrews 6:4–8. *Bibliotheca Sacra* 155:62–91.

———. 2000. The Old Testament Background of Rest in Hebrews 3:7–4:11. *Bibliotheca Sacra* 157:281–303.

Grant, F. C. 1953. *Hellenistic Religions: The Age of Syncreticism.* Indianapolis: Bobbs-Merrill.

Grant, Robert, with David Tracy. 1984. *A Short History of the Interpretation of the Bible.* 2nd ed. Philadelphia: Fortress.

Grässer, Erich. 1993. *An die Hebräer.* Evangelisch-katholischer Kommentar zum Neuen Testament. 3 vols. Zurich: Benziger; Neukirchen-Vluyn: Neukirchener.

Gray, Patrick. 2003. *Godly Fear: The Epistle to the Hebrews and Greco-Roman Critiques of Superstition.* Society of Biblical Literature Academia Biblica 16. Atlanta: Society of Biblical Literature.

Greene, John T. 1989. *The Role of the Messenger and Message in the Ancient Near East.* Atlanta: Scholars Press.

Greer, Rowan A. 1973. *The Captain of Our Salvation: A Study in the Patristic Exegesis of Hebrews.* Beiträge zur Geschichte der biblischen Exegese 15. Tübingen: Mohr Siebeck.

———. 2010. *Theodore of Mopsuestia: The Commentaries on the Minor Epistles of Paul.* Society of Biblical Literature Writings from the Greco-Roman World 26. Atlanta: Society of Biblical Literature.

Greimas, A. J. 1966. *Sémantique structural.* Paris: Larousse.

Guthrie, George H. 1994. *The Structure of Hebrews: A Text-Linguistic Analysis.* Supplements to Novum Testamentum 73. Leiden: Brill.

———. 2003. Hebrews' Use of the Old Testament: Recent Trends in Research. *Currents in Biblical Research* 1:271–94.

———. 2004. Hebrews in Its First-Century Contexts: Recent Research. Pages 414–43 in *The Face of New Testament Studies: A Survey of Recent Research.* Edited by S. McKnight and G. R. Osborne. Grand Rapids: Baker.

Hagner, Donald A. 1990. *Hebrews.* New International Bible Commentary on the New Testament. Peabody, Mass.: Hendrickson.

Hay, David M. 1973. *Glory at the Right Hand: Psalm 110 in Early Christianity.* Society of Biblical Literature Monograph Series 18. Nashville: Abingdon.

Hays, Richard B. 2002. *The Faith of Jesus Christ: An Investigation of the Narrative Substructure of Gal 3:1–4:11.* 2nd ed. Grand Rapids: Eerdmans.

———. 2005. Christ Prays the Psalms: Israel's Psalter as Matrix of Early Christology. Pages 101–18 in *The Conversion of the Imagination: Paul as Interpreter of Israel's Scriptures.* Edited by R. B. Hays. Grand Rapids: Eerdmans.

———. 2009. "Here We Have No Lasting City": New Covenantalism in Hebrews. Pages 151–73 in *The Epistle to the Hebrews and Christian Theology.* Edited by R. Bauckham et al. Grand Rapids: Eerdmans.

Heen, Erik M., and Philip D. W. Krey, eds. 2005. *Hebrews.* Ancient Christian Commentary on Scripture: New Testament 10. Downers Grove, Ill.: Intervarsity Press.

Hesiod. 1936. Translated by H. G. Evelyn-White. LCL. Cambridge: Harvard University Press.

Hill, Robert C. 2006. *Theodore of Mopsuestia: Commentary on Psalms 1–81*. Writings from the Greco-Roman World 5. Atlanta: Society of Biblical Literature.

Holladay, Carl R. 2005. *A Critical Introduction to the New Testament: Interpreting the Message and Meaning of Jesus Christ*. Nashville: Abingdon.

Holtz, Gudrun. 2009. Rabbinische Literatur und Neues Testament: Alte Schwierigkeiten und neue Möglichkeiten. *Zeitschrift für neutestamentliche Wissenschaft* 100:173–98.

Horst, Pieter Willem van der. 1990. Sarah's Seminal Emission: Hebrews 11:11 in the Light of Ancient Embryology. Pages 287–302 in *Greeks, Romans, and Christians: Essays in Honor of Abraham J. Malherbe*. Edited by D. L. Balch, E. Ferguson, and W. A. Meeks. Minneapolis: Fortress.

Horton, Fred L., Jr. 1976. *The Melchizedek Tradition: A Critical Examination of the Sources to the Fifth Century A.D. and in the Epistle to the Hebrews*. Society for New Testament Studies Monograph Series 30. Cambridge: Cambridge University Press.

Hughes, Dennis D. 1991. *Human Sacrifice in Ancient Greece*. London: Routledge.

Hurst, Lincoln D. 1987. The Christology of Hebrews 1 and 2. Pages 151–64 in *The Glory of Christ in the New Testament*. Edited by L. D. Hurst and N. T. Wright. Oxford: Clarendon.

———. 1990. *The Epistle to the Hebrews: Its Background of Thought*. Society for New Testament Studies Monograph Series 65. Cambridge: Cambridge University Press.

Isaacs, Marie E. 1992. *Sacred Space: An Approach to the Theology of the Epistle to the Hebrews*. Journal for the Study of the New Testament Supplement Series 73. Sheffield: JSOT Press.

———. 2002. *Reading Hebrews and James: A Literary and Theological Commentary*. Macon, Ga.: Smyth & Helwys.

Jasper, R. C. D., and G. J. Cuming. 1980. *Prayers of the Eucharist: Early and Reformed*. 2nd ed. New York: Oxford University Press.

Jensen, Robin Margaret. 2005. *Face to Face: Portraits of the Divine in Early Christianity*. Minneapolis: Fortress.

Johnson, Earl S., Jr. 2008. *Hebrews*. Interpretation Bible Studies. Louisville: Westminster John Knox.

Johnson, Luke Timothy. 2003. The Scriptural World of Hebrews. *Interpretation* 57:237–50.

———. 2006. *Hebrews: A Commentary*. New Testament Library. Louisville: Westminster John Knox.

Jonge, Marinus de, and Adam S. van der Woude. 1965–1966. 11Q Melchizedek and the New Testament. *New Testament Studies* 12:301–26.

Karrer, Martin. 2002–2008. *Der Brief an die Hebräer*. 2 vols. Ökumenischer Taschenbuchkommentar zum Neuen Testament 20; Gütersloher Taschenbücher 520. Gütersloh: Gütersloher Verlagshaus.

———. 2006. The Epistle to the Hebrews and the Septuagint. Pages 335–53 in *Septuagint Research: Issues and Challenges in the Study of the Greek Jewish Scriptures.* Edited by W. Kraus and R. G. Wooden. Socitey of Biblical Literature Septuagint and Cognate Studies 53. Atlanta: Society of Biblical Literature.

Käsemann, Ernst. 1984. *The Wandering People of God: An Investigation of the Letter to the Hebrews.* Translated by R. A. Harrisville and I. L. Sandberg. Minneapolis: Augsburg.

Kennedy, George A. 1972. *The Art of Rhetoric in the Roman World.* Princeton: Princeton University Press.

Kim, Lloyd. 2006. *Polemic in the Book of Hebrews: Anti-Semitism, Anti-Judaism, Supersessionism?* Princeton Theological Monographs 34. Eugene, Oreg.: Pickwick.

Kirschbaum, Engelbert, ed. 1968–1976. *Lexicon der christlichen Ikonographie.* 8 vols. Freiburg: Herder.

Kittel, Gerhard, and Gerhard Friedrich, eds. 1964–1976. *Theological Dictionary of the New Testament.* Translated by Geoffrey W. Bromiley. 10 vols. Grand Rapids: Eerdmans.

Klauck, Hans-Josef. 1994. *Alte Welt und neuer Glaube, Beiträge zur Religionsgeschichte, Forschungsgeschichte und Theologie des Neuen Testaments.* Novum Testamentum et Orbis Antiquus 29. Göttingen: Vandenhoeck & Ruprecht.

Knibb, Michael. 2000. Rule of the Community. Pages 793–94 in vol. 2 of *Encyclopedia of the Dead Sea Scrolls.* Edited by L. H. Schiffman and J. C. VanderKam. 2 vols. Oxford: Oxford University Press.

Kobelski, Paul J. 1981. *Melchizedek and Melchireša'.* Catholic Biblical Quarterly Monograph Series 10. Washington, D.C.: Catholic Biblical Association of America.

Koester, Craig R. 1994. The Epistle to the Hebrews in Recent Study. *Currents in Research: Biblical Studies* 2:123–45.

———. 2001. *Hebrews: A New Translation with Introduction and Commentary.* Anchor Bible 36. New York: Doubleday.

———. 2002. Hebrews, Rhetoric, and the Future of Humanity. *Catholic Biblical Quarterly* 64:103–23.

———. 2005. God's Purpose and God's Saving Work according to Hebrews. Pages 361–87 in *Salvation in the New Testament: Perspectives on Soteriology.* Edited by J. G. van der Watt. Supplements to Novum Testamentum 121. Leiden: Brill.

Kosmala, Hans. 1959. *Hebräer-Essener-Christen.* Studia post-biblica 1. Leiden: Brill.

Kowalski, Beate. 2005. Die Rezeption alttestamentlicher Theologie im Hebräerbrief. Pages 35–62 in *Ausharren in der Verheißung: Studien zum Hebräerbrief.* Edited by R. Kampling. Stuttgarter Bibelstudien 204. Stuttgart: Verlag Katholisches Bibelwerk.

Kugel, James L. 1998. *Traditions of the Bible: A Guide to the Bible as It Was at the Start of the Common Era.* Cambridge: Harvard University Press.

Kugler, Robert A. 1996. *From Patriarch to Priest: The Levi-Priestly Tradition from Aramaic Levi to Testament of Levi.* Society of Biblical Literature Early Judaism and Its Literature 9. Atlanta: Scholars Press.

Kümmel, Werner Georg. 1975. *Introduction to the New Testament.* Rev. ed. Translated by H. C. Kee. Nashville: Abingdon.

Lane, William L. 1991. *Hebrews.* 2 vols. Word Biblical Commentary 47. Waco, Tex.: Word.

Larson, Erik W. 2000. Michael. Pages 546–48 in vol. 1 of *Encyclopedia of the Dead Sea Scrolls.* Edited by L. H. Schiffman and J. C. VanderKam. 2 vols. Oxford: Oxford University Press.

Lausberg, Heinrich. 1998. *Handbook of Literary Rhetoric: A Foundation for Literary Study.* Edited by D. E. Orton and R. D. Anderson. Leiden: Brill.

Lee, John A. L. 1997. Hebrews 5:14 and "ΕΞΙΣ: A Century of Misunderstanding. *Novum Testamentum* 39:151–76.

Lehne, Susanne. 1990. *The New Covenant in Hebrews.* Journal for the Study of the New Testament Supplement Series 44. Sheffield: JSOT Press.

Levine, Lee I. 2005. *The Ancient Synagogue: The First Thousand Years.* 2nd ed. New Haven: Yale University Press.

Lincoln, Andrew. 2006. *Hebrews: A Guide.* London: T&T Clark.

Lindars, Barnabas. 1989. The Rhetorical Structure of Hebrews. *Novum Testamentum* 35:382–406.

———. 1991. *The Theology of the Letter to the Hebrews.* New Testament Theology. Cambridge: Cambridge University Press.

Löhr, Hermut. 2005. Reflections of Rhetorical Terminology in Hebrews. Pages 199–210 in *Hebrews: Contemporary Methods—New Insights.* Edited by G. Gelardini. Biblical Interpretation Series 75. Leiden: Brill. Repr., Atlanta: Society of Biblical Literature, 2008.

Longenecker, Bruce W. ed. 2002. *Narrative Dynamics in Paul: A Critical Assessment.* Louisville: Westminster John Knox.

Loofs, Friedrich, ed. 1905. *Nestoriana.* Halle: Niemeyer.

Lucian. 1913–1967. Translated by A. M. Harmon et al. 8 vols. LCL. Cambridge: Harvard University Press.

Lundbom, Jack. 2004. *Jeremiah 21–36: A New Translation with Introduction and Commentary* Anchor Bible 21B. New York: Doubleday.

Luther's Works. 1955–1986. American Edition. Edited by Jaroslav Pelikan and Helmut T. Lehman. 55 vols. Philadelphia: Muehlenberg and Fortress; St. Louis: Concordia.

Lyotard, Jean-François. 1984. *The Postmodern Condition: A Report on Knowledge.* Translated by G. Bennington and B. Massumi. Minneapolis: University of Minnesota Press.

Macaskill, Grant. 2007. Enoch, Second Book of. Page 265 in vol. 2 of *New Interpreter's Dictionary of the Bible.* Edited by K. D. Sakenfeld. 5 vols. Nashville: Abingdon, 2006–2009.

Mackie, Scott D. 2007. *Eschatology and Exhortation in the Epistle to the Hebrews.* WUNT 2/223. Tübingen: Mohr Siebeck.

MacRae, George W. 1978. Heavenly Temple and Eschatology in the Letter to the Hebrews. *Semeia* 12:179–99.

Malina, Bruce J. 1996. *The Social World of Jesus and the Gospels.* New York: Routledge.

Mann, Jacob. 1971. *The Bible as Read and Preached in the Old Synagogue: A Study in the Cycles of the Readings from Torah and Prophets, as well as from Psalms and in the Structure of Midrashic Homilies.* 2 vols. Library of Biblical Studies. Repr., New York: Ktav. [orig. 1940]

Marcus, Joel. 2003. Son of Man as Son of Adam, Part 1. *Revue biblique* 110:38–61.

Marshall, I. Howard. 2004. *New Testament Theology.* Downers Grove, Ill.: InterVarsity Press.

———. 2009. Soteriology in Hebrews. Pages 253–77 in *The Epistle to the Hebrews and Christian Theology.* Edited by Richard Bauckham et al. Grand Rapids: Eerdmans.

Martin, Dale B. 2008. *Pedagogy of the Bible: An Analysis and Proposal.* Louisville: Westminster John Knox.

März, Claus-Peter. 1990. *Hebräerbrief.* Die Neue Echter Bibel: Kommentar zum Neuen Testament mit der Einheitsübersetzung 16. 2nd ed. Würzburg: Echter.

———. 2006. Beobachtungen zur differenzierten Rezeption der "Schrift" im Hebräerbrief. Pages 389–403 in *Ein Herz so weit wie der Sand am Ufer des Meeres: Festschrift für Georg Hentschel.* Edited by S. Gillmayr-Bucher, A. Giercke, and C. Niessen. Erfurter theologische Studien 90. Würzburg: Echter.

Mason, Eric F. 2005. Hebrews 7:3 and the Relationship between Melchizedek and Jesus. *Biblical Research* 50:41–62.

———. 2008. *'You Are a Priest Forever': Second Temple Jewish Messianism and the Priestly Christology of the Epistle to the Hebrews.* Studies on the Texts of the Desert of Judah 74. Leiden: Brill.

———. 2009a. The Identification of *Mlky sdq* in 11QMelchizedek: A Survey of Recent Scholarship. *The Qumran Chronicle* 17.2–4:51–61.

———. 2009b. Psalm 2 in *4QFlorilegium* and in the New Testament. Pages 67–82 in *Echoes from the Caves: Qumran and the New Testament.* Edited by F. García Martínez. Studies on the Texts of the Desert of Judah 85. Leiden: Brill.

———. 2010a. The Epistle (Not Necessarily) to the "Hebrews": A Call to Renunciation of Judaism or Encouragement to Christian Commitment? *Perspectives in Religious Studies* 37:5–18.

———. 2010b. Hebrews and the Dead Sea Scrolls: Some Points of Comparison. *Perspectives in Religious Studies* 37:457–79.

———. 2012. "Sit at My Right Hand": Enthronement and the Heavenly Sanctuary in Hebrews. Pages 901–16 in vol. 2 of *A Teacher for All Generations: Essays in Honor of James C. VanderKam.* Edited by E. F. Mason et al. 2 vols. Supplements to the Journal for the Study of Judaism 153. Leiden: Brill.

Matera, Frank J. 1999. *New Testament Christology.* Louisville: Westminster John Knox.

———. 2007. *New Testament Theology: Exploring Diversity and Unity.* Louisville: Westminster John Knox.

McCullough, John C. 1980. The Old Testament Quotations in Hebrews. *New Testament Studies* 26:363–79.

———. 1994. Hebrews in Recent Scholarship (Part 1). *Irish Biblical Studies* 16:66–87.

McGuckin, John. 2004. *Saint Cyril of Alexandria and the Christological Controversy.* Crestwood, N.Y.: St. Vladimir's Seminary Press.

McLay, R. Timothy. 2003. *The Use of the Septuagint in New Testament Research.* Grand Rapids: Eerdmans.

Meijering, E. P. 1974. Wie Platonisierten Christen? Zur Grenzziehung zwischen Platonismus, kirchlichem Credo und patristischer Theologie. *Vigiliae Christianae* 28:15-28.

Metso, Sarianna. 1997. *The Textual Development of the Qumran Community Rule.* Studies on the Texts of the Desert of Judah 21. Leiden: Brill.

———. *The Serekh Texts.* 2007. Companion to the Qumran Scrolls 9. New York: T&T Clark.

Michel, Otto. 1975. *Der Brief an die Hebräer.* Kritisch-exegetischer Kommentar über das Neue Testament 13. 13th ed. Göttingen: Vandenhoeck & Ruprecht.

Milik, Józef. 1972a. 4Q Visions de 'Amram et une citation d'Origène. *Revue biblique* 79:77-97.

———. 1972b. *Milkî-sedek* et *Milkî-reša'* dans les anciens écrits juifs et chrétiens. *Journal for Jewish Studies* 23:95-144.

Miller, James C. 2005. Paul and Hebrews: A Comparison of Narrative Worlds. Pages 245-64 in *Hebrews: Contemporary Methods—New Insights.* Edited by G. Gelardini. Biblical Interpretation Series 75. Leiden: Brill. Repr., Atlanta: Society of Biblical Literature, 2008.

Mitchell, Alan C. 2007. *Hebrews.* Sacra Pagina 13. Collegeville, Minn.: Liturgical Press.

Mitchell, Margaret. 1992. New Testament Envoys in the Context of Greco-Roman Diplomatic and Epistolary Conventions: The Example of Timothy and Titus. *Journal of Biblical Literature* 111:641-62.

Moffatt, James. 1924. *A Critical and Exegetical Commentary on the Epistle to the Hebrews.* International Critical Commentary. Edinburgh: T&T Clark.

Moffitt, David M. 2008. "If Another Priest Arises": Jesus' Resurrection and the High Priestly Christology of Hebrews. Pages 68-79 in *A Cloud of Witnesses: The Theology of Hebrews in Its Ancient Contexts.* Edited by R. Bauckham et al. Library of New Testament Studies 387. London: T&T Clark.

———. 2011. *Atonement and the Logic of Resurrection in the Epistle to the Hebrews.* Supplements to Novum Testamentum 141. Leiden: Brill.

Montefiore, Hugh. 1964. *The Epistle to the Hebrews.* Harper's New Testament Commentaries. New York: Harper & Row.

Moore, Stephen D. 1989. *Literary Criticism and the Gospels: The Theoretical Challenge.* New Haven: Yale University Press.

Moulton, James H., Wilbert F. Howard, and Nigel Turner. 1906-1963. *A Grammar of New Testament Greek.* 4 vols. Edinburgh: T&T Clark.

Muir, Steven. 2008. The Anti-Imperial Rhetoric of Hebrews 1.3: *Charaktēr* as a "Double-Edged Sword." Pages 170-86 in *A Cloud of Witnesses: The Theology of Hebrews in Its Ancient Contexts.* Edited by R. Bauckham et al. Library of New Testament Studies 387. London: T&T Clark.

Nadeau, Ray. 1964. Hermogenes' *On Stases*: A Translation with an Introduction and Notes. *Speech Monographs* 31:361-424.

Nash, Ronald H. 1977. The Notion of Mediator in Alexandrian Judaism and the Epistle to the Hebrews. *Westminster Theological Journal* 40:89-115.

New Testament: New English Translation–Novum Testamentum Graece. 2004. English text and notes: The NET Bible. Text and notes edited by M. H. Burer, W. H. Harris

III, and D. B. Wallace. Greek text and critical apparatus: Nestle-Aland, *Novum Testamentum Graece*, 27th edition. Stuttgart: Deutsche Bibelgesellschaft; Dallas: NET Bible Press.

Newsom, Carol A. 1990. "Sectually Explicit" Literature from Qumran. Pages 167–87 in *The Hebrew Bible and Its Interpreters*. Edited by W. H. Propp, B. Halpern, and D. N. Freedman. Biblical and Judaic Studies from the University of California, San Diego 1. Winona Lake, Ind.: Eisenbrauns.

———. 1998. *Shirot 'Olat Hashabbat*. Pages 173–402 in *Qumran Cave 4.VI: Poetical and Liturgical Texts, Part 1*. Edited by Esther Eshel et al. in consultation with J. C. VanderKam and M. Brady. Discoveries in the Judaean Desert XI. Oxford: Clarendon.

———. 2000. Songs of the Sabbath Sacrifice. Pages 887–89 in vol. 2 of *Encyclopedia of the Dead Sea Scrolls*. Edited by L. H. Schiffman and J. C. VanderKam. 2 vols. Oxford: Oxford University Press.

Neyrey, J. H. 1991. "Without Beginning of Days or End of Life" (Hebrews 7:3): Topos for a True Deity. *Catholic Biblical Quarterly* 53:439–55.

———. 2005. God, Benefactor and Patron: The Major Cultural Model for Interpreting the Deity in Greco-Roman Antiquity. *Journal for the Study of the New Testament* 27:465–92.

———. 2007. "I Am the Door" (John 10:7, 9): Jesus the Broker in the Fourth Gospel. *Catholic Biblical Quarterly* 69:271–91.

Nock, Arthur Darby. 1972. *Essays on Religion and the Ancient World*. 2 vols. Oxford: Clarendon.

Oepke, A. 1967. "μεσίτης, κτλ." *TDNT* 4:598–624.

Olbricht, Thomas H. 1993. Hebrews as Amplification. Pages 375–87 in *Rhetoric and the New Testament*. Edited by S. E. Porter and T. H. Olbricht. Journal for the Study of the New Testament Supplement Series 90. Sheffield: JSOT Press.

Orlov, Andrei. 2007. The Heir of Righteousness and the King of Righteousness: The Priestly Noachic Polemics in 2 Enoch and the Epistle to the Hebrews. *Journal of Theological Studies* 58:45–65.

Pásztori-Kupán, István. 2006. *Theodoret of Cyrus*. Early Church Fathers. London: Routledge.

Pearson, Birger A. 1998. Melchizedek in Early Judaism, Christianity, and Gnosticism. Pages 176–202 in *Biblical Figures outside the Bible*. Edited by M. S. Stone and T. A. Bergren. Harrisburg, Pa.: Trinity Press International.

Pelikan, Jaroslav, ed. 1968. *Lectures on Titus, Philemon, and Hebrews*. Volume 29 of *Luther's Works*. Saint Louis: Concordia.

Perrot, Charles. 1988. The Reading of the Bible in the Ancient Synagogue. Pages 137–59 in *Mikra: Text, Translation, Reading and Interpretation of the Hebrew Bible in Ancient Judaism and Early Christianity*. Edited by M. J. Mulder and H. Sysling. Compendia Rerum Iudaicarum ad Novum Testamentum 2/1. Assen: Van Gorcum; Philadelphia: Fortress.

Peters, Melvin K. H. Septuagint. 1992. Pages 1093–1104 in vol. 5 of *The Anchor Bible Dictionary*. Edited by David Noel Freedman. 6 vols. New York: Doubleday.

Peterson, David. 1982. *Hebrews and Perfection: An Examination of the Concept of Perfection in the Epistle to the Hebrews*. Society for New Testament Studies Monograph Series 47. Cambridge: Cambridge University Press.

Philo. 1929–1953. Translated by F. H. Colson et al. 12 vols. LCL. Cambridge: Harvard University Press.

Pliny the Younger. 1969. Translated by Betty Radice. 2 vols. LCL. Cambridge: Harvard University Press.

Plutarch. 1914–2004. Translated by B. Perrin et al. 27 vols. LCL. Cambridge: Harvard University Press.

Powell, Mark A. 1990. *What Is Narrative Criticism?* Guides to Biblical Scholarship New Testament Series. Minneapolis: Fortress.

Presbyterian Church (U.S.A.). 1993. *Book of Common Worship*. Louisville: Westminster John Knox.

Puech, Émile, ed. 2001. *Qumrân Grotte 4.XXII: Textes Araméens Première Partie 4Q529–549*. Discoveries in the Judaean Desert XXXI. Oxford: Clarendon.

Pusey, Philip E., ed. 1875. *Sancti patris nostri Cyrilli archiepiscopi Alexandrini opera*. Vol. 6. Oxford: Oxford University Press.

Quintilian. 1921–1922. Translated by H. E. Butler. 4 vols. LCL. Cambridge: Harvard University Press.

Rascher, Angela. 2007. *Schriftauslegung und Christologie im Hebräerbrief*. Beihefte zur Zeitschrift für die neutestamentliche Wissenschaft und die Kunde der älteren Kirche 153. Berlin: de Gruyter.

Renoux, Athanese. 1969–1971. *Le codex arménian Jérusalem 121: Introduction et édition comparée du texte*. Patrologia Orientalis 35.1, 36.2. Turnhout: Brepols.

Rothschild, Clare K. 2009. *Hebrews as Pseudepigraphon: The History and Significance of the Pauline Attribution of Hebrews*. WUNT 235. Tübingen: Mohr Siebeck.

Russell, Norman. 2000. *Cyril of Alexandria*. Early Church Fathers. London: Routledge.

Scharbert, Josef. 1964. *Heilsmittler im Alten Testament und im Alten Orient*. Freiburg: Herder.

Schechter, Solomon. 1910. *Documents of Jewish Sectaries, Vol. 1: Fragments of a Zadokite Work*. Cambridge: Cambridge University Press.

Schenck, Kenneth. 2001. The Celebration of the Enthroned Son: The Catena of Hebrews 1:5–14. *Journal of Biblical Literature* 120:469–85.

———. 2002. *Philo and the Epistle to the Hebrews*: Ronald Williamson's Study after Thirty Years. *Studia Philonica Annual* 14:112–35.

———. 2003. *Understanding the Book of Hebrews: The Story behind the Sermon*. Louisville: Westminster John Knox.

———. 2007. *Cosmology and Eschatology in Hebrews: The Settings of the Sacrifice*. Society for New Testament Studies Monograph Series 143. Cambridge: Cambridge University Press.

———. 2009. God Has Spoken: Hebrews' Theology of the Scriptures. Pages 321–36 in *The Epistle to the Hebrews and Christian Theology*. Edited by Richard Bauckham et al. Grand Rapids: Eerdmans.

Schnelle, Udo. 2009. *Theology of the New Testament*. Grand Rapids: Baker.

Scholer, John M. 1991. *Proleptic Priests: Priesthood in the Epistle to the Hebrews*. Journal for the Study of the New Testament Supplement Series 49. Sheffield: Sheffield Academic.

Schrenk, Gottlob. 1965. "ἀρχιερεύς." *TDNT* 3:265–83.

Schröger, Friedrich. 1968. *Der Verfasser des Hebräerbriefes als Schriftausleger*. Biblische Untersuchungen 4. Regensburg: Pustet.

Scott, E. F. 1923. *The Epistle to the Hebrews*. Edinburgh: T&T Clark.

Seid, Timothy W. 1996. The Rhetorical Form of the Melchizedek/Christ Comparison in Hebrews 7. Ph.D. diss., Brown University.

———. 2007. The Rhetorical Function of Comparison in Hebrews. Paper presented at the Annual Meeting of the Society of Biblical Literature.

Seneca. 1917–2004. Translated by R. M. Gummere et al. 10 vols. LCL. Cambridge: Harvard University Press.

Simonetti, Manlio. 1994. *Biblical Interpretation in the Early Church: An Historical Introduction to Patristic Exegesis*. Translated by John A. Hughes. Edinburgh: T&T Clark.

Smith, Mark A. 2004. *The Memoirs of God: History, Memory, and the Experience of the Divine in Ancient Israel*. Minneapolis: Fortress.

Sobrino, Jon. 2001. *Christ the Liberator: A View from the Victims*. Translated by Paul Burns. Maryknoll, N.Y.: Orbis.

Soulen, R. Kendall. 1996. *The God of Israel and Christian Theology*. Minneapolis: Fortress.

Spicq, Ceslas. 1952–1953. *L'Epître aux Hébreux*. 2 vols. Paris: Gabalda.

———. 1958–1959. L'Épître aux Hébreux, Apollos, Jean-Baptiste, les Hellénistes et Qumrân. *Revue de Qumran* 1:365–90.

Spiegel, Shalom. 1967. *The Last Trial: On the Legends and Lore of the Command to Abraham to Offer Isaac as a Sacrifice: The Akedah*. Translated by Judah Goldin. New York: Pantheon.

Staab, Karl, ed. 1933. *Pauluskommentaren aus der Griechischen Kirche*. Münster: Aschendorff.

Sterling, Gregory E. 2001. Ontology Versus Eschatology: Tensions between Author and Community in Hebrews. *Studia Philonica Annual* 13:190–211.

Steudel, Annette. 1992. 4QMidrEschat: "A Midrash on Eschatology" (4Q174+4Q177). Pages 531–41 in vol. 2 of *The Madrid Qumran Congress: Proceedings of the International Congress on the Dead Sea Scrolls, Madrid 18–21 March, 1991*. Edited by J. Trebolle Barrera and L. Vegas Montaner. 2 vols. Studies on the Texts of the Desert of Judah 11. Leiden: Brill.

Steyn, Gert J. 2008. An Overview of the Extent and Diversity of Methods Utilised by the Author of Hebrews When Using the Old Testament. *Neotestamentica* 42:327–52.

Stökl Ben Ezra, Daniel. 2003. *The Impact of Yom Kippur on Early Christianity: The Day of Atonement from Second Temple Judaism to the Fifth Century*. WUNT 163. Tübingen: Mohr Siebeck.

Stone, Michael E. 2000. Amram. Pages 23–24 in vol. 1 of *Encyclopedia of the Dead Sea Scrolls*. Edited by L. H. Schiffman and J. C. VanderKam. 2 vols. Oxford: Oxford University Press.

Strack, H. L., and Günter Stemberger. 1996. *Introduction to the Talmud and Midrash*. 2nd ed. Edited and translated by M. Bockmuehl. Minneapolis: Fortress.

Strecker, Georg. 2000. *Theology of the New Testament*. Louisville: Westminster John Knox.

Strugnell, John. 1969–1970. Notes en marge du volume V des "Discoveries in the Judaean Desert of Jordan." *Revue de Qumran* 7:163–276 and plates I-VI.

Stuedel, Annette. 1993. אחרית הימים in the Texts from Qumran (1). *Revue de Qumran* 16:225–46.

Suetonius. 1914. Translated by J. C. Rolfe. 2 vols. LCL. Cambridge: Harvard University Press.

Swete, Henry B., ed. 1880–1882. *Theodori Mopsuesteni in Epistolas Beati Pauli Commentarii: The Latin Version with the Greek Fragments with an Introduction, Notes, and Indices*. 2 vols. Cambridge: Cambridge University Press.

Swetnam, James. 1981. *Jesus and Isaac: A Study of the Epistle to the Hebrews in the Light of the Aqedah*. Analecta Biblica 94. Rome: Pontifical Biblical Institute.

———. 1989. Christology and the Eucharist in the Epistle to the Hebrews. *Biblica* 70:74–95.

Tacitus. 1914–1937. Translated by M. Hutton et al. 5 vols. LCL. Cambridge: Harvard University Press.

Talmon, Shemaryahu. 1951. Yom Hakkippurim in the Habakkuk Scroll. *Biblica* 32:549–63.

———. 1994. The Community of the Renewed Covenant: Between Judaism and Christianity. Pages 3–24 in *The Community of the Renewed Covenant: The Notre Dame Symposium on the Dead Sea Scrolls*. Edited by E. Ulrich and J. C. VanderKam. Christianity and Judaism in Antiquity 10. Notre Dame, Ind.: University of Notre Dame Press.

Taut, Konrad. 1998. *Anleitung zum Schriftverständnis? Die heiligen Schriften nach dem Hebräerbrief*. Theos 20. Hamburg: Kovač.

Thielman, Frank. 2005. *Theology of the New Testament: A Canonical and Synthetic Approach*. Grand Rapids: Zondervan.

Thompson, James W. 1982. *The Beginnings of Christian Philosophy: The Epistle to the Hebrews*. Catholic Biblical Quarterly Monograph Series 13. Washington, D.C.: Catholic Biblical Association.

———. 1998. The Appropriate, the Necessary, and the Impossible: Faith and Reason in Hebrews. Pages 302–17 in *The Early Church in Its Context: Essays in Honor of Everett Ferguson*. Edited by A. J. Malherbe, F. W. Norris, and J. W. Thompson. Supplements to Novum Testamentum 90. Leiden: Brill.

———. 2007. *Ephapax*: The One and the Many in Hebrews. *New Testament Studies* 53:566–81.

———. 2008. *Hebrews*. Paideia Commentaries on the New Testament. Grand Rapids: Baker.

Tonneau, Raymond, ed. 1949. *Les Homélies Catéchétiques de Théodore de Mopsueste.* Studi e Testi 145. Vatican City: Vaticana.

Tov, Emmanuel, ed. 2006. *The Dead Sea Scrolls Electronic Library, Revised Edition 2006.* CD-ROM. Leiden: Brill.

Triennial Cycle. 2007. Pages 140–43 in vol. 20 of *Encyclopaedia Judaica.* Edited by M. Berenbaum and F. Skolnik. 2nd ed. 22 vols. Detroit: Macmillan Reference USA.

Trotter, Andrew H., Jr. 1997. *Interpreting the Epistle to the Hebrews.* Guides to New Testament Exegesis. Grand Rapids: Baker.

VanderKam, James C. 1994. Messianism in the Scrolls. Pages 211–34 in *The Community of the Renewed Covenant: The Notre Dame Symposium on the Dead Sea Scrolls.* Edited by E. Ulrich and J. C. VanderKam. Christianity and Judaism in Antiquity Series 10. Notre Dame, Ind.: University of Notre Dame Press.

———. 2000. Sabbatical Chronologies in the Dead Sea Scrolls and Related Literature. Pages 159–78 in *The Dead Sea Scrolls in Their Historical Context.* Edited by T. H. Lim. Edinburgh: T&T Clark.

———. 2010. *The Dead Sea Scrolls Today.* 2nd ed. Grand Rapids: Eerdmans.

Vanhoye, Albert. 1976. *La structure littéraire de L'epître aux Hébreux.* 2nd ed. Paris: Desclée de Brouwer.

———. 1989. *Structure and Message of the Epistle to the Hebrews.* Subsidia Biblica 12. Rome: Pontifical Biblical Institute.

Vogel, C. J. de. 1985. Platonism and Christianity: A Mere Antagonism or a Profound Common Ground? *Vigiliae Christianae* 39:1–61.

Volf, Miroslav. 2010. *Captive to the Word of God: Engaging the Scriptures for Contemporary Theological Reflection.* Grand Rapids: Eerdmans.

Vosté, Jacques M., ed. 1940. *Theodori Mopsuesteni Commentarius in Evangelium Johannis Apostoli.* Corpus Scriptorum Christianorum Orientalium 115–16; Scriptores Syri 4.3, vols. 62 and 63. Leuven: Officina Orientali.

Walters, John R. 1996. The Rhetorical Arrangement of Hebrews. *Asbury Theological Journal* 51:59–70.

Walz, Ernst Christian. 1832–1836. *Rhetores Graeci.* 9 vols. Stuttgart: Cottae.

Watson, Duane F. 1997. Rhetorical Criticism of Hebrews and the Catholic Epistles. *Currents in Research: Biblical Studies* 5:175–207.

Watson, Francis. 2002. Is There a Story in These Texts? Pages 231–39 in *Narrative Dynamics in Paul: A Critical Assessment.* Edited by B. W. Longenecker. Louisville: Westminster John Knox.

Webster, John. 2009. One Who Is Son: Theological Reflections on the Exordium to the Epistle to the Hebrews. Pages 69–94 in *The Epistle to the Hebrews and Christian Theology.* Edited by R. Bauckham et al. Grand Rapids: Eerdmans.

Weiss, Hans-Friedrich. 1991. *Der Brief an die Hebräer.* Kritisch-exegetischer Kommentar über das Neue Testament (Meyer Kommentar) 13. Göttingen: Vandenhoeck & Ruprecht.

Wendland, Paul. 1904. Σωτηρ. *Zeitschrift für die neutestamentliche Wissenschaft und die Kunde der älteren Kirche* 5:335–53.

Westcott, Brooke Foss. 1889. *The Epistle to the Hebrews: The Greek Text with Notes and Essays.* London: Macmillan. Repr., Eugene, Oreg.: Wipf & Stock, 2001.

Westfall, Cynthia Long. 2005. *A Discourse Analysis of the Letter to the Hebrews: The Relationship between Form and Meaning.* Library of Biblical Studies. London: T&T Clark.

Whitlark, Jason A. 2008. *Enabling Fidelity to God: Perseverance in Hebrews in Light of the Reciprocity Systems of the Ancient Mediterranean World.* Paternoster Biblical Monographs. Carlisle: Paternoster.

Whittaker, John. 1981. Plutarch, Platonism, and Christianity. Pages 50–63 in *Neoplatonism and Early Christian Thought: Essays in Honour of A. H. Armstrong.* Edited by H. J. Blumenthal and R. A. Markus. London: Variorum.

Wiles, Maurice F. 1967. *The Divine Apostle: The Interpretation of Saint Paul's Epistles in the Early Church.* Cambridge: Cambridge University Press.

Wilkinson, John. 1971. *Egeria's Travels.* London: SPCK.

Williamson, Ronald. 1975. The Eucharist and the Epistle to the Hebrews. *New Testament Studies* 21:300–312.

Windisch, Hans. 1931. *Der Hebräerbrief.* 2nd ed. Tübingen: Mohr Siebeck.

Witherington, Ben, III. 2009. *The Individual Witnesses.* Vol. 1 of *The Indelible Image: The Theological Thought World of the New Testament.* Downers Grove, Ill.: InterVarsity Press.

Woude, A. S. van der. 1965. Melchisedek als himmlische Erlösergestalt in den neugefundenen eschatologischen Midraschim aus Qumran Höhle XI. *Oudtestamentische Studiën* 14:354–73.

Wright, N. T. 1992. *The New Testament and the People of God.* Minneapolis: Fortress.

Wyller, Egil A. 1996. Plato/Platonismus III. Pages 677–702 in vol. 26 of *Theologische Realenzyklopädia.* Edited by G. Krause and G. Müller. 36 vols. Berlin: de Gruyer, 1976–2004.

Xeravits, Géza G. 2003. *King, Priest, Prophet: Positive Eschatological Protagonists of the Qumran Library.* Studies on the Texts of the Desert of Judah 67. Leiden: Brill.

Yadin, Yigael. 1958. The Dead Sea Scrolls and the Epistle to the Hebrews. *Scripta hierosolymitana* 4:36–55.

———. 1965. A Note on Melchizedek and Qumran. *Israel Exploration Journal* 15:152–54.

Yarnold, Edward. 1994. *The Awe-Inspiring Rites of Initiation: The Origins of the RCIA.* 2nd ed. Edinburgh: T&T Clark.

Young, Frances. 1989. The Rhetorical Schools and Their Influence on Patristic Exegesis. Pages 182–99 in *The Making of Orthodoxy: Essays in Honour of Henry Chadwick.* Edited by R. Williams. Cambridge: Cambridge University Press.

———. 1997. *Biblical Exegesis and the Formation of Christian Culture.* Cambridge: Cambridge University Press.

CONTRIBUTORS

Harold W. Attridge (Ph.D., Harvard University) is The Reverend Henry L. Slack Dean of Yale Divinity School and Lillian Claus Professor of New Testament, Yale University, New Haven, Connecticut.

Gabriella Gelardini (Dr. theol., University of Basel) is Senior Research Associate of New Testament at the University of Basel, Switzerland.

Patrick Gray (Ph.D., Emory University) is Associate Professor of Religious Studies, Rhodes College, Memphis, Tennessee.

Rowan A. Greer (Ph.D., Yale University) is Walter H. Gray Professor of Anglican Studies (emeritus), Yale Divinity School, Yale University, New Haven, Connecticut.

Craig R. Koester (Ph.D., Union Theological Seminary, New York) is Asher O. and Carrie Nasby Professor of New Testament at Luther Seminary, St. Paul, Minnesota.

Eric F. Mason (Ph.D., University of Notre Dame) is Associate Professor of Biblical Studies at Judson University, Elgin, Illinois.

Frank J. Matera (Ph.D., Union Theological Seminary, Virginia) is the Andrews-Kelley-Ryan Professor of Biblical Studies, The Catholic University of America, Washington, District of Columbia.

Kevin B. McCruden (Ph.D., Loyola University Chicago) is Associate Professor of Religious Studies, Gonzaga University, Spokane, Washington.

Alan C. Mitchell (Ph.D., Yale University) is Associate Professor of New Testament and Christian Origins, Georgetown University, Washington, District of Columbia.

David M. Moffitt (Ph.D., Duke University) is Assistant Professor of New Testament and Greek, Campbell University Divinity School, Buies Creek, North Carolina.

Jerome H. Neyrey, S.J. (Ph.D., Yale University) is Professor of New Testament Studies (emeritus), University of Notre Dame, Notre Dame, Indiana.

Kenneth Schenck (Ph.D., University of Durham) is Dean and Professor of New Testament and Christian Ministry, Wesley Seminary, Indiana Wesleyan University, Marion, Indiana.

James W. Thompson (Ph.D., Vanderbilt University) is the Robert and Kay Onstead Distinguished Professor of Biblical Studies and Associate Dean of the Graduate School of Theology, Abilene Christian University, Abilene, Texas.

Mark A. Torgerson (Ph.D., University of Notre Dame) is Professor of Worship Studies, Judson University, Elgin, Illinois.

Index of Ancient Sources

EARLY CHRISTIAN WRITERS

Index of Modern Authors

CPSIA information can be obtained at www.ICGtesting.com
Printed in the USA
BVOW030911230911

271890BV00002B/1/P